Children and Immigration

Cavendish
Publishing
Limited

Children and Immigration

JEREMY ROSENBLATT, BARRISTER
AND
IAN LEWIS, BARRISTER

Cavendish
Publishing
Limited

London • Sydney

First published in Great Britain 1997 by Cavendish Publishing Limited, The Glass House, Wharton Street, London WC1X 9PX.

Telephone: 0171-278 8000 Facsimile: 0171-278 8080

Rosenblatt, Jeremy

Children and Immigration

1. Children – Legal status, laws, etc – Great Britain

2. Emigration and immigration law – Great Britain

I. Title II. Lewis, Ian

344.1'0282'083

1-85941-197-5

Printed and bound in Great Britain by

Biddles Ltd, Guildford and King's Lynn

Preface

This book has been written to assist the family practitioner who may be unfamiliar with immigration law.

Jeremy Rosenblatt
Ian Lewis
Grays Inn Chambers
April 1997

Contents

Preface v

1 Introduction to the administration of immigration control in the United Kingdom 1
2 Family settlement 7
3 Children seeking limited leave to enter or remain as dependants 13
4 Independent children 17
5 Adoption 21
6 Asylum 25
7 Special cases 31
8 Contact 35
9 Deportation 43
10 British citizenship 45

Appendix I 47
- Immigration Act 1971 47
- Immigration Act 1988 111
- British Nationality Act 1981 120
- Asylum and Immigration Appeals Act 1993 194
- Asylum and Immigration Act 1996 211

Appendix II 233
- Statement of Changes in Immigration Rules – May 1994 233
- Statement of Changes in Immigration Rules – January 1996 343
- Statement of Changes in Immigration Rules – August 1996 344
- Statement of Changes in Immigration Rules – October 1996 353

Appendix III 355
- Home Office Circulars on Deportation 355

Index 369

1 Introduction to the administration of immigration control in the United Kingdom

The administration of immigration control is the responsibility of the Secretary of State for the Home Department, most usually acting through delegated officers.

The parameters within which control is exercised are delineated by a body of primary and secondary legislation. The Secretary of State retains a degree of discretion both within and without this framework.

Decisions made affecting those subject to immigration control may be challenged either by way of appeal to the independent immigration appellate authorities, or by way of judicial review. The appropriate forum will depend upon the nature of the decision.

Of increasing importance is the effect of European Community and European Economic Area measures, and international treaty or convention obligations such as the European Convention on Human Rights.

Immigration legislation

The principal piece of primary legislation governing the administration of immigration control is the Immigration Act 1971 (as amended). This Act, *inter alia*, stipulates who is subject to immigration control, the general provisions for regulation and control and the administration thereof, the structure and powers of the appellate authorities, and also creates certain criminal offences related to breaches of immigration control. (See Appendix I for primary legislation.)

It is pursuant to s 3(2) of this Act that the Secretary of State lays down 'the immigration rules' (more precisely *Statement of Changes in Immigration Rules* HC 395 as amended – see Appendix II). These rules are perhaps the single most important regulations with regard to the day-to-day administration of immigration control. They set out in detail the practice to be followed by the officers administering control, and indicate the requirements that applicants must satisfy to obtain entry or extension or variation of leave to remain in the United Kingdom.

The Immigration Act 1988 made certain amendments to the 1971 Act, and additionally, *inter alia*, introduced a restriction on the right of abode in cases of polygamy, and introduced a restriction on rights of appeal in certain deportation cases.

The Immigration (Carriers' Liability) Act 1987 is of limited application in the context of this book. It empowers the Secretary of State to impose financial penalties on the owners or agents of ships or aircraft upon which passengers reach the United Kingdom without requisite travel documents or visas.

The Asylum and Immigration Appeals Act 1993 had the important effect of incorporating directly into United Kingdom law the provisions of the 1951 Convention relating to the Status of Refugees, and the Protocol to that Convention. It also introduced a new appeals procedure in relation to asylum cases, as well as amending the 1971 Act to restrict the right of appeal in certain other cases.

The Asylum and Immigration Act 1996 was passed with the specific intent of 'tightening up' asylum procedures. It includes provisions creating new offences for fraudulent asylum seekers. It imposes obligations on employers to ensure that they do not employ anybody without permission to work, and imposes severe restrictions on entitlement to social security benefits. It also expands the 'fast track' system of appeals for asylum seekers who have travelled through deemed 'safe third countries' before arriving in the United Kingdom or who are fleeing from designated 'safe' countries.

In addition to the above pieces of primary legislation and the immigration rules, there are a number of statutory instruments concerned with the administration of immigration control, in particular governing procedures on appeals. However, a detailed exposition of these instruments is beyond the scope of this publication.

European directives and regulations pursuant to the Treaty of Rome (1959), and the Treaty itself are binding upon the United Kingdom. Of most significance in the context of immigration law are the provisions relating to the freedom of movement of persons. The right of free movement is exerciseable by citizens of the countries that have signed up to the European Economic Area Agreement (comprising Member States of the European Union and Liechtenstein and Norway). Family members of such people may also benefit from the right, even though not being a national of an EEA country, in circumstances where the EEA national is exercising the right to free movement. Family members are defined to include children under 21 years old or dependent on their parents, dependent grandchildren, and non-dependent grandchildren under 21 years old whose right is dependent upon the right of an EEA national exercising the right of freedom of movement for workers.

The European Convention on Human Rights has not been incorporated into United Kingdom law. However, it is recognised by the English courts as something to which the Secretary of State is to have regard in his own decision-making process. Indeed it is in particular with respect to Article 8 of the Convention (which is concerned with the right to respect of privacy and family life) that the Secretary of State has given written directions to immigration officers dealing with deportation decisions that affect spouses, co-habitees, and children (DP 2/93, DP 3/96, DP 4/96 and DP 5/96). (See further Chapter 9 and Appendix III.)

The British Nationality Act 1981, whilst not dealing directly with the administration of immigration control, is nonetheless of significance because it governs the manner in which individuals may obtain citizenship, and thereby cease to be subject to immigration control. (See further Chapter 10.)

Decision-making

The Secretary of State acts through delegated officers. It is only occasionally that he or she is likely to be involved directly with an immigration decision. It is a requirement that it be the Secretary of State who signs a deportation order, and so necessarily there is direct involvement at that final stage.

There are two types of officers: immigration officers (who are concerned with applications at ports or within the United Kingdom) and entry clearance officers (who are concerned with applications for visas or entry clearance made abroad).

The following broad types of decision may be identified:

(i) Decisions on applications for entry clearance made at an Embassy or High Commission abroad prior to travel. Visa nationals (see Appendix to HC 395 as amended) require entry clearance regardless of the purpose of their journey to the United Kingdom. Non-visa nationals will require prior entry clearance for certain categories of visit, eg working holiday-makers.

(ii) Decisions on applications for leave to enter the United Kingdom made at the port of entry. In a situation where an individual arrives with a prior entry clearance obtained at an Embassy or High Commission abroad, it is still open to an immigration officer at the port of entry to refuse leave to enter, eg if there has been a change of circumstance, or if the immigration officer is not satisfied the entry clearance was validly obtained.

(iii) Decisions on applications for variation or extension of leave to remain in the United Kingdom. An individual who has been granted leave to enter the United Kingdom may apply for the conditions attached to that leave to be varied, or for the length of the leave to be extended. In certain cases the immigration rules will not permit extension of leave beyond a certain time limit, eg visitors may not remain in that capacity for more than six months.

(iv) Decisions relating to deportation procedures. If an individual has entered the United Kingdom with leave, but has failed to secure any extension of that leave and remains without permission, it is open to the Secretary of State to consider the appropriateness of enforcing removal through deportation procedures. (See further Chapter 9.)

In considering the different types of decisions the officers will have regard to the detailed guidance contained in the immigration rules. It is to be noted that if an application is made for a purpose not covered by the rules then, in accordance with the rules, such an application is to be refused. However, it is possible to request that an application be considered outwith the rules, at the discretion and indulgence of the Secretary of State. If such a request is rejected the possibility of challenging such a decision will be limited.

Challenging decisions

The immigration appellate authority is a two-tier structure. Where there is a right of appeal, in the first instance it is to an immigration adjudicator (or immigration special adjudicator in the case of an asylum appeal). Save in limited deportation appeals (pursuant to s 5 of the Immigration Act 1988), an adjudicator may explore issues of fact and substitute his or her own findings and his or her own exercise of discretion for that of the decision-maker. He or she may also review the decision-maker's approach in law. (See further s 19 of the Immigration Act 1971.) However, where there has been a request to depart from the immigration rules (or to consider an application outwith the immigration rules) an adjudicator is not empowered to substitute his or her own discretion for that of the Secretary of State. (See s 19(2) of the 1971 Act). In such circumstances, challenge may be possible by way of judicial review, but the scope to seek such remedy is likely to be limited.

Procedures and time limits on appeal (both before the adjudicator and the Tribunal) is governed by the Immigration Appeals (Procedure) Rules 1984, and in the case of an asylum appeal by the Asylum Appeals (Procedure) Rules 1996.

A dissatisfied party to an appeal may seek leave to appeal to the Immigration Appeal Tribunal – the second tier of the appellate authorities. Although it is possible to apply for leave from the adjudicator, it is the usual practice to apply in writing to the Tribunal. The application is then considered by a single Tribunal chairman. In a non-asylum appeal it is necessary to establish an arguable error of law in order to obtain leave. Whilst this is not a strict requirement in an asylum appeal, in practice leave is unlikely to be obtained in the absence of an arguable point of law. Where there is an arguable point of law, leave to appeal does not follow automatically: the Tribunal retains a discretion to refuse leave if it considers that correction of the error would not make any material difference to the outcome of the appeal (rule 14(2)(b) of the 1984 Procedure Rules).

In the very limited circumstances referred to in s 22(5) of the 1971 Act, the Immigration Appeal Tribunal will grant leave to appeal as a matter of course.

Where leave to appeal is refused, remedy may lie by way of an application for judicial review against the refusal of leave. It will be necessary to impugn the refusal of leave on usual public law grounds (generally summarised as illegality, irrationality, and impropriety).

If leave is granted the matter proceeds to hearing before a three-man Tribunal. The appeal may be dismissed, allowed, or remitted for a *de novo* hearing before an adjudicator.

There is a further possibility of appeal, with leave, to the Court of Appeal against a final determination of the Tribunal (see s 9 of the 1993 Act), and of course thence ultimately to the House of Lords.

It is to be noted that appellants against decisions to refuse entry clearance or to refuse leave to enter are disadvantaged by having to pursue their appeals from abroad.

It is also to be noted that the right of appeal for an applicant in the United Kingdom with leave to enter is dependent upon the making of an application for variation or extension of leave before the expiry of the current leave. An 'out-of-time' application will be considered by the Home Office, but the right of appeal against any decision will have been lost.

Where there is no right of appeal to the appellate authorities then the only possibility of challenge in the domestic jurisdiction will be by way of judicial review. Again the usual public law principles will be applicable. This remedy may be of little value in many cases because it provides a supervisory or review jurisdiction rather than an appeal jurisdiction, and as such does not (save in the most exceptional circumstances) provide a forum within which to challenge factual findings of the decision-maker.

Decisions raising issues under the European Convention on Human Rights may be challenged in the European Court of Human Rights. However, it is necessary to exhaust all domestic remedies before commencing proceedings in that forum.

A word about 'children'

The immigration legislation does not provide any strict definition of 'child' or 'children'.

The applicability of control under any particular provision will not always depend upon a certain age limit. The immigration rules, for instance, impose an 18 year age limit on applications for leave to enter as a dependent child (see para 297 of HC 395 as amended), although there is no such age limit on an application for leave to remain if admitted before 18 years old (see para 298(ii)(b). Further, this age limit is qualified in circumstances where the 'child' is married or leading an independent life. By contrast, under European freedom of movement rights, the nominal age limit for 'children' is 21 years.

Further, in certain circumstances, individuals below the age of majority will fall to be considered in accordance with rules more usually associated with 'adults', eg fiancé(e)s and spouses.

Accordingly, this text does not seek to advance any strict definition of 'children'. The applicability of any particular provision will usually depend upon the circumstances of the individual case.

2 Family settlement

The majority of children seeking to settle in the United Kingdom will be doing so as members of families. This chapter is concerned with the requirements for admission to the United Kingdom and/or extension of leave to remain for those children subject to immigration control who are members of families either settled or seeking to settle. The requirements vary according to whether a child is born inside or outside the United Kingdom, and also in respect of European and non-European families.

It is to be noted that 'settlement' envisages the grant of indefinite leave to remain (which may lead to the acquisition of citizenship), and so is not concerned with non-temporary purposes (such as study or holiday).

Applications for indefinite leave to enter

It is necessary to obtain prior entry clearance from abroad in this category. (See para 299 of HC 395 as amended.)

To obtain indefinite leave it will be necessary to satisfy the entry clearance officer, and in turn the immigration officer at the port of entry that the child applicant is under 18 years of age, is not leading an independent life, is unmarried and has not formed an independent family unit, and can and will be maintained without recourse to public funds in suitable accommodation. Further, it is necessary to show that the child applicant is seeking leave to enter to accompany or join a relevant adult. (See para 297 of HC 395 as amended.)

The meaning of 'public funds' is defined in para 6 of the immigration rules (HC 395 as amended) and relates to various welfare benefits and housing provided under the homelessness provisions of the housing legislation (which does not therefore include all local authority accommodation *per se*).

Suitable accommodation is simply accommodation which the relevant adult or adults own or occupy exclusively.

Pursuant to para 297(i) of HC 395 as amended, the relevant adult is a parent, parents or a relative in one of the circumstances set out at sub-paras (a)–(f) of that provision. 'Parent' is further defined in para 6 of HC 395 as amended and includes step-parents (but only where the birth parent is dead), the father of an illegitimate child, adoptive parents, and in certain cases those to whom there has been a genuine transfer of parental responsibility.

It is to be noted that pursuant to para 297(i)(f) settlement may be with a relative other than a parent in circumstances where there are 'serious or compelling family or other considerations which make exclusion of the child undesirable and suitable arrangements have been made for the child's care'. There is no guidance in the immigration rules as to the approach to such considerations, and accordingly applications are dealt with on a case-by-case basis. The court decisions in *Secretary of State for the Home Department v Campbell* [1972] Imm AR 115, and *Rudolph v Entry Clearance Officer, Colombo* [1984] Imm AR 84 provide some broad principles of approach to what is essentially a subjective area. In this context it is to be recalled that on an appeal an adjudicator may substitute his or her own findings of fact and/or exercise of discretion for those of the entry clearance officer or immigration officer involved in the case.

Applications for indefinite leave to remain

The requirements under this category are similar (but not identical) to the requirements for indefinite leave to enter. (See para 298 of HC 395 as amended.)

Necessarily, because the application is being made 'in-country', there is no requirement of obtaining entry clearance, although in the case of a child of a family who is over 18 years old, it will be necessary to show that leave to enter or remain in the United Kingdom was previously obtained with a view to settlement. (See para 298(ii)(b) of HC 395 as amended.)

Applications for limited leave to enter or remain with a view to settlement

In many cases, a child's parent or parents will not be in a position to seek indefinite leave forthwith, but will have to seek some form of leave which in due course may permit them to apply for indefinite leave. Paragraph 301 of HC 395 as amended provides for such situations.

If leave to enter is being sought (as opposed to leave to remain) then prior entry clearance is required. If leave to remain is sought, then that applicant must have a current leave – this, in effect, excludes those who have allowed their leave to elapse.

The requirements for leave are again similar to those in para 297.

The relevant adult with whom settlement is envisaged is defined in para 301(i). It is to be noted that there is no reference to relatives other than parents. In such circumstances where it is envisaged that a child will need to live with a suitable relative, it is therefore appropriate to apply for indefinite leave forthwith, pursuant to either one of paras 297(i)(f) and 298(i)(d).

Where limited leave to enter or remain with a view to settlement is granted, it will usually be for an initial period of 12 months. Towards the end of that period an application may be made for indefinite leave pursuant to para 298.

Children born in the United Kingdom

Certain children will acquire British citizenship by virtue of their birth in the United Kingdom, or may subsequently apply for registration as a British citizen. (See further Chapter 10.) However, there will be other children who are subject to immigration control although they have never actually passed through a point of entry. If, for any reason, it is contemplated that such a child will leave the United Kingdom but will wish to seek to return, then it is necessary to consider the position pursuant to paras 304–09 of the immigration rules.

The relevant rules are more generous to the child applicant than the rules discussed above with regard to children generally, in that there is no requirement with regard to maintenance and accommodation. Also, where a child applicant is seeking leave to enter no prior entry clearance is required (save in the case of a visa national).

Otherwise, the requirements are, both for leave to remain and leave to enter, that the child applicant has been born in the United Kingdom, under 18 years of age, is not leading an independent life, is unmarried and has not formed an independent family unit, and there has been an absence from the United Kingdom of no more than two years (if two years' absence has elapsed then the child applicant will have to qualify under some other provision of the immigration rules), and either:

(i) the child applicant is accompanying or seeking to join or remain with either:

   (a) a parent or parents who have, or are given, leave to enter or remain; or

   (b) a parent or parents one of whom is a British citizen or has the right of abode in the United Kingdom;

   or

(ii) the child applicant is a child in respect of whom parental rights and duties are vested solely in a local authority.

Where the requirements of leave to enter or remain are met in the circumstances of (i)(a) above, then leave will be granted in accordance with the parent or parents. If the requirements of leave are not met in the circumstances of (i)(a) because neither parent has a current leave, there is nonetheless a discretion within the rules to grant leave to enter or remain for a period not exceeding three months if both parents are in the United Kingdom, it appears unlikely that they will be removed in the immediate future, and there is no other person outside the United Kingdom who might reasonably be expected to care for the child. (See para 307 of HC 395 as amended.)

In the case of (i)(b) and (ii) above, indefinite leave will be granted.

European Economic Area families

(See paras 255–62 of HC 395 as amended.)

If a child is a national of a European Economic Area country, then he or she may benefit directly from the provisions relating to freedom of movement: he or she is to be admitted along with, or to join, the principal exercising such a right, providing it may be evidenced that the child is such a national and is related to the principal as asserted.

If a child is not an EEA national then an EEA family permit will be required in accordance with paras 258–61 of HC 395 as amended. It is implicit in the rules that this permit has to be obtained before travel from an entry clearance officer.

Upon entry, residence permits are granted, which will usually be for five years in the first instance. However, a shorter permit may be issued in certain circumstances, eg short-term employment of the principal family member exercising his or her right to free movement.

The immigration rules provide for settlement in accordance with European Community directives after certain periods of residence and/or the fulfilment of other conditions. (See paras 255–57 of HC 395 as amended.)

Special vouchers scheme

A British Overseas citizen (see further Chapter 10) may obtain indefinite leave to enter the United Kingdom if a holder of a 'special voucher'. The spouse and/or children of such an individual may similarly be granted indefinite leave to enter if they can be adequately maintained and accommodated without recourse to public funds. (See paras 249–54 of HC 395 as amended.)

Whilst the special voucher scheme is referred to in the immigration rules, its operation is outwith the rules. It is limited in application to British overseas citizens and in practice is applied to East African and Indian BOCs.

Refusal of a voucher attracts no right of appeal, although may be subject to judicial review on the usual public law principles.

Something of the history and application of the scheme may be gleaned from the case of *Amin v Entry Clearance Officer, Bombay* (HL) [1983] 2 AC 818. It is to be noted that the scheme is limited both geographically and in terms of numbers.

Polygamous marriage

There is a general prohibition on the grant of any form of leave to enter or remain to a child of a mother in a polygamous marriage where the mother would not be entitled to such leave. (See HC 395 as amended at paras 296 and 278–80.)

Analysis of paras 278–80 indicates that there are narrow exceptions to this general rule. The prohibition applies if there is another surviving wife who has either been in the United Kingdom or has been granted a certificate of entitlement in respect of the right of abode or entry clearance as a wife. There is an exception if the mother of the child applicant was in the United Kingdom prior to 1 August 1988 (commencement of the Immigration Act 1988) having been permitted entry for the purpose of settlement as the spouse of her husband, or where the mother of the child applicant has been in the United Kingdom since her marriage at any time when there was no other wife living who had been granted either a certificate of entitlement or entry clearance.

Periods spent in the United Kingdom as a visitor or without formal leave are to be disregarded. (See para 280 of HC 395 as amended.)

'Primary purpose' marriages and intervening devotion

Under the rules relating to applications for leave to enter by spouses, it is necessary to demonstrate that 'the marriage was not entered into primarily to obtain admission to the United Kingdom'. (See para 281(ii) of HC 395 as amended). It is not at all uncommon to find that such applications are refused on the basis that the marriage was a device to circumvent immigration control – often referred to as a 'primary purpose case'.

In such cases the Home Office operates a policy outside the immigration rules where 'intervening devotion' is demonstrated by the married couple. Such devotion is deemed to be demonstrated by lapse of time (if the marriage is genuine and subsisting after five years), or by the birth of a child who has the right of abode in the United Kingdom. (See Parliamentary written answer in *Hansard* HC 30 June 1992, Vol 210 col 523.)

It is curious why intervening devotion should be considered to be demonstrated by the birth of a child with the right of abode, as opposed to the birth of any child. However, the wording of the concession is such that it may only apply to couples where one is already present and settled in the United Kingdom, and not to those seeking leave to enter for settlement at the same time.

However, it may be seen that in an appropriate case the birth of a child will be sufficient to obtain leave to enter for both the spouse and the child (providing the other provisions relating to maintenance and accommodation, etc are satisfied), in circumstances where the spouse alone might have been refused leave to enter.

3 Children seeking limited leave to enter or remain as dependants

There are a number of categories within the immigration rules relating to visits for temporary purposes. These categories may be summarised under the following heads:

(i) visitors;

(ii) students;

(iii) working holidaymakers;

(iv) trainees/those involved in work experience/employees;

(v) business people/investors;

(vi) writers/composers/artists.

As a general rule, if a parent or parents is seeking leave to enter or remain in any of these capacities, then any child or children will be permitted to enter or remain in accordance with the parent or parents.

Detailed consideration of each of these categories properly belongs in a more detailed text on general immigration procedures. However, a brief summary of these categories is included in this chapter, together with specific consideration of the position of children under these categories.

It is to be noted that transfer between categories is not always possible. Frequently, in order to obtain an extension of leave under a particular category, it is necessary to have first entered the United Kingdom in that particular category. Accordingly, it is not possible within the immigration rules to enter in a particular capacity, and then 'switch' to a different category in circumstances where there is such a requirement.

Visitors

(See paras 40–56 of HC 395 as amended.)

An applicant for entry as a visitor must demonstrate that he or she is genuinely seeking entry for the period stated, which cannot exceed six months, that he or she intends to leave the United Kingdom at the end of the period of the visit, that he or she does not intend to seek employment, or produce goods or supply services in the United Kingdom, that he or she does not intend to study at a maintained school, that he or she can adequately accommodate and maintain himself and any dependant without recourse to public funds (or will be so accommodated and maintained by relatives or friends), and that he or she can meet the cost of any onward or return journey.

Leave to enter will not be granted past six months, and no extension will be granted that would take the total period of leave past six months. (There is an exception to this rule for those seeking entry or leave to remain for private medical treatment – see paras 51–56 of HC 395 as amended – providing the treatment can be shown to be finite in duration.)

The immigration rules make no specific provisions for children as dependants, and as such they may be granted leave in their own right. There is no requirement that they be travelling with an adult providing, of course they can show that they will be maintained and accommodated in accordance with the rules.

Students

(See paras 79–81 of HC 395 as amended.)

Children may of course wish to travel to the United Kingdom independently for the purposes of study. This is given consideration in Chapter 4. In this chapter consideration is given to the children of students.

The children of a parent admitted to, or permitted to remain in the United Kingdom as a student, will be allowed to enter providing they are under 18 years old. They will be permitted to remain past their 18th birthdays providing they had leave to enter or remain in this capacity prior to reaching their majority.

Further, any such child must be unmarried and have not formed any independent family unit, or be leading an independent life. The child must not stay beyond the period of leave granted to the parent.

The requirements of maintenance and accommodation without recourse to public funds apply.

If leave is granted to enter or remain, the child will be prohibited from taking employment unless the period of leave is for 12 months or more.

Working holidaymakers

(See paras 100–03 of HC 395 as amended.)

To qualify as a working holidaymaker, it is necessary to be a Commonwealth citizen aged between 17 and 27 years. Any employment intended to be taken should be incidental to the holiday. Any grant of leave to enter or remain will not exceed two years.

If married, the potential working holidaymaker's spouse must also qualify under the rules, and the couple must intend to take a working holiday together.

There are requirements with regard to maintenance and accommodation without recourse to public funds, and an intention to leave at the end of the working holiday. (See further para 95 of HC 395 as amended.)

Leave will not be granted to applicants who have a dependent child over five years of age, or a child who will reach five years during the period of the working holiday.

It follows that only children under five will be admitted as the dependants of working holidaymakers. Further, children will only be admitted if both parents are being admitted or allowed to remain, save where one parent is deceased, or the accompanying parent has had sole responsibility for the child's upbringing, or there are compelling family or other considerations which would make exclusion undesirable and suitable arrangements for the child's care have been made.

Prior entry clearance is required for children seeking leave to enter under this category.

Trainees/those involved in work experience/ employees

(See paras 197–99 of HC 395 as amended.)

Paragraphs 128–93 of HC 395 as amended are concerned with the control of leave to enter and remain of various categories of worker. Pursuant to paras 197–99, the children of such workers may be given leave to enter or remain in line with their parent or parents.

Any children will be allowed to enter providing they are under 18 years old. They will be permitted to remain past their 18th birthdays providing they had leave to enter or remain in this capacity prior to reaching their majority.

Further, any such child must be unmarried and have not formed any independent family unit, or be leading an independent life. The child must not stay beyond the period of leave granted to the parent.

A requirement of maintenance and accommodation without recourse to public funds applies in accommodation which the parent or parents own or occupy exclusively.

Children will only be admitted if both parents are being admitted or allowed to remain, save where one parent is deceased, or the accompanying parent has had sole responsibility for the child's upbringing, or there are compelling family or other considerations which would make exclusion undesirable and suitable arrangements for the child's care have been made. (There is provision in paras 194–96 of HC 395 as amended for the spouse of a worker to be admitted or remain in line with the worker.)

Prior entry clearance is required for children seeking leave to enter under this category.

Work under these rules may in certain circumstances lead to the grant of indefinite leave to remain. A child of a worker granted indefinite leave may also be granted indefinite leave providing all the requirements for leave to enter or remain continue to be satisfied.

Business people/investors and writers/composers/artists

(See paras 243–45 of HC 395 as amended.)

Paragraphs 200–39 are concerned with the control of leave to enter and remain of the above various categories. Pursuant to paras 243–45 the children of such individuals may be given leave to enter or remain in line with their parent or parents.

The requirements of leave to enter or remain for such children are in accordance with the requirements for the workers referred to above.

4 Independent children

In practice, children are unlikely to be travelling to the United Kingdom independently of their parents except for purposes covered by the following categories:

(i) visitors;

(ii) working holidaymakers;

(iii) students (including schoolchildren);

(iv) fiancé(e)s/spouses.

The requirements for entry or leave to remain for visitors and working holiday-makers were dealt with in the previous chapter in respect of adults. The same requirements apply to independent children (although it is to be noted that a working holidaymaker must be at least 17 years old). Accordingly, these requirements are not repeated herein.

Students

(See paras 57–62 of HC 395 as amended.)

The student rules cover those accepted for a course of study at a publicly funded institution of further or higher education, or at a private education institution which maintains satisfactory records of enrolment and attendance (such as a language school or private accountancy tutors), or an independent fee-paying school outside the maintained sector. It is the latter type of study that is likely to be applicable to children.

To qualify under the rules for leave to enter the United Kingdom, an applicant must show that he or she has been accepted at such a school, is able and intends to follow a full-time course of study at the school (which, if he or she is under 16 years of age, must meet the requirements of the Education Act 1944), and intends to leave the United Kingdom at the end of his or her studies.

Further, there must be no intention to work except part-time or vacation work undertaken with the consent of the Secretary of State for Employment. In practice, this requirement should present no difficulty for potential school pupils who are unlikely to be of working age.

There is also a requirement that the costs of the course of study and any accommodation and maintenance can be met without working or having recourse to public funds.

If an applicant qualifies under the rules, he or she will likely be admitted for a period appropriate to the length of the course and his or her means.

Extensions of stay as a school pupil may also be obtained providing that regular attendance is demonstrated and satisfactory progress is being made on the course, and the requirements for initial leave to enter continue to be satisfied.

It is to be noted that non-visa nationals may 'switch' to studies from other categories within the immigration rules.

After completion of a school course it may be possible for an individual to continue to higher or further education, or tuition at a private institution, providing the relevant rules are satisfied. However, there is a continuing expectation that a student will leave the United Kingdom on completion of all his or her studies.

Extensions may be refused where a student has a record of failure in examinations (which is not 'satisfactory progress' and casts doubt on his or her ability to follow his or her course) or if a student would be spending more than four years on 'short courses'. (See para 60(vi) of HC 395 as amended.)

Fiancé(e)s/spouses

(See paras 277–95 of HC 395 as amended.)

Whilst those entering marriages are not usually considered to be 'children', as indicated earlier in this work there is no strict definition of 'children' in the immigration legislation, and of course many under-18-year-olds do enter marriages. As such, brief consideration is given herein to the rules relating to fiancé(e)s and spouses.

In line with United Kingdom law, the immigration rules specifically state that they are not to be construed in any way to permit entry or leave to remain for a spouse where any party to the marriage will be under 16 years of age on the date of arrival or grant of leave to remain.

However, there is no such age restriction on the admission of fiancé(e)s, who may be granted up to six months leave to enter for the purpose of marriage. Accordingly, a fiancé(e) technically might qualify for admission at the age of 15 years and six months, and may subsequently apply for extension of leave to remain as a spouse following marriage and his or her 16th birthday.

Apart from this distinction on age, the rules relating to spouses and fiancé(e)s are very similar.

The requirements for leave to enter may be summarised as follows:

(i) the applicant for entry must be married or planning to be married to a person present and settled in the United Kingdom or being admitted at the same time for settlement;

(ii) the marriage or proposed marriage must not have been contracted primarily to obtain admission to the United Kingdom (the 'primary purpose rule');

(iii) the parties to the marriage must have met;

(iv) the parties must each have an intention to live together permanently as man and wife;

(v) there must be adequate accommodation for the parties and any dependants without recourse to public funds in accommodation that they own or occupy exclusively, and the parties must similarly be able to maintain themselves and any dependants without recourse to public funds. (Additionally, in the case of a fiancé(e), there must be adequate accommodation and maintenance without recourse to public funds pending the marriage.)

Both a fiancé(e) and a spouse require prior entry clearance if seeking leave to enter.

On entry, a fiancé(e) will be granted no more than six months leave to enter, with a prohibition on employment.

A fiancé(e) seeking variation of leave to remain will only be granted such a variation if he or she entered the United Kingdom with entry clearance as a fiancé(e) and can show good reason why the marriage did not take place as planned within the currency of the leave granted on entry, and there is satisfactory evidence that the marriage will presently take place at an early date.

There is no provision for an individual to 'switch' to the fiancé(e) category, eg a student at the end of studies cannot obtain an extension of leave as a fiancé(e) under the rules.

A spouse on entry will be granted 12 months' leave to enter. There is usually no prohibition on taking employment. Indefinite leave to remain may be obtained at the end of the initial 12-month period if the marriage is subsisting, both parties still intend to live permanently with each other as man and wife, and the requirements as to accommodation and maintenance continue to be satisfied.

An individual with valid leave under some other category may apply for a variation of leave as a spouse, eg a student who marries may apply to 'switch' categories. The same requirements detailed above for leave to enter will apply (save of course for the requirement of prior entry clearance). Additionally the applicant must have valid limited leave to remain in the United Kingdom and not to have breached any of the immigration laws or contracted the marriage after a decision to deport the applicant has been made by the Secretary of State for the Home Department, or a court recommendation for deportation following a criminal conviction has been made. If the rules are satisfied, an initial 12-month variation of leave will be granted, and indefinite leave may be granted thereafter if the marriage subsists, the parties still intend to live permanently with each other as man and wife, and the requirements as to maintenance and accommodation continue to be satisfied.

5 Adoption

There are immigration rules that govern applications for leave to enter or remain as an adopted child. (See paras 310–16 of HC 395 as amended.)

However, there are no rules relating to applicants seeking leave to enter for the purpose of adoption. Such applications are dealt with pursuant to a policy outwith the rules.

Applications within the rules

Under the immigration rules there are four types of application in respect of an adopted child:

(i) An application for indefinite leave to enter as the adopted child of a parent or parents present and settled or being admitted for settlement in the United Kingdom;

(ii) An application for indefinite leave to remain as the adopted child of a parent or parents present and settled in the United Kingdom;

(iii) An application for limited leave to enter with a view to settlement as the adopted child of a parent or parents given limited leave to enter or remain in the United Kingdom with a view to settlement;

(iv) An application for limited leave to remain with a view to settlement as the adopted child of a parent or parents given limited leave to enter or remain in the United Kingdom with a view to settlement.

All of these situations presuppose that an adoption has taken place.

The applicable rules are very similar to the rules governing children generally: para 310(i)–(iv) and (xi) compares with para 297(i)–(iv) and (v) (with a modification to (i)(f)); para 311(i)–(iv) compares with para 298(i)–(iv) (with a modification to (i)(d)); para 314(i)–(iv), (xi) and (xii) compares with para 301(i)–(iv), (v) and (vi). For guidance on these common requirements, see Chapter 2.

In addition to these matters, there are stipulations with regard to the circumstances of the adoption and the adoption process. The requirements are common to each of the four types of application identified above. They are:

(i) The applicant is to have been adopted in accordance with a decision taken by the competent administrative authority or court in his or her country of origin or the country in which he or she is resident;

(ii) The adoption is to have taken place at a time when either:

(a) both adoptive parents were resident together abroad; or

(b) either or both adoptive parents were settled in the United Kingdom;

(iii) The adopted child is to have the same rights and obligations as any other child of the marriage;

(iv) The applicant is to have been adopted due to the inability of the original parent or parents or current carer to care for him and there is to have been a genuine transfer of parental responsibility to the adoptive parents;

(v) The adopted child is to have lost or broken his or her ties with his or her family of origin;

(vi) The adoption is not to have been one of convenience arranged to facilitate the adopted child's admission or remaining in the United Kingdom.

It is plain that these requirements are aimed at ensuring that the circumstances surrounding the adoption of the applicant are broadly consistent with the principles applied in the United Kingdom before a court will approve an adoption order.

What is of note is that what is acceptable as an adoption is not limited to 'overseas' adoptions specifically recognised under the Adoption Act 1976 and the Adoptions (Designation of Overseas Adoptions) Order 1973.

Applications outwith the rules

If prospective adoptive parents wish to adopt a child living abroad, and wish to do so through the domestic courts, then they must comply with the procedures of the Home Office's policy set up outwith the immigration rules, and set out in a standard letter denoted as RON 117. If successful, this may culminate in the grant of entry clearance to the child, who will then usually be given six months' leave to enter, subsequent to which an adoption order may be sought through the courts.

The whole procedure is lengthy because a number of different agencies are involved.

Following the application for entry clearance (made pursuant to the appendices to the RON 117 letter), the entry clearance officer will make enquiries as to the child's circumstances in his or her home country: most obviously whether or not the child is free for adoption. The results of such enquiries are then referred to the Home Office, which makes a general check on whether there are any immigration bars to the application proceeding any further. If there are no apparent difficulties the application is passed to the Department of Health (or the Welsh Office if the prospective parents live in Wales).

The Department of Health is primarily concerned with welfare issues relating to the proposed adoption. In pursuit of this enquiries will be made of the prospective parents' local authority, which will in turn make a 'homestudy' of the circumstances of the prospective adoptive parents. The homestudy report is concerned with the suitability of the adults as parents, and will be concerned with such issues as their ages and capabilities, the suitability of their accommodation, their commitment and intentions. It is to be noted that this report is distinct from the report pursuant to Schedule 2 of the Adoption Rules 1984 (the report used by the domestic courts in considering the making of an adoption order). The latter report will be required at a later stage, and is a wider report in that it considers the suitability of the match between parents and child.

The local authority will report and make a recommendation to the Department of Health, who will in turn pass the matter back to the Home Office. If the recommendation is satisfactory, if the Department of Health has no concerns over the adoption being likely to safeguard and promote the welfare of the child concerned, and if there are no other immigration bars, then it is likely that the entry clearance officer will be authorised to issue entry clearance.

In considering any immigration bars, the Home Office and entry clearance officer will likely have regard to the provisions relating to children and adopted children within the rules, and apply them by analogy: for instance, the Home Office will wish to be satisfied that any proposed adoption will indeed involve a transfer of parental responsibility.

If entry clearance is granted, then after entry it will be necessary to seek an adoption order through the domestic courts in the usual manner. It is at this stage that the Schedule 2 report will be compiled by the local authority. The Home Office should be kept informed of the progress of the adoption application and of any court hearing dates. If the process will not be completed by the expiry of the period of leave to enter, an application for variation of leave to remain should be made to the Home Office.

The future

It is noted that at the time of writing there is a draft Adoption Bill which contains provisions in relation to intercountry adoptions. In particular, it would enable the United Kingdom to ratify the 1993 Hague Convention on Protection of Children and Co-operation in respect of Intercountry Adoption. This would promote mutual recognition of adoption orders by signatory countries.

It is suggested that advisers should always check on the current position of the law and any Home Office policy outside the rules, either by contacting the Home Office directly, or by making enquiries at the Embassy or High Commission in the child's country.

6 Asylum

The United Kingdom is a signatory to the 1951 Convention and 1967 Protocol relating to the Status of Refugees. Although it has for some time applied the terms of the Convention and Protocol, it was not until the coming into force of the Asylum and Immigration Appeals Act 1993 that the Convention was directly incorporated into domestic law.

The 1993 Act and paras 327–52 of HC 395 as amended provide the procedures in respect of applications for asylum. In addition, there is published by the Office of the United Nations High Commissioner for Refugees a *Handbook on Procedures and Criteria for Determining Refugee Status*. The *Handbook* does not have the force of law in the United Kingdom but is frequently used as guidance by the immigration appellate authorities, and is a useful tool to assist in interpretation of the Convention.

Asylum applications have increased worldwide in recent years as a result of instability and the wider availability of international transport. The introduction of the 1993 Act has meant an increased asylum workload for the immigration appellate authorities. The Asylum and Immigration Act 1996 introduced further measures in relation to asylum seekers, in particular in relation to entitlement to social security benefits. As far as the processing of applications is concerned, it made some important amendments to 'fast track' appeal procedures in relation to those passing through 'safe third countries' and from designated safe countries. It is an exciting and continually evolving area of law, both in terms of national and international jurisprudence. As such, a full treatment of the topic is beyond the scope of this publication. An overview of the general criteria applied in the United Kingdom is presented, together with an analysis of the impact on children.

It is to be noted that children may seek asylum in their own right, or more frequently may benefit as the dependants of adult asylum seekers.

General criteria

The Convention definition of a refugee that is generally applied in the United Kingdom is a person who:

> owing to a well-founded fear of being persecuted for reasons of race, religion, nationality, membership of a particular social group or political opinion, is outside the country of his nationality and is unable, or owing to such fear, is unwilling to avail himself of the protection of that country.

(See Article 1A(2) of the Convention.)

This definition requires that an applicant have a subjective fear, and that that fear is objectively well-founded.

The fear is to be of persecution. There has never been any satisfactory definition of what amounts to persecution. A recent authoritative *dictum* is that of Simon Brown LJ in *Sandralingam & Ravichandran v Secretary of State for the Home Department* [1996] Imm AR 97, where he stated:

> the issue ... raises a single composite question. It is, as it seems to me, unhelpful and potentially misleading to try to reach separate conclusions as to whether certain conduct amounts to persecution, and as to what reasons underlie it. Rather, the question whether someone is at risk of persecution for a Convention reason should be looked at in the round and all the relevant circumstances brought into account.

In *R v Immigration Appeal Tribunal ex parte Jonah* [1985] Imm AR 7 it was held that the word was to be given its ordinary dictionary definition: to pursue with malignancy or injurious action, especially to oppress for holding a heretical opinion or belief. In *Lazarevic and others v Secretary of State for the Home Department* (unreported – 13 February 1997) the Court of Appeal approved a definition of persecution as 'the sustained or systematic violation of human rights demonstrative of a failure of State protection'.

It is apparent that the drafters of the Convention deliberately avoided defining the word 'persecution' too strictly. It is perhaps now generally recognised that it is to be considered in accordance with prevailing circumstances and the object and purpose of the Convention. In this way the Convention can evolve to meet the changing world order.

The UNHCR *Handbook* suggests that a threat to life or freedom would always constitute persecution. At the lower end of the scale, it is suggested that mere discrimination is unlikely to be sufficient, although if it is against a background of instability and insecurity, or if it is of a nature that is substantially prejudicial, such as affecting the right to earn a living, then discrimination may too amount to persecution.

It is to be noted that to establish a well-founded fear of persecution, it is not necessary to demonstrate that persecution *will* take place: it is sufficient that there be a reasonable degree of likelihood of future persecution. (See *Sivakumaran v Secretary of State for the Home Department* [1988] AC 958.)

The feared persecution must also arise for one or more of the 'Convention grounds', ie for reasons of race, religion, nationality, membership of a particular social group, or political opinion. With the exception of 'social group' these categories are largely self-explanatory. 'Social group' seems to have been introduced as a 'catch-all' provision, and so again there has been a resistance to giving it any strict definition. In broad terms, it might be said that individuals who share a common, immutable characteristic (which may include a shared past experience), which may be defined by objective criteria, form a social group for the purposes of the Convention.

An applicant need not have left his or her home country because of a well-founded fear. It is possible to become a refugee '*sur place*' where events after leaving give rise to the requisite well-founded fear.

If an applicant is able to return to his or her home country but is unwilling, then the well-founded fear must be current. However, the position is different with regard to an applicant who is unable to return. If the fear or actuality of past persecution still plays a causative part in the applicant's presence in the United Kingdom, it is not necessary to demonstrate a current risk of persecution. (See *Lazarevic and others v Secretary of State for the Home Department* (unreported – 13 February 1997)). In the same case, the Court of Appeal held that the denial of return may constitute an act of persecution in itself.

It is not necessary to demonstrate that the risk of persecution extends throughout the country from which the applicant seeks refuge. If the risk is established in one area of the country, it may then become an issue of whether or not it is reasonable to expect the applicant to seek refuge within his or her country the internal flight alternative. (See para 343 of HC 395 as amended and *R v Immigration Appeal Tribunal ex parte Anandanadarajah* [1996] Imm AR 514.)

The risk of persecution need not emanate directly from the State. It is sufficient if the risk emanates from other sections of the community in circumstances where the State is unwilling or unable to offer effective protection from the risk.

Consideration of applications

An application for asylum may be at any stage upon or after arrival in the United Kingdom, and it must be referred to the Secretary of State by the immigration officer receiving the application. However, there is a tendency by the Home Office to doubt the credibility of applicants who do not apply at the first available opportunity, ie upon arrival, or in the case of a refugee '*sur place*' at or about the time that the situation in the applicant's home country gave rise to his or her fear of persecution if returned. In many cases such scepticism is misplaced: many applicants are unaware of the procedures for claiming asylum, or if they already have current leave to enter or remain do not think it necessary to seek to alter their current status – they are after all not at risk of return during the pendency of any leave, and may have a better prospect of avoiding return by extending their current status than they do of succeeding with an asylum claim.

An application made at the port of entry may be refused without substantive consideration of its merits if it is considered by the Home Office that the applicant had an opportunity to claim asylum in another country en route to the United Kingdom and it would be safe to return the applicant to that country to pursue an asylum claim; safe in the sense that the Secretary of State is satisfied that that country would fulfil its Convention obligations in respect of the applicant. (See para 345 of HC 395 as amended – Third country cases.) An application may also be refused without substantive consideration if it is considered frivolous. There is a special 'fast track' appeal procedure in these types of cases.

If an application is considered substantively by the Home Office, the applicant will ordinarily complete a questionnaire about his or her circumstances and reasons for seeking asylum, and subsequently be interviewed by an immigration officer. (However, see the comments below in relation to children.)

Any adverse decision will lead to a further immigration decision (to refuse leave to enter, to refuse variation of leave to remain, to decide to make a deportation order, or to give removal directions) and that applicant will be entitled to appeal to the immigration appellate authorities against that latter decision on the ground that any removal in consequence of the decision would be contrary to the United Kingdom's obligations under the Convention. (See s 8 of the Asylum and Immigration Appeals Act 1993.)

In some circumstances, the Home Office will refuse asylum, but grant exceptional leave to remain outside the immigration rules. For instance, the Secretary of State is unlikely to return applicants to war zones, or may grant exceptional leave to give effect to other international obligations outside the Refugee Convention, such as the European Convention on Human Rights or the United Nations Convention on Torture, or may grant exceptional leave if there are some compelling humanitarian or compassionate circumstances in respect of the individual applicant.

The position of children

A child may fall for consideration under the provisions of para 349 of HC 395 as amended as the dependant of an adult applicant. In such circumstances, there is unlikely to be separate consideration of the child's position. If the adult is granted asylum, then the child is likely to be given leave to remain in accordance with the adult, although this will not technically be a grant of asylum to the child.

Paragraphs 350–52 are concerned with applications made by unaccompanied children. Paragraph 351 suggests in certain circumstances it is not necessary for a child to have understood the nature of any risk, or have any subjective fear, if objectively there is indeed a well-founded risk of persecution. Paragraph 352 advocates the obtaining of information from sources other than the child if at all possible.

In certain circumstances, it may be advantageous for an application for asylum to be explicitly made on behalf of a child who is present as a dependant of another adult who fears persecution. An adult may fear persecution, but that persecution may not be for a Convention reason. However, because of the risk to the adult, it may be that members of the family are also at risk by reason of association. It is then possible to argue that, for instance, the child is at risk because of family membership, and that constitutes a Convention reason, a family being a social group. The child would be entitled to asylum, even if the principal adult were not. (See, for example, the recent Immigration Appeal Tribunal decision in *Hernandez* (12773).)

The principle of family unity

Often, because of circumstances in the home country, an asylum seeker will arrive without his or her family members. If asylum is granted then he or she will be entitled to apply for family reunion. 'Family' is usually restricted to spouses and unmarried dependent children. An application for entry clearance may be made forthwith upon the grant of asylum.

However, those individuals granted exceptional leave are not usually accorded the same entitlement. Ordinarily, they are not permitted to have family members join them until four years have been spent with exceptional leave. It may be arguable that this is contrary to Article 8 of the European Convention on Human Rights.

7 Special cases

Children in care

Occasionally a child will arrive in the United Kingdom with his or her family, and during the course of the child's stay concerns over his or her welfare will become apparent, leading to local authority social services involvement and intervention.

This may culminate in the making of a care order or supervision order, if the situation is such that the criteria in s 31(2) of the Children Act 1989 are satisfied:

> (a) that the child concerned is suffering, or likely to suffer, significant harm; and
>
> (b) that the harm or likelihood of harm is attributable to:
>
> > (i) the care given to the child, or likely to be given to him if the order were not made, not being what it would be reasonable to expect a parent to give to him; or
> >
> > (ii) the child's being beyond parental control.

It is to be noted that the assessment of what it is reasonable to expect a parent to give will likely be measured in accordance with domestic standards and customs, eg female circumcision would be a possible ground for making a care order.

A care order gives parental responsibility to the local authority, whereas a supervision order does not, it allowing the local authority involvement in planning and monitoring the child's welfare arrangements.

Following the making of an order, the local authority will have a duty to attempt to facilitate the rehabilitation of the child with his or her family. If successful rehabilitation is completed during the currency of any leave to enter or remain that the child and the family have, then the child will simply rejoin his or her family, and any further immigration application be considered in accordance with the general rules.

However, questions of status will arise where leave expires before rehabilitation is complete, or where rehabilitation is going to be unlikely.

In such circumstances the local authority will have a duty to ascertain the country of origin of the child, and the likely welfare provisions in that country. If the social service system is likely to be deemed acceptable to a United

Kingdom court, then the local authority should communicate its concerns over the child's welfare with the relevant social services department abroad. If the domestic court is satisfied as to the provision of adequate welfare services abroad, it is unlikely that the court will allow the local authority to retain the child in the United Kingdom.

Further, in any event the Home Office will be aware of the factual background when considering any immigration application in respect of the child, and will likely take the attitude that any rehabilitation is best continued in the country of origin; if there is to be no rehabilitation, in any event the child's interests are better served by being looked after by the social services in the country of origin.

However, concerns can arise where the social services standard might be deemed to be unacceptable, or where due to the length of Home Office deliberations (eg on an asylum case) a child might be in care for some considerable time.

Where there is cause for concern over the standard of care in the country of origin, it is likely that the domestic court will be anxious to avoid return, particularly if any care plan of the local authority that offers the child an alternative to rehabilitation is going to benefit his or her welfare (eg if the child is thriving with foster parents who may wish to (or have applied to) adopt).

Any order that the domestic court makes in respect of a child cannot fetter the power and discretion of the Secretary of State to enforce the removal of a child in such a situation. (See *R v Secretary of State for the Home Department ex parte T* [1995] 1 FLR 293.) However, the domestic court does have power to consider its jurisdiction under the Children Act (or wardship as appropriate). Whilst the Court of Appeal in *ex parte T* stated that it would not be appropriate for a court to use its jurisdiction to influence the Secretary of State, it would appear that in a suitable case where the Children Act criteria were satisfied, the court could make an appropriate order, which although in no way binding on the Secretary of State's approach, would nonetheless be a matter to which the Secretary of State should have proper regard when considering the exercise of his power to enforce departure.

Abandoned children

A new-born abandoned child may be deemed to have acquired British Citizenship by virtue of s 1(2) of the British Nationality Act 1981. Such will be the case unless it can be shown that the child was not born in the United Kingdom or was not the child of a parent with citizenship or settled in the United Kingdom. In such circumstances, the child will not be subject to immigration control and the local authority will fall to deal with the child in accordance with its general duties to provide services for children.

An older abandoned child will fall for consideration in much the same was as a child the subject of a care or supervision plan. However, in some circumstances, it will not be possible to ascertain the country of origin of the abandoned child. In such a case removal from the United Kingdom will be inappropriate.

Long-term residence concessions

There are policy concessions outside the immigration rules in relation to long-term residence, which may result in the grant of indefinite leave to remain.

If an individual has a period of 10 years' lawful residence in the United Kingdom there is a discretion to grant indefinite leave to remain. It may be seen that a child who is a long-term student, or a pupil who commenced schooling in the United Kingdom at the age of six years, might qualify under this concession. (Similarly, a child born in the United Kingdom may acquire citizenship by registration if he or she has spent no more than 90 days abroad in each of the first 10 years of his or her life – see s 1(4) of the British Nationality Act 1984.) At one stage, there was a presumption in favour of the grant of indefinite leave, but the policy has been toughened and now it is merely a matter of discretion to be exercised on the merits of the individual case.

Similarly, at one stage, 14 years' residence, even where some of that period was unlawful, was considered sufficient to warrant indefinite leave. It is now extremely difficult to obtain such leave if any of the period were unlawful.

When deportation procedure is contemplated against adults, the fact of there being children with lengthy residence is a factor that is to be taken into consideration as militating against deportation. DP 5/96 sets out the matters to which immigration officers should have regard. (See Appendix III.)

8 Contact

The immigration rules

Until 1 October 1994, the introduction of HC 395 as amended, the immigration rules made no provision in respect of individuals seeking to visit the United Kingdom for the purposes of exercising contact with their children. Parents could simply avail themselves of the 'visitor' rule.

However, paras 246–48 of HC 395 as amended introduced specific requirements for 'persons exercising rights of access to a child resident in the United Kingdom'. (The rules insist on using the now outmoded term 'access' throughout.)

These rules appear to have been introduced because the absence of a specific provision was causing difficulties to the Home Office in the context of seeking to remove parents who were not entitled to remain here, but had children settled here with a former partner. It was being argued that such parents had no remedy to permit them to remain for the purposes of seeing their children. The rule appears to have been designed to allow the Home Office to remove such a parent and yet be able to say that such removal would not deprive the parent of contact as he or she could reapply for entry under the new rules.

The main requirements of the rule are:

(i) that there is a contact order from a United Kingdom court;

(ii) that the applicant is seeking leave to enter for the purposes of exercising contact;

(iii) that the applicant is either divorced or legally separated from the other parent;

(iv) that the applicant intends to leave the United Kingdom at the expiry of his or her leave to enter;

(v) that the applicant does not intend to work in the United Kingdom;

(vi) that the applicant will maintain him or herself and any dependants without recourse to public funds or work, or alternatively will be so maintained by friends or relatives;

(vii) that the applicant can meet the cost of the journey out of the United Kingdom.

Entry clearance must be obtained prior to travelling to the United Kingdom.

If the rules are satisfied, and the applicant has already obtained entry clearance, then leave to enter will ordinarily be granted with a condition prohibiting employment. Leave should be granted for a suitable period to enable the exercise of the contact rights, but will be for no longer than 12 months.

There is no rule governing an application for an extension of leave to remain in this capacity. (See 'Parent seeking contact when already present in the United Kingdom' below.)

Limitations of the rule

The most obvious limitation of the rule is that it is restricted to parents who either have been or are married (but separated) to the other parent of their child or children. It thereby excludes all those parents who are seeking to exercise contact to children born outside wedlock, no matter how long or stable a relationship was enjoyed with the other parent. (See 'Parents who were not married' below.)

Further, the rule is limited to those who have already obtained a contact order from a United Kingdom court. If there is no current order, an order should be sought by applying to the Family Division of the High Court (the appropriate forum for applications of an international nature). The prospects of obtaining such an order whilst abroad are slight because:

(i) the applicant, being absent will not have the opportunity of being assessed by a court welfare officer, whose opinion will be highly regarded by the court;

(ii) if the applicant is absent from the hearing, the court will not make any order for contact as it too will not be in a position to assess the merits of the application and the applicant – additionally if the court requires any undertakings from the applicant in any respect these cannot be taken as they should be given in person;

(iii) further, in most cases, it will be very difficult to put forward any meaningful plans for the exercise of contact.

If faced with such a situation, a parent may have to apply for leave to enter as a visitor, and pursue contact proceedings during that period of leave. It may even be possible to instruct a United Kingdom solicitor whilst abroad to conduct the preliminary aspects of the contact application, and then visit the United Kingdom only for the purposes of assessment and the hearing. Legal aid may be available, subject to means, even from abroad. Such a process is unwieldy and potentially expensive in terms of travel costs, but would appear to be the only option as the rules stand at the moment.

An overseas parent is also presented with the potential uncertainty of being able to obtain a contact order on the merits of his or her case in circumstances such as where contact would be extremely limited and there is the competing interest of a new partner of the other parent.

In circumstances where there is no dispute between parents as to the desirability of contact, there may often not be any order as it is not considered necessary. As the rules specifically require a court order, it would be advisable to obtain such an order. Even though the principle of the Children Act 1989 is not to record an order where parties agree, if the purpose of the order is to facilitate immigration clearance, with the purpose being to facilitate contact, and there no suggestion of any improper ulterior motive, then it is unlikely that the court will refuse to make such an order. Whilst the High Court will not want (and cannot) fetter the discretion of the Home Office in its decision to grant or refuse entry clearance or leave to enter, if the purpose of the application is simply to record the genuine wish of both parents through a consent order the High Court is likely to do so. If, however, the court is reluctant to make a Children Act order, such a consent order could be applied for in wardship or under the inherent jurisdiction of the High Court. (See further 'Impact of immigration status on the decision to make a contact order' below.)

A further difficulty will arise for many by reason of the prohibition on employment. In practical terms, this means that for most parents, although 12 months' leave may be 'on offer' they will only be in a position, after the expense of air fares and maintaining and accommodating themselves at their own expense in the United Kingdom, to visit for relatively short periods, only occasionally. This, of course, undermines the whole purpose of contact in seeking to preserve the relationship between parent and child, which will be particularly crucial where the child is very young.

Where an applicant lives abroad and gains an order for contact to be exercised either within or without the jurisdiction, the court is likely to expect the applicant to give undertakings to return the child to the other parent's care and control at the end of the contact period, and to return the child to the jurisdiction of England and Wales if the child is to be taken abroad for any duration of the contact period.

The court can also order that the contact order of the English court be registered abroad, or obtain a 'mirror' order in the court local to where the applicant resides abroad. A mirror order is likely to be especially preferred where the applicant resides in a country whose legal system does not own any comity with the English system, or where the country is not a signatory to the Hague Convention on the Civil Aspects of International Child Abduction 1985. Even if the country is such a signatory, mirror orders can still be required as unfortunately some signatory countries are not complying with orders already obtained in the English courts to the same standard as the English courts do in dealing with orders obtained abroad.

Children coming to the United Kingdom for the purpose of contact with a United Kingdom-resident parent

There is no specific rule that covers this category. As such, it will be necessary to consider the position either within one of the existing categories, or exceptionally outside the rules. There is a potential problem in that on a strict interpretation of the immigration rules entry clearance or leave to enter is to be refused if entry is being sought for a purpose not covered by the rules. (See para 320(1) of HC 395 as amended.) This would suggest that if the sole purpose of any visit was contact no entry clearance or leave should be granted. However, it is likely that in practice contact would be considered to be collateral with some other purpose, eg a holiday.

Indeed, in most cases an application as a visitor is likely to suffice. Necessarily this directs itself towards short-term contact and will not enable regular long-term contact to be exercised.

In some cases, the child will be visiting the United Kingdom unaccompanied to stay throughout with the United Kingdom-resident parent (eg during school holidays). In other cases, the parent with care and control may wish to accompany the child, and the child to stay with him or her and visit the United Kingdom-resident parent only occasionally. There may be practical difficulties in the latter case, in particular arising from the prohibition on employment and recourse to public funds under the visitor rules, which may, again, have the effect of limiting the period and frequency of contact.

On the positive side, however, it would appear that there would be no necessity for there to be any form of court order (in this jurisdiction or any other) in order to obtain leave in this capacity.

Parent seeking contact when already present in the United Kingdom

There is no provision in the immigration rules for a parent to seek a variation of leave, or leave to remain for the purpose of exercising contact with a child in the United Kingdom. As such, at the expiry of any current leave, and in the absence of being able to extend that leave under the rules, the parent will become liable to removal/deportation procedures as he or she will have no legal status in the United Kingdom. An example might be a student whose studies have now concluded, but who has been in the United Kingdom for five years during which time he has fathered a child with whom he has enjoyed close contact. In such circumstances the Home Office circulars DP2/93, DP3/96 and DP4/96 are likely to be of application. (See Appendix III.)

It is now settled law that the Secretary of State must have regard to his own guidelines as set out within these documents in exercising his discretion when considering whether or not removal or deportation is appropriate. This does not mean that he must follow the guidelines in every case, but where he does not, in the absence of any explanation for departing from the guidelines, there may be scope for challenge of such a decision. (See further para 1(3) of Schedule 2 to the Immigration Act 1971: 'In the exercise of their functions under this Act immigration officers shall act in accordance with such instructions (not inconsistent with the immigration rules) as may be given them by the Secretary of State ...'.)

The Home Office circulars seek to give effect to the attitude of the European Court of Human Rights towards the right to respect for family life provided for by Article 8 of the European Convention on Human Rights (see further below). This does not have the effect of incorporating Article 8 into English law, but it does mean that the Home Office must at least have regard to Article 8. (See further *Hlomodor* [1993] Imm AR 534.)

In this context the most important passage in DP2/93 is at para 5. Providing that there is 'frequent and regular access currently by either parent', it is recommended that removal action be abandoned. This would seem to apply regardless of whether it is the parent with residence or the parent exercising contact who is the potential subject of removal or deportation action.

However, the policy under DP4/96 represents a hardening of attitude. See especially at para 7, where it suggests that enforcement action should only be abandoned in exceptional cases. The absurdity of this change of policy and the contact rules is underlined by the fact that para 8 recognises the difficulties for those not married and those facing a potential three-year bar from return to the United Kingdom: it implicitly recognises that the never-married parents should be less susceptible to removal than divorced or separated parents.

The precise meanings of 'frequent and regular' (DP2/93) and 'quality and regularity' (DP4/96) would appear to be a matter for the Secretary of State, who will often require proof of such contact. A court order will assist in discharging this proof, but is not a prerequisite. However, if the parent with residence is uncooperative he or she may take advantage of the situation by failing to provide corroborative evidence of contact, or actually misinforming the Home Office. It may be possible to argue that the 'frequent and regular' test puts the matter higher than is required on a strict interpretation of Article 8 (see further below), but as Article 8 has not been incorporated this argument encounters difficulties in the domestic jurisdiction!

The Home Office tends to be suspicious of contact applications made around the time of curtailment of leave, and may seek to intervene in contact proceedings. It is now settled that regardless of any order made in the family courts, the Secretary of State's discretion to proceed with deportation or removal cannot be usurped. (See *R v Secretary of State for the Home Department ex parte T* [1995] 1 FLR 293.)

In circumstances where the parent exercising contact is still entitled to remain in the United Kingdom (eg continuing studies), the guidance of the Home Office circulars will have no application.

European Convention on Human Rights, Article 8

Article 8 provides:

> 1. Everyone has the right to respect for private and family life, his home and his correspondence.
>
> 2. There shall be no interference by public authority with the exercise of this right except such as is in accordance with the law and is necessary in a democratic society in the interests of national security, public safety, or the economic well-being of the country, for the prevention of disorder or crime, for the protection of health or morals, or for the protection of the rights and freedoms of others.

As indicated above, Article 8 has not been incorporated into English law, although it is something to which the Secretary of State is to have regard.

Attempts to incorporate the provisions of the Convention have met with little success in the courts to date. The leading case at present is *Brind* [1991] 1 AC 696. This would suggest that if the Home Office is not going to follow the provisions of the Convention it needs to provide some justification for not doing so. It may be seen that the domestic jurisdiction is approaching the somewhat absurd position where there is no need to follow the Convention, if an explanation is given, but that in such circumstances the government will be implicitly admitting it is not following the Convention, and thereby opening itself up for challenge in the European Court. This area of law has been the subject of recent judicial consideration in the immigration context and the application of Article 8. The approach of the courts at the present time seems to be to allow the Secretary of State a very wide margin of discretion, and not to impose any great due of justification of departure from the ECHR. (See further *Patel* [1995] Imm AR 223 and *Mbatube* [1996] Imm AR 184.)

The European case law is such that it may be argued that the meaning of 'family life' provides a lower test than does the phrase 'frequent and regular access'. The test for 'family life' may be advanced as being the existence of close ties amounting to a real and genuine bond. In the context of a parent/child relationship such a bond is likely to have arisen where there has been significant contact in the past. In order to found a case under Article 8, it would be necessary to demonstrate that there is continuing significant contact, and that the bond would likely be effectively broken were either the parent or child required to leave the country. (See *Berrehab v Netherlands* (1988) 11 EHRR 322.)

It may also be argued that 'family life' extends beyond the parent/child relationship to grandparents and uncles and aunts. There is some support for this proposition to be found in the provisions of the Children Act 1989. Para 15(1) of Schedule 2 requires a local authority that is looking after a child to endeavour to promote contact with, *inter alia*, relatives, and 'relative' is defined in s 105 as including grandparents, uncles and aunts. This would indicate a recognition by Parliament of the importance of contact with the extended family. Further support to this proposition is lent by the European case of *Marckx v Belgium* (1979) 2 EHRR 330.

Impact of immigration status on the decision to make a contact order

As indicated above the Home Office is often suspicious, sometimes with good reason, of applications made for contact, or other applications involving children, in the English courts, particularly if they coincide with curtailment of leave in some capacity. Such applications are sometimes seen as attempts to evade or frustrate removal or deportation procedures. In some circumstances, the Home Office will seek leave to intervene in the proceedings in the family courts.

It was held in *ex parte T* that the court has jurisdiction to entertain Children Act applications or to invoke its wardship jurisdiction, notwithstanding the prospect, or the fact, of there being an adverse immigration decision. However, because any order in such proceedings could not deprive the Secretary of State of his powers to remove or deport under the Immigration Act 1971, such jurisdiction of the family courts was to be used sparingly, and not as a means of influencing the decision of the Secretary of State. In a hopeless case where it is plain the jurisdiction is being invoked as a device to frustrate immigration actions, advisers should pay heed to the possibility of a wasted costs order being made against them. In *Ridehalgh v Horsefield* it was observed by the Court of Appeal that whilst it was 'one thing' for a representative to present a hopeless case on instructions, it is 'quite another' to lend assistance to proceedings which are an abuse of the process of the court: a representative is not entitled to use litigious procedures for purposes for which they were not intended.

However, it is suggested that there can be little scope for criticism where there are genuine concerns for the welfare of a child.

Parents who were not married

There is no provision in the immigration rules for a parent of a child who was never married to the other parent, to apply for entry clearance or leave to enter for the purpose of contact. Such a parent would fall to be refused entry accordingly.

In such circumstances, an application for consideration exceptionally outside the immigration rules would have to be made. In the absence of a favourable decision, there is little scope for challenge within the domestic jurisdiction. This is plainly a regrettable lacuna in the present legislation and rules for which there is no apparent justification. It is not clear whether this is a matter of deliberate policy or oversight. In either event it is to be hoped that the rules will be revised in the near future.

It has already been indicated above that the Home Office circulars underline the inconsistency of the present policies and rules. An example of this, which indicates that a never-married parent might be in a better position than a divorced or separated parent is to be found in the case of *Zighem* [1996] Imm AR 194.

Residence

In circumstances where a parent resident abroad wishes to obtain a residence order, with a parallel order of leave to remove the child from the jurisdiction permanently (ie wishes to take child home with him to live), then that parent will be in a similar position to the parent from abroad seeking a contact order.

Legal aid

Any applicant from abroad is entitled to seek legal aid for representation in proceedings in the English family courts. The legal aid board will consider the means of the applicant, taking into account moneys/income within this jurisdiction and abroad before deciding upon whether legal aid should be granted with or without a contribution, or refused altogether.

9 Deportation

General procedure

The Secretary of State's power to deport is founded in s 3 of the Immigration Act 1971 (see sub-ss (5) and (6)). Four circumstances in which the power may be exercised are stipulated:

(i) breach of a condition of leave (including overstaying that leave);

(ii) removal deemed conducive to the public good;

(iii) following recommendation for deportation by a criminal court;

(iv) by reason of being a member of the family of a person ordered to be deported.

(See also para 363 of HC 395 as amended.)

Paragraphs 362–95 of HC 395 as amended offer guidance as to the manner in which the power is exercised.

Deportation involves a two-stage process. Initially, there is a decision in principle to make a deportation order. Subsequently, and depending on intervening events, there is the signing of the deportation order.

After the initial decision there is a right of appeal (except in 'conducive to the public good' cases), and an opportunity to make arrangements for voluntary or supervised departure. The right of appeal is limited by virtue of s 5 of the Immigration Act 1988 if an individual last entered the United Kingdom less than seven years before the decision (save in cases involving asylum claims or the curtailment of leave). On a limited appeal, the appellate authorities will not investigate the merits of a case but confine themselves to whether or not on the facts of the case there is the power in law to deport for the stated reason.

If the matter gets to the stage of a deportation order being signed, then the deportee will not be allowed to return to the United Kingdom until such time as the order is revoked. Ordinarily, an order will not be revoked until at least three years have passed. (See further paras 390–95 of HC 395 as amended.)

In considering whether deportation is appropriate, the Secretary of State is to have regard to the factors set out at para 364 of HC 395 as amended. It is to be noted that this paragraph indicates that there is a presumption in favour of deportation where there has been a failure to comply with conditions of leave, or a period of remaining without leave ('overstaying').

The position of children

Children are not usually the subject of deportation proceedings in their own right. However, abandoned children or children taken into care may be so subjected. In such circumstances, the Secretary of State will wish to ascertain that there is sufficient child care provision for the deportee in the country of origin. (See similarly Chapter 7, Special cases.)

Where a child may be subject to deportation by reason of being a member of the family of an adult deportee, then the provisions of paras 366 and 367 of HC 395 as amended must be taken into consideration. Deportation may be avoided if the child is living apart from the deportee with his or her mother or father, or is otherwise leading a life independent of the deportee. In addition to the criteria in para 364, the Secretary of State should also have regard to the likely effect on a child's education, and the effect on plans for the child's care and maintenance.

Further, the Home Office circulars provide further guidance for decision-makers. In particular, the provisions of para 7 of DP3/96, paras 2–9 of DP4/96, and the whole of DP5/96 may impact on any decision to deport children, or indeed to refrain from deporting an adult on the basis of the presence in the United Kingdom of children of the family.

It is to be noted that the Home Office does not consider the removal of children with their parents to be an interference with family life contrary to Article 8 of the European Convention on Human Rights. This is on the basis that, providing it is reasonable to expect the children to accompany the departing parent or parents, there is no reason why family life cannot continue outside the United Kingdom.

It is to be noted that, as with so many matters, the discretion of the Secretary of State is at large when considering what course to take, although para 364 makes reference to aiming for a consistent and fair exercise of power.

If a deportation order is signed, the usual minimum three-year period before revocation may not apply in the case of a child, the order in respect of whom is revoked upon his or her reaching 18 years of age. (See para 389(i).)

10 British citizenship

A child with British citizenship will be exempt from immigration control. This does not necessarily mean that it might not be considered reasonable by the Secretary of State to expect a child to leave the United Kingdom with a parent who is subject to immigration control, but the fact of the child's citizenship will be an important countervailing factor against the enforced departure of a parent. It will also necessarily mean that the child will have no difficulty entering the United Kingdom at some future time, without the requirement of obtaining any form of entry clearance or leave.

British citizenship is governed by the provisions of the British Nationality Act 1981. (See Appendix I.) The Act provides for:

(i) Acquisition by birth;

(ii) Acquisition by adoption;

(iii) Acquisition by descent;

(iv) Acquisition by registration;

(v) Acquisition by naturalisation.

(The categories under the Act of British Dependent Territory citizens, British Overseas citizens, British subjects, and citizens of independent Commonwealth countries, do not confer any exemption from immigration control. As such they have been excluded from analysis in this publication.)

Acquisition by birth

A person born at the present time in the United Kingdom will be a British citizen if his or her father or mother is a British citizen, or is settled in the United Kingdom. (See s 1(1) of the Act.)

Similarly, there is a presumption of citizenship in the case of a foundling. (See s 1(2).)

A person who is born in the United Kingdom at the present time who is not a British citizen is entitled to register if whilst still a minor his or her father or mother becomes a British citizen or becomes settled in the United Kingdom. (See s 1(3).)

It is to be noted that where a child is born out of wedlock the relationship of father/child is not recognised by virtue of s 50(9) and so a father could not pass citizenship. However, in accordance with s 47, the child may be 'legitimated' as from birth if there is a subsequent marriage of his or her parents.

A person may also register by reason of his or her birth if, not being a British citizen he or she spent no more than 90 days each year for the first 10 years of his or her life outside the United Kingdom. (See s 1(4).) The 90-day requirement may be varied more generously at the discretion of the Secretary of State. (See s 1(7).)

Acquisition by adoption

Where a person is adopted by order of a United Kingdom court and where the adopter, or if a joint adoption one of the adopters, is a British citizen, then the adopted child shall acquire British citizenship. (See s 1(5).)

It is to be noted that a foreign adoption order will not confer such citizenship. A child in such circumstances may apply for registration as a citizen at the discretion of the Secretary of State pursuant to s 3(1) of the Act.

Acquisition by descent

A person born outside the United Kingdom may acquire citizenship by descent if his or her father or mother (subject to s 50(9)) is a British citizen otherwise than by descent, or is involved in Crown service, European Community service or some other designated service, in accordance with the provisions of s 2 of the Act.

Acquisition by registration

Under s 3(1), the Secretary of State has a discretion to permit a minor to register as a British citizen 'if he thinks fit'.

There is an entitlement to registration if the criteria referred to in sub-ss (2) and (5) are satisfied.

Further, there is an entitlement to registration by any person (including a minor) who is a British Dependent Territories citizen, a British Overseas citizen, a British subject or a British protected person if he or she can satisfy the criteria as to residence specified in s 4(2) of the Act.

Both s 3 and s 4 provide the Secretary of State with a discretion to relax certain of the criteria applicable.

Acquisition by naturalisation

Providing certain criteria as set out in Schedule 1 of the Act are met, then naturalisation is at the discretion of the Secretary of State.

However, it is to be noted that an applicant for naturalisation must be of full age and capacity. (See s 6(1) and (2).) As such it is not possible for a child to acquire citizenship in this manner.

Appendix I

Immigration Act 1971

CHAPTER 77

ARRANGEMENT OF SECTIONS

PART I

REGULATION OF ENTRY INTO AND STAY IN UNITED KINGDOM

Section

1. General principles.
2. Statement of right of abode, and related amendments as to citizenship by registration.
3. General provisions for regulation and control.
4. Administration of control.
5. Procedure for, and further provisions as to, deportation.
6. Recommendations by court for deportation.
7. Exemption from deportation for certain existing residents.
8. Exceptions for seamen, aircrews and other special cases.
9. Further provisions as to common travel area.
10. Entry otherwise than by sea or air.
11. Construction of references to entry, and other phrases relating to travel.

PART II

APPEALS

The appellate authorities

12. Immigration Appeal Tribunal and adjudicators.

Appeals to adjudicator or Tribunal in first instance

13. Appeals against exclusion from United Kingdom.
14. Appeals against conditions.
15. Appeals in respect of deportation orders.
16. Appeals against validity of directions for removal.
17. Appeals against removal on objection to destination.
18. Notice of matters in respect of which there are rights of appeal.
19. Determination of appeals by adjudicators.

Section

Appeals from adjudicator to Tribunal, and review of decisions

20. Appeal to Tribunal from determination of adjudicator.
21. Reference of cases for further consideration.

Supplementary

22. Procedure.
23. Financial support for organisations helping persons with rights of appeal.

PART III

CRIMINAL PROCEEDINGS

24. Illegal entry and similar offences.
25. Assisting illegal entry, and harbouring.
26. General offences in connection with administration of Act.
27. Offences by persons connected with ships or aircraft or with ports.
28. Proceedings.

PART IV

SUPPLEMENTARY

29. Contributions for expenses of persons returning abroad.
30. Return of mental patients.
31. Expenses.
32. General provisions as to Orders in Council, etc.
33. Interpretation.
34. Repeal, transitional and temporary.
35. Commencement, and interim provisions.
36. Power to extend to Islands.
37. Short title and extent.

SCHEDULES:

Schedule 1—Registration as citizen by reason of residence, Crown service, etc.

Schedule 2—Administrative provisions as to control on entry and departure.

Part I—General provisions.

Part II—Effect of appeals.

Schedule 3—Supplementary provisions as to deportation.

Schedule 4—Integration with United Kingdom law of immigration law of Islands.

Schedule 5—The adjudicators and the Tribunal.

Part I—The adjudicators.

Part II—The Tribunal.

Part III—Staff and expenses.

Schedule 6—Repeals.

1971 CHAPTER 77

An Act to amend and replace the present immigration laws, to make certain related changes in the citizenship law and enable help to be given to those wishing to return abroad, and for purposes connected therewith.

[28 October 1911]

BE IT ENACTED by the Queen's most Excellent Majesty, by and with the advice and consent of the Lords Spiritual and Temporal, and Commons, in this present Parliament assembled, and by the authority of the same, as follows—

PART I

REGULATION OF ENTRY INTO AND STAY IN UNITED KINGDOM

General principles

1.—(1) All those who are in this Act expressed to have the right of abode in the United Kingdom shall be free to live in, and to come and go into and from, the United Kingdom without let or hindrance except such as may be required under and in accordance with this Act to enable their right to be established or as may be otherwise lawfully imposed on any person.

(2) Those not having that right may live, work and settle in the United Kingdom by permission and subject to such regulation and control of their entry into, stay in and departure from the United Kingdom as is imposed by this Act; and indefinite leave to enter or remain in the United Kingdom shall, by virtue of this provision, be treated as having been given under this Act to those in the United Kingdom at its coming into force, if they are then settled there (and not exempt under this Act from the provisions relating to leave to enter or remain).

(3) Arrival in and departure from the United Kingdom on a local journey from or to any of the Islands (that is to say, the Channel Islands and Isle of Man) or the Republic of Ireland shall not be subject to control under this Act, nor shall a person require leave to enter the United Kingdom on so arriving, except in so far as any of those places is for any purpose excluded from this subsection under the powers conferred by this Act; and in this Act

the United Kingdom and those places, or such of them as are not so excluded, are collectively referred to as 'the common travel area'.

(4) The rules laid down by the Secretary of State as to the practice to be followed in the administration of this Act for regulating the entry into and stay in the United Kingdom of persons not having the right of abode shall include provision for admitting (in such cases and subject to such restrictions as may be provided by the rules, and subject or not to conditions as to length of stay or otherwise) persons coming for the purpose of taking employment, or for purposes of study, or as visitors, or as dependants of persons lawfully in or entering the United Kingdom.

(5) The rules shall be so framed that Commonwealth citizens settled in the United Kingdom at the coming into force of this Act and their wives and children are not, by virtue of anything in the rules, any less free to come into and go from the United Kingdom than if this Act had not been passed.

Statement of right of abode, and related amendments as to citizenship by registration

2.—(1) A person is under this Act to have the right of abode in the United Kingdom if—

(a) he is a citizen of the United Kingdom and Colonies who has that citizenship by his birth, adoption, naturalisation or (except as mentioned below) registration in the United Kingdom or in any of the Islands; or

(b) he is a citizen of the United Kingdom and Colonies born to or legally adopted by a parent who had that citizenship at the time of the birth or adoption, and the parent either—

(i) then had that citizenship by his birth, adoption, naturalisation or (except as mentioned below) registration in the United Kingdom or in any of the Islands; or

(ii) had been born to or legally adopted by a parent who at the time of that birth or adoption so had it; or

(c) he is a citizen of the United Kingdom and Colonies who has at any time been settled in the United Kingdom and Islands and had at that time (and while such a citizen) been ordinarily resident there for the last five years or more; or

(d) he is a Commonwealth citizen born to or legally adopted by a parent who at the time of the birth or adoption had citizenship of the United Kingdom and Colonies by his birth in the United Kingdom or in any of the Islands.

(2) A woman is under this Act also to have the right of abode in the United Kingdom if she is a Commonwealth citizen and either—

(a) is the wife of any such citizen of the United Kingdom and Colonies as is mentioned in subsection (1)(a), (b) or (c) above or any such Commonwealth citizen as is mentioned in subsection (1)(d); or

(b) has at any time been the wife—

(i) of a person then being such a citizen of the United Kingdom and Colonies or Commonwealth citizen; or

(ii) of a British subject who but for his death would on the date of commencement of the British Nationality Act 1948 have been such a citizen of the United Kingdom and Colonies as is mentioned in subsection (1)(a) or (b);

but in subsection (1)(a) and (b) above references to registration as a citizen of the United Kingdom and Colonies shall not, in the case of a woman, include registration after the passing of this Act under or by virtue of s 6(2) (wives) of the British Nationality Act 1948 unless she is so registered by virtue of her marriage to a citizen of the United Kingdom and Colonies before the passing of this Act.

(3) In relation to the parent of a child born after the parent's death, references in subsection (1) above to the time of the child's birth shall be replaced by references to the time of the parent's death; and for purposes of that subsection—

(a) 'parent' includes the mother of an illegitimate child; and

(b) references to birth in the United Kingdom shall include birth on a ship or aircraft registered in the United Kingdom, or on an unregistered ship or aircraft of the government of the United Kingdom, and similarly with references to birth in any of the Islands; and

(c) references to citizenship of the United Kingdom and Colonies shall, in relation to a time before the year 1949, be construed as references to British nationality and, in relation to British nationality and to a time before the 31 March 1922, 'the United Kingdom' shall mean Great Britain and Ireland; and

(d) subject to s 8(5) below, references to a person being settled in the United Kingdom and Islands are references to his being ordinarily resident there without being subject under the immigration laws to any restriction on the period for which he may remain.

(4) In subsection (1) above, any reference to registration in the United Kingdom shall extend also to registration under arrangements made by virtue of s 8(2) of the British Nationality Act 1948 (registration in independent Commonwealth country by United Kingdom High Commissioner), but, in the case of a registration by virtue of s 7 (children) of that Act, only if the registration was effected before the passing of this Act.

(5) The law with respect to registration as a citizen of the United Kingdom and Colonies shall be modified as provided by Schedule 1 to this Act.

(6) In the following provisions of this Act the word 'patrial' is used of persons having the right of abode in the United Kingdom.

General provisions for regulation and control

3.—(1) Except as otherwise provided by or under this Act, where a person is not patrial—

(a) he shall not enter the United Kingdom unless given leave to do so in accordance with this Act;

(b) he may be given leave to enter the United Kingdom (or, when already there, leave to remain in the United Kingdom) either for a limited or for an indefinite period;

(c) if he is given a limited leave to enter or remain in the United Kingdom, it may be given subject to conditions restricting his employment or occupation in the United Kingdom, or requiring him to register with the police, or both.

(2) The Secretary of State shall from time to time (and as soon as may be) lay before Parliament statements of the rules, or of any changes in the rules, laid down by him as to the practice to be followed in the administration of this Act for regulating the entry into and stay in the United Kingdom of persons required by this Act to have leave to enter, including any rules as to the period for which leave is to be given and the conditions to be attached in different circumstances; and s 1(4) above shall not be taken to require uniform provision to be made by the rules as regards admission of persons for a purpose or in a capacity specified in s 1(4) (and in particular, for this as well as other purposes of this Act, account may be taken of citizenship or nationality).

If a statement laid before either House of Parliament under this subsection is disapproved by a resolution of that House passed within the period of 40 days beginning with the date of laying (and exclusive of any period during which Parliament is dissolved or prorogued or during which both Houses are adjourned for more than four days), then the Secretary of State shall as soon as may be make such changes or further changes in the rules as appear to him to be required in the circumstances, so that the statement of those changes be laid before Parliament at latest by the end of the period of 40 days beginning with the date of the resolution (but exclusive as aforesaid).

(3) In the case of a limited leave to enter or remain in the United Kingdom—

(a) a person's leave may be varied, whether by restricting, enlarging or removing the limit on its duration, or by adding, varying or revoking, conditions, but if the limit on its duration is removed, any conditions attached to the leave shall cease to apply; and

(b) the limitation on and any conditions attached to a person's leave may be imposed (whether originally or on a variation) so that they will, if not superseded, apply also to any subsequent leave he may obtain after an absence from the United Kingdom within the period limited for the duration of the earlier leave.

(4) A person's leave to enter or remain in the United Kingdom shall lapse on his going to a country or territory outside the common travel area (whether or not he lands there), unless within the period for which he had leave he returns to the United Kingdom in circumstances in which he is not required to obtain leave to enter; but, if he does so return, his previous leave (and any limitation on it or conditions attached to it) shall continue to apply.

(5) A person who is not patrial shall be liable to deportation from the United Kingdom—

(a) if, having only a limited leave to enter or remain, he does not observe a condition attached to the leave or remains beyond the time limited by the leave; or

(b) if the Secretary of State deems his deportation to be conducive to the public good; or

(c) if another person to whose family he belongs is or has been ordered to be deported.

(6) Without prejudice to the operation of subsection (5) above, a person who is not patrial shall also be liable to deportation from the United Kingdom if, after he has attained the age of 17, he is convicted of an offence for which he is punishable with imprisonment and on his conviction is recommended for deportation by a court empowered by this Act to do so.

(7) Where it appears to Her Majesty proper so to do by reason of restrictions or conditions imposed on citizens of the United Kingdom and Colonies when leaving or seeking to leave any country or the territory subject to the government of any country, Her Majesty may by Order in Council make provision for prohibiting persons who are nationals or citizens of that country and are not patrial from embarking in the United Kingdom, or from doing so elsewhere than at a port of exit, or for imposing restrictions or conditions on them when embarking or about to embark in the United Kingdom; and Her Majesty may also make provision by Order in Council to enable those who are not patrial to be, in such cases as may be prescribed by the Order, prohibited in the interests of safety from so embarking on a ship or aircraft specified or indicated in the prohibition.

Any Order in Council under this subsection shall be subject to annulment in pursuance of a resolution of either House of Parliament.

(8) When any question arises under this Act whether or not a person is patrial, or is entitled to any exemption under this Act, it shall lie on the person asserting it to prove that he is.

(9) A person seeking to enter the United Kingdom and claiming to be patrial by virtue of s 2(1)(c) or (d) or s 2(2) above shall prove it by means of such certificate of patriality as may be specified in the immigration rules,

unless in the case of a woman claiming to be patrial by virtue of s 2(2) she shows that she is a citizen of the United Kingdom and Colonies and is patrial by virtue of s 2(2) apart from any reference therein to s 2(1)(c) or (d).

Administration of control

4.—(1) The power under this Act to give or refuse leave to enter the United Kingdom shall be exercised by immigration officers, and the power to give leave to remain in the United Kingdom, or to vary any leave under s 3(3)(a) (whether as regards duration or conditions), shall be exercised by the Secretary of State; and, unless otherwise allowed by this Act, those powers shall be exercised by notice in writing given to the person affected, except that the powers under s 3(3)(a) may be exercised generally in respect of any class of persons by order made by statutory instrument.

(2) The provisions of Schedule 2 to this Act shall have effect with respect to—

(a) the appointment and powers of immigration officers and medical inspectors for purposes of this Act;

(b) the examination of persons arriving in or leaving the United Kingdom by ship or aircraft, and the special powers exerciseable in the case of those who arrive as, or with a view to becoming, members of the crews of ships and aircraft; and

(c) the exercise by immigration officers of their powers in relation to entry into the United Kingdom, and the removal from the United Kingdom of persons refused leave to enter or entering or remaining unlawfully; and

(d) the detention of persons pending examination or pending removal from the United Kingdom;

and for other purposes supplementary to the foregoing provisions of this Act.

(3) The Secretary of State may by regulations made by statutory instrument, which shall be subject to annulment in pursuance of a resolution of either House of Parliament, make provision as to the effect of a condition under this Act requiring a person to register with the police; and the regulations may include provision—

(a) as to the officers of police by whom registers are to be maintained, and as to the form and content of the registers;

(b) as to the place and manner in which anyone is to register and as to the documents and information to be furnished by him, whether on registration or on any change of circumstances;

(c) as to the issue of certificates of registration and as to the payment of fees for certificates of registration;

and the regulations may require anyone who is for the time being subject to such a condition to produce a certificate of registration to such persons and in such circumstances as may be prescribed by the regulations.

(4) The Secretary of State may by order made by statutory instrument, which shall be subject to annulment in pursuance of a resolution of either House of Parliament, make such provision as appears to him to be expedient in connection with this Act for records to be made and kept of persons staying at hotels and other premises where lodging or sleeping accommodation is provided, and for persons (whether patrial or not) who stay at any such premises to supply the necessary information.

Procedure for, and further provisions as to, deportation

5.—(1) Where a person is under s 3(5) or (6) above liable to deportation, then subject to the following provisions of this Act the Secretary of State may make a deportation order against him, that is to say an order requiring him to leave and prohibiting him from entering the United Kingdom; and a deportation order against a person shall invalidate any leave to enter or remain in the United Kingdom given him before the order is made or while it is in force.

(2) A deportation order against a person may at any time be revoked by a further order of the Secretary of State, and shall cease to have effect if he becomes patrial.

(3) A deportation order shall not be made against a person as belonging to the family of another person if more than eight weeks have elapsed since the other person left the United Kingdom after the making of the deportation order against him; and a deportation order made against a person on that ground shall cease to have effect if he ceases to belong to the family of the other person, or if the deportation order made against the other person ceases to have effect.

(4) For purposes of deportation the following shall be those who are regarded as belonging to another person's family—

(a) where that other person is a man, his wife and his or her children under the age of 18; and

(b) where that other person is a woman, her children under the age of 18;

and for purposes of this subsection an adopted child, whether legally adopted or not, may be treated as the child of the adopter and, if legally adopted, shall be regarded as the child only of the adopter; an illegitimate child (subject to the foregoing rule as to adoptions) shall be regarded as the child of the mother; and 'wife' includes each of two or more wives.

(5) The provisions of Schedule 3 to this Act shall have effect with respect to the removal from the United Kingdom of persons against whom deportation

orders are in force and with respect to the detention or control of persons in connection with deportation.

(6) Where a person is liable to deportation under s 3(5)(c) or (6) above but, without a deportation order being made against him, leaves the United Kingdom to live permanently abroad, the Secretary of State may make payments of such amounts as he may determine to meet that person's expenses in so leaving the United Kingdom, including travelling expenses for members of his family or household.

Recommendations by court for deportation

6.—(1) Where under s 3(6) above a person convicted of an offence is liable to deportation on the recommendation of a court, he may be recommended for deportation by any court having power to sentence him for the offence unless the court commits him to be sentenced or further dealt with for that offence by another court.

Provided that in Scotland the power to recommend a person for deportation shall be exerciseable only by the sheriff or the High Court of Justiciary, and shall not be exerciseable by the latter on an appeal unless the appeal is against a conviction on indictment or against a sentence upon such a conviction.

(2) A court shall not recommend a person for deportation unless he has been given not less than seven days notice in writing stating that a person is not liable to deportation if he is patrial, describing the persons who are patrial and stating (so far as material) the effect of s 3(8) above and s 7 below; but the powers of adjournment conferred by s 14(3) of the Magistrates' Courts Act 1952, s 26 of the Criminal Justice (Scotland) Act 1949 or any corresponding enactment for the time being in force in Northern Ireland shall include power to adjourn, after convicting an offender, for the purpose of enabling a notice to be given to him under this subsection or, if a notice was so given to him less than seven days previously, for the purpose of enabling the necessary seven days to elapse.

(3) For purposes of s 3(6) above—

(a) a person shall be deemed to have attained the age of 17 at the time of his conviction if, on consideration of any available evidence, he appears to have done so to the court making or considering a recommendation for deportation; and

(b) the question whether an offence is one for which a person is punishable with imprisonment shall be determined without regard to any enactment restricting the imprisonment of young offenders or first offenders;

and for purposes of deportation a person who on being charged with an offence is found to have committed it shall, notwithstanding any enactment to the contrary and notwithstanding that the court does not proceed to conviction, be regarded as a person convicted of the offence, and references to conviction shall be construed accordingly.

(4) Notwithstanding any rule of practice restricting the matters which ought to be taken into account in dealing with an offender who is sentenced to imprisonment, a recommendation for deportation may be made in respect of an offender who is sentenced to imprisonment for life.

(5) Where a court recommends or purports to recommend a person for deportation, the validity of the recommendation shall not be called in question except on an appeal against the recommendation or against the conviction on which it is made; but—

(a) except in Scotland, the recommendation shall be treated as a sentence for the purpose of any enactment providing an appeal against sentence; and

(b) in Scotland, a person recommended for deportation may, without prejudice to any other form of appeal under any rule of law, appeal against the recommendation in the same manner as against a conviction.

(6) A deportation order shall not be made on the recommendation of a court so long as an appeal or further appeal is pending against the recommendation or against the conviction on which it was made; and for this purpose an appeal or further appeal shall be treated as pending (where one is competent but has not been brought) until the expiration of the time for bringing that appeal or, in Scotland, until the expiration of 28 days from the date of the recommendation.

(7) For the purpose of giving effect to any of the provisions of this section in its application to Scotland, the High Court of Justiciary shall have power to make rules by act of adjournal.

Exemption from deportation for certain existing residents

7.—(1) Notwithstanding anything in s 3(5) or (6) above but subject to the provisions of this section, a Commonwealth citizen or citizen of the Republic of Ireland who was such a citizen at the coming into force of this Act and was then ordinarily resident in the United Kingdom—

(a) shall not be liable to deportation under s 3(5)(b) if at the time of the Secretary of State's decision he had at all times since the coming into force of this Act been ordinarily resident in the United Kingdom and Islands; and

(b) shall not be liable to deportation under s 3(5)(a), (b) or (c) if at the time of the Secretary of State's decision he had for the last five years been ordinarily resident in the United Kingdom and Islands; and

(c) shall not on conviction of an offence be recommended for deportation under s 3(6) if at the time of the conviction he had for the last five years been ordinarily resident in the United Kingdom and Islands.

(2) A person who has at any time become ordinarily resident in the United Kingdom or in any of the Islands shall not be treated for the purposes of this section as having ceased to be so by reason only of his having remained there in breach of the immigration laws.

(3) The 'last five years' before the material time under subsection (1)(b) or (c) above is to be taken as a period amounting in total to five years exclusive of any time during which the person claiming exemption under this section was undergoing imprisonment or detention by virtue of a sentence passed for an offence on a conviction in the United Kingdom and Islands, and the period for which he was imprisoned or detained by virtue of the sentence amounted to six months or more.

(4) For purposes of subsection (3) above—

(a) 'sentence' includes any order made on conviction of an offence; and

(b) two or more sentences for consecutive (or partly consecutive) terms shall be treated as a single sentence; and

(c) a person shall be deemed to be detained by virtue of a sentence—

(i) at any time when he is liable to imprisonment or detention by virtue of the sentence, but is unlawfully at large; and

(ii) (unless the sentence is passed after the material time) during any period of custody by which under any relevant enactment the term to be served under the sentence is reduced.

In para (c)(ii) above 'relevant enactment' means s 67 of the Criminal Justice Act 1967 (or, before that section operated, s 17(2) of the Criminal Justice Administration Act 1962) and any similar enactment which is for the time being or has (before or after the passing of this Act) been in force in any part of the United Kingdom and Islands.

(5) Nothing in this section shall be taken to exclude the operation of s 3(8) above in relation to an exemption under this section.

Exceptions for seamen, aircrews and other special cases

8.—(1) Where a person arrives at a place in the United Kingdom as a member of the crew of a ship or aircraft under an engagement requiring him to leave on that ship as a member of the crew, or to leave within seven days on that or another, aircraft as a member of its crew, then unless either—

(a) there is in force a deportation order made against him; or

(b) he has at any time been refused leave to enter the United Kingdom and has not since then been given leave to enter or remain in the United Kingdom; or

(c) an immigration officer requires him to submit to examination in accordance with Schedule 2 to this Act;

he may without leave enter the United Kingdom at that place and remain until the departure of the ship or aircraft on which he is required by his engagement to leave.

(2) The Secretary of State may by order exempt any person or class of persons, either unconditionally or subject to such conditions as may be imposed by or under the order, from all or any of the provisions of this Act relating to those who are not patrial.

An order under this subsection, if made with respect to a class of persons, shall be made by statutory instrument, which shall be subject to annulment in pursuance of a resolution of either House of Parliament.

(3) The provisions of this Act relating to those who are not patrial shall not apply to any person so long as he is a member of a mission (within the meaning of the Diplomatic Privileges Act 1964), a person who is a member of the family and forms part of the household of such a member, or a person otherwise entitled to the like immunity from jurisdiction as is conferred by that Act on a diplomatic agent.

(4) The provisions of this Act relating to those who are not patrial, other than the provisions relating to deportation, shall also not apply to any person so long as either—

(a) he is subject, as a member of the home forces, to service law; or

(b) being a member of a Commonwealth force or of a force raised under the law of any associated State, colony, protectorate or protected State, is undergoing or about to undergo training in the United Kingdom with any body, contingent or detachment of the home forces; or

(c) he is serving or posted for service in the United Kingdom as a member of a visiting force or of any force raised as aforesaid or as a member of an international headquarters or defence organisation designated for the time being by an Order in Council under s 1 of the International Headquarters and Defence Organisations Act 1964.

(5) Where a person having a limited leave to enter or remain in the United Kingdom becomes entitled to an exemption under this section, that leave shall continue to apply after he ceases to be entitled to the exemption, unless it has by then expired; and a person is not to be regarded for purposes of this Act as having been settled in the United Kingdom and Islands at any time when he was entitled to an exemption under subsection (3) or (4)(b) or (c) above or, unless the order otherwise provides, under subsection (2) or to any corresponding exemption under the former immigration laws or under the immigration laws of any of the Islands.

(6) In this section 'the home forces' means any of Her Majesty's forces other than a Commonwealth force or a force raised under the law of any associated state, colony, protectorate or protected state; 'Commonwealth force' means a force of any country to which provisions of the Visiting Forces Act 1952

apply without an Order in Council under s 1 of the Act; and 'visiting force' means a body, contingent or detachment of the forces of a country to which any of those provisions apply, being a body, contingent or detachment for the time being present in the United Kingdom on the invitation of Her Majesty's government in the United Kingdom.

Further provisions as to common travel area

9.—(1) Subject to subsection (5) below, the provisions of Schedule 4 to this Act shall have effect for the purpose of taking account in the United Kingdom of the operation in any of the Islands of the immigration laws there.

(2) Persons who lawfully enter the United Kingdom on a local journey from a place in the common travel area after having either—

(a) entered any of the Islands or the Republic of Ireland on coming from a place outside the common travel area; or

(b) left the United Kingdom while having a limited leave to enter or remain which has since expired;

if they are not patrial (and are not to be regarded under Schedule 4 to this Act as having leave to enter the United Kingdom), shall be subject in the United Kingdom to such restrictions on the period for which they may remain, and such conditions restricting their employment or occupation or requiring them to register with the police or both, as may be imposed by an order of the Secretary of State and may be applicable to them.

(3) Any provision of this Act applying to a limited leave or to conditions attached to a limited leave shall, unless otherwise provided, have effect in relation to a person subject to any restriction or condition by virtue of an order under subsection (2) above as if the provisions of the order applicable to him were terms on which he had been given leave under this Act to enter the United Kingdom.

(4) Section 1(3) above shall not be taken to affect the operation of a deportation order; and, subject to Schedule 4 to this Act, a person who is not patrial may not by virtue of s 1(3) enter the United Kingdom without leave on a local journey from a place in the common travel area if either—

(a) he is on arrival in the United Kingdom given written notice by an immigration officer stating that, the Secretary of State having issued directions for him not to be given entry to the United Kingdom on the ground that his exclusion is conducive to the public good as being in the interests of national security, he is accordingly refused leave to enter the United Kingdom; or

(b) he has at any time been refused leave to enter the United Kingdom and has not since then been given leave to enter or remain in the United Kingdom.

(5) If it appears to the Secretary of State necessary so to do by reason of differences between the immigration laws of the United Kingdom and any

of the Islands, he may by order exclude that island from s 1(3) above for such purposes as may be specified in the order, and references in this Act to the Islands other than any reference in s 2 shall apply to an island so excluded so far only as may be provided by order of the Secretary of State.

(6) The Secretary of State shall also have power by order to exclude the Republic of Ireland from s 1(3) for such purposes as may be specified in the order.

(7) An order of the Secretary of State under this section shall be made by statutory instrument, which shall be subject to annulment in pursuance of a resolution of either House of Parliament.

Entry otherwise than by sea or air

10.—(1) Her Majesty may by Order in Council direct that any of the provisions of this Act shall have effect in relation to persons entering or seeking to enter the United Kingdom on arrival otherwise than by ship or aircraft as they have effect in the case of a person arriving by ship or aircraft; and any such Order may make such adaptations or modifications of those provisions, and such provisions supplementary thereto, as appear to Her Majesty to be necessary or expedient for the purposes of the Order.

(2) The provision made by an Order in Council under this section may include provision for excluding the Republic of Ireland from s 1(3) of this Act either generally or for any specified purposes.

(3) No recommendation shall be made to Her Majesty to make an Order in Council under this section unless a draft of the Order has been laid before Parliament and approved by a resolution of each House of Parliament.

Construction of references to entry, and other phrases relating to travel

11.—(1) A person arriving in the United Kingdom by ship or aircraft shall for purposes of this Act be deemed not to enter the United Kingdom unless and until he disembarks, and on disembarkation at a port shall further be deemed not to enter the United Kingdom so long as he remains in such area (if any) at the port as may be approved for this purpose by an immigration officer; and a person who has not otherwise entered the United Kingdom shall be deemed not to do so as long as he is detained, or temporarily admitted or released while liable to detention, under the powers conferred by Schedule 2 to this Act.

(2) In this Act 'disembark' means disembark from a ship or aircraft, and 'embark' means embark in a ship or aircraft; and, except in subsection (1) above,—

(a) references to disembarking in the United Kingdom do not apply to disembarking after a local journey from a place in the United Kingdom or elsewhere in the common travel area; and

(b) references to embarking in the United Kingdom do not apply to embarking for a local journey to a place in the United Kingdom or elsewhere in the common travel area.

(3) Except in so far as the context otherwise requires, references in this Act to arriving in the United Kingdom by ship shall extend to arrival by any floating structure, and 'disembark' shall be construed accordingly; but the provisions of this Act specially relating to members of the crew of a ship shall not by virtue of this provision apply in relation to any floating structure not being a ship.

(4) For purposes of this Act 'common travel area' has the meaning given by s 1(3), and a journey is, in relation to the common travel area, a local journey if but only if it begins and ends in the common travel area and is not made by a ship or aircraft which—

(a) in the case of a journey to a place in the United Kingdom, began its voyage from, or has during its voyage called at, a place not in the common travel area; or

(b) in the case of a journey from a place in the United Kingdom, is due to end its voyage in, or call in the course of its voyage at, a place not in the common travel area.

(5) A person who enters the United Kingdom lawfully by virtue of s 8(1) above, and seeks to remain beyond the time limited by s 8(1), shall be treated for purposes of this Act as seeking to enter the United Kingdom.

PART II

APPEALS

The appellate authorities

Immigration Appeal Tribunal and adjudicators

12. The Immigration Appeal Tribunal and adjudicators provided for by the Immigration Appeals Act 1969 shall continue for purposes of this Act, and—

(a) members of the Tribunal shall continue to be appointed by the Lord Chancellor and adjudicators by the Secretary of State; and

(b) the provisions of Schedule 1 to that Act shall continue to apply, as set out in Schedule 5 to this Act with the required adaptation of references to that Act, but with the substitution also of references to the Minister for the Civil Service for references to the Treasury.

Appeals to adjudicator or Tribunal in first instance

Appeals against exclusion from United Kingdom

13.—(1) Subject to the provisions of this Part of this Act, a person who is refused leave to enter the United Kingdom under this Act may appeal to an adjudicator against the decision that he requires leave or against the refusal.

(2) Subject to the provisions of this Part of this Act, a person who, on an application duly made, is refused a certificate of patriality or an entry clearance may appeal to an adjudicator against the refusal.

(3) A person not holding a certificate of patriality shall not be entitled to appeal on the ground that he is patrial by virtue of s 2(1)(c) or (d) or s 2(2) above against a decision that he requires leave to enter the United Kingdom unless in the case of a woman who is a citizen of the United Kingdom and Colonies the ground of appeal is that she is patrial by virtue of s 2(2) apart from any reference therein to s 2(1)(c) or (a); and a person shall not be entitled to appeal against a refusal of leave to enter so long as he is in the United Kingdom, unless he was refused leave at a port of entry and at a time when he held a current entry clearance or was a person named in a current work permit.

(4) An appeal against a refusal of leave to enter shall be dismissed by the adjudicator if he is satisfied that the appellant was at the time of the refusal an illegal entrant, and an appeal against a refusal of an entry clearance shall be dismissed by the adjudicator if he is satisfied that a deportation order was at the time of the refusal in force in respect of the appellant.

(5) A person shall not be entitled to appeal against a refusal of leave to enter, or against a refusal of an entry clearance, if the Secretary of State certifies that directions have been given by the Secretary of State (and not by a person acting under his authority) for the appellant not to be given entry to the United Kingdom on the ground that his exclusion is conducive to the public good, or if the leave to enter or entry clearance was refused in obedience to any such directions.

Appeals against conditions

14.—(1) Subject to the provisions of this Part of this Act, a person who has a limited leave under this Act to enter or remain in the United Kingdom may appeal to an adjudicator against any variation of the leave (whether as regards duration or conditions), or against any refusal to vary it; and a variation shall not take effect so long as an appeal is pending under this subsection against the variation, nor shall an appellant be required to leave the United Kingdom by reason of the expiration of his leave so long as his appeal is pending under this subsection against a refusal to enlarge or remove the limit on the duration of the leave.

(2) Subject to the provisions of this Part of this Act, a person who, on ceasing to be entitled to an exemption under any provision of s 8 above other than s 8(1), or on ceasing while in the United Kingdom to be patrial, is given a limited leave to remain may appeal to an adjudicator against any provision limiting the duration of the leave or attaching a condition to it; and so long as an appeal is pending under this subsection against any provision, effect shall not be given to that provision.

(3) A person shall not be entitled to appeal under subsection (1) above against any variation of his leave which reduces its duration, or against any refusal to enlarge or remove the limit on its duration, if the Secretary of State certifies that the appellant's departure from the United Kingdom would be conducive to the public good, as being in the interests of national security or of the relations between the United Kingdom and any other country or for other reasons of a political nature, or the decision questioned by the appeal was taken on that ground by the Secretary of State (and not by a person acting under his authority).

(4) A person shall not be entitled to appeal under subsection (1) above against any variation made by statutory instrument, or against any refusal of the Secretary of State to make a statutory instrument.

Appeals in respect of deportation orders

15.—(1) Subject to the provisions of this Part of this Act, a person may appeal to an adjudicator against—

(a) a decision of the Secretary of State to make a deportation order against him by virtue of s 3(5) above; or

(b) a refusal by the Secretary of State to revoke a deportation order made against him.

(2) A deportation order shall not be made against a person by virtue of s 3(5) above so long as an appeal may be brought against the decision to make it nor, if such an appeal is duly brought, so long as the appeal is pending; but, in calculating the period of eight weeks limited by s 5 (3) above for making a deportation order against a person as belonging to the family of another person, there shall be disregarded any period during which there is pending an appeal against the decision to make it.

(3) A person shall not be entitled to appeal against a decision to make a deportation order against him if the ground of the decision was that his deportation is conducive to the public good as being in the interests of national security or of the relations between the United Kingdom and any other country or for other reasons of a political nature.

(4) A person shall not be entitled to appeal under this section against a refusal to revoke a deportation order, if the Secretary of State certifies that the appellant's exclusion from the United Kingdom is conducive to the public

good or if revocation was refused on that ground by the Secretary of State (and not by a person acting under his authority).

(5) A person shall not be entitled to appeal under this section against a refusal to revoke a deportation order so long as he is in the United Kingdom, whether because he has not complied with the requirement to leave or because he has contravened the prohibition on entering.

(6) On an appeal against a decision to make a deportation order against a person as belonging to the family of another person, or an appeal against a refusal to revoke a deportation order so made, the appellant shall not be allowed, for the purpose of showing that he does not or did not belong to another person's family, to dispute any statement made with a view to obtaining leave for the appellant to enter or remain in the United Kingdom (including any statement made to obtain an entry clearance) unless the appellant shows that the statement was not so made by him or by any person acting with his authority and that, when he took the benefit of the leave, he did not know any such statement had been made to obtain it or, if he did know, was under the age of 18.

(7) An appeal under this section shall be to the Appeal Tribunal in the first instance, instead of to an adjudicator, if—

(a it is an appeal against a decision to make a deportation order and the ground of the decision was that the deportation of the appellant is conducive to the public good; or

(b) it is an appeal against a decision to make a deportation order against a person as belonging to the family of another person, or an appeal against a refusal to revoke a deportation order so made; or

(c) there is pending a related appeal to which para (b) above applies.

(8) Where an appeal to an adjudicator is pending under this section, and before the adjudicator has begun to hear it a related appeal is brought, the appeal to the adjudicator shall be dealt with instead by the Appeal Tribunal and be treated as an appeal duly made to the Tribunal in the first instance.

(9) In relation to an appeal under this section in respect of a deportation order against any person (whether an appeal against a decision to make or against a refusal to revoke the order), any other appeal under this section is a 'related appeal' if it is an appeal in respect of a deportation order against another person as belonging to the family of the first-mentioned person.

Appeals against validity of directions for removal

16.—(1) Subject to the provisions of this Part of this Act where directions are given under this Act for a person's removal from the United Kingdom either—

(a) on the ground that he is an illegal entrant or on the ground specifically that he has entered the United Kingdom in breach of a deportation order; or

(b) under the special powers conferred by Schedule 2 to this Act in relation to members of the crew of a ship or aircraft or persons coming to the United Kingdom to join a ship or aircraft as a member of the crew;

then he may appeal to an adjudicator against those directions on the ground that in the facts of his case there was in law no power to give them on the ground on which they were given.

(2) A person shall not be entitled to appeal under this section so long as he is in the United Kingdom, unless he is appealing against directions given by virtue of a deportation order (whether on the ground specifically that he has returned in breach of that order or on the ground that he is an illegal entrant) and is appealing on the ground that he is not the person named in that order.

(3) Where a person appeals under this section against directions given by virtue of a deportation order, he shall not be allowed to dispute the original validity of that order.

(4) An appeal under this section against directions given as mentioned in subsection (1)(b) shall be dismissed by the adjudicator, notwithstanding that the ground of appeal may be made out, if he is satisfied that there was power to give the like directions on the ground that the appellant was an illegal entrant.

Appeals against removal on objection to destination

17.—(1) Subject to the provisions of this Part of this Act, where directions are given under this Act for a person's removal from the United Kingdom either—

(a) on his being refused leave to enter; or

(b) on a deportation order being made against him; or

(c) on his having entered the United Kingdom in breach of a deportation order;

he may appeal to an adjudicator against the directions on the ground that he ought to be removed (if at all) to a different country or territory specified by him.

(2) Where a person appeals under s 13(1) above on being refused leave to enter the United Kingdom, and either—

(a) before he does so, directions have been given for his removal from the United Kingdom to any country or territory; or

(b) before or after he does so, the Secretary of State or an immigration officer serves on him notice that any directions which may be given for his removal by virtue of the refusal will be for his removal to a country or territory or one of several countries or territories specified in the notice;

then he may on that appeal object to the country or territory to which he would be removed in pursuance of the directions, or to that specified in the notice (or to one or more of those specified), and claim that he ought to be removed (if at all) to a different country or territory specified by him.

(3) Where a person appeals under s 15 above against a decision to make a deportation order against him, and before or after he does so the Secretary of State serves on him notice that any directions which may be given for his removal by virtue of the deportation order will be for his removal to a country or territory or one of several countries or territories specified in the notice, then he may on that appeal object to the country or territory specified in the notice (or to one or more of those specified), and claim that he ought to be removed (if at all) to a different country or territory specified by him.

(4) Where by virtue of subsection (2) or (3) above a person is able to object to a country or territory on an appeal under s 13(1) or 15, and either he does not object to it on that appeal or his objection to it on that appeal is not sustained, then he shall not be entitled to appeal under this section against any directions subsequently given by virtue of the refusal or order in question, if their effect will be his removal to that country or territory.

(5) A person shall not be entitled to appeal under this section against any directions given on his being refused leave to enter the United Kingdom, unless either he is also appealing under s 13(1) against the decision that he requires leave to enter or he was refused leave at a port of entry and at a time when he held a current entry clearance or was a person named in a current work permit.

Notice of matters in respect of which there are rights of appeal

18.—(1) The Secretary of State may by regulations provide—

(a) for written notice to be given to a person of any such decision or action taken in respect of him as is appealable under this Part of this Act (whether or not he is in the facts of his case entitled to appeal) or would be so appealable but for the ground on which it is taken;

(b) for any such notice to include a statement of the reasons for the decision or action and, where the action is the giving of directions for the removal of any person from the United Kingdom, of the country or territory to which he is to be removed;

(c) for any such notice to be accompanied by a statement containing particulars of the rights of appeal available under this Part of this Act and of the procedure by which those rights may be exercised;

(d) for the form of any such notice or statement and the way in which a notice is to be or may be given.

(2) For the purpose of any proceedings under this Part of this Act a statement included in a notice in pursuance of regulations under this section shall be conclusive of the person by whom and of the ground on which any decision or action was taken.

(3) The power to make regulations under this section shall be exerciseable by statutory instrument, and any statutory instrument containing such regulations shall be subject to annulment in pursuance of a resolution of either House of Parliament.

Determination of appeals by adjudicators

19.—(1) Subject to ss 13(4) and 16(4) above, and to any restriction on the grounds of appeal, an adjudicator on an appeal to him under this Part of this Act—

(a) shall allow the appeal if he considers—

(i) that the decision or action against which the appeal is brought was not in accordance with the law or with any immigration rules applicable to the case; or

(ii) where the decision or action involved the exercise of a discretion by the Secretary of State or an officer, that the discretion should have been exercised differently; and

(b) in any other case, shall dismiss the appeal.

(2) For the purposes of subsection (1)(a) above the adjudicator may review any determination of a question of fact on which the decision or action was based; and for the purposes of subsection (1)(a)(ii) no decision or action which is in accordance with the immigration rules shall be treated as having involved the exercise of a discretion by the Secretary of State by reason only of the fact that he has been requested by or on behalf of the appellant to depart, or to authorise an officer to depart, from the rules and has refused to do so.

(3) Where an appeal is allowed, the adjudicator shall give such directions for giving effect to the determination as the adjudicator thinks requisite, and may also make recommendations with respect to any other action which the adjudicator considers should be taken in the case under this Act; and, subject to s 20(2) below, it shall be the duty of the Secretary of State and of any officer to whom directions are given under this subsection to comply with them.

(4) Where in accordance with s 15 above a person appeals to the Appeal Tribunal in the first instance, this section shall apply with the substitution of references to the Tribunal for references to an adjudicator.

Appeals from adjudicator to Tribunal, and review of decisions

Appeal to Tribunal from determination of adjudicator

20.—(1) Subject to any requirement of rules of procedure as to leave to appeal, any party to an appeal to an adjudicator may, if dissatisfied with his determination thereon, appeal to the Appeal Tribunal, and the Tribunal may affirm the determination or make any other determination which could have been made by the adjudicator.

(2) Directions given by an adjudicator under s 19(3) above need not be complied with so long as an appeal can be brought against his determination and, if such an appeal is duly brought, so long as the appeal is pending; and if the Tribunal affirm his determination allowing the appeal, they may alter or add to his directions and recommendations under s 19(3) or replace them with their own directions and recommendations, and the provisions of that subsection shall apply to directions given by them accordingly.

(3) Where an appeal is dismissed by an adjudicator but allowed by the Tribunal, s 19(3) above shall apply with the substitution of references to the Tribunal for references to the adjudicator.

Reference of cases for further consideration

21.—(1) Where in any case—

(a) an adjudicator has dismissed an appeal, and there has been no further appeal to the Appeal Tribunal, or the Tribunal has dismissed an appeal made to them in the first instance by virtue of s 15 above; or

(b) the Appeal Tribunal has affirmed the determination of an adjudicator dismissing an appeal, or reversed the determination of an adjudicator allowing an appeal;

the Secretary of State may at any time refer for consideration under this section any matter relating to the case which was not before the adjudicator or Tribunal.

(2) Any reference under this section shall be to an adjudicator or to the Appeal Tribunal, and the adjudicator or Tribunal shall consider the matter which is the subject of the reference and report to the Secretary of State the opinion of the adjudicator or Tribunal thereon.

Supplementary

Procedure

22.—(1) The Secretary of State may make rules (in this Act referred to as 'rules of procedure')—

(a) for regulating the exercise of the rights of appeal conferred by this Part of this Act;

(b) for prescribing the practice and procedure to be followed on or in connection with appeals thereunder, including the mode and burden of proof and admissibility of evidence on such an appeal; and

(c) for other matters preliminary or incidental to or arising out of such appeals, including proof of the decisions of adjudicators or the Appeal Tribunal.

(2) Rules of procedure may include provision—

(a) enabling the Tribunal, on an appeal from an adjudicator, to remit the appeal to an adjudicator for determination by him in accordance with any directions of the Tribunal, or for further evidence to be obtained with a view to determination by the Tribunal; or

(b) enabling any functions of the Tribunal which relate to matters preliminary or incidental to an appeal, or which are conferred by Part II of Schedule 2 to this Act, to be performed by a single member of the Tribunal; or

(c) conferring on adjudicators or the Tribunal such ancillary powers as the Secretary of State thinks necessary for the purposes of the exercise of their functions.

(3) The rules of procedure shall provide that any appellant shall have the right to be legally represented.

(4) Where on an appeal under this Part of this Act it is alleged—

(a) that a passport or other travel document, certificate of patriality, entry clearance or work permit (or any part thereof or entry therein) on which a party relies is a forgery; and

(b) that the disclosure to that party of any matters relating to the method of detection would be contrary to the public interest;

then (without prejudice to the generality of the power to make rules of procedure) the adjudicator or Tribunal shall arrange for the proceedings to take place in the absence of that party and his representatives while the allegation at (b) above is inquired into by the adjudicator or Tribunal and, if it appears to the adjudicator or Tribunal that the allegation is made out, for such further period as appears necessary in order to ensure that those matters can be presented to the adjudicator or Tribunal without any disclosure being directly or indirectly made contrary to the public interest.

(5) If, under the rules of procedure, leave to appeal to the Tribunal is required in cases where an adjudicator dismisses an appeal under s 13 above, then the authority having power to grant leave to appeal shall grant it—

(a) in any case where the appeal was against a decision that the appellant required leave to enter the United Kingdom, and the authority is satisfied that at the time of the decision he held a certificate of patriality; and

(b) in any case where the appeal was against a refusal of leave to enter, and the authority is satisfied that at the time of the refusal the appellant held an entry clearance and that the dismissal of the appeal was not required by s 13(4).

(6) A person who is required under or in accordance with rules of procedure to attend and give evidence or produce documents before an adjudicator or

the Tribunal, and fails without reasonable excuse to comply with the requirement, shall be guilty of an offence and liable on summary conviction to a fine not exceeding £100.

(7) The power to make rules of procedure shall be exerciseable by statutory instrument, which shall be subject to annulment in pursuance of a resolution of either House of Parliament.

Financial support for organisations helping persons with rights of appeal

23. The Secretary of State may with the consent of the Treasury make grants to any voluntary organisation which provides advice or assistance for, or other services for the welfare of, persons who have rights of appeal under this Part of this Act.

PART III

CRIMINAL PROCEEDINGS

Illegal entry and similar offences

24.—(1) A person who is not patrial shall be guilty of an offence punishable on summary conviction with a fine of not more than £200 or with imprisonment for not more than six months, or with both, in any of the following cases—

(a) if contrary to this Act he knowingly enters the United Kingdom in breach of a deportation order or without leave;

(b) if, having only a limited leave to enter or remain in the United Kingdom, he knowingly either—

   (i) remains beyond the time limited by the leave; or

   (ii) fails to observe a condition of the leave;

(c) if, having lawfully entered the United Kingdom without leave by virtue of s 8(1) above, he remains without leave beyond the time allowed by s 8(1);

(d) if, without reasonable excuse, he fails to comply with any requirement imposed on him under Schedule 2 to this Act to report to a medical officer of health, or to attend, or submit to a test or examination, as required by such an officer;

(e) if, without reasonable excuse, he fails to observe any restriction imposed on him under Schedule 2 or 3 to this Act as to residence or as to reporting to the police or to an immigration officer;

(f) if he disembarks in the United Kingdom from a ship or aircraft after being placed on board under Schedule 2 or 3 to this Act with a view to his removal from the United Kingdom;

(g) if he embarks in contravention of a restriction imposed by or under an Order in Council under s 3(7) of this Act.

(2) A constable or immigration officer may arrest without warrant anyone who has, or whom he, with reasonable cause, suspects to have, committed or attempted to commit an offence under this section other than an offence under subsection (1)(d) above.

(3) The extended time limit for prosecutions which is provided for by s 28 below shall apply to offences under subsection (1)(a), (b)(i) and (c) above.

(4) In proceedings for an offence against subsection (1)(a) above of entering the United Kingdom without leave—

(a) any stamp purporting to have been imprinted on a passport or other travel document by an immigration officer on a particular date for the purpose of giving leave shall be presumed to have been duly so imprinted, unless the contrary is proved;

(b) proof that a person had leave to enter the United Kingdom shall lie on the defence if, but only if, he is shown to have entered within six months before the date when the proceedings were commenced.

Assisting illegal entry, and harbouring

25.—(1) Any person knowingly concerned in making or carrying out arrangements for securing or facilitating the entry into the United Kingdom of anyone whom he knows or has reasonable cause for believing to be an illegal entrant shall be guilty of an offence, punishable on summary conviction with a fine of not more than £400 or with imprisonment for not more than six months, or with both, or on conviction on indictment with a fine or with imprisonment for not more than seven years, or with both.

(2) Without prejudice to subsection (1) above a person knowingly harbouring anyone whom he knows or has reasonable cause for believing to be either an illegal entrant or a person who has committed an offence under s 24(1)(b) or (c) above, shall be guilty of an offence, punishable on summary conviction with a fine of not more than £400 or with imprisonment for not more than six months, or with both.

(3) A constable or immigration officer may arrest without warrant anyone who has, or whom he, with reasonable cause, suspects to have, committed an offence under subsection (1) above.

(4) The extended time limit for prosecutions which is provided for by s 28 below shall apply to offences under this section.

(5) Subsection (1) above shall apply to things done outside as well as to things done in the United Kingdom where they are done—

(a) by a citizen of the United Kingdom and Colonies;

(b) by a British subject by virtue of s 2 of the British Nationality Act 1948 (continuance of certain subjects of the Republic of Ireland as British subjects);

(c) by a British subject without citizenship by virtue of s 13 or 16 of that Act (which relate respectively to British subjects whose citizenship had not been ascertained at the commencement of that Act and to persons who had ceased to be British on loss of British nationality by a parent);

(d) by a British subject by virtue of the British Nationality Act 1965; or

(e) by a British protected person (within the meaning of the British Nationality Act 1948).

(6) Where a person convicted on indictment of an offence under subsection (1) above is at the time of the offence—

(a) the owner or one of the owners of a ship, aircraft or vehicle used or intended to be used in carrying out the arrangements in respect of which the offence is committed; or

(b) a director or manager of a company which is the owner or one of the owners of any such ship, aircraft or vehicle; or

(c) captain of any such ship or aircraft;

then subject to subsections (7) and (8) below the court before which he is convicted may order the forfeiture of the ship, aircraft or vehicle.

In this subsection (but not in subsection (7) below) 'owner' in relation to a ship, aircraft or vehicle which is the subject of a hire-purchase agreement, includes the person in possession of it under that agreement and, in relation to a ship or aircraft, includes a charterer.

(7) A court shall not order a ship or aircraft to be forfeited under subsection (6) above on a person's conviction, unless—

(a) in the case of a ship, it is of less than 500 tons gross tonnage or, in the case of an aircraft (not being a hovercraft), it is of less than 5,700 kilogrammes operating weight; or

(b) the person convicted is at the time of the offence the owner or one of the owners, or a director or manager of a company which is the owner or one of the owners, of the ship or aircraft; or

(c) the ship or aircraft, under the arrangements in respect of which the offence is committed, has been used for bringing more than 20 persons at one time to the United Kingdom as illegal entrants, and the intention to use the ship or aircraft in bringing persons to the United Kingdom as illegal entrants was known to, or could by the exercise of reasonable diligence, have been discovered by, some person on whose conviction the ship or aircraft would have been liable to forfeiture in accordance with para (b) above.

In this subsection 'operating weight' means in relation to an aircraft the maximum total weight of the aircraft and its contents at which the aircraft may take off anywhere in the world, in the most favourable circumstances, in accordance with the certificate of airworthiness in force in respect of the aircraft.

(8) A court shall not order a ship, aircraft or vehicle to be forfeited under subsection (6) above, where a person claiming to be the owner of the ship, aircraft or vehicle or otherwise interested in it applies to be heard by the court, unless an opportunity has been given to him to show cause why the order should not be made.

General offences in connection with administration of the Act

26.—(1) A person shall be guilty of an offence punishable on summary conviction with a fine of not more than £200 or with imprisonment for not more than six months, or with both, in any of the following cases—

(a) if, without reasonable excuse, he refuses or fails to submit to examination under Schedule 2 to this Act;

(b) if, without reasonable excuse, he refuses or fails to furnish or produce any information in his possession, or any documents in his possession or control, which he is on an examination under that Schedule required to furnish or produce;

(c) if, on any such examination or otherwise, he makes or causes to be made to an immigration officer or other person lawfully acting in the execution of this Act a return, statement or representation which he knows to be false or does not believe to be true;

(d) if, without lawful authority, he alters any certificate of patriality, entry clearance, work permit or other document issued or made under or for the purposes of this Act, or uses for the purposes of this Act, or has in his possession for such use, any passport, certificate of patriality, entry clearance, work permit or other document which he knows or has reasonable cause to believe to be false;

(e) if, without reasonable excuse, he fails to complete and produce a landing or embarkation card in accordance with any order under Schedule 2 to this Act;

(f) if, without reasonable excuse, he fails to comply with any requirement of regulations under s 4(3) or of an order under s 4(4) above;

(g) if, without reasonable excuse, he obstructs an immigration officer or other person lawfully acting in the execution of this Act.

(2) The extended time limit for prosecutions which is provided for by s 28 below shall apply to offences under subsection (1)(c) and (d) above.

Offences by persons connected with ships or aircraft or with ports

27. A person shall be guilty of an offence punishable on summary conviction with a fine of not more than £200 or with imprisonment for not more than six months, or with both, in any of the following cases—

(a) if, being the captain of a ship or aircraft—

(i) he knowingly permits a person to disembark in the United Kingdom when required under Schedule 2 or 3 to this Act to prevent it, or fails without reasonable excuse to take any steps he is required by or under Schedule 2 to take in connection with the disembarkation or examination of passengers or for furnishing a passenger list or particulars of members of the crew; or

(ii) he fails, without reasonable excuse, to comply with any directions given him under Schedule 2 or 3 with respect to the removal of a person from the United Kingdom;

(b) if, as owner or agent of a ship or aircraft—

(i) he arranges, or is knowingly concerned in any arrangements, for the ship or aircraft to call at a port other than a port of entry contrary to any provision of Schedule 2 to this Act; or

(ii) he fails, without reasonable excuse, to take any steps required by an order under Schedule 2 for the supply to passengers of landing or embarkation cards; or

(iii) he fails, without reasonable excuse, to make arrangements for the removal of a person from the United Kingdom when required to do so by directions given under Schedule 2 or 3 to this Act.

(c) if, as owner or agent of a ship or aircraft or as a person concerned in the management of a port, he fails, without reasonable excuse, to take any steps required by Schedule 2 in relation to the embarkation or disembarkation of passengers where a control area is designated.

Proceedings

28.—(1) Where the offence is one to which, under s 24, 25 or 26 above, an extended time limit for prosecutions is to apply, then—

(a) an information relating to the offence may in England and Wales be tried by a magistrates' court if it is laid within six months after the commission of the offence, or if it is laid within three years after the commission of the offence and not more than two months after the date certified by a chief officer of police to be the date on which evidence sufficient to justify proceedings came to the notice of an officer of his police force; and

(b) summary proceedings for the offence may in Scotland be commenced within six months after the commission of the offence, or within three years after the commission of the offence and not more than two months after the date on which evidence sufficient in the opinion of the Lord Advocate to justify proceedings came to his knowledge; and

(c) a complaint charging the commission of the offence may in Northern Ireland be heard and determined by a magistrates' court if it is made within six months after the commission of the offence, or if it is made within three years after the commission of the offence and not more than two months after the date certified by an officer of police not below the rank of assistant chief constable to be the date on which evidence sufficient to justify the proceedings came to the notice of the police in Northern Ireland.

(2) For purposes of subsection (1)(b) above proceedings shall be deemed to be commenced on the date on which a warrant to apprehend or to cite the accused is granted, if such warrant is executed without undue delay; and a certificate of the Lord Advocate as to the date on which such evidence as is mentioned in subsection (1)(b) came to his knowledge shall be conclusive evidence.

(3) For the purposes of the trial of a person for an offence under this Part of this Act, the offence shall be deemed to have been committed either at the place at which it actually was committed or at any place at which he may be.

(4) Any powers exerciseable under this Act in the case of any person may be exercised notwithstanding that proceedings for an offence under this Part of this Act have been taken against him.

PART IV

SUPPLEMENTARY

Contributions for expenses of persons returning abroad

29.—(1) The Secretary of State may, in such cases as he may with the approval of the Treasury determine, make payments of such amount as may be so determined to meet or provide for expenses of persons who are not patrial in leaving the United Kingdom for a country or territory where they intend to reside permanently, including travelling expenses for members of their families or households.

(2) The Secretary of State shall, so far as practicable, administer this section so as to secure that a person's expenses in leaving the United Kingdom are not met by or out of a payment made by the Secretary of State unless it is shown that it is in that person's interest to leave the United Kingdom and that he wishes to do so.

Return of mental patients

30.—(1) In the following enactments (which provide in relation to England, Wales and Northern Ireland and in relation to Scotland, respectively, for aliens receiving treatment for mental illness as in-patients to be removed, where proper arrangements have been made, to a country or territory outside the United Kingdom and Islands), that is to say—

(a) s 90 of the Mental Health Act 1959; and

(b) s 82 of the Mental Health (Scotland) Act 1960;

there shall in each case be substituted for the words 'any patient being an alien' the words 'any patient who is not patrial within the meaning of the Immigration Act 1971 and'.

(2) Under s 90 of the Mental Health Act 1959 (as under s 82 of the Mental Health (Scotland) Act 1960) the Secretary of State shall only authorise the removal of a patient if it appears to him to be in the interests of the patient; and accordingly in s 90 after the words 'and for his care or treatment there' there shall be inserted the words 'and that it is in the interests of the patient to remove him'.

Expenses

31. There shall be defrayed out of moneys provided by Parliament any expenses incurred by a Secretary of State under or by virtue of this Act—

(a) by way of administrative expenses (including any additional expenses under the British Nationality Acts 1948–65 which are attributable to Schedule 1 to this Act); or

(b) in connection with the removal of any person from the United Kingdom under Schedule 2 or 3 to this Act or the departure with him of his dependants, or his or their maintenance pending departure; or

(c) on account of the remuneration, allowances and other sums payable to or in respect of the adjudicators and members of the Immigration Appeal Tribunal, or of the remuneration of the officers and servants appointed for the adjudicators or Tribunal, or of the expenses of the adjudicators or Tribunal; or

(d) on the making of any grants or payments under s 23 or 29 above.

General provisions as to Orders in Council, etc

32.—(1) Any power conferred by Part I of this Act to make an Order in Council or order (other than a deportation order) or to give any directions includes power to revoke or vary the Order in Council, order or directions.

(2) Any document purporting to be an order, notice or direction made or given by the Secretary of State for the purposes of this Act and to be signed by him or on his behalf, and any document purporting to be a certificate of the Secretary of State so given and to be signed by him, shall be received in evidence, and shall, until the contrary is proved, be deemed to be made or issued by him.

(3) *Prima facie* evidence of any such order, notice, direction or certificate as aforesaid may, in any legal proceedings or proceedings under Part II of this

Act, be given by the production of a document bearing a certificate purporting to be signed by or on behalf of the Secretary of State and stating that the document is a true copy of the order, notice, direction or certificate.

(4) Where an order under s 8(2) above applies to persons specified in a schedule to the order, or any directions of the Secretary of State given for the purposes of this Act apply to persons specified in a schedule to the directions, prima facie evidence of the provisions of the order or directions other than the schedule and of any entry contained in the schedule may, in any legal proceedings or proceedings under Part II of this Act, be given by the production of a document purporting to be signed by or on behalf of the Secretary of State and stating that the document is a true copy of the said provisions and of the relevant entry.

Interpretation

33.—(1) For purposes of this Act, except in so far as the context otherwise requires—

'aircraft' includes hovercraft, 'airport' includes hoverport and 'port' includes airport;

'captain' means master (of a ship) or commander (of an aircraft);

'certificate of patriality' means such a certificate as is referred to in s 3(9) above;

'crew', in relation to a ship or aircraft, means all persons actually employed in the working or service of the ship or aircraft, including the captain, and 'member of the crew' shall be construed accordingly;

'entrant' means a person entering or seeking to enter the United Kingdom, and 'illegal entrant' means a person unlawfully entering or seeking to enter in breach of a deportation order or of the immigration laws, and includes also a person who has so entered;

'entry clearance' means a visa, entry certificate or other document which, in accordance with the immigration rules, is to be taken as evidence of a person's eligibility, though not patrial, for entry into the United Kingdom (but does not include a work permit);

'immigration laws' means this Act and any law for purposes similar to this Act which is for the time being or has (before or after the passing of this Act) been in force in any part of the United Kingdom and Islands;

'immigration rules' means the rules for the time being laid down as mentioned in s 3(2) above;

'the Islands' means the Channel Islands and the Isle of Man, and 'the United Kingdom and Islands' means the United Kingdom and the Islands taken together;

'legally adopted' means adopted in pursuance of an order made by any court in the United Kingdom and Islands or by any adoption specified as an overseas adoption by order of the Secretary of State under s 4 of the Adoption Act 1968;

'limited leave' and 'indefinite leave' mean respectively leave under this Act to enter or remain in the United Kingdom which is, and one which is not, limited as to duration;

'settled' shall be construed in accordance with s 2(3)(d) above but, where used in relation to the United Kingdom only, as if any reference in s 2(3)(d or in s 8(5) to the Islands were omitted;

'ship' includes every description of vessel used in navigation;

'work permit' means a permit indicating, in accordance with the immigration rules, that a person named in it is eligible, though not patrial, for entry into the United Kingdom for the purpose of taking employment.

(2) It is hereby declared that, except as otherwise provided in this Act, a person is not to be treated for the purposes of any provision of this Act as ordinarily resident in the United Kingdom or in any of the Islands at a time when he is there in breach of the immigration laws.

(3) The ports of entry for purposes of this Act, and the ports of exit for purposes of any Order in Council under s 3(7) above, shall be such ports as may from time to time be designated for the purpose by order of the Secretary of State made by statutory instrument.

(4) For purposes of this Act an appeal under Part II shall, subject to any express provision to the contrary, be treated as pending during the period beginning when notice of appeal is duly given and ending when the appeal is finally determined or withdrawn; and in the case of an appeal to an adjudicator, the appeal shall not be treated as finally determined so long as a further appeal can be brought by virtue of s 20 nor, if such an appeal is duly brought, until it is determined or withdrawn.

(5) This Act shall not be taken to supersede or impair any power exerciseable by Her Majesty in relation to aliens by virtue of Her prerogative.

Repeal, transitional and temporary

34.—(1) Subject to the following provisions of this section, the enactments mentioned in Schedule 6 to this Act are hereby repealed, as from the coming into force of this Act, to the extent mentioned in column 3 of the Schedule; and—

(a) this Act, as from its coming into force, shall apply in relation to entrants or others arriving in the United Kingdom at whatever date before or after it comes into force; and

(b) after this Act comes into force anything done under or for the purposes of the former immigration laws shall have effect, in so far as any corresponding action could be taken under or for the purposes of this Act, as if done by way of action so taken, and in relation to anything so done this Act shall apply accordingly.

(2) Without prejudice to the generality of subsection (1)(a) and (b) above, a person refused leave to land by virtue of the Aliens Restriction Act 1914 shall be treated as having been refused leave to enter under this Act, and a person given leave to land by virtue of that Act shall be treated as having been given leave to enter under this Act; and similarly with the Commonwealth Immigrants Acts 1962 and 1968.

(3) A person treated in accordance with subsection (2) above as having leave to enter the United Kingdom—

(a) shall be treated as having an indefinite leave, if he is not at the coming into force of this Act subject to a condition limiting his stay in the United Kingdom; and

(b) shall be treated, if he is then subject to such a condition, as having a limited leave of such duration, and subject to such conditions (capable of being attached to leave under this Act), as correspond to the conditions to which he is then subject, but not to conditions not capable of being so attached.

This subsection shall have effect in relation to any restriction or requirement imposed by Order in Council under the Aliens Restriction Act 1914 as if it had been imposed by way of a landing condition.

(4) Notwithstanding anything in the foregoing provisions of this Act, the former immigration laws shall continue to apply, and this Act shall not apply—

(a) in relation to the making of deportation orders and matters connected therewith in any case where a decision to make the order has been notified to the person concerned before the coming into force of this Act;

(b) in relation to removal from the United Kingdom and matters connected therewith (including detention pending removal or pending the giving of directions for removal) in any case where a person is to be removed in pursuance of a decision taken before the coming into force of this Act or in pursuance of a deportation order to the making of which para (a) above applies;

(c) in relation to appeals against any decision taken or other thing done under the former immigration laws, whether taken or done before the coming into force of this Act or by virtue of this subsection.

(5) Subsection (1) above shall not be taken as empowering a court on appeal to recommend for deportation a person whom the court below could not recommend for deportation, or as affecting any right of appeal in respect of a recommendation for deportation made before this Act comes into force, or as enabling a notice given before this Act comes into force and not complying

with s 6(2) to take the place of the notice required by s 6(2) to be given before a person is recommended for deportation.

(6) So long as s 2 of the Southern Rhodesia Act 1965 remains in force, this Act shall have effect subject to such provision as may (before or after this Act comes into force) be made by Order in Council under and for the purposes of that section.

Commencement, and interim provisions

35.—(1) Except as otherwise provided by this Act, Parts I–III of this Act shall come into force on such day as the Secretary of State may appoint by order made by statutory instrument; and references to the coming into force of this Act shall be construed as references to the beginning of the day so appointed.

(2) Section 25 above, except s 25(2), and s 28 in its application to offences under s 25(1) shall come into force at the end of one month beginning with the date this Act is passed.

(3) The provisions of s 28(1) and (2) above shall have effect, as from the passing of this Act, in relation to offences under s 4A (unauthorised landing) of the Commonwealth Immigrants Act 1962 as amended by the Commonwealth Immigrants Act 1968, other than offences committed six months or more before the passing of this Act, as those provisions are expressed to have effect in relation to offences to which the extended time limit for prosecutions is to apply under ss 24, 25 and 26 above; but where proceedings for an offence under s 4A of the Commonwealth Immigrants Act 1962 would have been out of time but for this subsection, s 4A(4) (under which, in certain cases, a person not producing a passport duly stamped by an immigration officer is presumed for purposes of that section to have landed in contravention of it, unless the contrary is proved) shall not apply.

(4) Section 1(2A)(d) of the Commonwealth Immigrants Act 1962 (which was inserted by s 1 of the Commonwealth Immigrants Act 1968, and excludes from the control on immigration under those Acts, among other persons, certain persons registered in the United Kingdom or in an independent country of the Commonwealth as citizens of the United Kingdom and Colonies) shall not apply—

- (a) to a woman registered after the passing of this Act under or by virtue of s 6(2) (wives) of the British Nationality Act 1948, unless so registered either—
  - (i) by virtue of her marriage to a citizen of the United Kingdom and Colonies before the passing of this Act; or
  - (ii) by virtue of her marriage to such a citizen who at the time of her registration or at his death before that time was excluded

from the control on immigration under the Commonwealth Immigrants Acts 1962 and 1968 by s 1(2) of the 1962 Act; nor

(b) to anyone registered after the passing of this Act under or by virtue of s 7 (children) of the British Nationality Act 1948, unless so registered in the United Kingdom.

(5) So much of s 1 of the Aliens Restriction (Amendment) Act 1919 as limits the duration of that section, and s 5 of the Commonwealth Immigrants Act 1962 in so far as it limits the duration of Part I of that Act, shall cease to have effect on the passing of this Act.

Power to extend to Islands

36. Her Majesty may by Order in Council direct that any of the provisions of this Act shall extend, with such exceptions, adaptations and modifications, if any, as may be specified in the Order, to any of the Islands; and any Order in Council under this subsection may be varied or revoked by a further Order in Council.

Short title and extent

37.—(1) This Act may be cited as the Immigration Act 1971.

(2) It is hereby declared that this Act extends to Northern Ireland, and (without prejudice to any provision of Schedule l to this Act as to the extent of that Schedule) where an enactment repealed by this Act extends outside the United Kingdom the repeal shall be of like extent.

SCHEDULES

SCHEDULE 1

REGISTRATION AS CITIZEN BY REASON OF RESIDENCE, CROWN SERVICE, ETC

1. The law with respect to registration as a citizen of the United Kingdom and Colonies shall be modified as follows—

(a) in the British Nationality Act 1948, immediately before s 6, there shall be inserted as s 5A the provisions set out in Appendix A to this Schedule, and no person shall be entitled to be registered under or by virtue of s 6(1) of that Act except in the transitional cases allowed for by para 2 below; and

(b) in s 8 of the British Nationality Act 1948 (registration outside United Kingdom)—

(i) after the words 'foregoing sections' there shall be inserted in subsection (1) the words 'or, subject to subsection (1A) of this section, under s 5A' and in subsection (2) the words 'or under s 5A of this Act'; and

(ii) there shall be omitted in subsection (1) the words from 'and as if' onwards (except for purposes of registration by virtue of para 2 below), and there shall be inserted as subsections (1A) and (1B) the provisions set out in Appendix B to this Schedule; and

(c) for s 9 of the British Nationality Act 1948 there shall be substituted the provisions set out in Appendix C to this Schedule (which insert in the section a reference to the new s 5A and add a requirement for the taking in certain cases of an oath of allegiance).

2. Notwithstanding anything in para 1 above or any repeal made by this Act (but subject to para 3 below), a person who would but for this Act have been entitled under or by virtue of s 6(1) of the British Nationality Act 1948 to be registered as a citizen of the United Kingdom and Colonies shall be entitled to be so registered in the United Kingdom if he satisfies the Secretary of State that at the date of his application to be registered he had throughout the last five years or, if it is more than five years, throughout the period since the coming into force of this Act been ordinarily resident in the United Kingdom without being subject, by virtue of any law relating to immigration, to any restriction on the period for which he might remain.

3.—(1) A person in respect of whom a recommendation for deportation is at the date of his application in force shall not be entitled to be registered as a citizen of the United Kingdom and Colonies by virtue of para 2 above.

(2) Where, in accordance with any regulations relating to appeals, a person, when he applies to be so registered by virtue of para 2 above, has been given notice of a decision to make a deportation order in respect of him, he shall not be entitled to be so registered by virtue of that paragraph, unless before the date of his application an appeal by him against that decision has been finally determined in his favour or the Secretary of State has notified him that the order will not be made.

(3) References in this paragraph to recommendations for deportation, deportation orders and other matters shall include any such recommendation, order or matter under the enactments repealed by this Act; and accordingly this paragraph shall apply for purposes of para 2 above in place of the corresponding provision made by s 12(1) of the Commonwealth Immigrants Act 1962 and s 18 of the Immigration Appeals Act 1969.

4.—(1) Paragraph 2 above shall apply in relation to a colony or protectorate with the substitution for references to the United Kingdom and to the Secretary of State of references to that colony or protectorate and to the Governor; and in relation to a colony or protectorate para 3(1) and (2) shall have effect (with any necessary adaptations) with reference to deportation from the colony or protectorate.

(2) In this paragraph 'colony', 'protectorate' and 'Governor' have the same meanings as they have for purposes of the British Nationality Act 1948, except that 'colony' does not include an associated State.

5.—(1) It is hereby declared that this Schedule extends to each of the associated States; and in the application of paras 2 and 3 to an associated state—

(a) in para 2 references to the associated State shall be substituted for references to the United Kingdom; and

(b) para 3(1) and (2) shall have effect (with any necessary adaptations) with reference to deportation from the associated State.

(2) In para 4 of Schedule 3 to the West Indies Act 1967 (which provides for a person other than the Secretary of State to be given in relation to an associated State certain functions of the Secretary of State, including those under sections of the British Nationality Act 1948 listed in para 4(3)(a)) there shall be inserted at the beginning of sub-para (3)(a) the words 'section 5A except as regards registration under s 5A(1) and', and where by virtue of that paragraph the functions of the Secretary of State under s 6(1) of the British Nationality Act 1948 are exerciseable by another person the reference in para 2 above to the Secretary of State shall have effect as a reference to that person.

APPENDIX A TO SCHEDULE 1

Provisions to have effect as s 5A of British Nationality Act 1948

5A.—(1) Subject to the provisions of subsections (5) and (6) below, a citizen of any country mentioned in s 1(3) of this Act, being a person of full age and capacity, shall be entitled, on making application therefore to the Secretary of State in the prescribed manner, to be registered as a citizen of the United Kingdom and Colonies if he satisfies the Secretary of State that—

(a) he is patrial within the meaning of the Immigration Act 1971 by virtue of s 2(1)(d) of that Act or of the reference thereto in s 2(2); and

(b) he fulfils the condition in subsection (3) below.

(2) On an application made to the Secretary of State in the prescribed manner, the Secretary of State may cause to be registered as a citizen of the United Kingdom and Colonies any person of full age and capacity who satisfies the Secretary of State that—

(a) he is a citizen of a country mentioned in s 1(3) of this Act or of Eire; and

(b) he fulfils the condition in subsection (3) below; and

(c) he is of good character; and

(d) he has sufficient knowledge of the English or Welsh language; and

(e) he intends in the event of his being registered to reside in the United Kingdom or a colony or protectorate or to enter into or continue in relevant employment.

(3) The condition that a person is required by subsection (1)(b) or (2)(b) above to fulfil is that throughout the period of five years ending with the date of his application to be registered, or such shorter period so ending as the Secretary of State may in the special circumstances of any particular case accept, he has been ordinarily resident in the United Kingdom, or engaged in relevant employment, or partly the one and partly the other.

(4) For purposes of this section 'relevant employment' means—

(a) Crown service under Her Majesty's government in the United Kingdom; or

(b) service under an international organisation of which Her Majesty's government in the United Kingdom is a member; or

(c) service in the employment of a society, company or body of persons established in the United Kingdom;

and in subsection (2)(e) includes service in the employment of a society, company or body of persons established either in the United Kingdom or in a colony or protectorate.

(5) A person shall not be registered under this section wholly or partly by reason of service within subsection (4)(b) or (c) above unless it seems to the Secretary of State fitting that he should be so registered by reason of his close connection with the United Kingdom or, if he is applying for registration under subsection (2), his close connection with the United Kingdom and Colonies.

(6) A person who has renounced citizenship of the United Kingdom and Colonies under this Act shall not be entitled to be registered as a citizen thereof under subsection (1) above, but may be so registered with the approval of the Secretary of State.

(7) Where a person is a British subject without citizenship by virtue of s 13 or 16 of this Act or (being a woman) is a British subject by virtue of s 1 of the British Nationality Act 1965 by virtue of her having satisfied the Secretary of State that she has been married to a man who was, or but for his death would have been, a British subject as aforesaid, this section shall apply to that person as it applies to a citizen of a country mentioned in s 1(3) of this Act.

APPENDIX B TO SCHEDULE 1

Provisions to have effect as s 8(1A) and (1B) of the British Nationality Act 1948

(1A) Except in the Channel Islands and the Isle of Man, subsection (1) above shall not apply to the functions of the Secretary of State as regards registration under s 5A(1) of this Act; and in its application to any of those islands that section shall have effect as if a reference to that island were substituted in s 5A(5) for the first reference to the United Kingdom.

(1B) Subject to subsection (1A) above, s 5A of this Act shall in its application to any colony or protectorate, have effect as if for the references in subsection (3) and in subsection (4)(c) to the United Kingdom there were substituted references to that colony or protectorate, and as if for the reference to the English or Welsh language in subsection (2)(d) there were substituted a reference to the English language or any other language in current use in that colony or protectorate.

APPENDIX C TO SCHEDULE 1

Provisions to have effect as s 9 of British Nationality Act 1948

9.—(1) A person registered under any of the three last foregoing sections or under s 5A of this Act shall, on taking an oath of allegiance in accordance with subsection (2) below if so required by that subsection, be a citizen of the United Kingdom and Colonies by registration as from the date on which he is registered.

(2) A person of full age and capacity shall on registration as mentioned in subsection (1) above, if not already a citizen of a country of which Her Majesty is Queen nor a British subject by virtue of s 1 of the British Nationality Act 1965, take an oath of allegiance in the form specified in the First Schedule to this Act.

SCHEDULE 2

ADMINISTRATIVE PROVISIONS AS TO CONTROL ON ENTRY, ETC

PART I

GENERAL PROVISIONS

Immigration officers and medical inspectors

1.—(1) Immigration officers for the purposes of this Act shall be appointed by the Secretary of State, and he may arrange with the Commissioners of Customs and Excise for the employment of officers of customs and excise as immigration officers under this Act.

(2) Medical inspectors for the purposes of this Act may be appointed by the Secretary of State or, in Northern Ireland, by the Minister of Health and Social Services or other appropriate Minister of the government of Northern Ireland in pursuance of arrangements made between that Minister and the Secretary of State, and shall be fully qualified medical practitioners.

(3) In the exercise of their functions under this Act immigration officers shall act in accordance with such instructions (not inconsistent with the immigration rules) as may be given them by the Secretary of State, and medical inspectors shall act in accordance with such instructions as may be given them by the Secretary of State or, in Northern Ireland, as may be given in pursuance of the arrangements mentioned in sub-para (2) above by the Minister making appointments of medical inspectors in Northern Ireland.

(4) An immigration officer or medical inspector may board any ship or aircraft for the purpose of exercising his functions under this Act.

(5) An immigration officer, for the purpose of satisfying himself whether there are persons he may wish to examine under para 2 below, may search any ship or aircraft and anything on board it, or any vehicle taken off a ship or aircraft on which it has been brought to the United Kingdom.

Examination by immigration officers, and medical examination

2.—(1) An immigration officer may examine any persons who have arrived in the United Kingdom by ship or aircraft (including transit passengers, members of the crew and others not seeking to enter the United Kingdom) for the purpose of determining—

(a) whether any of them is or is not patrial; and

(b) whether, if he is not, he may or may not enter the United Kingdom without leave; and

(c) whether, if he may not, he should be given leave and for what period and on what conditions (if any), or should be refused leave.

(2) Any such person, if he is seeking to enter the United Kingdom, may be examined also by a medical inspector or by any qualified person carrying out a test or examination required by a medical inspector.

(3) A person, on being examined under this paragraph by an immigration officer or medical inspector, may be required in writing by him to submit to further examination; but a requirement under this sub-paragraph shall not prevent a person who arrives as a transit passenger, or as a member of the crew of a ship or aircraft, or for the purpose of joining a ship or aircraft as a member of the crew, from leaving by his intended ship or aircraft.

3.—(1) An immigration officer may examine any person who is embarking or seeking to embark in the United Kingdom for the purpose of determining whether he is patrial and, if he is not, for the purpose of establishing his identity.

(2) So long as any Order in Council is in force under s 3(7) of this Act, an immigration officer may examine any person who is embarking or seeking to embark in the United Kingdom for the purpose of determining—

(a) whether any of the provisions of the Order apply to him; and

(b) whether, if so, any power conferred by the Order should be exercised in relation to him and in what way.

Information and documents

4.—(1) It shall be the duty of any person examined under para 2 or 3 above to furnish to the person carrying out the examination all such information in his possession as that person may require for the purpose of his functions under that paragraph.

(2) A person on his examination under para 2 or 3 above by an immigration officer shall, if so required by the immigration officer—

(a) produce either a valid passport with photograph or some other document satisfactorily establishing his identity and nationality or citizenship; and

(b) declare whether or not he is carrying or conveying documents of any relevant description specified by the immigration officer, and produce any documents of that description which he is carrying or conveying.

In para (b), 'relevant description' means any description appearing to the immigration officer to be relevant for the purposes of the examination.

(3) Where under sub-para (2)(b) above a person has been required to declare whether or not he is carrying or conveying documents of any description, he and any baggage belonging to him or under his control may be searched with a view to ascertaining whether he is doing so by the immigration officer or a person acting under the directions of the officer—

Provided that no woman or girl shall be searched except by a woman.

(4) An immigration officer may examine any documents produced pursuant to sub-para (2)(b) above or found on a search under sub-para (3), and may for that purpose detain them for any period not exceeding seven days; and if on examination of any document so produced or found the immigration officer is of the opinion that it may be needed in connection with proceedings on an appeal under this Act or for an offence, he may detain it until he is satisfied that it will not be so needed.

5. The Secretary of State may by order made by statutory instrument make provision for requiring passengers disembarking or embarking in the United Kingdom, or any class of such passengers, to produce to an immigration officer, if so required, landing or embarkation cards in such form as the Secretary of State may direct, and for requiring the owners or agents of ships and aircraft to supply such cards to those passengers.

Notice of leave to enter or of refusal of leave

6.—(1) Subject to sub-para (3) below, where a person examined by an immigration officer under para 2 above is to be given a limited leave to enter the United Kingdom or is to be refused leave, the notice giving or refusing leave shall be given not later than 12 hours after the conclusion of his examination (including any further examination) in pursuance of that paragraph; and if notice giving or refusing leave is not given him before the end of those 12 hours, he shall (if not patrial) be deemed to have been given indefinite leave to enter the United Kingdom and the immigration officer shall as soon as may be give him written notice of that leave.

(2) Where on a person's examination under para 2 above he is given notice of leave to enter the United Kingdom, then at any time before the end of 12 hours from the conclusion of the examination he may be given a further notice in writing by an immigration officer cancelling the earlier notice and refusing him leave to enter.

(3) Where in accordance with this paragraph a person is given notice refusing him leave to enter the United Kingdom, that notice may at any time be cancelled by notice in writing given him by an immigration officer; and where a person is given a notice of cancellation under this sub-paragraph, the immigration officer may at the same time give him a limited leave to enter, but in the absence of a notice giving a limited leave the notice of cancellation shall be deemed to be a notice giving him indefinite leave to enter.

(4) Where an entrant is a member of a party in charge of a person appearing to the immigration officer to be a responsible person, any notice to be given in relation to that entrant in accordance with this paragraph shall be duly given if delivered to the person in charge of the party.

Power to require medical examination after entry

7. If, on a person's examination by an immigration officer under para 2 above, the immigration officer—

(a) determines that he may be given leave to enter the United Kingdom; but

(b) is of opinion, on the advice of a medical inspector or, where no medical inspector is available, on that of any other fully qualified medical practitioner, that a further medical test or examination may be required in the interests of public health;

then the immigration officer, on giving that person leave to enter the United Kingdom, may by notice in writing require him to report his arrival to such medical officer of health as may be specified in the notice and thereafter to attend at such place and time, and submit to such test or examination (if any), as that medical officer of health may require.

Removal of persons refused leave to enter and illegal entrants

8.—(1) Where a person arriving in the United Kingdom is refused leave to enter, an immigration officer may, subject to sub-para (2) below—

(a) give the captain of the ship or aircraft in which he arrives directions requiring the captain to remove him from the United Kingdom in that ship or aircraft; or

(b) give the owners or agents of that ship or aircraft directions requiring them to remove him from the United Kingdom in any ship or aircraft specified or indicated in the directions, being a ship or aircraft of which they are the owners or agents; or

(c) give those owners or agents directions requiring them to make arrangements for his removal from the United Kingdom in any ship or aircraft specified or indicated in the directions to a country or territory so specified, being either—

(i) a country of which he is a national or citizen; or

(ii) a country or territory in which he has obtained a passport or other document of identity; or

(iii) a country or territory in which he embarked for the United Kingdom; or

(iv) a country or territory to which there is reason to believe that he will be admitted.

(2) No directions shall be given under this paragraph in respect of anyone after the expiration of two months beginning with the date on which he was refused leave to enter the United Kingdom.

9. Where an illegal entrant is not given leave to enter or remain in the United Kingdom, an immigration officer may give any such directions in respect of him as in a case within para 8 above are authorised by para 8(1).

10.—(1) Where it appears to the Secretary of State either—

(a) that directions might be given in respect of a person under para 8 or 9 above, but that it is not practicable for them to be given or that, if given, they would be ineffective; or

(b) that directions might have been given in respect of a person under para 8 above but that the time limited by para 8(2) has passed;

then the Secretary of State may give to the owners or agents of any ship or aircraft any such directions in respect of that person as are authorised by para 8(1)(c).

(2) Where the Secretary of State may give directions for a person's removal in accordance with sub-para (1) above, he may instead give directions for his removal in accordance with arrangements to be made by the Secretary of

State to any country or territory to which he could be removed under sub-para (1).

(3) The costs of complying with any directions given under this paragraph shall be defrayed by the Secretary of State.

11. A person in respect of whom directions are given under any of paras 8–10 above may be placed, under the authority of an immigration officer, on board any ship or aircraft in which he is to be removed in accordance with the directions.

Seamen and aircrews

12.—(1) If, on a person's examination by an immigration officer under para 2 above, the immigration officer is satisfied that he has come to the United Kingdom for the purpose of joining a ship or aircraft as a member of the crew, then the immigration officer may limit the duration of any leave he gives that person to enter the United Kingdom by requiring him to leave the United Kingdom in a ship or aircraft specified or indicated by the notice giving leave.

(2) Where a person (not being patrial) arrives in the United Kingdom for the purpose of joining a ship or aircraft as a member of the crew and, having been given leave to enter as mentioned in sub-para (1) above, remains beyond the time limited by that leave, or is reasonably suspected by an immigration officer of intending to do so, an immigration officer may—

(a) give the captain of that ship or aircraft directions requiring the captain to remove him from the United Kingdom in that ship or aircraft; or

(b) give the owners or agents of that ship or aircraft directions requiring them to remove him from the United Kingdom in any ship or aircraft specified or indicated in the directions, being a ship or aircraft of which they are the owners or agents; or

(c) give those owners or agents directions requiring them to make arrangements for his removal from the United Kingdom in any ship or aircraft specified or indicated in the directions to a country or territory so specified, being either—

(i) a country of which he is a national or citizen; or

(ii) a country or territory in which he has obtained a passport or other document of identity; or

(iii) a country or territory in which he embarked for the United Kingdom; or

(iv) a country or territory where he was engaged as a member of the crew of the ship or aircraft which he arrived in the United Kingdom to join; or

(v) a country or territory to which there is reason to believe that he will be admitted.

13.—(1) Where a person being a member of the crew of a ship or aircraft is examined by an immigration officer under para 2 above, the immigration officer may limit the duration of any leave he gives that person to enter the United Kingdom—

(a) in the manner authorised by para 12 (1) above; or

(b) if that person is to be allowed to enter the United Kingdom in order to receive hospital treatment, by requiring him, on completion of that treatment, to leave the United Kingdom in accordance with arrangements to be made for his repatriation; or

(c) by requiring him to leave the United Kingdom within a specified period in accordance with arrangements to be made for his repatriation.

(2) Where a person (not being patrial) arrives in the United Kingdom as a member of the crew of a ship or aircraft, and either—

(A) having lawfully entered the United Kingdom without leave by virtue of s 8(1) of this Act, he remains without leave beyond the time allowed by s 8(1), or is reasonably suspected by an immigration officer of intending to do so; or

(B) having been given leave limited as mentioned in sub-para (1) above, he remains beyond the time limited by that leave, or is reasonably suspected by an immigration officer of intending to do so;

an immigration officer may—

(a) give the captain of the ship or aircraft in which he arrived directions requiring the captain to remove him from the United Kingdom in that ship or aircraft; or

(b) give the owners or agents of that ship or aircraft directions requiring them to remove him from the United Kingdom in any ship or aircraft specified or indicated in the directions, being a ship or aircraft of which they are the owners or agents; or

(c) give those owners or agents directions requiring them to make arrangements for his removal from the United Kingdom in any ship or aircraft specified or indicated in the directions to a country or territory so specified, being either—

(i) a country of which he is a national or citizen; or

(ii) a country or territory in which he has obtained a passport or other document of identity; or

(iii) a country in which he embarked for the United Kingdom; or

(iv) a country or territory in which he was engaged as a member of the crew of the ship or aircraft in which he arrived in the United Kingdom; or

(v) a country or territory to which there is reason to believe that he will be admitted.

14.—(1) Where it appears to the Secretary of State that directions might be given in respect of a person under para 12 or 13 above, but that it is not practicable for them to be given or that, if given, they would be ineffective, then the Secretary of State may give to the owners or agents of any ship or aircraft any such directions in respect of that person as are authorised by para 12(2)(c) or 13(2)(c).

(2) Where the Secretary of State may give directions for a person's removal in accordance with sub-para (1) above, he may instead give directions for his removal in accordance with arrangements to be made by the Secretary of State to any country or territory to which he could be removed under sub-para (1).

(3) The costs of complying with any directions given under this paragraph shall be defrayed by the Secretary of State.

15. A person in respect of whom directions are given under any of paras 12–14 above may be placed, under the authority of an immigration officer, on board any ship or aircraft in which he is to be removed in accordance with the directions.

Detention of persons liable to examination or removal

16.—(1) A person who may be required to submit to examination under para 2 above may be detained under the authority of an immigration officer pending his examination and pending a decision to give or refuse him leave to enter.

(2) A person in respect of whom directions may be given under any of paras 8–14 above may be detained under the authority of an immigration officer pending the giving of directions and pending his removal in pursuance of any directions given.

(3) A person on board a ship or aircraft may, under the authority of an immigration officer, be removed from the ship or aircraft for detention under this paragraph but if an immigration officer so requires the captain of a ship or aircraft shall prevent from disembarking in the United Kingdom any person who has arrived in the United Kingdom in the ship or aircraft and been refused leave to enter, and the captain may for that purpose detain him in custody on board the ship or aircraft.

(4) The captain of a ship or aircraft, if so required by an immigration officer, shall prevent from disembarking in the United Kingdom or before

the directions for his removal have been fulfilled any person placed on board the ship or aircraft under para 11 or 15 above, and the captain may for that purpose detain him in custody on board the ship or aircraft.

17.—(1) A person liable to be detained under para 16 above may be arrested without warrant by a constable or by an immigration officer.

(2) If—

(a) a justice of the peace is by written information on oath satisfied that there is reasonable ground for suspecting that a person liable to be arrested under this paragraph is to be found on any premises; or

(b) in Scotland, a sheriff, or a magistrate or justice of the peace, having jurisdiction in the place where the premises are situated is by evidence on oath so satisfied;

he may grant a warrant authorising any constable acting for the police area in which the premises are situated, or in Northern Ireland any constable, at any time or times within one month from the date of the warrant to enter, if need be by force, the premises named in the warrant for the purpose of searching for and arresting that person.

18.—(1) Persons may be detained under para 16 above in such places as the Secretary of State may direct (when not detained in accordance with para 16 on board a ship or aircraft).

(2) Where a person is detained under para 16, any immigration officer, constable or prison officer, or any other person authorised by the Secretary of State, may take all such steps as may be reasonably necessary for photographing, measuring or otherwise identifying him.

(3) Any person detained under para 16 may be taken in the custody of a constable, or of any person acting under the authority of an immigration officer, to and from any place where his attendance is required for the purpose of ascertaining his citizenship or nationality or of making arrangements for his admission to a country or territory other than the United Kingdom, or where he is required to be for any other purpose connected with the operation of this Act.

(4) A person shall be deemed to be in legal custody at any time when he is detained under para 16 or is being removed in pursuance of sub-para (3) above.

19.—(1) Where a person is refused leave to enter the United Kingdom and directions are given in respect of him under para 8 or 10 above, then subject to the provisions of this paragraph the owners or agents of the ship or aircraft in which he arrived shall be liable to pay the Secretary of State on demand any expenses incurred by the latter in respect of the custody, accommodation or maintenance of that person at any time after his arrival while he was detained or liable to be detained under para 16 above.

(2) Sub-para (1) above shall not apply to expenses in respect of a person who, when he arrived in the United Kingdom, held a certificate of patriality or a current entry clearance or was the person named in a current work permit; and for this purpose a document purporting to be a certificate of patriality, entry clearance or work permit is to be regarded as being one unless its falsity is reasonably apparent.

(3) If, before the directions for a person's removal under para 8 or 10 above have been carried out, he is given leave to enter the United Kingdom, or if he is afterwards given that leave in consequence of the determination in his favour of an appeal under this Act (being an appeal against a refusal of leave to enter by virtue of which the directions were given), or it is determined on an appeal under this Act that he does not require leave to enter (being an appeal occasioned by such a refusal), no sum shall be demanded under sub-para (1) above for expenses incurred in respect of that person and any sum already demanded and paid shall be refunded.

(4) Sub-para (1) above shall not have effect in relation to directions which, in consequence of an appeal under this Act, have ceased to have effect or are for the time being of no effect; and the expenses to which that sub-paragraph applies include expenses in conveying the person in question to and from the place where he is detained or accommodated unless the journey is made for the purpose of attending an appeal by him under this Act.

20.—(1) Subject to the provisions of this paragraph, in either of the following cases, that is to say—

(a) where directions are given in respect of an illegal entrant under para 9 or 10 above; and

(b) where a person has lawfully entered the United Kingdom without leave by virtue of s 8(1) of this Act, but directions are given in respect of him under para 13(2)(A) above or, in a case within para 13(2)(A), under para 14;

the owners or agents of the ship or aircraft in which he arrived in the United Kingdom shall be liable to pay the Secretary of State on demand any expenses incurred by the latter in respect of the custody, accommodation or maintenance of that person at any time after his arrival while he was detained or liable to be detained under para 16 above.

(2) If, before the directions for a person's removal from the United Kingdom have been carried out, he is given leave to remain in the United Kingdom, no sum shall be demanded under sub-para (1) above for expenses incurred in respect of that person and any sum already demanded and paid shall be refunded.

(3) Sub-para (1) above shall not have effect in relation to directions which, in consequence of an appeal under this Act, are for the time being of no

effect; and the expenses to which that sub-paragraph applies include expenses in conveying the person in question to and from the place where he is detained or accommodated unless the journey is made for the purpose of attending an appeal by him under this Act.

Temporary admission or release of persons liable to detention

21.—(1) A person liable to detention or detained under para 16 above may, under the written authority of an immigration officer, be temporarily admitted to the United Kingdom without being detained or be released from detention; but this shall not prejudice a later exercise of the power to detain him.

(2) So long as a person is at large in the United Kingdom by virtue of this paragraph, he shall be subject to such restrictions as to residence and as to reporting to the police or an immigration officer as may from time to time be notified to him in writing by an immigration officer.

22.—(1) A person detained under para 16(1) above pending examination may, if seven days have elapsed since the date of his arrival in the United Kingdom, be released on bail by an adjudicator on his entering into a recognizance or, in Scotland, bail bond conditioned for his appearance before an immigration officer at a time and place named in the recognizance or bail bond or at such other time or place as may in the meantime be notified to him in writing by an immigration officer.

(2) The conditions of a recognizance or bail bond taken under this paragraph may include conditions appearing to the adjudicator to be likely to result in the appearance of the person bailed at the required time and place; and any recognizance shall be with or without sureties as the adjudicator may determine.

(3) In any case in which an adjudicator has power under this paragraph to release a person on bail, the adjudicator may, instead of taking the bail, fix the amount and conditions of the bail (including the amount in which any sureties are to be bound) with a view to its being taken subsequently by any such person as may be specified by the adjudicator; and on the recognizance or bail bond being so taken the person to be bailed shall be released.

23.—(1) Where a recognizance entered into under para 22 above appears to an adjudicator to be forfeited, the adjudicator may by order declare it to be forfeited and adjudge the persons bound thereby, whether as principal or sureties, or any of them, to pay the sum in which they are respectively bound or such part of it, if any, as the adjudicator thinks fit; and an order under this sub-paragraph shall specify a magistrates' court or, in Northern Ireland, court of summary jurisdiction, and—

(a) the recognizance shall be treated for the purposes of collection, enforcement and remission of the sum forfeited as having been forfeited by the court so specified; and

(b) the adjudicator shall, as soon as practicable, give particulars of the recognizance to the clerk of that court.

(2) Where a person released on bail under para 22 above as it applies in Scotland fails to comply with the terms of his bail bond, an adjudicator may declare the bail to be forfeited, and any bail so forfeited shall be transmitted by the adjudicator to the sheriff court having jurisdiction in the area where the proceedings took place, and shall be treated as having been forfeited by that court.

(3) Any sum the payment of which is enforceable by a magistrates' court in England or Wales by virtue of this paragraph shall be treated for the purposes of the Justices of the Peace Act 1949 and, in particular, s 27 thereof as being due under a recognizance forfeited by such a court and as being Exchequer moneys.

(4) Any sum the payment of which is enforceable by virtue of this paragraph by a court of summary jurisdiction in Northern Ireland shall, for the purposes of s 20(5) of the Administration of Justice Act (Northern Ireland) 1954, be treated as a forfeited recognizance.

24.—(1) An immigration officer or constable may arrest without warrant a person who has been released by virtue of para 22 above—

(a) if he has reasonable grounds for believing that that person is likely to break the condition of his recognizance or bail bond that he will appear at the time and place required or to break any other condition of it, or has reasonable ground to suspect that that person is breaking or has broken any such other condition; or

(b) if, a recognizance with sureties having been taken, he is notified in writing by any surety of the surety's belief that that person is likely to break the first-mentioned condition, and of the surety's wish for that reason to be relieved of his obligations as a surety;

and para 17(2) above shall apply for the arrest of a person under this paragraph as it applies for the arrest of a person under para 17.

(2) A person arrested under this paragraph—

(a) if not required by a condition on which he was released to appear before an immigration officer within 24 hours after the time of his arrest, shall as soon as practicable be brought before an adjudicator or, if that is not practicable within those 24 hours, before a justice of the peace acting for the petty sessions area in which he is arrested or, in Scotland, the sheriff; and

(b) if required by such a condition to appear within those 24 hours before an immigration officer, shall be brought before that officer.

(3) An adjudicator, justice of the peace or sheriff before whom a person is brought by virtue of sub-para (2)(a) above—

(a) if of the opinion that that person has broken or is likely to break any condition on which he was released, may either—

   (i) direct that he be detained under the authority of the person by whom he was arrested; or

   (ii) release him, on his original recognizance or on a new recognizance, with or without sureties, or, in Scotland, on his original bail or on new bail; and

(b) if not of that opinion, shall release him on his original recognizance or bail.

25. The power to make rules of procedure conferred by s 22 of this Act shall include power to make rules with respect to applications to an adjudicator under paras 22–24 above and matters arising out of such applications.

Supplementary duties of those connected with ships or aircraft or with ports

26.—(1) The owners or agents of a ship or aircraft employed to carry passengers for reward shall not, without the approval of the Secretary of State, arrange for the ship or aircraft to call at a port in the United Kingdom other than a port of entry for the purpose of disembarking passengers, if any of the passengers on board may not enter the United Kingdom without leave and having not been given leave, or for the purpose of embarking passengers unless the owners or agents have reasonable cause to believe all of them to be patrial.

(2) The Secretary of State may from time to time give written notice to the owners or agents of any ships or aircraft designating control areas for the embarkation or disembarkation of passengers in any port in the United Kingdom, and specifying the conditions and restrictions (if any) to be observed in any control area; and where by notice given to any owners or agents a control area is for the time being designated for the embarkation or disembarkation of passengers at any port, the owners or agents shall take all reasonable steps to secure that, in the case of their ships or aircraft, passengers do not embark or disembark, as the case may be, at the port outside the control area and that any conditions or restrictions notified to them are observed.

(3) The Secretary of State may also from time to time give to any persons concerned with the management of a port in the United Kingdom written notice designating control areas in the port and specifying conditions or restrictions to be observed in any control area, and any such person shall take all reasonable steps to secure that any conditions or restrictions as notified to him are observed.

27.—(1) The captain of a ship or aircraft arriving in the United Kingdom—

(a) shall take such steps as may be necessary to secure that persons on board do not disembark there unless either they have been examined by an immigration officer, or they disembark in accordance with arrangements approved by an immigration officer, or they are members of the crew who may lawfully enter the United Kingdom without leave by virtue of s 8(1) of this Act; and

(b) where the examination of persons on board is to be carried out on the ship or aircraft, shall take such steps as may be necessary to secure that those to be examined are presented for the purpose in an orderly manner.

(2) The Secretary of State may by order made by statutory instrument make provision for requiring captains of ships or aircraft arriving in the United Kingdom, or of such of them as arrive from or by way of countries or places specified in the order, to furnish to immigration officers—

(a) a passenger list showing the names and nationality or citizenship of passengers arriving on board the ship or aircraft;

(b) particulars of members of the crew of the ship or aircraft;

and for enabling an immigration officer to dispense with the furnishing of any such list or particulars.

PART II

EFFECT OF APPEALS

Stay on directions for removal

28.—(1) Where a person in the United Kingdom appeals under s 13(1) of this Act on being refused leave to enter, any directions previously given by virtue of the refusal for his removal from the United Kingdom shall cease to have effect, except in so far as they have already been carried out, and no directions shall be so given so long as the appeal is pending.

(2) Where a person in the United Kingdom appeals under s 16 or 17 of this Act against any directions given under Part I of this Schedule for his removal from the United Kingdom, those directions, except in so far as they have already been carried out, shall be of no effect so long as the appeal is pending.

(3) Notwithstanding sub-para (1) or (2) above, the provisions of Part I of this Schedule with respect to detention and persons liable to detention shall apply to a person appealing under s 13(1), 16 or 17 of this Act as if there were in force directions for his removal from the United Kingdom, except that he shall not be detained on board a ship or aircraft so as to compel him to leave the United Kingdom while the appeal is pending.

(4) In calculating the period of two months limited by para 8(2) above for the giving of directions under that paragraph for the removal of a person

from the United Kingdom, there shall be disregarded any period during which there is pending an appeal by him under s 13(1) or 17 of this Act.

(5) For purposes of sub-paras (1)–(3) above (but not for purposes of sub-para (4)), where an appeal to an adjudicator is dismissed, an appeal shall not be regarded as pending unless forthwith after the dismissal—

(a) the appellant duly gives notice of appeal against the determination of the adjudicator; or

(b) in a case in which leave to appeal against that determination is required and the adjudicator has power to grant leave, the appellant duly applies for and obtains the leave of the adjudicator.

(6) Where directions are given under Part I of this Schedule for anyone's removal from the United Kingdom, and directions are also so given for the removal with him of persons belonging to his family then if any of them appeals under s 13(1), 16 or 17 of this Act, the appeal shall have the like effect under this paragraph in relation to the directions given in respect of each of the others as it has in relation to the directions given in respect of the appellant.

Grant of bail pending appeal

29.—(1) Where a person (in the following provisions of this Schedule referred to as 'an appellant') has an appeal pending under s 13(1), 16 or 17 of this Act and is for the time being detained under Part I of this Schedule, he may be released on bail in accordance with this paragraph.

(2) An immigration officer not below the rank of chief immigration officer or a police officer not below the rank of inspector may release an appellant on his entering into a recognizance or, in Scotland, bail bond conditioned for his appearance before an adjudicator or the Appeal Tribunal at a time and place named in the recognizance or bail bond.

(3) An adjudicator may release an appellant on his entering into a recognizance or, in Scotland, bail bond conditioned for his appearance before that or any other adjudicator or the Appeal Tribunal at a time and place named in the recognizance or bail bond; and where an adjudicator dismisses an appeal but grants leave to the appellant to appeal to the Tribunal, or, in a case in which leave to appeal is not required, the appellant has duly given notice of appeal to the Tribunal, the adjudicator shall, if the appellant so requests, exercise his powers under this sub-paragraph.

(4) Where an appellant has duly applied for leave to appeal to the Appeal Tribunal, the Tribunal may release him on his entering into a recognizance or, in Scotland, bail bond conditioned for his appearance before the Tribunal at a time and place named in the recognizance or bail bond; and where—

(a) the Tribunal grants leave to an appellant to appeal to the Tribunal; or

(b) in a case in which leave to appeal is not required, the appellant has duly given notice of appeal to the Tribunal; the Tribunal shall, if the appellant so requests, release him as aforesaid.

(5) The conditions of a recognizance or bail bond taken under this paragraph may include conditions appearing to the person fixing the bail to be likely to result in the appearance of the appellant at the time and place named; and any recognizance shall be with or without sureties as that person may determine.

(6) In any case in which an adjudicator or the Tribunal has power or is required by this paragraph to release an appellant on bail, the adjudicator or Tribunal may, instead of taking the bail, fix the amount and conditions of the bail (including the amount in which any sureties are to be bound) with a view to its being taken subsequently by any such person as may be specified by the adjudicator or the Tribunal and on the recognizance or bail bond being so taken the appellant shall be released.

Restrictions on grant of bail

30.—(1) An appellant shall not be released under para 29 above without the consent of the Secretary of State if directions for the removal of the appellant from the United Kingdom are for the time being in force, or the power to give such directions is for the time being exerciseable.

(2) Notwithstanding para 29(3) or (4) above, an adjudicator and the Tribunal shall not be obliged to release an appellant unless the appellant enters into a proper recognizance, with sufficient and satisfactory sureties if required, or in Scotland sufficient and satisfactory bail is found if so required; and an adjudicator and the Tribunal shall not be obliged to release an appellant if it appears to the adjudicator or the Tribunal, as the case may be—

(a) that the appellant, having on any previous occasion been released on bail (whether under para 24 or under any other provision), has failed to comply with the conditions of any recognizance or bail bond entered into by him on that occasion;

(b) that the appellant is likely to commit an offence unless he is retained in detention;

(c) that the release of the appellant is likely to cause danger to public health;

(d) that the appellant is suffering from mental disorder and that his continued detention is necessary in his own interests or for the protection of any other person; or

(e) that the appellant is under the age of 17, that arrangements ought to be made for his care in the event of his release and that no satisfactory arrangements for that purpose have been made.

Forfeiture of recognizances

31.—(1) Where under para 29 above (as it applies in England and Wales or in Northern Ireland) a recognizance is entered into conditioned for the appearance of an appellant before an adjudicator or the Tribunal, and it appears to the adjudicator or the Tribunal as the case may be, to be forfeited, the adjudicator or Tribunal may by order declare it to be forfeited and adjudge the persons bound thereby, whether as principal or sureties, or any of them, to pay the sum in which they are respectively bound or such part of it, if any, as the adjudicator or Tribunal thinks fit.

(2) An order under this paragraph shall, for the purposes of this sub-paragraph, specify a magistrates' court or, in Northern Ireland, court of summary jurisdiction; and the recognizance shall be treated for the purposes of collection, enforcement and remission of the sum forfeited as having been forfeited by the court so specified.

(3) Where an adjudicator or the Tribunal makes an order under this paragraph the adjudicator or Tribunal shall, as soon as practicable, give particulars of the recognizance to the clerk of the court specified in the order in pursuance of sub-para (2) above.

(4) Any sum the payment of which is enforceable by a magistrates' court in England or Wales by virtue of this paragraph shall be treated for the purposes of the Justices of the Peace Act 1949 and, in particular, s 27 thereof as being due under a recognizance forfeited by such a court and as being Exchequer moneys.

(5) Any sum the payment of which is enforceable by virtue of this paragraph by a court of summary jurisdiction in Northern Ireland shall, for the purposes of s 20(5) of the Administration of Justice Act (Northern Ireland) 1954, be treated as a forfeited recognizance.

32. Where under para 29 above (as it applies in Scotland) a person released on bail fails to comply with the terms of a bail bond conditioned for his appearance before an adjudicator or the Tribunal, the adjudicator or Tribunal may declare the bail to be forfeited, and any bail so forfeited shall be transmitted by the adjudicator or the Tribunal to the sheriff court having jurisdiction in the area where the proceedings took place, and shall be treated as having been forfeited by that court.

Arrest of appellants released on bail

33.—(1) An immigration officer or constable may arrest without warrant a person who has been released by virtue of this Part of this Schedule—

(a) if he has reasonable grounds for believing that that person is likely to break the condition of his recognizance or bail bond that he will appear at the time and place required or to break any other condition of it, or has reasonable ground to suspect that that person is breaking or has broken any such other condition; or

(b) if, a recognizance with sureties having been taken, he is notified in writing by any surety of the surety's belief that that person is likely to break the first-mentioned condition, and of the surety's wish for that reason to be relieved of his obligations as a surety;

and para 17(2) above shall apply for the arrest of a person under this paragraph as it applies for the arrest of a person under para 17.

(2) A person arrested under this paragraph—

(a) if not required by a condition on which he was released to appear before an adjudicator or Tribunal within 24 hours after the time of his arrest, shall as soon as practicable be brought before an adjudicator or, if that is not practicable within those 24 hours, before a justice of the peace acting for the petty sessions area in which he is arrested or, in Scotland, the sheriff; and

(b) if required by such a condition to appear within those 24 hours before an adjudicator or before the Tribunal, shall be brought before that adjudicator or before the Tribunal, as the case may be.

(3) An adjudicator, justice of the peace or sheriff before whom a person is brought by virtue of sub-para (2)(a) above—

(a) if of the opinion that that person has broken or is likely to break any condition on which he was released, may either—

(i) direct that he be detained under the authority of the person by whom he was arrested; or

(ii) release him on his original recognizance or on a new recognizance, with or without sureties, or, in Scotland, on his original bail or on new bail; and

(b) if not of that opinion, shall release him on his original recognizance or bail.

SCHEDULE 3

SUPPLEMENTARY PROVISIONS AS TO DEPORTATION

Removal of persons liable to deportation

1.—(1) Where a deportation order is in force against any person, the Secretary of State may give directions for his removal to a country or territory specified in the directions being either—

(a) a country of which he is a national or citizen; or

(b) a country or territory to which there is reason to believe that he will be admitted.

(2) The directions under sub-para (1) above may be either—

(a) directions given to the captain of a ship or aircraft about to leave the United Kingdom requiring him to remove the person in question in that ship or aircraft; or

(b) directions given to the owners or agents of any ship or aircraft requiring them to make arrangements for his removal in a ship or aircraft specified or indicated in the directions; or

(c) directions for his removal in accordance with arrangements to be made by the Secretary of State.

(3) In relation to directions given under this paragraph, paras 11 and 16(4) of Schedule 2 to this Act shall apply, with the substitution of references to the Secretary of State for references to an immigration officer, as they apply in relation to directions for removal given under para 8 of that Schedule.

(4) The Secretary of State, if he thinks fit, may apply in or towards payment of the expenses of or incidental to the voyage from the United Kingdom of a person against whom a deportation order is in force, or the maintenance until departure of such a person and his dependants, if any, any money belonging to that person; and except so far as they are paid as aforesaid, those expenses shall be defrayed by the Secretary of State.

Detention or control pending deportation

2.—(1) Where a recommendation for deportation made by a court is in force in respect of any person, and that person is neither detained in pursuance of the sentence or order of any court nor for the time being released on bail by any court having power so to release him, he shall, unless the court by which the recommendation is made otherwise directs, be detained pending the making of a deportation order in pursuance of the recommendation, unless the Secretary of State directs him to be released pending further consideration of his case.

(2) Where notice has been given to a person in accordance with regulations under s 18 of this Act of a decision to make a deportation order against him, and he is neither detained in pursuance of the sentence or order of a court nor for the time being released on bail by a court having power so to release him, he may be detained under the authority of the Secretary of State pending the making of the deportation order.

(3) Where a deportation order is in force against any person, he may be detained under the authority of the Secretary of State pending his removal or departure from the United Kingdom (and if already detained by virtue of sub-para (1) or (2) above when the order is made, shall continue to be detained unless the Secretary of State directs otherwise).

(4) In relation to detention under sub-para (2) or (3) above, paras 17 and 18 of Schedule 2 to this Act shall apply as they apply in relation to detention under para 16 of that Schedule.

(5) A person liable to be detained under sub-para (2) or (3) above shall, while not so detained, be subject to such restrictions as to residence and as to reporting to the police as may from time to time be notified to him in writing by the Secretary of State.

Effect of appeals

3. Part II of Schedule 2 to this Act, so far as it relates to appeals under s 16 or 17, shall apply for purposes of this Schedule as if the references in para 28(2), (3) and (6) and in para 29(1) of Part I of that Schedule were references to this Schedule; and paras 29–33 shall apply in like manner in relation to appeals under s 15(1)(a).

SCHEDULE 4

INTEGRATION WITH UNITED KINGDOM LAW OF IMMIGRATION LAW OF ISLANDS

Leave to enter

1.—(1) Where under the immigration laws of any of the Islands a person is or has been given leave to enter or remain in the island, or is or has been refused leave, this Act shall have effect in relation to him, if he is not patrial, as if the leave were leave (of like duration) given under this Act to enter or remain in the United Kingdom, or, as the case may be, as if he had under this Act been refused leave to enter the United Kingdom.

(2) Where under the immigration laws of any of the Islands a person has a limited leave to enter or remain in the island subject to any such conditions as are authorised in the United Kingdom by s 3(1) of this Act (being conditions imposed by notice given to him, whether the notice of leave or a subsequent notice), then on his coming to the United Kingdom this Act shall apply, if he is not patrial, as if those conditions related to his stay in the United Kingdom and had been imposed by notice under this Act.

(3) Without prejudice to the generality of sub-paras (1) and (2) above, anything having effect in the United Kingdom by virtue of either of those sub-paragraphs may in relation to the United Kingdom be varied or revoked under this Act in like manner, and subject to the like appeal (if any), as if it had originated under this Act as mentioned in that sub-paragraph.

(4) Where anything having effect in the United Kingdom by virtue of sub-para (1) or (2) above ceases to have effect or is altered in effect as mentioned in sub-para (3) or otherwise by anything done under this Act, sub-para (1)

or (2) shall not thereafter apply to it or, as the case may be, shall apply to it as so altered in effect.

(5) Nothing in this paragraph shall be taken as conferring on a person a right of appeal under this Act against any decision or action taken in any of the Islands.

2. Notwithstanding s 3(4) of this Act, leave given to a person under this Act to enter or remain in the United Kingdom shall not continue to apply on his return to the United Kingdom after an absence if he has during that absence entered any of the Islands in circumstances in which he is required under the immigration laws of that island to obtain leave to enter.

Deportation

3.—(1) Subject to sub-para (2) below, where under the immigration laws of any of the Islands, a person is or has been ordered to leave the island and forbidden to return, then, if he is not patrial, this Act shall have effect in relation to him as if the order were a deportation order made against him under this Act.

(2) The Secretary of State shall not by virtue of sub-para (1) above have power to revoke a deportation order made in any of the Islands, but may in any particular case direct that sub-para (1) shall not apply in relation to an order so made; and nothing in this paragraph shall render it unlawful for a person in respect of whom such an order is in force in any of the Islands to enter the United Kingdom on his way from that island to a place outside the United Kingdom.

Illegal entrants

4. Notwithstanding anything in s 1(3) of this Act, it shall not be lawful for a person who is not patrial to enter the United Kingdom from any of the Islands where his presence was unlawful under the immigration laws of that island, unless he is given leave to enter.

SCHEDULE 5

THE ADJUDICATORS AND THE TRIBUNAL

PART I

THE ADJUDICATORS

1. There shall be such number of adjudicators as the Secretary of State may with the consent of the Minister for the Civil Service determine, and the Secretary of State shall appoint one of them as chief adjudicator.

2.—(1) An adjudicator shall hold and vacate his office in accordance with the terms of his appointment and shall, on ceasing to hold office, be eligible for re-appointment.

(2) An adjudicator may at any time by notice in writing to the Secretary of State resign his office.

3. The Secretary of State shall pay—

(a) to the adjudicators, such remuneration and allowances as he may, with the approval of the Minister for the Civil Service, determine;

(b) as regards any of the adjudicators in whose case he may so determine with the approval of the Minister for the Civil Service, such pension, allowance or gratuity to or in respect of him, or such sums towards the provision of such pension, allowance or gratuity, as may be so determined;

and, if a person ceases to be an adjudicator and it appears to the Secretary of State that there are special circumstances which make it right that that person should receive compensation, the Secretary of State may, with the approval of the said Minister, pay to that person a sum of such amount as the Secretary of State may, with the approval of that Minister, determine.

4. In Part III of Schedule 1 to the House of Commons Disqualification Act 1957 (which lists offices the holders of which are disqualified for membership of the House of Commons), and in the said Part III as it applies by virtue of Schedule 3 to that Act in relation to the Senate and House of Commons of Northern Ireland, there shall be inserted at the appropriate point the words 'Adjudicator appointed for the purposes of the Immigration Act 1971'.

5. The adjudicators shall sit at such times and in such places as the Secretary of State may direct; and the chief adjudicator shall allocate duties among the adjudicators and have such other functions as may be conferred on him by the Secretary of State.

PART II

THE TRIBUNAL

Members

6. The Tribunal shall consist of such number of members as the Lord Chancellor may determine, and the Lord Chancellor shall appoint one of them to be president.

7. The president and such number of the other members of the Tribunal as the Lord Chancellor may determine shall be barristers, advocates or solicitors, in each case of not less than seven years standing.

8.—(1) A member of the Tribunal shall hold and vacate his office in accordance with the terms of his appointment and shall on ceasing to hold office, be eligible for re-appointment.

(2) Any member of the Tribunal may at any time by notice in writing to the Lord Chancellor resign his office.

9. The Secretary of State shall pay—

(a) to the members of the Tribunal, such remuneration and allowances as he may, with the approval of the Minister for the Civil Service, determine;

(b) as regards any member in whose case he may so determine with the approval of the Minister for the Civil Service, such pension, allowance or gratuity to or in respect of him, or such sums towards the provision of such pension, allowance or gratuity, as may be so determined;

and, if a person ceases to be a member of the Tribunal and it appears to the Secretary of State that there are special circumstances which make it right that that person should receive compensation, the Secretary of State may, with the approval of the said Minister, pay to that person a sum of such amount as the Secretary of State may, with the approval of that Minister, determine.

10. In Part II of Schedule 1 to the House of Commons Disqualification Act 1957 (which lists bodies of which all members are disqualified for membership of the House of Commons), and in the said Part II as it applies by virtue of Schedule 3 to that Act in relation to the Senate and House of Commons of Northern Ireland, there shall be inserted at the appropriate point the words 'The Immigration Appeal Tribunal'.

Proceedings

11. For the purpose of hearing and determining appeals under Part II of this Act or any matter preliminary or incidental to any such appeal, the Tribunal shall sit at such times and in such place or places as the Lord Chancellor may direct, and may sit in two or more divisions.

12. Subject to rules of procedure, the Tribunal shall be deemed to be duly constituted if it consists of three members (or a greater uneven number of members) of whom at least one is qualified as mentioned in para 7 of this Schedule; and the determination of any question before the Tribunal shall be according to the opinion of the majority of the members hearing the case.

13. The Lord Chancellor may appoint members of the Tribunal who are qualified as mentioned in para 7 of this Schedule to act on behalf of the president in his temporary absence or inability to act.

14. The president or, in his absence, the member qualified as mentioned in para 7 of this Schedule (or, if there is more than one such member present, the senior of them) shall preside at a sitting of the Tribunal.

Part III

Staff and Expenses

15. The Secretary of State may appoint such officers and servants for the adjudicators and the Tribunal as he may, with the approval of the Minister for the Civil Service as to remuneration and numbers, determine.

16. The remuneration of officers and servants appointed as aforesaid, and such expenses of the adjudicators and the Tribunal as the Secretary of State may with the approval of the Minister for the Civil Service determine, shall be defrayed by the Secretary of State.

SCHEDULE 6

REPEALS

Chapter	Short title	Extent of repeal
4 & 5 Geo. 5 c. 12.	The Aliens Restriction Act 1914.	The whole Act.
9 & 10 Geo. 5. c. 92.	The Aliens Restriction (Amendment) Act 1919.	Section 1. Section 2(1). Section 13(3). Section 14(1).
11 & 12 Geo. 6. c. 56.	The British Nationality Act 1948.	Section 6(1). In s 6(2), the words from 'and, if' to 'Act'. Section 8(1) from 'and as if' onwards.
6 & 7 Eliz. 2. c. 10.	The British Nationality Act 1958.	Section 3(2). In s 5(3) the words from 'including' to 'this Act'.
10 & 11 Eliz. 2. c. 21.	The Commonwealth Immigrants Act 1962.	The whole Act, except s 12(2) and (4) and s 20(1) and (3). In s 12(2) the words from the beginning to 'six, and'.
1964 c. 81.	The Diplomatic Privileges Act 1964.	Section 5(1).
1965 c. 34.	The British Nationality Act 1965.	Section 2(3).
1967 c. 4.	The West Indies Act 1967.	In Schedule 3, para 3.
1967 c. 80.	The Criminal Justice Act 1967.	Section 58.
1968 c. 9.	The Commonwealth Immigrants Act 1968.	The whole Act.
1968 c. 19.	The Criminal Appeal Act 1968.	In s 51(1), the definition of 'recommendation for deportation'.
1968 c. 59.	The Hovercraft Act 1968.	In para I of the Schedule, sub-para (f) and the words from 'and 1962' to '1968'.
1969 c. 21.	The Immigration Appeals Act 1969.	The whole Act.
1970 c. 58.	The Expiring Laws Continuance Act 1970.	The whole Act.

Immigration Act 1988

CHAPTER 14

ARRANGEMENT OF SECTIONS

Section

1. Termination of saving in respect of Commonwealth citizens settled before 1973.
2. Restriction on exercise of right of abode in cases of polygamy.
3. Proof of right of abode.
4. Members of diplomatic missions.
5. Restricted right of appeal against deportation in cases of breach of limited leave.
6. Knowingly overstaying limited leave.
7. Persons exercising Community rights and nationals of member States.
8. Examination of passengers prior to arrival.
9. Charges.
10. Miscellaneous minor amendments.
11. Expenses and receipts.
12. Short title, interpretation, commencement and extent.
Schedule—Minor Amendments.

Immigration Act 1988

1988 CHAPTER 14

An Act to make further provision for the regulation of immigration into the United Kingdom; and for connected purposes.

[10 May 1988]

BE IT ENACTED by the Queen's most Excellent Majesty, by and with the advice and consent of the Lords Spiritual and Temporal, and Commons, in this present Parliament assembled, and by the authority of the same, as follows—

Termination of saving in respect of Commonwealth citizens settled before 1973

1. Section 1(5) of the Immigration Act 1971 (in this Act referred to as 'the principal Act') is hereby repealed.

Restriction on exercise of right of abode in cases of polygamy

2.—(1) This section applies to any woman who—

(a) has the right of abode in the United Kingdom under s 2(1)(b) of the principal Act as, or as having been, the wife of a polygamous man ('the husband')—

(i) to whom she is or was polygamously married; and

(ii) who is or was such a citizen of the United Kingdom and Colonies, Commonwealth citizen or British subject as is mentioned in s 2(2)(a) or (b) of that Act as in force immediately before the commencement of the British Nationality Act 1981; and

(b) has not before the coming into force of this section and since her marriage to the husband been in the United Kingdom.

(2) A woman to whom this section applies shall not be entitled to enter the United Kingdom in the exercise of the right of abode mentioned in subsection (1)(a) above or to be granted a certificate of entitlement in respect of that right if there is another woman living (whether or not one to whom this section applies) who is the wife or widow of the husband and who—

(a) is, or at any time since her marriage to the husband has been, in the United Kingdom; or

(b) has been granted a certificate of entitlement in respect of the right of abode mentioned in subsection (1)(a) above or an entry clearance to enter the United Kingdom as the wife of the husband.

(3) So long as a woman is precluded by subsection (2) above from entering the United Kingdom in the exercise of her right of abode or being granted a certificate of entitlement in respect of that right the principal Act shall apply to her as it applies to a person not having a right of abode.

(4) Subsection (2) above shall not preclude a woman from re-entering the United Kingdom if since her marriage to the husband she has at any time previously been in the United Kingdom and there was at that time no such other woman living as is mentioned in that subsection.

(5) Where a woman claims that this section does not apply to her because she had been in the United Kingdom before the coming into force of this section and since her marriage to the husband it shall be for her to prove that fact.

(6) For the purposes of this section a marriage may be polygamous although at its inception neither party has any spouse additional to the other.

(7) For the purposes of subsections (1)(b), (2)(a), (4) and (5) above there shall be disregarded presence in the United Kingdom as a visitor or an illegal entrant and presence in circumstances in which a person is deemed by s 11(1) of the principal Act not to have entered the United Kingdom.

(8) In subsection (2)(b) above the reference to a certificate of entitlement includes a reference to a certificate treated as such a certificate by virtue of s 39(8) of the British Nationality Act 1981.

(9) No application by a woman for a certificate of entitlement in respect of such a right of abode as is mentioned in subsection (1)(a) above or for an

entry clearance shall be granted if another application for such a certificate or clearance is pending and that application is made by a woman as the wife or widow of the same husband.

(10) For the purposes of subsection (9) above an application shall be regarded as pending so long as it and any appeal proceedings relating to it have not been finally determined.

Proof of right of abode

3.—(1) For s 3(9) and (9A) of the principal Act there shall be substituted—

'(9) A person seeking to enter the United Kingdom and claiming to have the right of abode there shall prove that he has that right by means of either—

(a) a United Kingdom passport describing him as a British citizen or as a citizen of the United Kingdom and Colonies having the right of abode in the United Kingdom; or

(b) a certificate of entitlement issued by or on behalf of the government of the United Kingdom certifying that he has such a right of abode.'

(2) For the provisions of s 13(3) of that Act up to the end of para (b) there shall be substituted—

'(3) A person shall not be entitled to appeal, on the ground that he has a right of abode in the United Kingdom, against a decision that he requires leave to enter the United Kingdom unless he holds such a passport or certificate as is mentioned in s 3(9) above'.

(3) In s 2(2) of that Act for the words 'sections 3(9) and (9A), 5(2) and 13(3)' there shall be substituted the words 'section 5(2)', subsections (3) and (5) of s 39 of the British Nationality Act 1981 are hereby repealed and in subsection (8) of that section for the words 'as amended by this section' there shall be substituted the words 'as in force after commencement'.

Members of diplomatic missions

4. At the beginning of subsection (3) of s 8 of the principal Act (exemption from immigration control for members of diplomatic missions , etc) there shall be inserted the words 'Subject to subsection (3A) below,' and after that subsection there shall be inserted—

'(3A) In the case of a member of a mission other than a diplomatic agent (within the meaning of the said Act of 1964) subsection (3) above shall apply only if he enters or has entered the United Kingdom—

(a) as a member of that mission; or

(b) in order to take up a post as such a member which was offered to him before his arrival;

and references in that subsection to a member of a mission shall be construed accordingly.'

Restricted right of appeal against deportation in cases of breach of limited leave

5.—(1) A person to whom this subsection applies shall not be entitled to Restricted right of appeal under s 15 of the principal Act against a decision to make a deportation order against him—

(a) by virtue of s 3(5)(a) of that Act (breach of limited leave); or

(b) by virtue of s 3(5)(c) of that Act as belonging to the family of a person who is or has been ordered to be deported by virtue of s 3(5)(a),

except on the ground that on the facts of his case there is in law no power to make the deportation order for the reasons stated in the notice of the decision.

(2) Subsection (1) above applies to any person who was last given leave to enter the United Kingdom less than seven years before the date of the decision in question but the Secretary of State may by order exempt any such persons from that subsection in such circumstances and to such extent as may be specified in the order.

(3) The power to make an order under subsection (2) above shall be exerciseable by statutory instrument subject to annulment in pursuance of a resolution of either House of Parliament.

(4) It shall be presumed for the purposes of this section that a person was last given leave as mentioned in subsection (2) above unless he proves the contrary.

(5) Subsection (1) above shall not affect the grounds on which a person may appeal where written notice of the decision in question was given to him before the coming into force of this section.

Knowingly overstaying limited leave

6.—(1) After subsection (1) of s 24 of the principal Act (illegal entry and similar offences) there shall be inserted—

'(1A) A person commits an offence under subsection (1)(b)(i) above on the day when he first knows that the time limited by his leave has expired and continues to commit it throughout any period during which he is in the United Kingdom thereafter; but a person shall not be prosecuted under that provision more than once in respect of the same limited leave.'

(2) In subsection (3) of that section (extension of time limit for prosecutions) for the words 'subsection (1)(a), (b)(i) and (c)' there shall be substituted the words 'subsection (1)(a) and (c)'.

(3) These amendments do not apply in relation to a person whose leave has expired before the coming into force of this section.

Persons exercising Community rights and nationals of member States

7.—(1) A person shall not under the principal Act require leave to enter or remain in the United Kingdom in any case in which he is entitled to do so by virtue of an enforceable Community right or of any provision made under s 2(2) of the European Communities Act 1972.

(2) The Secretary of State may by order made by statutory instrument give leave to enter the United Kingdom for a limited period to any class of persons who are nationals of member States but who are not entitled to enter the United Kingdom as mentioned in subsection (1) above; and any such order may give leave subject to such conditions as may be imposed by the order.

(3) References in the principal Act to limited leave shall include references to leave given by an order under subsection (2) above and a person having leave by virtue of such an order shall be treated as having been given that leave by a notice given to him by an immigration officer within the period specified in para 6(1) of Schedule 2 to that Act.

Examination of passengers prior to arrival

8.—(1) This section applies to a person who arrives in the United Kingdom with a passport or other travel document bearing a stamp which—

(a) has been placed there by an immigration officer before that person's departure on his journey to the United Kingdom or in the course of that journey; and

(b) states that the person may enter the United Kingdom either for an indefinite or a limited period and, if for a limited period, subject to specified conditions.

(2) A person to whom this section applies shall for the purposes of the principal Act be deemed to have been given on arrival in the United Kingdom indefinite or, as the case may be, limited leave in terms corresponding to those of the stamp.

(3) A person who is deemed to have leave by virtue of this section shall be treated as having been given it by a notice given to him by an immigration officer within the period specified in para 6(1) of Schedule 2 to the principal Act.

(4) A person deemed to have leave by virtue of this section shall not on his arrival in the United Kingdom be subject to examination under para 2 of Schedule 2 to the principal Act but may be examined by an immigration officer for the purpose of establishing that he is such a person.

(5) The leave which a person is deemed to have by virtue of this section may, at any time before the end of the period of 24 hours from his arrival at the port at which he seeks to enter the United Kingdom or, if he has been examined under subsection (4) above, from the conclusion of that examination, be cancelled by an immigration officer by giving him a notice in writing refusing him leave to enter.

(6) Sub-paras (3) and (4) of para 6 of Schedule 2 to the principal Act shall have effect as if any notice under subsection (5) above were a notice under that paragraph.

(7) References in this section to a person's arrival in the United Kingdom are to the first occasion on which he arrives after the time when the stamp in question was placed in his passport or travel document, being an occasion not later than seven days after that time.

Charges

9.—(1) The Secretary of State may with the consent of the Treasury make regulations prescribing fees to be paid, at such times as may be prescribed, in connection with any application for indefinite leave to remain in the United Kingdom or the grant of such leave; and no such leave shall be granted unless any fee payable in connection with the grant of that leave has been paid.

(2) Regulations under subsection (1) above may make different provision for different cases, including provision for cases in which no fee is to be paid.

(3) The power to make regulations under subsection (1) above shall be exerciseable by statutory instrument subject to annulment in pursuance of a resolution of either House of Parliament.

(4) The Secretary of State may, at the request of any person and in consideration of such charges as he may determine, make arrangements for the provision at any port of additional immigration officers or for the provision of immigration officers for dealing with passengers of a particular description or in particular circumstances.

Miscellaneous minor amendments

10. The principal Act shall have effect with the amendments specified in the Schedule to this Act.

Expenses and receipts

11.—(1) There shall be paid out of money provided by Parliament any expenses incurred by the Secretary of State in consequence of this Act.

(2) Any sums received by the Secretary of State by virtue of this Act shall be paid into the Consolidated Fund.

Short title, interpretation, commencement and extent

12.—(1) This Act may be cited as the Immigration Act 1988.

(2) In this Act 'the principal Act' means the Immigration Act 1971 and any expression which is also used in the Act has the same meaning as in that Act.

(3) Except as provided in subsection (4) below this Act shall come into force at the end of the period of two months beginning with the day on which it is passed.

(4) Sections 1, 2, 3, 4, 5 and 7(1) and para 1 of the Schedule shall come into force on such day as may be appointed by the Secretary of State by an order made by statutory instrument; and such an order may appoint different days for different provisions and contain such transitional provisions and savings as the Secretary of State thinks necessary or expedient in connection with any provision brought into force.

(5) This Act extends to Northern Ireland and s 36 of the principal Act (power to extend any of its provisions to the Channel Islands or the Isle of Man) shall apply also to the provisions of this Act.

SCHEDULE

MINOR AMENDMENTS

Limitation and conditions on leave to be applicable also to subsequent leave granted after absence within period of earlier leave

1. In s 3(3)(b) for the words 'may be imposed (whether originally or on a variation) so that they will' there shall be substituted the words '(whether imposed originally or on a variation) shall'.

Power to pay expenses of persons liable to deportation who voluntarily leave the United Kingdom

2. In s 5(6) for '3(5)(c)' there shall be substituted '3(5)'.

Deportation order to terminate appeal pending in respect of limited leave

3. At the end of s 14 there shall be inserted—

> '(5) Where a deportation order is made against a person any pending appeal by that person under subsection (1) above shall lapse.'

Time-limit for proceedings

4. In s 28(1)(a) for the words 'a chief officer of police' there shall be substituted the words 'an officer of police above the rank of chief superintendent' and for the words 'his police force' there shall be substituted the words 'the police force to which he belongs'.

Entry clearance as requisite evidence of eligibility

5. In s 33(1), in the definition of 'entry clearance', after the word 'evidence' there shall be inserted the words 'or the requisite evidence'.

Power to detain passport, etc

6.—(1) After para 4(2) of Schedule 2 there shall be inserted—

> '(2A) An immigration officer may detain any passport or other document produced pursuant to sub-para (2)(a) above until the person concerned is given leave to enter the United Kingdom or is about to depart or be removed following refusal of leave.'

(2) This amendment does not apply in relation to any person whose examination under para 2 or 3 of Schedule 2 began before the coming into force of this paragraph.

Time-limit for giving, refusing or cancelling leave to enter

7.—(1) In para 6(1) and (2) of Schedule 2 for the words 'twelve hours', wherever they occur, there shall be substituted the words 'twenty-four hours'.

(2) This amendment does not apply in relation to any person whose examination under para 2 began before the coming into force of this paragraph.

Leave in default of notice giving or refusing leave or cancelling refusal

8.—(1) In para 6(1) of Schedule 2 for the words 'indefinite leave to enter the United Kingdom' there shall be substituted the words 'leave to enter the United Kingdom for a period of six months subject to a condition prohibiting his taking employment'.

(2) In para 6(3) of Schedule 2 for the words from 'the immigration officer may' onwards there shall be substituted the words 'and the immigration officer does not at the same time give him indefinite or limited leave to enter, he shall be deemed to have been given leave to enter for a period of six months subject to a condition prohibiting his taking employment and the immigration officer shall as soon as may be give him written notice of that leave.'

(3) The amendment in sub-para (1) above does not apply in relation to any person in whose case the time-limit in para 6(1) of Schedule 2 has expired before the coming into force of this paragraph; and the amendment in sub-para (2) above does not apply in relation to a person given a notice of cancellation under para 6(3) of Schedule 2 before the coming into force of this paragraph.

Time-limit for removal directions

9.—(1) At the end of para 8(2) of Schedule 2 there shall be inserted the words 'except that directions may be given under sub-para (1)(b) or (c) after the end of that period if the immigration officer has within that period given written notice to the owners or agents in question of his intention to give directions to them in respect of that person'.

(2) In para 10(1)(b) of Schedule 2 for the words 'but that the time limited by para 8(2) has passed' there shall be substituted the words 'but that the requirements of para 8(2) have not been complied with'.

(3) In para 28(4) of Schedule 2 after the words 'directions under that paragraph for the removal of a person from the United Kingdom' there shall be inserted the words 'and for the giving of a notice of intention to give such directions'.

(4) These amendments do not apply in relation to any person refused leave to enter the United Kingdom before the coming into force of this paragraph.

Restriction on work in case of persons temporarily admitted, etc

10—(1) In para 21(2) of Schedule 2 after the words 'as to residence' there shall be inserted the words ', as to his employment or occupation'.

(2) In paras 2(5) and 4 of Schedule 3 after the words 'as to residence' there shall be inserted the words ', as to his employment or occupation'.

(3) In s 24(1)(e) after the words 'as to residence' there shall be inserted the words ', as to his employment or occupation'.

(4) These amendments apply in relation to persons granted temporary admission or released from detention under para 21 of Schedule 2, becoming liable to detention under para 2(2) or (3) of Schedule 3, or directed to be released as mentioned in para 4 of that Schedule, as the case may be, before as well as after the coming into force of this paragraph.

British Nationality Act 1981

1981 CHAPTER 61

ARRANGEMENT OF SECTIONS

PART I

BRITISH CITIZENSHIP

Acquisition after commencement

Section

1. Acquisition by birth or adoption.
2. Acquisition by descent.
3. Acquisition by registration: minors.
4. Acquisition by registration: British Dependent Territories citizens, etc.
5. Acquisition by registration: nationals for purposes of the Community Treaties.
6. Acquisition by naturalisation.

Acquisition after commencement: special cases

7. Right to registration by virtue of residence in the United Kingdom or relevant employment.
8. Registration by virtue of marriage.
9. Right to registration by virtue of father's citizenship, etc.
10. Registration following renunciation of citizenship of the United Kingdom and Colonies.

Acquisition at commencement

11. Citizens of the United Kingdom and Colonies who are to become British citizens at commencement.

Renunciation and resumption

12. Renunciation.
13. Resumption.

Supplementary

14. Meaning of British citizen 'by descent'.

PART II

BRITISH DEPENDENT TERRITORIES CITIZENSHIP

Acquisition after commencement

Section

15. Acquisition by birth or adoption.
16. Acquisition by descent.

17. Acquisition by registration: minors.
18. Acquisition by naturalisation.

Acquisition after commencement: special cases

19. Right to registration by virtue of residence in dependent territory.
20. Registration by virtue of marriage.
21. Right to registration by virtue of father's citizenship, etc.
22. Right to registration replacing right to resume citizenship of the United Kingdom and Colonies.

Acquisition at commencement

23. Citizens of the United Kingdom and Colonies who are to become British Dependent Territories citizens at commencement.

Renunciation and resumption

24. Renunciation and resumption.

Supplementary

25. Meaning of British Dependent Territories citizen 'by descent'.

PART III

BRITISH OVERSEAS CITIZENSHIP

26. Citizens of the United Kingdom and Colonies who are to become British Overseas citizens at commencement.
27. Registration of minors.
28. Registration by virtue of marriage.
29. Renunciation.

PART IV

BRITISH SUBJECTS

30. Continuance as British subjects of existing British subjects of certain descriptions.
31. Continuance as British subjects of certain former citizens of Eire.
32. Registration of minors.
33. Registration of certain alien women entitled to registration as British subjects immediately before commencement.
34. Renunciation.
35. Circumstances in which British subjects are to lose that status.

PART V

MISCELLANEOUS AND SUPPLEMENTARY

36. Provisions for reducing statelessness.
37. Commonwealth citizenship.

38. British protected persons.
39. Amendment of Immigration Act 1971.
40. Deprivation of citizenship.
41. Regulations and Orders in Council.
42. Registration and naturalisation: general provisions.
43. Exercise of functions of Secretary of State by Governors and others.
44. Decisions involving exercise of discretion.
45. Evidence.
46. Offences and proceedings.
47. Legitimated children.
48. Posthumous children.
49. Registration and naturalisation under British Nationality Acts 1948–65.
50. Interpretation.
51. Meaning of certain expressions relating to nationality in other Acts and instruments.
52. Consequential amendments, transitional provisions, repeals and savings.
53. Citation, commencement and extent.

SCHEDULES—

Schedule 1—Requirements for naturalisation.

Schedule 2—Provisions for reducing statelessness.

Schedule 3—Countries whose citizens are Commonwealth citizens.

Schedule 4—Amendments of Immigration Act 1971.

Schedule 5—Form of oath of allegiance.

Schedule 6—British Dependent Territories.

Schedule 7—Consequential amendments.

Schedule 8—Transitional provisions.

Schedule 9—Repeals.

British Nationality Act 1981

1981 CHAPTER 61

An Act to make fresh provision about citizenship and nationality, and to amend the Immigration Act 1971 as regards the right of abode in the United Kingdom.

[30 October 1981]

BE IT ENACTED by the Queen's most Excellent Majesty, by and with the advice and consent of the Lords Spiritual and Temporal, and Commons, in this present Parliament assembled, and by the authority of the same, as follows—

PART I

BRITISH CITIZENSHIP

Acquisition after commencement

Acquisition by birth or adoption

1.—(1) A person born in the United Kingdom after commencement shall be a British citizen if at the time of the birth his father or mother is—

(a) a British citizen; or

(b) settled in the United Kingdom.

(2) A new-born infant who, after commencement, is found abandoned in the United Kingdom shall, unless the contrary is shown, be deemed for the purposes of subsection (1)—

(a) to have been born in the United Kingdom after commencement; and

(b) to have been born to a parent who at the time of the birth was a British citizen or settled in the United Kingdom.

(3) A person born in the United Kingdom after commencement who is not a British citizen by virtue of subsection (1) or (2) shall be entitled to be registered as a British citizen if, while he is a minor—

(a) his father or mother becomes a British citizen or becomes settled in the United Kingdom; and

(b) an application is made for his registration as a British citizen.

(4) A person born in the United Kingdom after commencement who is not a British citizen by virtue of subsection (1) or (2) shall be entitled, on an application for his registration as a British citizen made at any time after he has attained the age of 10 years, to be registered as such a citizen if, as regards each of the first 10 years of that person's life, the number of days on which he was absent from the United Kingdom in that year does not exceed 90.

(5) Where after commencement an order authorising the adoption of a minor who is not a British citizen is made by any court in the United Kingdom, he shall be a British citizen as from the date on which the order is made if the adopter or, in the case of a joint adoption, one of the adopters is a British citizen on that date.

(6) Where an order in consequence of which any person became a British citizen by virtue of subsection (5) ceases to have effect whether on annulment or otherwise, the cesser shall not affect the status of that person as a British citizen.

(7) If, in the special circumstances of any particular case, the Secretary of State thinks fit, he may for the purposes of subsection (4) treat the person to whom the application relates as fulfilling the requirement specified in that subsection although, as regards any one or more of the first 10 years of that person's life, the number of days on which he was absent from the United Kingdom in that year or each of the years in question exceeds 90.

(8) In this section and elsewhere in this Act 'settled' has the meaning given by s 50.

Acquisition by descent

2.—(1) A person born outside the United Kingdom after commencement shall be a British citizen if at the time of the birth his father or mother—

(a) is a British citizen otherwise than by descent; or

(b) is a British citizen and is serving outside the United Kingdom in service to which this paragraph applies, his or her recruitment for that service having taken place in the United Kingdom; or

(c) is a British citizen and is serving outside the United Kingdom in service under a Community institution, his or her recruitment for that service having taken place in a country which at the time of the recruitment was a member of the Community.

(2) Paragraph (b) of subsection (1) applies to—

(a) Crown service under the government of the United Kingdom; and

(b) service of any description for the time being designated under subsection (3).

(3) For the purposes of this section the Secretary of State may by order made by statutory instrument designate any description of service which he considers to be closely associated with the activities outside the United Kingdom of Her Majesty's government in the United Kingdom.

(4) Any order made under subsection (3) shall be subject to annulment in pursuance of a resolution of either House of Parliament.

Acquisition by registration: minors

3.—(1) If, while a person is a minor, an application is made for his registration as a British citizen, the Secretary of State may, if he thinks fit, cause him to be registered as such a citizen.

(2) A person born outside the United Kingdom shall be entitled, on an application for his registration as a British citizen made within the period of 12 months from the date of the birth, to be registered as such a citizen if the requirements specified in subsection (3) or, in the case of a person born stateless, the requirements specified in paras (a) and (b) of that subsection, are fulfilled in the case of either that person's father or his mother ('the parent in question').

(3) The requirements referred to in subsection (2) are—

(a) that the parent in question was a British citizen by descent at the time of the birth; and

(b) that the father or mother of the parent in question—

(i) was a British citizen otherwise than by descent at the time of the birth of the parent in question; or

(ii) became a British citizen otherwise than by descent at commencement, or would have become such a citizen otherwise than by descent at commencement but for his or her death; and

(c) that, as regards some period of three years ending with a date not later than the date of the birth—

(i) the parent in question was in the United Kingdom at the beginning of that period; and

(ii) the number of days on which the parent in question was absent from the United Kingdom in that period does not exceed 270.

(4) If, in the special circumstances of any particular case, the Secretary of State thinks fit, he may treat subsection (2) as if the reference to 12 months were a reference to six years.

(5) A person born outside the United Kingdom shall be entitled, on an application for his registration as a British citizen made while he is a minor, to be registered as such a citizen if the following requirements are satisfied, namely—

(a) that at the time of that person's birth his father or mother was a British citizen by descent; and

(b) subject to subsection (6), that that person and his father and mother were in the United Kingdom at the beginning of the period of three years ending with the date of the application and that, in the case of each of them, the number of days on which the person in question was absent from the United Kingdom in that period does not exceed 270; and

(c) subject to subsection (6), that the consent of his father and mother to the registration has been signified in the prescribed manner.

(6) In the case of an application under subsection (5) for the registration of a person as a British citizen—

(a) if his father or mother died, or their marriage was terminated, on or before the date of the application, or his father and mother were legally separated on that date, the references to his father and mother in para (b) of that subsection shall be read either as references to his father or as references to his mother;

(b) if his father or mother died on or before that date, the reference to his father and mother in para (c) of that subsection shall be read as a reference to either of them; and

(c) if he was born illegitimate, all those references shall be read as references to his mother.

Acquisition by registration: British Dependent Territories citizens, etc

4.—(1) This section applies to any person who is a British Dependent Territories citizen, a British Overseas citizen, a British subject under this Act or a British protected person.

(2) A person to whom this section applies shall be entitled, on an application for his registration as a British citizen, to be registered as such a citizen if the following requirements are satisfied in the case of that person, namely—

(a) subject to subsection (3), that he was in the United Kingdom at the beginning of the period of five years ending with the date of the application and that the number of days on which he was absent from the United Kingdom in that period does not exceed 450; and

(b) that the number of days on which he was absent from the United Kingdom in the period of 12 months so ending does not exceed 90; and

(c) that he was not at any time in the period of 12 months so ending subject under the immigration laws to any restriction on the period for which he might remain in the United Kingdom; and

(d) that he was not at any time in the period of five years so ending in the United Kingdom in breach of the immigration laws.

(3) So much of subsection (2)(a) as requires the person in question to have been in the United Kingdom at the beginning of the period there mentioned shall not apply in relation to a person who was settled in the United Kingdom immediately before commencement.

(4) If, in the special circumstances of any particular case, the Secretary of State thinks fit, he may for the purposes of subsection (2) do all or any of the following things, namely—

(a) treat the person to whom the application relates as fulfilling the requirement specified in subsection (2)(a) or subsection (2)(b), or both, although the number of days on which he was absent from the United Kingdom in the period there mentioned exceeds the number there mentioned;

(b) disregard any such restriction as is mentioned in subsection (2)(c), not being a restriction to which that person was subject on the date of the application;

(c) treat that person as fulfilling the requirement specified in subsection (2)(d) although he was in the United Kingdom in breach of the immigration laws in the period there mentioned.

(5) If, on an application for registration as a British citizen made by a person to whom this section applies, the Secretary of State is satisfied that the applicant has at any time served in service to which this subsection applies, he may, if he thinks fit in the special circumstances of the applicant's case, cause him to be registered as such a citizen.

6) Subsection (5) applies to—

(a) Crown service under the government of a dependent territory; and

(b) paid or unpaid service (not falling within para (a)) as a member of any body established by law in a dependent territory members of which are appointed by or on behalf of the Crown.

Acquisition by registration: nationals for purposes of the Community Treaties

5. A British Dependent Territories citizen who falls to be treated as a national of the United Kingdom for the purposes of the Community Treaties shall be entitled to be registered as a British citizen if an application is made for his registration as such a citizen.

Acquisition by naturalisation

6.—(1) If, on an application for naturalisation as a British citizen made by a person of full age and capacity, the Secretary of State is satisfied that the applicant fulfils the requirements of Schedule 1 for naturalisation as such a citizen under this subsection, he may, if he thinks fit, grant to him a certificate of naturalisation as such a citizen.

(2) If, on an application for naturalisation as a British citizen made by a person of full age and capacity who on the date of the application is married to a British citizen, the Secretary of State is satisfied that the applicant fulfils the requirements of Schedule 1 for naturalisation as such a citizen under this subsection, he may, if he thinks fit, grant to him a certificate of naturalisation as such a citizen.

Acquisition after commencement: special cases

Right to registration by virtue of residence in the United Kingdom or relevant employment

7.—(1) A person shall be entitled, on an application for his registration as a British citizen made (subject to subsections (6) and (7)) within five years after commencement, to be registered as such a citizen if either of the following requirements is satisfied in his case, namely—

(a) that, if paras 2 and 3 (but not para 4 or 5) of Schedule 1 to the Immigration Act 1971 had remained in force, he would (had he applied for it) have been, on the date of the application under this subsection, entitled under the said para 2 to be registered in the United Kingdom as a citizen of the United Kingdom and Colonies; or

(b) that, if s 5A of the 1948 Act (and s 2 of the Immigration Act 1971 as in force immediately before commencement) had remained in force, he would (had he applied for it) have been, both at commencement and on the date of the application under this subsection, entitled under s 5A(1) of the 1948 Act to be registered as a citizen of the United Kingdom and Colonies.

(2) A person shall be entitled, on an application for his registration as a British citizen made (subject to subsection (8)) within six years after commencement, to be registered as such a citizen if he—

(a) was ordinarily resident in the United Kingdom throughout a period ending at commencement but not amounting to five years; and

(b) throughout the period from commencement to the date of the application—

(i) remained ordinarily resident in the United Kingdom; and

(ii) had the right of abode in the United Kingdom under the Immigration Act 1971; and

(c) had on the date of the application been ordinarily resident in the United Kingdom for the last five years or more.

(3) Subject to subsection (5), if, in the case of an application for the registration of a person under subsection (2) as a British citizen, that person has been engaged in relevant service throughout any period (of whatever length), that period shall for the purposes of subsection (2) be treated as a period throughout which he was ordinarily resident in the United Kingdom.

(4) For the purposes of subsection (3) 'relevant service' means—

(a) Crown service under the government of the United Kingdom; or

(b) service under any international organisation of which the United Kingdom or Her Majesty's government therein is a member; or

(c) service in the employment of any company or association established in the United Kingdom.

(5) A person shall not be registered under subsection (2) wholly or partly by reason of service within subsection (4)(b) or (c) unless it seems to the Secretary of State fitting that he should be so registered by reason of his close connection with the United Kingdom.

(6) If, in the special circumstances of any particular case, the Secretary of State thinks fit, he may treat subsection (1) as if—

(a) the reference to five years after commencement were a reference to eight years after commencement; or

(b) where subsection (7) applies, as if the reference to five years from the date on which the person to whom the application relates attains full age were a reference to eight years from that date,

but shall not do so in the case of an application based on para (b) of subsection (1) unless the person to whom the application relates would have been entitled to be registered under that subsection on an application so based made immediately before the end of the five years after commencement.

(7) In the case of any person who is a minor at commencement, the reference to five years after commencement in subsection (1) above shall be treated as a reference to five years from the date on which he attains full age.

(8) If, in the special circumstances of any particular case, the Secretary of State thinks fit, he may treat subsection (2) as if the reference to six years after commencement were a reference to eight years after commencement.

Registration by virtue of marriage

8.—(1) A woman who immediately before commencement was the wife of a citizen of the United Kingdom and Colonies shall be entitled, on an application for her registration as a British citizen made within five years after commencement, to be registered as a British citizen if—

(a) immediately before commencement she would (if she had applied for it) have been entitled under s 6(2) of the 1948 Act to be registered as a citizen of the United Kingdom and Colonies by virtue of her marriage to the man who was then her husband; and

(b) that man became a British citizen at commencement and did not at any time in the period from commencement to the date of the application under this subsection cease to be such a citizen as a result of a declaration of renunciation; and

(c) she remained married to him throughout that period.

(2) On an application for her registration as a British citizen made within five years after commencement, the Secretary of State may if he thinks fit, cause a woman to be registered as such a citizen if—

(a) immediately before commencement she would (if she had applied for it) have been entitled under s 6(2) of the 1948 Act to be registered as a citizen of the United Kingdom and Colonies by virtue of having been married to a man to whom she is no longer married on the date of the application under this subsection; and

(b) that man became a British citizen at commencement or would have done so but for his death.

(3) On an application for her registration as a British citizen made within five years after commencement by a woman who at the time of the application is married, the Secretary of State may, if he thinks fit, cause her to be registered as such a citizen if—

(a) immediately before commencement she would (if she had applied for it) have been entitled under s 6(2) of the 1948 Act to be registered as a citizen of the United Kingdom and Colonies by virtue of her being or having been married to the man who is her husband on the date of the application under this subsection; and

(b) that man either—

(i) became a British citizen at commencement but has ceased to be such a citizen as a result of a declaration of renunciation; or

(ii) would have become a British citizen at commencement but for his having ceased to be a citizen of the United Kingdom and Colonies as a result of a declaration of renunciation.

Right to registration by virtue of father's citizenship, etc

9.—(1) A person born in a foreign country within five years after commencement shall be entitled, on an application for his registration as a British citizen made within the period of 12 months from the date of the birth, to be registered as such a citizen if—

(a) the requirements specified in subsection (2) are fulfilled in the case of that person's father; and

(b) had that person been born before commencement and become a citizen of the United Kingdom and Colonies by virtue of s 5 of the 1948 Act (citizenship by descent) as a result of the registration of his birth at a United Kingdom consulate under para (b) of the proviso to s 5(1) of that Act, he would immediately before commencement have had the right of abode in the United Kingdom by virtue of s 2(1)(b) of the Immigration Act 1971 as then in force (connection with United Kingdom through parent or grandparent).

(2) The requirements referred to in subsection (1)(a) are that the father of the person to whom the application relates—

(a) immediately before commencement or at his death (whichever was earlier)—

(i) was a citizen of the United Kingdom and Colonies by virtue of s 5 of the 1948 Act (citizenship by descent) or was a person who, under any provision of the British Nationality Acts 1948–65, was deemed for the purposes of the proviso to s 5(1) of the 1948 Act to be a citizen of the United Kingdom and Colonies by descent only; and

(ii) was married to that person's mother; and

(iii) was ordinarily resident in a foreign country (no matter which) within the meaning of the 1948 Act; and

(b) either—

(i) became a British citizen at commencement and remained such a citizen throughout the period from commencement to the date of the application or, if he died during that period, throughout the period from commencement to his death; or

(ii) would have become a British citizen at commencement but for his death.

Registration following renunciation of citizenship of the United Kingdom and Colonies

10.—(1) Subject to subsection (3), a person shall be entitled, on an application for his registration as a British citizen, to be registered as such a citizen if immediately before commencement he would (had he applied for it) have been entitled under s 1(1) of the British Nationality Act 1964 (resumption of citizenship) to be registered as a citizen of the United Kingdom and Colonies by virtue of having an appropriate qualifying connection with the United Kingdom or, if a woman, by virtue of having been married before commencement to a person who has, or would if living have, such a connection.

(2) On an application for his registration as a British citizen made by a person of full capacity who had before commencement ceased to be a citizen of the United Kingdom and Colonies as a result of a declaration of renunciation, the Secretary of State may, if he thinks fit, cause that person to be registered as a British citizen if that person—

(a) has an appropriate qualifying connection with the United Kingdom; or

(b) if a woman, has been married to a person who has, or would if living have, such a connection.

(3) A person shall not be entitled to registration under subsection (1) on more than one occasion.

(4) For the purposes of this section a person shall be taken to have an appropriate qualifying connection with the United Kingdom if he, his father or his father's father—

(a) was born in the United Kingdom; or

(b) is or was a person naturalised in the United Kingdom; or

(c) was registered as a citizen of the United Kingdom and Colonies in the United Kingdom or in a country which at the time was mentioned in s 1(3) of the 1948 Act.

Acquisition at commencement

Citizens of the United Kingdom and Colonies who are to become British citizens at commencement

11.—(1) Subject to subsection (2), a person who immediately before commencement—

(a) was a citizen of the United Kingdom and Colonies; and

(b) had the right of abode in the United Kingdom under the Immigration Act 1971 as then in force,

shall at commencement become a British citizen.

(2) A person who was registered as a citizen of the United Kingdom and Colonies under s 1 of the British Nationality 1964 c. 54. (No. 2) Act 1964 (stateless persons) on the ground mentioned in subsection (1)(a) of that section (namely that his mother was a citizen of the United Kingdom and Colonies at the time when he was born) shall not become a British citizen under subsection (1) unless—

(a) his mother becomes a British citizen under subsection (1) or would have done so but for her death; or

(b) immediately before commencement he had the right of abode in the United Kingdom by virtue of s 2(1)(c) of the Immigration Act 1971 as then in force (settlement in United Kingdom, combined with five or more years' ordinary residence there as a citizen of the United Kingdom and Colonies).

(3) A person who—

(a) immediately before commencement was a citizen of the United Kingdom and Colonies by virtue of having been registered under subsection (6) of s 12 of the 1948 Act (British subjects before commencement of 1948 Act becoming citizens of United Kingdom and Colonies) under arrangements made by virtue of subsection (7) of that section (registration in independent Commonwealth country by United Kingdom High Commissioner); and

(b) was so registered on an application under the said subsection (6) based on the applicant's descent in the male line from a person ('the relevant person') possessing one of the qualifications specified in subsection (1)(a) and (b) of that section (birth or naturalisation in the United Kingdom and Colonies), shall at commencement become a British citizen if the relevant person was born or naturalised in the United Kingdom.

Renunciation and resumption

Renunciation

12.—(1) If any British citizen of full age and capacity makes in the prescribed manner a declaration of renunciation of British citizenship, then, subject to subsections (3) and (4), the Secretary of State shall cause the declaration to be registered.

(2) On the registration of a declaration made in pursuance of this section the person who made it shall cease to be a British citizen.

(3) A declaration made by a person in pursuance of this section shall not be registered unless the Secretary of State is satisfied that the person who made it will after the registration have or acquire some citizenship or nationality other than British citizenship; and if that person does not have any such citizenship or nationality on the date of registration and does not acquire some such citizenship or nationality within six months from that date, he shall be, and be deemed to have remained, a British citizen notwithstanding the registration.

(4) The Secretary of State may withhold registration of any declaration made in pursuance of this section if it is made during any war in which Her Majesty may be engaged in right of Her Majesty's government in the United Kingdom.

(5) For the purposes of this section any person who has been married shall be deemed to be of full age.

Resumption

13.—(1) Subject to subsection (2), a person who has ceased to be a British citizen as a result of a declaration of renunciation shall be entitled, on an application for his registration as a British citizen, to be registered as such a citizen if—

(a) he is of full capacity; and

(b) his renunciation of British citizenship was necessary to enable him to retain or acquire some other citizenship or nationality.

(2) A person shall not be entitled to registration under subsection (1) on more than one occasion.

(3) If a person of full capacity who has ceased to be a British citizen as a result of a declaration of renunciation (for whatever reason made) makes an application for his registration as such a citizen, the Secretary of State may, if he thinks fit, cause him to be registered as such a citizen.

Supplementary

Meaning of British citizen 'by descent'

14.—(1) For the purposes of this Act a British citizen is a British citizen if and only if—

(a) he is a person born outside the United Kingdom after commencement who is a British citizen by virtue of s 2(1)(a) only or by virtue of registration under s 3(2) or 9; or

(b) subject to subsection (2), he is a person born outside the United Kingdom before commencement who became a British citizen at commencement and immediately before commencement—

(i) was a citizen of the United Kingdom and Colonies by virtue of s 5 of the 1948 Act (citizenship by descent); or

(ii) was a person who, under any provision of the British Nationality Acts 1948–65, was deemed for the purposes of the proviso to s 5(1) of the 1948 Act to be a citizen of the United Kingdom and Colonies by descent only, or would have been so deemed if male; or

(iii) had the right of abode in the United Kingdom by virtue only of para (b) of subsection (1) of s 2 of the Immigration Act 1971 as then in force (connection with United Kingdom through parent or grandparent), or by virtue only of that paragraph and para (c) of that subsection (settlement in United Kingdom with five years' ordinary residence there), or by virtue only of being or having been the wife of a person who immediately before commencement had that right by virtue only of the said para (b) or the said paras (b) and (c); or

(iv) being a woman, was a citizen of the United Kingdom and Colonies as a result of her registration as such a citizen under s 6(2) of the 1948 Act by virtue of having been married to a man who at commencement became a British citizen by descent or would have done so but for his having died or ceased to be a citizen of the United Kingdom and Colonies as a result of a declaration of renunciation; or

(c) he is a British citizen by virtue of registration under s 3(1) and either—

(i) his father or mother was a British citizen at the time of the birth; or

(ii) his father or mother was a citizen of the United Kingdom and Colonies at that time and became a British citizen at commencement, or would have done so but for his or her death; or

(d) he is a British citizen by virtue of registration under s 5; or

(e) subject to subsection (2), being a woman born outside the United Kingdom before commencement, she is a British citizen as a result of her registration as such a citizen under s 8 by virtue of being or having been married to a man who at commencement became a British citizen by descent or would have done so but for his having died or ceased to be a citizen of the United Kingdom and Colonies as a result of a declaration of renunciation; or

(f) he is a British citizen by virtue of registration under s 10 who, having before commencement ceased to be a citizen of the United Kingdom and Colonies as a result of a declaration of renunciation, would, if he had not so ceased, have at commencement become a British citizen by descent by virtue of para (b); or

(g) he is a British citizen by virtue of registration under s 13 who, immediately before he ceased to be a British citizen as a result of a declaration of renunciation, was such a citizen by descent; or

(h) he is a person born in a dependent territory after commencement who is a British citizen by virtue of para 2 of Schedule 2.

(2) A person born outside the United Kingdom before commencement is not a British citizen 'by descent' by virtue of subsection (1)(b) or (e) if his father was at the time of his birth serving outside the United Kingdom—

(a) in service of a description mentioned in subsection (3), his recruitment for the service in question having taken place in the United Kingdom; or

(b) in service under a Community institution, his recruitment for that service having taken place in a country which at the time of the recruitment was a member of the Community.

(3) The descriptions of service referred to in subsection (2) are—

(a) Crown service under the government of the United Kingdom; and

(b) service of any description at any time designated under s 2(3).

PART II

BRITISH DEPENDENT TERRITORIES CITIZENSHIP

Acquisition after commencement

Acquisition by birth or adoption

15.—(1) A person born in a dependent territory after commencement shall be a British Dependent Territories citizen if at the time of the birth his father or mother is—

(a) a British Dependent Territories citizen; or

(b) settled in a dependent territory.

(2) A new-born infant who, after commencement, is found abandoned in a dependent territory shall, unless the contrary is shown, be deemed for the purposes of subsection (1)—

(a) to have been born in that territory after commencement; and

(b) to have been born to a parent who at the time of the birth was a British Dependent Territories citizen or settled in a dependent territory.

(3) A person born in a dependent territory after commencement who is not a British Dependent Territories citizen by virtue of subsection (1) or (2) shall be entitled to be registered as such a citizen if, while he is a minor—

(a) his father or mother becomes such a citizen or becomes settled in a dependent territory; and

(b) an application is made for his registration as such a citizen.

(4) A person born in a dependent territory after commencement who is not a British Dependent Territories citizen by virtue of subsection (1) or (2) shall be entitled, on an application for his registration as a British Dependent Territories citizen made at any time after he has attained the age of 10 years, to be registered as such a citizen if, as regards each of the first 10 years of that person's life, the number of days on which he was absent from that territory in that year does not exceed 90.

(5) Where after commencement an order authorising the adoption of a minor who is not a British Dependent Territories citizen is made by a court in any dependent territory, he shall be a British Dependent Territories citizen as from the date on which the order is made if the adopter or, in the case of a joint adoption, one of the adopters, is a British Dependent Territories citizen on that date.

(6) Where an order in consequence of which any person became a British Dependent Territories citizen by virtue of subsection (5) ceases to have effect, whether on annulment or otherwise, the cesser shall not affect the status of that person as such a citizen.

(7) If in the special circumstances of any particular case the Secretary of State thinks fit, he may for the purposes of subsection (4) treat the person to whom the application relates as fulfilling the requirements specified in that subsection although, as regards any one or more of the first 10 years of that person's life, the number of days on which he was absent from the dependent territory there mentioned in that year or each of the years in question exceeds 90.

Acquisition by descent

16.—(1) A person born outside the dependent territories after commencement shall be a British Dependent Territories citizen if at the time of the birth his father or mother—

(a) is such a citizen otherwise than by descent; or

(b) is such a citizen and is serving outside the dependent territories in service to which this paragraph applies, his or her recruitment for that service having taken place in a dependent territory.

(2) Paragraph (b) of subsection (1) applies to—

(a) Crown service under the government of a dependent territory; and

(b) service of any description for the time being designated under subsection (3).

(3) For the purposes of this section the Secretary of State may by order made by statutory instrument designate any description of service which he considers to be closely associated with the activities outside the dependent territories of the government of any dependent territory.

(4) Any order made under subsection (3) shall be subject to annulment in pursuance of a resolution of either House of Parliament.

Acquisition by registration: minors

17.—(1) If while a person is a minor an application is made for his registration as a British Dependent Territories citizen the Secretary of State may, if he thinks fit, cause him to be registered as such a citizen.

(2) A person born outside the dependent territories shall be entitled, on an application for his registration as a British Dependent Territories citizen made within the period of 12 months from the date of the birth, to be registered as such a citizen if the requirements specified in subsection (3) or, in the case of a person born stateless, the requirements specified in paras (a) and (b) of that subsection, are fulfilled in the case of either that person's father or his mother ('the parent in question').

(3) The requirements referred to in subsection (2) are—

(a) that the parent in question was a British Dependent Territories citizen by descent at the time of the birth; and

(b) that the father or mother of the parent in question—

(i) was a British Dependent Territories citizen otherwise than by descent at the time of the birth of the parent in question; or

(ii) became a British Dependent Territories citizen otherwise than by descent at commencement, or would have become such a citizen otherwise than by descent at commencement but for his or her death; and

(c) that, as regards some period of three years ending with a date not later than the date of the birth—

(i) the parent in question was in a dependent territory at the beginning of that period; and

(ii) the number of days on which the parent in question was absent from that territory in that period does not exceed 270.

(4) If in the special circumstances of any particular case the Secretary of State thinks fit, he may treat subsection (2) as if the reference to 12 months were a reference to six years.

(5) A person born outside the dependent territories shall be entitled, an on application for his registration as a British Dependent Territories citizen made while he is a minor, to be registered as such a citizen if the following requirements are satisfied, namely—

(a) that at the time of that person's birth his father or mother was a British Dependent Territories citizen by descent; and

(b) subject to subsection (6), that that person and his father and mother were in one and the same dependent territory (no matter which) at the beginning of the period of three years ending with the date of the application and that, in the case of each of them, the number of days on which the person in question was absent from the last-mentioned territory in that period does not exceed 270; and

(c) subject to subsection (6), that the consent of his father and mother to the registration has been signified in the prescribed manner.

(6) In the case of an application under subsection (5) for the registration of a person as a British Dependent Territories citizen—

(a) if his father or mother died, or their marriage was terminated, on or before the date of the application, or his father and mother were legally separated on that date, the references to his father and mother in para (b) of that subsection shall be read either as references to his father or as references to his mother;

(b) if his father or mother died on or before that date, the reference to his father and mother in para (c) of that subsection shall be read as a reference to either of them; and

(c) if he was born illegitimate, all those references shall be read as references to his mother.

Acquisition by naturalisation

18.—(1) If, on an application for naturalisation as a British Dependent Territories citizen made by a person of full age and capacity, the Secretary of State is satisfied that the applicant fulfils the requirements of Schedule 1 for naturalisation as such a citizen under this subsection, he may, if he thinks fit, grant to him a certificate of naturalisation as such a citizen.

(2) If, on an application for naturalisation as a British Dependent Territories citizen made by a person of full age and capacity who on the date of the application is married to such a citizen, the Secretary of State is satisfied that the applicant fulfils the requirements of Schedule 1 for naturalisation as such

a citizen under this subsection, he may, if he thinks fit, grant to him a certificate of naturalisation as such a citizen.

(3) Every application under this section shall specify the dependent territory which is to be treated as the relevant territory for the purposes of that application; and, in relation to any such application, references in Schedule 1 to the relevant territory shall be construed accordingly.

Acquisition after commencement: special cases

Right to registration by virtue of residence in dependent territory

19.—(1) A person shall be entitled, on an application for his registration as a British Dependent Territories citizen made within five years after commencement, to be registered as such a citizen if, had paras 2–5 of Schedule 1 to the Immigration Act 1971 remained in force, he would (had he applied for it) have been on the date of the application under this subsection, entitled under the said para 2 to be registered in a dependent territory as a citizen of the United Kingdom and Colonies.

(2) In the case of any person who is a minor at commencement, the reference to five years after commencement in subsection (1) shall be treated as a reference to five years from the date on which he attains full age.

(3) If in the special circumstances of any particular case the Secretary of State thinks fit, he may treat subsection (1) as if—

(a) the reference to five years after commencement were a reference to eight years after commencement; or

(b) where subsection (2) applies, as if the reference to five years from the date on which the person to whom the application relates attains full age were a reference to eight years from that date.

Registration by virtue of marriage

20.—(1) A woman who immediately before commencement was the wife of a citizen of the United Kingdom and Colonies shall be entitled, on an application for her registration as a British Dependent Territories citizen made within five years after commencement, to be registered as a British Dependent Territories citizen if—

(a) immediately before commencement she would (if she had applied for it) have been entitled under s 6(2) of the 1948 Act to be registered as a citizen of the United Kingdom and Colonies by virtue of her marriage to the man who was then her husband; and

(b) that man became a British Dependent Territories citizen at commencement and did not at any time in the period from commencement to the date of the application under this subsection cease to be such a citizen as a result of a declaration of renunciation; and

(c) she remained married to him throughout that period.

(2) On such an application for her registration as a British Dependent Territories citizen made within five years after commencement the Secretary of State may, if he thinks fit, cause a woman to be registered as such a citizen if—

(a) immediately before commencement she would (if she had applied for it) have been entitled under s 6(2) of the 1948 Act to be registered as a citizen of the United Kingdom and Colonies by virtue of having been married to a man to whom she is no longer married on the date of the application under this subsection; and

(b) that man became a British Dependent Territories citizen at commencement or would have done so but for his death.

(3) On an application for her registration as a British Dependent Territories citizen made within five years after commencement by a woman who at the time of the application is married, the Secretary of State shall, if he thinks fit, cause her to be registered as such a citizen if—

(a) immediately before commencement she would (if she had applied for it) have been entitled under s 6(2) of the 1948 Act to be registered as a citizen of the United Kingdom and Colonies by virtue of her being or having been married to the man who is her husband on the date of the application under this subsection; and

(b) that man either—

(i) became a British Dependent Territories citizen at commencement but has ceased to be such a citizen as a result of a declaration of renunciation; or

(ii) would have become a British Dependent Territories citizen at commencement but for his having ceased to be a citizen of the United Kingdom and Colonies as a result of a declaration of renunciation.

Right to registration by virtue of father's citizenship, etc

21.—A person born in a foreign country within five years after commencement shall be entitled, on an application for his registration as a British Dependent Territories citizen made within the period of 12 months from the date of the birth, to be registered as such a citizen if—

(a) the requirements referred to in subsection (1)(a) of s 9 are fulfilled in the case of that person's father, subsection (2)(b) of that section being for the purposes of this paragraph read as if any reference to becoming or remaining a British citizen were a reference to becoming or, as the case may be, remaining a British Dependent Territories citizen; and

(b) had that person been born before commencement and become a citizen of the United Kingdom and Colonies as mentioned in subsection (1)(b) of that section, he would at commencement have become a British Dependent Territories citizen by virtue of s 23(1)(b).

Right to registration replacing right to resume citizenship of the United Kingdom and Colonies

22.—(1) Subject to subsection (3), a person shall be entitled, on an application for his registration as a British Dependent Territories citizen, to be registered as such a citizen if immediately before commencement he would (had he applied for it) have been entitled under s 1(1) of the British Nationality Act 1964 (resumption of citizenship) to be registered as a citizen of the United Kingdom and Colonies by virtue of having an appropriate qualifying connection with a dependent territory or, if a woman, by virtue of having been married before commencement to a person who has, or would if living have, such a connection.

(2) On an application for his registration as a British Dependent Territories citizen made by a person of full capacity who had before commencement ceased to be a citizen of the United Kingdom and Colonies as a result of a declaration of renunciation, the Secretary of State may, if he thinks fit, cause that person to be registered as a British Dependent Territories citizen if that person—

(a) has an appropriate qualifying connection with a dependent territory; or

(b) if a woman, has been married to a person who has, or would if living have, such a connection.

(3) A person shall not be entitled to registration under subsection (1) on more than one occasion.

(4) For the purposes of this section a person shall be taken to have an appropriate qualifying connection with a dependent territory if he, his father or his father's father—

(a) was born in that territory; or

(b) is or was a person naturalised in that territory; or

(c) was registered as a citizen of the United Kingdom and Colonies in that territory; or

(d) became a British subject by reason of the annexation of any territory included in that territory.

Acquisition at commencement

Citizens of the United Kingdom and Colonies who are to become British Dependent Territories citizens at commencement

23.—(1) A person shall at commencement become a British citizen of Dependent Territories citizen if—

(a) immediately before commencement he was a citizen of the United Kingdom and Colonies who had that citizenship by his birth, naturalisation or registration in a dependent territory; or

(b) he was immediately before commencement a citizen of the United Kingdom and Colonies, and was born to a parent—

(i) who at the time of the birth ('the material time') was a citizen of the United Kingdom and Colonies; and

(ii) who either had that citizenship at the material time by his birth, naturalisation or registration in a dependent territory or was himself born to a parent who at the time of that birth so had that citizenship; or

(c) being a woman, she was immediately before commencement a citizen of the United Kingdom and Colonies and either was then, or had at any time been, the wife of a man who under para (a) or (b) becomes a British Dependent Territories citizen at commencement or would have done so but for his death.

(2) A person shall at commencement become a British Dependent Territories citizen if—

(a) immediately before commencement he was a citizen of the United Kingdom and Colonies by virtue of registration under s 7 of the 1948 Act (minor children) or s 1 of the British Nationality (No. 2) Act 1964 (stateless persons); and

(b) he was so registered otherwise than in a dependent territory; and

(c) his father or mother (in the case of a person registered under the said s 7) or his mother (in the case of a person registered under the said s 1)—

(i) was a citizen of the United Kingdom and Colonies at the time of the registration or would have been such a citizen at that time but for his or her death; and

(ii) becomes a British Dependent Territories citizen at commencement or would have done so but for his or her death.

(3) A person who—

(a) immediately before commencement was a citizen of the United Kingdom and Colonies by virtue of having been registered under subsection (6) of s 12 of the 1948 Act (British subjects before commencement of 1948 Act becoming citizens of United Kingdom and Colonies) otherwise than in a dependent territory; and

(b) was so registered on an application under that subsection based on the applicant's descent in the male line from a person ('the relevant person') possessing one of the qualifications specified in subsection (1) of that section (birth or naturalisation in the United Kingdom and Colonies, or acquisition of the status of British subject by reason of annexation of territory),

shall at commencement become a British Dependent Territories citizen if the relevant person—

(i) was born or naturalised in a dependent territory; or

(ii) became a British subject by reason of the annexation of any territory included in a dependent territory.

(4) A person who—

(a) immediately before commencement was a citizen of the United Kingdom and Colonies by virtue of registration under s 1 of the British Nationality Act 1964 (resumption of citizenship); and

(b) was so registered otherwise than in a dependent territory; and

(c) was so registered by virtue of having an appropriate qualifying connection with a dependent territory or, if a woman, by virtue of having been married to a person who at the time of the registration had or would, if then living, have had such a connection,

shall at commencement become a British Dependent Territories citizen.

(5) For the purposes of subsection (4) a person shall be taken to have an appropriate qualifying connection with a dependent territory if he, his father or his father's father—

(a) was born in a dependent territory; or

(b) is or was a person naturalised in a dependent territory; or

(c) was registered as a citizen of the United Kingdom and Colonies in a dependent territory; or

(d) became a British subject by reason of the annexation of any territory included in a dependent territory.

(6) For the purposes of subsection (1)(b) references to citizenship of the United Kingdom and Colonies shall, in relation to a time before the year 1949, be construed as references to British nationality.

Renunciation and resumption

Renunciation and resumption

24. The provisions of ss 12 and 13 shall apply in relation to British Dependent Territories citizens and British Dependent Territories citizenship as they apply in relation to British citizens and British citizenship.

Supplementary

Meaning of British Dependent Territories citizen 'by descent'

25.—(1) For the purposes of this Act a British Dependent Territories citizen is such a citizen 'by descent' if and only if—

(a) he is a person born outside the dependent territories after commencement who is a British Dependent Territories citizen by virtue of s 16(1)(a) only or by virtue of registration under s 17(2) or 21; or

(b) subject to subsection (2), he is a person born outside the dependent territories before commencement who became a British Dependent Territories citizen at commencement and immediately before commencement—

(i) was a citizen of the United Kingdom and Colonies by virtue of s 5 of the 1948 Act (citizenship by descent); or

(ii) was a person who, under any provision of the British Nationality Acts 1948–65, was deemed for the purposes of the proviso to s 5(l) of the 1948 Act to be a citizen of the United Kingdom and Colonies by descent only, or would have been so deemed if male; or

(c) he is a British Dependent Territories citizen by virtue of registration under s 17(1) and either—

(i) his father or mother was a British Dependent Territories citizen at the time of the birth; or

(ii) his father or mother was a citizen of the United Kingdom and Colonies at that time and became a British Dependent Territories citizen at commencement, or would have done so but for his or her death; or

(d) subject to subsection (2), he is a person born outside the dependent territories before commencement who became a British Dependent Territories citizen at commencement under s 23(1)(b) only; or

(e) subject to subsection (2), being a woman, she became a British Dependent Territories citizen at commencement under s 23(1)(c) only, and did so only by virtue of having been, immediately before commencement or earlier, the wife of a man who immediately after commencement was, or would but for his death have been, a British Dependent Territories citizen by descent by virtue of para (b) or (d) of this subsection; or

(f) subject to subsection (2), being a woman born outside the dependent territories before commencement, she is a British Dependent Territories citizen as a result of her registration as such a citizen under s 20 by virtue of being or having been married to a man who at commencement became such a citizen by descent or would have done so but for his having died or ceased to be a citizen of the United Kingdom and Colonies as a result of a declaration of renunciation; or

(g) he is a British Dependent Territories citizen by virtue of registration under s 22 who, having before commencement ceased to be a citizen of the United Kingdom and Colonies as a result of a declaration of renunciation, would, if he had not so ceased, have at commencement become a British Dependent Territories citizen by descent by virtue of para (b), (d) or (e);

(h) he is a British Dependent Territories citizen by virtue of registration under s 13 (as applied by s 24) who, immediately before he ceased to be a British Dependent Territories citizen as a result of a declaration of renunciation, was such a citizen by descent; or

(i) he is a person born in the United Kingdom after commencement who is a British Dependent Territories citizen by virtue of para 1 of Schedule 2.

(2) A person born outside the dependent territories before commencement is not a British Dependent Territories citizen 'by descent' by virtue of subsection (1)(b), (d), (e) or (f) if his father was at the time of his birth serving outside the dependent territories in service of a description mentioned in subsection (3), his recruitment for the service in question having taken place in a dependent territory.

(3) The descriptions of service referred to in subsection (2) are—

(a) Crown service under the government of a dependent territory; and

(b) service of any description at any time designated under s 16(3).

PART III

BRITISH OVERSEAS CITIZENSHIP

Citizens of THE UNITED KINGDOM and Colonies who are to become British Overseas citizens at commencement

26. Any person who was a citizen of the United Kingdom and Colonies immediately before commencement and who does not at commencement become either a British citizen or a British Dependent Territories citizen shall at commencement become a British Overseas citizen.

Registration of minors

27.—(1) If while a person is a minor an application is made for his registration as a British Overseas citizen, the Secretary of State may, if he thinks fit, cause him to be registered as such a citizen.

(2) A person born in a foreign country within five years after commencement shall be entitled, on an application for his registration as a British Overseas

citizen made within the period of 12 months from the date of the birth, to be registered as such a citizen if—

(a) the requirements referred to in subsection (1)(a) of s 9 are fulfilled in the case of that person's father, subsection (2)(b) of that section being for the purposes of this paragraph read as if—

(i) any reference to becoming a British citizen were a reference to becoming a citizen of any of the following descriptions, namely a British citizen, a British Dependent Territories citizen and a British Overseas citizen; and

(ii) the reference to remaining a British citizen throughout any period were a reference to being throughout that period a citizen of at least one of those descriptions (though not necessarily the same one) throughout that period; and

(b) had that person been born before commencement and become a citizen of the United Kingdom and Colonies as mentioned in subsection (1)(b) of that section, he would at commencement have become a British Overseas citizen by virtue of s 26.

Registration by virtue of marriage

28.—(1) A woman who immediately before commencement was the wife of a citizen of the United Kingdom and Colonies shall be entitled, on an application for her registration as a British Overseas citizen made within five years after commencement, to be registered as a British Overseas citizen if—

(a) immediately before commencement she would (if she had applied for it) have been entitled under s 6(2) of the 1948 Act to be registered as a citizen of the United Kingdom and Colonies by virtue of her marriage to the man who was then her husband; and

(b) that man became a British Overseas citizen at commencement and did not at any time in the period from commencement to the date of the application under this subsection cease to be such a citizen as a result of a declaration of renunciation; and

(c) she remained married to him throughout that period.

(2) On an application for her registration as a British Overseas citizen made within five years after commencement, the Secretary of State may, if he thinks fit, cause a woman to be registered as such a citizen if—

(a) immediately before commencement she would (if she had applied for it) have been entitled under s 6(2) of the 1948 Act to be registered as a citizen of the United Kingdom and Colonies by virtue of having been married to a man to whom she is no longer married on the date of the application under this subsection; and

(b) that man became a British Overseas citizen at commencement or would have done so but for his death.

(3) On an application for her registration as a British Overseas citizen made within five years after commencement by a woman who at the time of the application is married, the Secretary of State may, if he thinks fit, cause her to be registered as such a citizen if—

(a) immediately before commencement she would (if she had applied for it) have been entitled under s 6(2) of the 1948 Act to be registered as a citizen of the United Kingdom and Colonies by virtue of her being or having been married to the man who is her husband on the date of the application under this subsection; and

(b) that man either—

(i) became a British Overseas citizen at commencement but has ceased to be such a citizen as a result of a declaration of renunciation; or

(ii) would have become a British Overseas citizen at commencement but for his having ceased to be a citizen of the United Kingdom and Colonies as a result of a declaration of renunciation.

Renunciation

29. The provisions of s 12 shall apply in relation to British Overseas citizens and British Overseas citizenship as they apply in relation to British citizens and British citizenship.

PART IV

BRITISH SUBJECTS

Continuance as British subjects of existing British subjects of certain descriptions

30. A person who immediately before commencement was—

(a) a British subject without citizenship by virtue of s 13 or 16 of the 1948 Act; or

(b) a British subject by virtue of s 1 of the British Nationality Act 1965 (registration of alien women who have been married to British subjects of certain descriptions),

shall as from commencement be a British subject by virtue of this section.

Continuance as British subjects of certain former citizens of Eire

31.—(1) A person is within this subsection if immediately before 1 January 1949 he was both a citizen of Eire and a British subject.

(2) A person within subsection (1) who immediately before commencement was a British subject by virtue of s 2 of the 1948 Act (continuance of certain citizens of Eire as British subjects) shall as from commencement be a British subject by virtue of this subsection.

(3) If at any time after commencement a citizen of the Republic of Ireland who is within subsection (1) but is not a British subject by virtue of subsection (2) gives notice in writing to the Secretary of State claiming to remain a British subject on either or both of the following grounds, namely—

(a) that he is or has been in Crown Service under the government of the United Kingdom; and

(b) that he has associations by way of descent, residence or otherwise with the United Kingdom or with any dependent territory,

he shall as from that time be a British subject by virtue of this subsection.

(4) A person who is a British subject by virtue of subsection (2) or (3) shall be deemed to have remained a British subject from 1 January 1949 to the time when (whether already a British subject by virtue of the said s 2 or not) he became a British subject by virtue of that subsection.

Registration of minors

32. If while a person is a minor an application is made for his registration as a British subject, the Secretary of State may, if he thinks fit, cause him to be registered as a British subject.

Registration of certain alien women entitled to registration as British subjects immediately before commencement

33. A woman who immediately before commencement was the wife of a British subject shall be entitled, on an application for her registration as a British subject made within five years after commencement, to be registered as a British subject if—

(a) immediately before commencement she would (if she had applied for it) have been entitled under s 1 of the British Nationality Act 1965 to be registered as a British subject by virtue of her marriage to the man who was then her husband; and

(b) on the date of the application under this section that man is a British subject; and

(c) she remained married to him throughout the period from commencement to that date.

Renunciation

34. The provisions of s 12 shall apply in relation to British subjects and the status of a British subject as they apply in relation to British citizens and British citizenship.

Circumstances in which British subjects are to lose that status

35. A person who under this Act is a British subject otherwise than by virtue of s 31 shall cease to be such a subject if, in whatever circumstances and whether under this Act or otherwise, he acquires any other citizenship or nationality whatever.

PART V

MISCELLANEOUS AND SUPPLEMENTARY

Provisions for reducing statelessness

36. The provisions of Schedule 2 shall have effect for the purpose of reducing statelessness.

Commonwealth citizenship

37.—(1) Every person who—

(a) under this Act is a British citizen, a British Dependent Territories citizen, a British Overseas citizen or a British subject; or

(b) under any enactment for the time being in force in any country mentioned in Schedule 3 is a citizen of that country,

shall have the status of a Commonwealth citizen.

(2) Her Majesty may by Order in Council amend Schedule 3 by the alteration of any entry, the removal of any entry, or the insertion of any additional entry.

(3) Any Order in Council made under this section shall be subject to annulment in pursuance of a resolution of either House of Parliament.

(4) After commencement no person shall have the status of a Commonwealth citizen or the status of a British subject otherwise than under this Act.

British protected persons

38.—(1) Her Majesty may by Order in Council made in relation to any territory which was at any time before commencement—

(a) a protectorate or protected State for the purposes of the 1948 Act; or

(b) a United Kingdom trust territory within the meaning of that Act,

declare to be British protected persons for the purposes of this Act any class of persons who are connected with that territory and are not citizens of any country mentioned in Schedule 3 which consists of or includes that territory.

(2) Any Order in Council made under this section shall be subject to annulment in pursuance of a resolution of either House of Parliament.

Amendment of Immigration Act 1971

39.—(1) The Immigration Act 1971 shall be amended in accordance with the following provisions of this section.

(2) For s 2 (statement of right of abode) there shall be substituted—

> **'Statement of right of abode in United Kingdom**
>
> 2.—(1) A person is under this Act to have the right of abode in the United Kingdom if—

(a) he is a British citizen; or

(b) he is a Commonwealth citizen who—

(i) immediately before the commencement of the British Nationality Act 1981 was a Commonwealth citizen having the right of abode in the United Kingdom by virtue of s 2(1)(d) or s 2(2) of this Act as then in force; and

(ii) has not ceased to be a Commonwealth citizen in the meanwhile.

(2) In relation to Commonwealth citizens who have the right of abode in the United Kingdom by virtue of subsection (l)(b) above, this Act, except this section and ss 3(9) and (9A), 5(2) and 13(3), shall apply as if they were British citizens; and in this Act (except as aforesaid) "British citizen" shall be construed accordingly.'.

(3) For s 3(9) (certificates of patriality) there shall be substituted—

'(9) A person within this subsection seeking to enter the United Kingdom and claiming to have the right of abode there shall prove that he has that right by means of such certificate of entitlement as may be specified in the immigration rules, unless–

(a) he claims to be a British citizen and produces (or is present when there is produced) a United Kingdom passport describing him as such a citizen or a United Kingdom passport describing him as a citizen of the United Kingdom and Colonies having the right of abode in the United Kingdom; or

(b) in the case of a woman falling within subsection (9A)(b) below who claims to be a British citizen as there mentioned by virtue of s 2(2) of this Act as in force immediately before the commencement of the British Nationality Act 1981, she shows that immediately before that commencement she—

(i) was a citizen of the United Kingdom and Colonies; and

(ii) had the right of abode in the United Kingdom by virtue of s 2(2) of this Act, as then in force, apart from any reference therein to s 2(1)(c) or (d) as then in force.

(9A) A person is within subsection (9) above if—

(a) he is not a British citizen; or

(b) he claims to be a British citizen by virtue of s 11(1) of the British Nationality Act 1981 on the ground that immediately before the commencement of that Act he had the right of abode in the United Kingdom by virtue of s 2(1)(c) or s 2(2) of this Act, as then in force.'.

(4) In s 8 (exceptions for special cases), after subsection (5) there shall be inserted—

'(5A) An order under subsection (2) above may, as regards any person or class of persons to whom it applies, provide for that person or class to be in specified circumstances regarded (notwithstanding the order) as settled in the United Kingdom for the purposes of s 1(1) of the British Nationality Act 1981.'.

(5) For so much of s 13(3) as precedes the words 'and a person' (restriction of right of appeal against decision that leave to enter the United Kingdom is required) there shall be substituted—

'(3) A person within s 3(9) above who does not hold a certificate of entitlement shall not be entitled to appeal on the ground that he has the right of abode in the United Kingdom against a decision that he requires leave to enter the United Kingdom unless—

(a) he claims to be a British citizen and produces (or is present when there is produced) a United Kingdom passport describing him as such a citizen or a United Kingdom passport describing him as a citizen of the United Kingdom and Colonies having the right of abode in the United Kingdom; or

(b) in the case of such a woman as is mentioned in para (b) of s 3(9) above, she shows that immediately before the commencement of the British Nationality Act 1981 she satisfied the conditions specified in sub-paras (i) and (ii) of that paragraph;'.

(6) Schedule 4 (which contains further amendments of the Immigration Act 1971) shall have effect.

(7) In s 90 of the Mental Health Act 1959 and s 82 of the Mental Health (Scotland) Act 1960 (removal of nonpatrial in-patients to places outside the United Kingdom), for the words from 'any patient' to '1971 and' (which were substituted for 'any person being an alien' by s 30(1) of the Immigration Act 1971) there shall be substituted 'any patient who is neither a British citizen nor a Commonwealth citizen having the right of abode in the United Kingdom by virtue of s 2(1)(b) of the Immigration Act 1971, being a patient'.

(8) A certificate of patriality issued under the Immigration Act 1971 and in force immediately before commencement shall have effect after commencement as if it were a certificate of entitlement issued under that Act as amended by this section, unless at commencement the holder ceases to have the right of abode in the United Kingdom.

Deprivation of citizenship

40.—(1) Subject to the provisions of this section, the Secretary of State may by order deprive any British citizen to whom this subsection applies of his British citizenship if the Secretary of State is satisfied that the registration or certificate of naturalisation by virtue of which he is such a citizen was obtained by means of fraud, false representation or the concealment of any material fact.

(2) Subsection (1) applies to any British citizen who—

(a) became a British citizen after commencement by virtue of—

(i) his registration as a British citizen under any provision of this Act; or

(ii) a certificate of naturalisation granted to him under s 6; or

(b) being immediately before commencement a citizen of the United Kingdom and Colonies by virtue of registration as such a citizen under any provision of the British Nationality Acts 1948–64, became at commencement a British citizen; or

(c) at any time before commencement became a British subject (within the meaning of that expression at that time), or a citizen of Eire or of the Republic of Ireland, by virtue of a certificate of naturalisation granted to him or in which his name was included.

(3) Subject to the provisions of this section, the Secretary of State may by order deprive any British citizen to whom this subsection applies of his British citizenship if the Secretary of State is satisfied that that citizen—

(a) has shown himself by act or speech to be disloyal or disaffected towards Her Majesty; or

(b) has, during any war in which Her Majesty was engaged, unlawfully traded or communicated with an enemy or been engaged in or associated with any business that was to his knowledge carried on in such a manner as to assist an enemy in that war; or

(c) has, within the period of five years from the relevant date been sentenced in any country to imprisonment for a term of not less than 12 months.

(4) Subsection (3) applies to any British citizen who falls within para (a) or (c) of subsection (2); and in subsection (3) 'the relevant date', in relation to a British citizen to whom subsection (3) applies, means the date of the registration by virtue of which he is such a citizen or, as the case may be, the date of the grant of the certificate of naturalisation by virtue of which he is such a citizen.

(5) The Secretary of State—

(a) shall not deprive a person of British citizenship under this section unless he is satisfied that it is not conducive to the public good that that person should continue to be a British citizen; and

(b) shall not deprive a person of British citizenship under subsection (3) on the ground mentioned in para (c) of that subsection if it appears to him that that person would thereupon become stateless.

(6) Before making an order under this section the Secretary of State shall give the person against whom the order is proposed to be made notice in writing informing him of the ground or grounds on which it is proposed to be made and of his right to an inquiry under this section.

(7) If the person against whom the order is proposed to be made applies in the prescribed manner for an inquiry, the Secretary of State shall, and in any other case the Secretary of State may, refer the case to a committee of inquiry consisting of a chairman, being a person possessing judicial experience, appointed by the Secretary of State and of such other members appointed by the Secretary of State as he thinks proper.

(8) The Secretary of State may make rules for the practice and procedure to be followed in connection with references under subsection (7) to a committee of inquiry; and such rules may, in particular, provide for conferring on any such committee any powers, rights or privileges of any court, and for enabling any powers so conferred to be exercised by one or more members of the committee.

(9) The power of the Secretary of State to make rules under subsection (8) shall be exerciseable by statutory instrument subject to annulment in pursuance of a resolution of either House of Parliament.

(10) The preceding provisions of this section shall apply in relation to British Dependent Territories citizens and British Dependent Territories citizenship as they apply in relation to British citizens and British citizenship, but as if in subsection (2)(a)(ii) the reference to s 6 were a reference to s 18.

Regulations and Orders in Council

41.—(1) The Secretary of State may by regulations make provision generally for carrying into effect the purposes of this Act, and in particular provision—

(a) for prescribing anything which under this Act is to be prescribed;

(b) for prescribing the manner in which, and the persons to and by whom, applications for registration or naturalisation under any provision of this Act may or must be made;

(c) for the registration of anything required or authorised by or under this Act to be registered;

(d) for the administration and taking of oaths of allegiance under this Act, as to the time within which oaths of allegiance must be taken, and for the registration of oaths of allegiance;

(e) for the giving of any notice required or authorised to be given to any person under this Act;

(f) for the cancellation of the registration of, and the cancellation and amendment of certificates of naturalisation relating to, persons deprived of citizenship under this Act, and for requiring such certificates to be delivered up for those purposes;

(g) for the births and deaths of persons of any class or description born or dying in a country mentioned in Schedule 3 to be registered there by the High Commissioner for Her Majesty's government in the United Kingdom or by members of his official staff;

(h) for the births and deaths of persons of any class or description born or dying in a foreign country to be registered there by consular officers or other officers in the service of Her Majesty's government in the United Kingdom;

(i) for enabling the births and deaths of British citizens, British Dependent Territories citizens, British Overseas citizens, British subjects and British protected persons born or dying in any country in which Her Majesty's government in the United Kingdom has for the time being no diplomatic or consular representatives to be registered—

(i) by persons serving in the diplomatic, consular or other foreign service of any country which, by arrangement with Her Majesty's government in the United Kingdom, has undertaken to represent that government's interest in that country, or

(ii) by a person authorised in that behalf by the Secretary of State.

(2) The Secretary of State may with the consent of the Treasury by regulations make provision for the imposition, recovery and application of fees in connection with any of the following matters, namely—

(a) any application made to the Secretary of State under this Act;

(b) the effecting in the United Kingdom of any registration authorised by or under this Act;

(c) the making in the United Kingdom of any declaration, the grant there of any certificate, or the taking there of any oath of allegiance authorised to be made, granted or taken by or under this Act;

(d) the supplying in the United Kingdom of a certified or other copy of any notice, certificate, order, declaration or entry given, granted or made under or by virtue of this Act or any of the former nationality Acts;

(e) the carrying out of searches in or of any registers or other records, being registers or records held in the United Kingdom by or on behalf of the Secretary of State, which are or may be relevant for the purpose of determining the status of any person under this Act or any of the former nationality Acts;

(f) the supplying by or on behalf of the Secretary of State of an opinion in writing concerning the status of any person under this Act or any of the former nationality Acts, or a certified or other copy of such an opinion.

(3) Regulations under subsection (1) or (2) may make different provision for different circumstances; and—

(a) regulations under subsection (1) may provide for the extension of any time-limit for the taking of oaths of allegiance; and

(b) regulations under subsection (2) may provide for any fees imposed by the regulations to be payable at such times as may be prescribed.

(4) Her Majesty may by Order in Council provide for any Act or Northern Ireland legislation to which this subsection applies to apply, with such adaptations and modifications as appear to Her Majesty necessary, to births and deaths registered—

(a) in accordance with regulations made in pursuance of subsection (1)(g)–(i) of this section or subsection (1)(f) and (g) of s 29 of the 1948 Act; or

(b) at a consulate of Her Majesty in accordance with regulations made under the British Nationality and Status of Aliens Acts 1914–43 or in accordance with instructions of the Secretary of State; or

(c) by a High Commissioner for Her Majesty's government in the United Kingdom or members of his official staff in accordance with instructions of the Secretary of State;

and an Order in Council under this subsection may exclude, in relation to births and deaths so registered, any of the provisions of s 45.

(5) Subsection (4) applies to—

(a) the Births and Deaths Registration Act 1953, the Registration Service Act 1953 and the Registration of Births, Deaths and Marriages (Scotland) Act 1965; and

(b) so much of any Northern Ireland legislation for the time being in force (whether passed or made before or after commencement) as relates to the registration of births and deaths.

(6) The power to make regulations under subsection (1) or (2) shall be exerciseable by statutory instrument.

(7) Any regulations or Order in Council made under this section shall be subject to annulment in pursuance of a resolution of either House of Parliament.

Registration and naturalisation: general provisions

42.—(1) Subject to subsection (2)—

(a) a person shall not be registered under any provision of this Act as a citizen of any description or as a British subject; and

(b) a certificate of naturalisation shall not be granted to a person under any provision of this Act,

unless—

(i) any fee payable by virtue of this Act in connection with the registration or, as the case may be, the grant of the certificate has been paid; and

(ii) the person concerned has within the prescribed time taken an oath of allegiance in the form indicated in Schedule 5.

(2) So much of subsection (1) as requires the taking of an oath of allegiance shall not apply to a person who—

(a) is not of full age; or

(b) is already a British citizen, a British Dependent Territories citizen, a British Overseas citizen, a British subject, or a citizen of any country of which Her Majesty is Queen.

(3) Any provision of this Act which provides for a person to be entitled to registration as a citizen of any description or as a British subject shall have effect subject to the preceding provisions of this section.

(4) A person registered under any provision of this Act as a British citizen, or as a British Dependent Territories citizen or as a British Overseas citizen, or as a British subject, shall be a citizen of that description or, as the case may be, a British subject as from the date on which he is so registered.

(5) A person to whom a certificate of naturalisation as a British citizen or as a British Dependent Territories citizen is granted under any provision of this Act shall be a citizen of that description as from the date on which the certificate is granted.

Exercise of functions of Secretary of State by Governors and others

43.—(1) Subject to subsection (3), the Secretary of State may, in the case of any of his functions under this Act with respect to any of the matters mentioned in subsection (2), make arrangements for that function to be exercised—

(a) in any of the Islands, by the Lieutenant-Governor in cases concerning British citizens or British citizenship;

(b) in any dependent territory which is for the time being a colony, by the Governor in cases concerning British Dependent Territories citizens or British Dependent Territories citizenship.

(2) The said matters are—

(a) registration and naturalisation; and

(b) renunciation, resumption and deprivation of British citizenship or British Dependent Territories citizenship.

(3) Nothing in this section applies in the case of any power to make regulations or rules conferred on the Secretary of State by this Act.

(4) Arrangements under subsection (1) may provide for any such function as is there mentioned to be exerciseable only with the approval of the Secretary of State.

Decisions involving exercise of discretion

44.—(1) Any discretion vested by or under this Act in the Secretary of State, a Governor or a Lieutenant-Governor shall be exercised without regard to the race, colour or religion of any person who may be affected by its exercise.

(2) The Secretary of State, a Governor or a Lieutenant-Governor, as the case may be, shall not be required to assign any reason for the grant or refusal of any application under this Act the decision on which is at his discretion, and the decision of the Secretary of State or a Governor or Lieutenant-Governor on any such application shall not be subject to appeal to, or review in, any court.

(3) Nothing in this section affects the jurisdiction of any court to entertain proceedings of any description concerning the rights of any person under any provision of this Act.

Evidence

45.—(1) Every document purporting to be a notice, certificate, order or declaration, or an entry in a register, or a subscription of an oath of allegiance, given, granted or made under this Act or any of the former nationality Acts shall be received in evidence and shall, unless the contrary is proved, be deemed to have been given, granted or made by or on behalf of the person by whom or on whose behalf it purports to have been given, granted or made.

(2) *Prima facie* evidence of any such document may be given by the production of a document purporting to be certified as a true copy of it by such person and in such manner as may be prescribed.

(3) Any entry in a register made under this Act or any of the former nationality Acts shall be received as evidence (and in Scotland as sufficient evidence) of the matters stated in the entry.

(4) A certificate given by or on behalf of the Secretary of State that a person was at any time in Crown service under the government of the United Kingdom or that a person's recruitment for such service took place in the United Kingdom shall, for the purposes of this Act, be conclusive evidence of that fact.

Offences and proceedings

46.—(1) Any person who for the purpose of procuring anything to be done or not to be done under this Act—

(a) makes any statement which he knows to be false in a material particular; or

(b) recklessly makes any statement which is false in a material particular,

shall be liable on summary conviction in the United Kingdom to imprisonment for a term not exceeding three months or to a fine not exceeding £1,000, or both.

(2) Any person who without reasonable excuse fails to comply with any requirement imposed on him by regulations made under this Act with respect to the delivering up of certificates of naturalisation shall be liable on summary conviction in the United Kingdom to a fine not exceeding £500.

(3) In the case of an offence under subsection (1)—

(a) any information relating to the offence may in England and Wales be tried by a magistrates' court if it is laid within six months after the commission of the offence, or if it is laid within three years after the commission of the offence and not more than two months after the date certified by a chief officer of police to be the date on which evidence sufficient to justify proceedings came to the notice of an officer of his police force; and

(b) summary proceedings for the offence may in Scotland be commenced within six months after the commission of the offence, or within three years after the commission of the offence and not more than two months after the date on which evidence sufficient in the opinion of the Lord Advocate to justify proceedings came to his knowledge; and

(c) a complaint charging the commission of the offence may in Northern Ireland be heard and determined by a magistrates' court if it is made within six months after the commission of the offence, or if it is made within three years after the commission of the offence and not more than two months after the date certified by an officer of police not below the rank of assistant chief constable to be the date on which evidence sufficient to justify the proceedings came to the notice of the police in Northern Ireland.

(4) For the purposes of subsection (3)(b) proceedings shall be deemed to be commenced on the date on which a warrant to apprehend or to cite the accused is granted, if such warrant is executed without undue delay; and a certificate of the Lord Advocate as to the date on which such evidence as is mentioned in subsection (3)(b) came to his knowledge shall be conclusive evidence.

(5) For the purposes of the trial of a person for an offence under subsection (1) or (2), the offence shall be deemed to have been committed either at the place at which it actually was committed or at any place at which he may be.

(6) In their application to the Bailiwick of Jersey subsections (1) and (2) shall have effect with the omission of the words 'on summary conviction'.

Legitimated children

47.—(1) A person born out of wedlock and legitimated by the subsequent marriage of his parents shall, as from the date of the marriage, be treated for the purposes of this Act as if he had been born legitimate.

(2) A person shall be deemed for the purposes of this section to have been legitimated by the subsequent marriage of his parents if by the law of the place in which his father was domiciled at the time of the marriage the marriage operated immediately or subsequently to legitimate him, and not otherwise.

Posthumous children

48. Any reference in this Act to the status or description of the father or mother of a person at the time of that person's birth shall, in relation to a person born after the death of his father or mother, be construed as a reference to the status or description of the parent in question at the time of that parent's death; and where that death occurred before, and the birth occurs after, commencement, the status or description which would have been applicable to the father or mother had he or she died after commencement shall be deemed to be the status or description applicable to him or her at the time of his or her death.

Registration and naturalisation under British Nationality Acts 1948–65

49.—(1) After the passing of this Act—

(a) a person shall not be registered under any provision of the existing nationality Acts as a citizen of the United Kingdom and Colonies or a British subject; and

(b) a certificate of naturalisation shall not be granted to a person under any provision of those Acts,

unless—

(i) any fee payable by virtue of those Acts in connection with the registration or, as the case may be, the grant of the certificate has been paid; and

(ii) where applicable, the person in question has taken the oath of allegiance which, but for this section, he would have been required by those Acts to take in connection with the registration or, as the case may be, the grant to him of the certificate.

(2) Any provision of the existing nationality Acts which provides for a person to be entitled to registration as a citizen of the United Kingdom and Colonies or a British subject shall have effect subject to subsection (1).

(3) A person registered after the passing of this Act under any provision of the existing nationality Acts as a citizen of the United Kingdom and Colonies or a British subject shall be such a citizen by registration or, as the case may be, a British subject by virtue of that provision as from the date on which he is so registered; and a person to whom a certificate of naturalisation is after the passing of this Act granted under any such provision shall be a citizen of the United Kingdom and Colonies by naturalisation as from the date on which the certificate is granted.

(4) The following provisions of the existing nationality Acts, namely—

(a) in the 1948 Act, s 9 and, in s 10(1), the words from 'and the person' onwards; and

(b) s 1(2) of the British Nationality Act 1965,

shall not apply in relation to any application for registration or for a certificate of naturalisation under any provision of the existing nationality Acts, whenever made, unless the person to whom that application relates has been registered or, as the case may be, granted such a certificate before the passing of this Act.

(5) In this section 'the existing nationality Acts' means the British Nationality Acts 1948–65.

Interpretation

50.—(1) In this Act, unless the context otherwise requires—

'the 1948 Act' means the British Nationality Act 1948;

'alien' means a person who is neither a Commonwealth citizen nor a British protected person nor a citizen of the Republic of Ireland;

'association' means an unincorporated body of persons;

'British protected person' means a person who is a member of any class of persons declared to be British protected persons by an Order in Council for the time being in force under s 38 or is a British protected person by virtue of the Solomon Islands Act 1978;

'commencement', without more, means the commencement of this Act;

'Commonwealth citizen' means a person who has the status of a Commonwealth citizen under this Act;

'company' means a body corporate;

'Crown service' means the service of the Crown, whether within Her Majesty's dominions or elsewhere;

'Crown service under the government of the United Kingdom' means Crown service under Her Majesty's government in the United Kingdom or under Her Majesty's government in Northern Ireland;

'dependent territory' means a territory mentioned in Schedule 6;

'enactment' includes an enactment comprised in Northern Ireland legislation;

'foreign country' means a country other than the United Kingdom, a dependent territory, a country mentioned in Schedule 3 and the Republic of Ireland;

'the former nationality Acts' means—

(a) the British Nationality Acts 1948–65;

(b) the British Nationality and Status of Aliens Acts 1914–43; and

(c) any Act repealed by the said Acts of 1914–43 or by the Naturalisation Act 1870;

'Governor', in relation to a dependent territory, includes the officer for the time being administering the government of that territory;

'High Commissioner' includes an acting High Commissioner;

'immigration laws'—

(a) in relation to the United Kingdom, means the Immigration Act 1971 and any law for purposes similar to that Act which is for the time being or has at any time been in force in any part of the United Kingdom;

(b) in relation to a dependent territory, means any law for purposes similar to the Immigration Act 1971 which is for the time being or has at any time been in force in that territory;

'the Islands' means the Channel Islands and the Isle of Man;

'minor' means a person who has not attained the age of 18 years;

'prescribed' means prescribed by regulations made under s 41;

'settled' shall be construed in accordance with subsections (2)–(4);

'ship' includes a hovercraft;

'statutory provision' means any enactment or any provision contained in—

(a) subordinate legislation (as defined in s 21(1) of the Interpretation Act 1978); or

(b) any instrument of a legislative character made under any Northern Ireland legislation;

'the United Kingdom' means Great Britain, Northern Ireland and the Islands, taken together;

'United Kingdom consulate' means the office of a consular officer of Her Majesty's government in the United Kingdom where a register of births is kept or, where there is no such office, such office as may be prescribed.

(2) Subject to subsection (3), references in this Act to a person being settled in the United Kingdom or in a dependent territory are references to his being

ordinarily resident in the United Kingdom or, as the case may be, in that territory without being subject under the immigration laws to any restriction on the period for which he may remain.

(3) Subject to subsection (4), a person is not to be regarded for the purposes of this Act—

(a) as having been settled in the United Kingdom at any time when he was entitled to an exemption under s 8(3) or (4)(b) or (c) of the Immigration Act 1971 or, unless the order under s 8(2) of that Act conferring the exemption in question provides otherwise to an exemption under the said s 8(2), or to any corresponding exemption under the former immigration laws; or

(b) as having been settled in a dependent territory at any time when he was under the immigration laws entitled to any exemption corresponding to any such exemption as is mentioned in para (a) (that paragraph being for the purposes of this paragraph read as if the words from 'unless' to 'otherwise' were omitted).

(4) A person to whom a child is born in the United Kingdom after commencement is to be regarded for the purposes of s 1(1) as being settled in the United Kingdom at the time of the birth if—

(a) he would fall to be so regarded but for his being at that time entitled to an exemption under s 8 (3) of the Immigration Act 1971; and

(b) immediately before he became entitled to that exemption he was settled in the United Kingdom; and

(c) he was ordinarily resident in the United Kingdom from the time when he became entitled to that exemption to the time of the birth;

but this subsection shall not apply if at the time of the birth the child's father or mother is a person on whom any immunity from jurisdiction is conferred by or under the Diplomatic Privileges Act 1964.

(5) It is hereby declared that a person is not to be treated for the purpose of any provision of this Act as ordinarily resident in the United Kingdom or in a dependent territory at a time when he is in the United Kingdom or, as the case may be, in that territory in breach of the immigration laws.

(6) For the purposes of this Act—

(a) a person shall be taken to have been naturalised in the United Kingdom if, but only if, he is—

(i) a person to whom a certificate of naturalisation was granted under any of the former nationality Acts by the Secretary of State or, in any of the Islands, by the Lieutenant-Governor; or

(ii) a person who by virtue of s 27(2) of the British Nationality and Status of Aliens Act 1914 was deemed to be a person to whom a certificate of naturalisation was granted, if the certificate of naturalisation in which his name was included was granted by the Secretary of State; or

(iii) a person who by virtue of s 10(5) of the Naturalization Act 1870 was deemed to be a naturalised British subject by reason of his residence with his father or mother;

(b) a person shall be taken to have been naturalised in a dependent territory if, but only if, he is—

(i) a person to whom a certificate of naturalisation was granted under any of the former nationality Acts by the Governor of that territory or by a person for the time being specified in a direction given in relation to that territory under para 4 of Schedule 3 to the West Indies Act 1967 or for the time being holding an office so specified; or

(ii) a person who by virtue of the said s 27(2) was deemed to be a person to whom a certificate of naturalisation was granted, if the certificate of naturalisation in which his name was included was granted by the Governor of that territory; or

(iii) a person who by the law in force in that territory enjoyed the privileges of naturalisation within that territory only;

and references in this Act to naturalisation in the United Kingdom or in a dependent territory shall be construed accordingly.

(7) For the purposes of this Act a person born outside the United Kingdom aboard a ship or aircraft—

(a) shall be deemed to have been born in the United Kingdom if—

(i) at the time of the birth his father or mother was a British citizen; or

(ii) he would, but for this subsection, have been born stateless,

and (in either case) at the time of the birth the ship or aircraft was registered in the United Kingdom or was an unregistered ship or aircraft of the government of the United Kingdom; but

(b) subject to para (a), is to be regarded as born outside the United Kingdom, whoever was the owner of the ship or aircraft at that time, and irrespective of whether or where it was then registered.

The preceding provisions of this subsection shall apply in relation to each dependent territory with the substitution for the references to the United Kingdom and to a British citizen of references to that territory and to a British Dependent Territories citizen respectively.

(8) For the purposes of this Act an application under any provision thereof shall be taken to have been made at the time of its receipt by a person authorised to receive it on behalf of the person to whom it is made; and

references in this Act to the date of such an application are references to the date of its receipt by a person so authorised.

(9) For the purposes of this Act—

(a) the relationship of mother and child shall be taken to exist between a woman and any child (legitimate or illegitimate) born to her; but

(b) subject to s 47, the relationship of father and child shall be taken to exist only between a man and any legitimate child born to him;

and the expressions 'mother', 'father', 'parent', 'child' and 'descended' shall be construed accordingly.

(10) For the purposes of this Act—

(a) a period 'from' or 'to' a specified date includes that date; and

(b) any reference to a day on which a person was absent from the United Kingdom or from a dependent territory or from the dependent territories is a reference to a day for the whole of which he was so absent.

(11) For the purposes of this Act—

(a) a person is of full age if he has attained the age of 18 years, and of full capacity if he is not of unsound mind; and

(b) a person attains any particular age at the beginning of the relevant anniversary of the date of his birth.

(12) References in this Act to any country mentioned in Schedule 3 include references to the dependencies of that country.

(13) Her Majesty may by Order in Council subject to annulment in pursuance of a resolution of either House of Parliament amend Schedule 6 in any of the following circumstances, namely—

(a) where the name of any territory mentioned in it is altered; or

(b) where any territory mentioned in it is divided into two or more territories.

Meaning of certain expressions relating to nationality in other Acts and instruments

51.—(1) Without prejudice to subsection (3)(c), in any enactment or instrument whatever passed or made before commencement 'British subject' and 'Commonwealth citizen' have the same meaning, that is—

(a) in relation to any time before commencement—

(i) a person who under the 1948 Act was at that time a citizen of the United Kingdom and Colonies or who, under any enactment then in force in a country mentioned in s 1(3) of that Act as then in force, was at that time a citizen of that country; and

(ii) any other person who had at that time the status of a British subject under that Act or any other enactment then in force;

(b) in relation to any time after commencement, a person who has the status of a Commonwealth citizen under this Act.

(2) In any enactment or instrument whatever passed or made after commencement—

'British subject' means a person who has the status of a British subject under this Act;

'Commonwealth citizen' means a person who has the status of a Commonwealth citizen under this Act.

(3) In any enactment or instrument whatever passed or made before commencement—

(a) 'citizen of the United Kingdom and Colonies'—

(i) in relation to any time before commencement, means a person who under the 1948 Act was at that time a citizen of the United Kingdom and Colonies;

(ii) in relation to any time after commencement, means a person who under this Act is a British citizen, a British Dependent Territories citizen or a British Overseas citizen;

(b) any reference to ceasing to be a citizen of the United Kingdom and Colonies shall, in relation to any time after commencement, be construed as a reference to becoming a person who is neither a British citizen nor a British Dependent Territories citizen nor a British Overseas citizen;

(c) any reference to a person who is a British subject (or a British subject without citizenship) by virtue of s 2, 13, or 16 of the 1948 Act or by virtue of, or of s 1 of, the British Nationality Act 1965 shall, in relation to any time after commencement, be construed as a reference to a person who under this Act is a British subject.

(4) In any statutory provision, whether passed or made before or after commencement, and in any other instrument whatever made after commencement 'alien', in relation to any time after commencement, means a person who is neither a Commonwealth citizen nor a British protected person nor a citizen of the Republic of Ireland.

(5) The preceding provisions of this section—

(a) shall not apply in cases where the context otherwise requires; and

(b) shall not apply to this Act or to any instrument made under this Act.

Consequential amendments, transitional provisions, repeals and savings

52.—(1) In any enactment or instrument whatever passed or made before commencement, for any reference to s 1(3) of the 1948 Act (list of countries whose citizens are Commonwealth citizens under that Act) there shall be substituted a reference to Schedule 3 to this Act, unless the context makes that substitution inappropriate.

(2) Subject to subsection (3), Her Majesty may by Order in Council make such consequential modifications of—

(a) any enactment of the Parliament of the United Kingdom passed before commencement;

(b) any provision contained in any Northern Ireland legislation passed or made before commencement; or

(c) any instrument made before commencement under any such enactment or provision,

as appear to Her Majesty necessary or expedient for preserving after commencement the substantive effect of that enactment, provision or instrument.

(3) Subsection (2) shall not apply in relation to—

(a) the Immigration Act 1971; or

(b) any provision of this Act not contained in Schedule 7.

(4) Any Order in Council made under subsection (2) shall be subject to annulment in pursuance of a resolution of either House of Parliament.

(5) Any provision made by Order in Council under subsection (2) after commencement may be made with retrospective effect as from commencement or any later date.

(6) The enactments specified in Schedule 7 shall have effect subject to the amendments there specified, being amendments consequential on the provisions of this Act.

(7) This Act shall have effect subject to the transitional provisions contained in Schedule 8.

(8) The enactments mentioned in Schedule 9 are hereby repealed to the extent specified in the third column of that Schedule.

(9) Without prejudice to s 51, nothing in this Act affects the operation, in relation to any time before commencement, of any statutory provision passed or made before commencement.

(10) Nothing in this Act shall be taken as prejudicing the operation of ss 16 and 17 of the Interpretation Act 1978 (which relate to the effect of repeals).

(11) In this section 'modifications' includes additions, omissions and alterations.

Citation, commencement and extent

53.—(1) This Act may be cited as the British Nationality Act 1981.

(2) This Act, except the provisions mentioned in subsection (3), shall come into force on such day as the Secretary of State may by order made by statutory instrument appoint; and references to the commencement of this Act shall be construed as references to the beginning of that day.

(3) Section 49 and this section shall come into force on the passing of this Act.

(4) This Act extends to Northern Ireland.

(5) The provisions of this Act, except those mentioned in subsection (7), extend to the Islands and all dependent territories; and s 36 of the Immigration Act 1971 (power to extend provisions of that Act to Islands) shall apply to the said excepted provisions as if they were provisions of that Act.

(6) For the purposes of s 3(3) of the West Indies Act 1967 it is hereby declared that the provisions of this Act, except those mentioned in subsection (7), extend to all associated States.

(7) The provisions referred to in subsections (5) and (6) are—

(a) s 39 and Schedule 4;

(b) s 52(7) and Schedule 8 so far as they relate to the Immigration Act 1971; and

(c) s 52(8) and Schedule 9 so far as they relate to provisions of the Immigration Act 1971 other than Schedule 1.

SCHEDULES

SCHEDULE 1

REQUIREMENTS FOR NATURALISATION

Naturalisation as a British citizen under s 6(1)

1.—(1) Subject to para 2, the requirements for naturalisation as a British citizen under s 6(1) are, in the case of any person who applies for it—

(a) the requirements specified in sub-para (2) of this paragraph, or the alternative requirement specified in sub-para (3) of this paragraph; and

(b) that he is of good character; and

(c) that he has a sufficient knowledge of the English, Welsh or Scottish Gaelic language; and

(d) that either—

(i) his intentions are such that, in the event of a certificate of naturalisation as a British citizen being granted to him, his home or (if he has more than one) his principal home will be in the United Kingdom; or

(ii) he intends, in the event of such a certificate being granted to him, to enter into, or continue in, Crown service under the government of the United Kingdom, or service under an international organisation of which the United Kingdom or Her Majesty's government therein is a member, or service in the employment of a company or association established in the United Kingdom.

(2) The requirements referred to in sub-para (1)(a) of this paragraph are—

(a) that the applicant was in the United Kingdom at the beginning of the period of five years ending with the date of the application, and that the number of days on which he was absent from the United Kingdom in that period does not exceed 450; and

(b) that the number of days on which he was absent from the United Kingdom in the period of 12 months so ending does not exceed 90; and

(c) that he was not at any time in the period of 12 months so ending subject under the immigration laws to any restriction on the period for which he might remain in the United Kingdom; and

(d) that he was not at any time in the period of five years so ending in the United Kingdom in breach of the immigration laws.

(3) The alternative requirement referred to in sub-para (1)(a) of this paragraph is that on the date of the application he is serving outside the United Kingdom in Crown service under the government of the United Kingdom.

2. If in the special circumstances of any particular case the Secretary of State thinks fit, he may for the purposes of para 1 do all or any of the following things, namely—

(a) treat the applicant as fulfilling the requirement specified in para 1(2)(a) or para 1(2)(b), or both, although the number of days on which he was absent from the United Kingdom in the period there mentioned exceeds the number there mentioned;

(b) treat the applicant as having been in the United Kingdom for the whole or any part of any period during which he would otherwise fall to be treated under para 9(1) as having been absent;

(c) disregard any such restriction as is mentioned in para 1(2)(c), not being a restriction to which the applicant was subject on the date of the application;

(d) treat the applicant as fulfilling the requirement specified in para 1(2)(d) although he was in the United Kingdom in breach of the immigration laws in the period there mentioned;

(e) waive the need to fulfil the requirement specified in para 1(1)(c) if he considers that because of the applicant's age or physical or mental condition it would be unreasonable to expect him to fulfil it.

Naturalisation as a British citizen under s 6(2)

3. Subject to para 4, the requirements for naturalisation as a British citizen under s 6(2) are, in the case of any person who applies for it—

(a) that he was in the United Kingdom at the beginning of the period of three years ending with the date of the application, and that the number of days on which he was absent from the United Kingdom in that period does not exceed 270; and

(b) that the number of days on which he was absent from the United Kingdom in the period of 12 months so ending does not exceed 90; and

(c) that on the date of the application he was not subject under the immigration laws to any restriction on the period for which he might remain in the United Kingdom; and

(d) that he was not at any time in the period of three years ending with the date of the application in the United Kingdom in breach of the immigration laws; and

(e) the requirement specified in para (l)(b).

4. Paragraph 2 shall apply in relation to para 3 with the following modifications, namely—

(a) the reference to the purposes of para 1 shall be read as a reference to the purposes of para 3;

(b) the references to paras 1(2)(a), 1(2)(b) and 1(2)(d) shall be read as references to paras 3(a), 3(b) and 3(d) respectively;

(c) para 2(c) and (e) shall be omitted; and

(d) after para (e) there shall be added—

> '(f) waive the need to fulfil all or any of the requirements specified in para 3(a) and (b) if on the date of the application the person to whom the applicant is married is serving in service to which s 2(1)(b) applies, that person's recruitment for that service having taken place in the United Kingdom.'.

Naturalisation as a British Dependent Territories citizen under s 18(1)

5.—(1) Subject to para 6, the requirements for naturalisation as a British Dependent Territories citizen under s 18(1) are, in the case of any person who applies for it—

(a) the requirements specified in sub-para (2) of this paragraph, or the alternative requirement specified in sub-para (3) of this paragraph; and

(b) that he is of good character; and

(c) that he has a sufficient knowledge of the English language or any other language recognised for official purposes in the relevant territory; and

(d) that either—

(i) his intentions are such that, in the event of a certificate of naturalisation as a British Dependent Territories citizen being granted to him, his home or (if he has more than one) his principal home will be in the relevant territory; or

(ii) he intends, in the event of such a certificate being granted to him, to enter into, or continue in, Crown service under the government of that territory, or service under an international organisation of which that territory or the government of that territory is a member, or service in the employment of a company or association established in that territory.

(2) The requirements referred to in sub-para (1)(a) of this paragraph are—

(a) that he was in the relevant territory at the beginning of the period of five years ending with the date of the application,. and that the number of days on which he was absent from that territory in that period does not exceed 450; and

(b) that the number of days on which he was absent from that territory in the period of 12 months so ending does not exceed 90; and

(c) that he was not at any time in the period of 12 months so ending subject under the immigration laws to any restriction on the period for which he might remain in that territory; and

(d) that he was not at any time in the period of five years so ending in that territory in breach of the immigration laws.

(3) The alternative requirement referred to in sub-para (1)(a) of this paragraph is that on the date of the application he is serving outside the relevant territory in Crown service under the government of that territory.

6. If in the special circumstances of any particular case the Secretary of State thinks fit, he may for the purposes of para 5 do all or any of the following things, namely—

(a) treat the applicant as fulfilling the requirement specified in para 5(2)(a) or para 5(2)(b), or both, although the number of days on which he was absent from the relevant territory in the period there mentioned exceeds the number there mentioned;

(b) treat the applicant as having been in the relevant territory for the whole or any part of any period during which he would otherwise fall to be treated under para 9(2) as having been absent;

(c) disregard any such restriction as is mentioned in para 5(2)(c), not being a restriction to which the applicant was subject on the date of the application;

(d) treat the applicant as fulfilling the requirement specified in para 5(2)(d) although he was in the relevant territory in breach of the immigration laws in the period there mentioned;

(e) waive the need to fulfil the requirement specified in para 5(1)(c) if he considers that because of the applicant's age or physical or mental condition it would be unreasonable to expect him to fulfil it.

Naturalisation as a British Dependent Territories citizen under s 18(2)

7. Subject to para 8, the requirements for naturalisation as a British Dependent Territories citizen under s 18(2) are, in the case of any person who applies for it—

(a) that he was in the relevant territory at the beginning of the period of three years ending with the date of the application, and that the number of days on which he was absent from that territory in that period does not exceed 270; and

(b) that the number of days on which he was absent from that territory in the period of 12 months so ending does not exceed 90; and

(c) that on the date of the application he was not subject under the immigration laws to any restriction on the period for which he might remain in that territory; and

(d) that he was not at any time in the period of three years ending with the date of the application in that territory in breach of the immigration laws; and

(e) the requirement specified in para 5(1)(b).

8. Paragraph 6 shall apply in relation to para 7 with the following modifications, namely—

(a) the reference to the purposes of paragraph as a reference to the purposes of para 7;

(b) the references to paras 5(2)(a), 5(2)(b) and 5(2)(d) shall be read as references to paras 7(a), 7(b) and 7(d) respectively;

(c) para 6(c) and (e) shall be omitted; and

(d) after para (e) there shall be added—

> '(f) waive the need to fulfil all or any of the requirements specified in para 7(a) and (b) if on the date of the application the person to whom the applicant is married is serving in service to which s 16(1)(b) applies, that person's recruitment for that service having taken place in a dependent territory.'.

Periods to be treated as periods of absence from the United Kingdom or a dependent territory

9.—(1) For the purposes of this Schedule a person shall (subject to para 2(b)) be treated as having been absent from the United Kingdom during any of the following periods, that is to say—

(a) any period when he was in the United Kingdom and either was entitled to an exemption under s 8(3) or (4) of the Immigration Act 1971 (exemptions for diplomatic agents, etc and members of the forces) or was a member of the family and formed part of the household of a person so entitled;

(b) any period when he was detained—

(i) in any place of detention in the United Kingdom in pursuance of a sentence passed on him by a court in the United Kingdom or elsewhere for any offence;

(ii) in any hospital in the United Kingdom under a hospital order made under Part V of the Mental Health Act 1959 or s 175 or 376 of the Criminal Procedure (Scotland) Act 1975 or Part III of the Mental Health Act (Northern Ireland) 1961, being an order made in connection with his conviction of an offence; or

(iii) under any power of detention conferred by the immigration laws of the United Kingdom;

(c) any period when, being liable to be detained as mentioned in para (b)(i) or (ii) of this sub-paragraph, he was unlawfully at large or absent without leave and for that reason liable to be arrested or taken into custody;

(d) any period when, his actual detention under any such power as is mentioned in para (b)(iii) of this sub-paragraph being required or specifically authorised, he was unlawfully at large and for that reason liable to be arrested.

(2) For the purposes of this Schedule a person shall (subject to para 6(b)) be treated as having been absent from any particular dependent territory during any of the following periods, that is to say—

(a) any period when he was in that territory and either was entitled to an exemption under the immigration laws of that territory corresponding to any such exemption as is mentioned in sub-para (1)(a) or was a member of the family and formed part of the household of a person so entitled;

(b) any period when he was detained—

(i) in any place of detention in the relevant territory in pursuance of a sentence passed on him by a court in that territory or elsewhere for any offence;

(ii) in any hospital in that territory under a direction (however described) made under any law for purposes similar to Part V of the Mental Health Act 1959 which was for the time being in force in that territory, being a direction made in connection with his conviction of an offence and corresponding to a hospital order under that Part; or

(iii) under any power of detention conferred by the immigration laws of that territory;

(c) any period when, being liable to be detained as mentioned in para (b)(i) or (ii) of this sub-paragraph, he was unlawfully at large or absent without leave and for that reason liable to be arrested or taken into custody;

(d) any period when, his actual detention under any such power as is mentioned in para (b)(iii) of this sub-paragraph being required or specifically authorised, he was unlawfully at large and for that reason liable to be arrested.

Interpretation

10. In this Schedule 'the relevant territory' has the meaning given by s 18(3).

SCHEDULE 2

PROVISIONS FOR REDUCING STATELESSNESS

Persons born in the United Kingdom after commencement

1.—(1) Where a person born in the United Kingdom after commencement would, but for this paragraph, be born stateless, then, subject to sub-para (3)—

(a) if at the time of the birth his father or mother is a citizen or subject of a description mentioned in sub-para (2), he shall be a citizen or subject of that description; and accordingly

(b) if he is born legitimate and at the time of the birth each of his parents is a citizen or subject of a different description so mentioned, he shall be a citizen or subject of the same description so mentioned as each of them is respectively at that time.

(2) The descriptions referred to in sub-para (1) are a British Dependent Territories citizen, a British Overseas citizen and a British subject under this Act.

(3) A person shall not be a British subject by virtue of this paragraph if by virtue of it he is a citizen of a description mentioned in sub-para (2).

Persons born in a dependent territory after commencement

2.—(1) Where a person born in a dependent territory after commencement would, but for this paragraph, be born stateless, then, subject to sub-para (3)—

(a) if at the time of the birth his father or mother is a citizen or subject of a description mentioned in sub-para (2), he shall be a citizen or subject of that description; and accordingly

(b) if he is born legitimate and at the time of the birth each of his parents is a citizen or subject of a different description so mentioned, he shall be a citizen or subject of the same description so mentioned as each of them is respectively at that time.

(2) The descriptions referred to in sub-para (1) are a British citizen, a British Overseas citizen and a British subject Act.

(3) A person shall not be a British subject by virtue of this paragraph if by virtue of it he is a citizen of a description mentioned in sub-para (2).

Persons born in the United Kingdom or a dependent territory after commencement

3.—(1) A person born in the United Kingdom or a dependent territory after commencement shall be entitled, on an application for his registration under this paragraph, to be so registered if the following requirements are satisfied in his case, namely—

(a) that he is and always has been stateless; and

(b) that on the date of the application he had attained the age of 10 but was under the age of 22; and

(c) that he was in the United Kingdom or a dependent territory (no matter which) at the beginning of the period of five years ending with that date and that (subject to para 6) the number of days on which he was absent from both the United Kingdom and the dependent territories in that period does not exceed 450.

(2) A person entitled to registration under this paragraph—

(a) shall be registered under it as a British citizen if, in the period of five years mentioned in sub-para (1), the number of days wholly or partly spent by him in the United Kingdom exceeds the number of days wholly or partly spent by him in the dependent territories;

(b) in any other case, shall be registered under it as a British Dependent Territories citizen.

Persons born outside the United Kingdom and the dependent territories after commencement

4.—(1) A person born outside the United Kingdom and the dependent territories after commencement shall be entitled, on an application for his registration under this paragraph, to be so registered if the following requirements are satisfied, namely—

(a) that that person is and always has been stateless; and

(b) that at the time of that person's birth his father or mother was a citizen or subject of a description mentioned in sub-para (4); and

(c) that that person was in the United Kingdom or a dependent territory (no matter which) at the beginning of the period of three years ending with the date of the application and that (subject to para 6) the number of days on which he was absent from both the United Kingdom and the dependent territories in that period does not exceed 270.

(2) A person entitled to registration under this paragraph—

(a) shall be registered under it as a citizen or subject of a description available to him in accordance with sub-para (3); and

(b) if more than one description is so available to him, shall be registered under this paragraph as a citizen of whichever one or more of the descriptions so available to him is or are stated in the application under this paragraph to be wanted.

(3) For the purposes of this paragraph the descriptions of citizen or subject available to a person entitled to registration under this paragraph are—

(a) in the case of a person whose father or mother was at the time of that person's birth a citizen of a description mentioned in sub-para (4), any description of citizen so mentioned which applied to his father or mother at that time;

(b) in any other case, a British subject under this Act.

(4) The descriptions referred to in sub-paras (1)–(3) are a British citizen, a British Dependent Territories citizen, a British Overseas citizen and a British subject under this Act.

Persons born stateless before commencement

5.—(1) A person born before commencement shall be entitled, on an application for his registration under this paragraph, to be so registered if the circumstances are such that, if—

(a) this Act had not been passed, and the enactments repealed or amended by this Act had continued in force accordingly; and

(b) an application for the registration of that person under s 1 of the British Nationality (No 2) Act 1964 (stateless persons) as a citizen of the United Kingdom and Colonies had been made on the date of the application under this paragraph,

that person would have been entitled under that section to be registered as such a citizen.

(2) A person entitled to registration under this paragraph shall be registered under it as such a citizen as he would have become at commencement if, immediately before commencement, he had been registered as a citizen of the United Kingdom and Colonies under s 1 of the British Nationality (No 2) Act 1964 on whichever of the grounds mentioned in subsection (1)(a)–(c) of that section he would have been entitled to be so registered on in the circumstances described in sub-para (1)(a) and (b) of this paragraph.

Supplementary

6. If in the special circumstances of any particular case the Secretary of State thinks fit, he may for the purposes of para 3 or 4 treat the person who is the subject of the application as fulfilling the requirement specified in sub-para (1)(c) of that paragraph although the number of days on which he was absent from both the United Kingdom and the dependent territories in the period there mentioned exceeds the number there mentioned.

SCHEDULE 3

COUNTRIES WHOSE CITIZENS ARE COMMONWEALTH CITIZENS

Antigua and Barbuda
Australia
The Bahamas
Bangladesh
Barbados
Belize
Botswana
Canada
Republic of Cyprus
Dominica
Fiji
The Gambia
Ghana
Mauritius
Nauru
New Zealand
Nigeria
Papua New Guinea
Saint Lucia
Saint Vincent and the Grenadines
Seychelles
Sierra Leone
Singapore
Solomon Islands
Sri Lanka

Grenada	Swaziland
Guyana	Tanzania
India	Tonga
Jamaica	Trinidad and Tobago
Kenya	Tuvalu
Kiribati	Uganda
Lesotho	Vanuatu
Malawi	Western Samoa
Malaysia	Zambia
Malta	Zimbabwe

SCHEDULE 4

AMENDMENTS OF IMMIGRATION ACT 1971

1. In this Schedule 'the 1971 Act', means the Immigration Act 1971.

2. For 'patrial'—

(a) where it occurs in the provisions of the 1971 Act listed in the first column of the following table, and where it first occurs in s 6(2) of that Act, substitute 'a British citizen';

(b) where it occurs in the provisions of that Act listed in the second column of that table, and where it last occurs in s 6(2) of that Act, substitute 'British citizens'.

TABLE

(1) 'a British citizen'	(2) 'British citizens'
Section 3(1), (5), (6), (8);	Section 3(7) (twice);
Section 5(2);	Section 4(4);
Section 9(4);	Section 8(2), (3), (4);
Section 14(2);	Section 9(2);
Section 24(1);	Section 29(1);
In s 33(1), the definitions of 'entry clearance' and 'work permit';	In Schedule 2, para 26(1)
In Schedule 2, paras 2(1)(a), 3(1), 6(1), 12(2) and 13(2).	
In Schedule 4, paras 1(1) and (2), 3(1) and 4.	

3.—(1) For 'certificate of patriality', wherever (except in s 33(1)) it occurs in the 1971 Act (that is, in ss 13(2), 22(4)(a) and (5)(a), 26(1)(d) (twice) and para 19(2) of Schedule 2 (twice)) substitute 'certificate of entitlement'.

(2) In the entry in s 33(1) which defines 'certificate of patriality', for 'patriality' substitute 'entitlement'.

4. In s 3(7) of the 1971 Act (powers available where restrictions or conditions are imposed on citizens of the United Kingdom and Colonies when leaving or seeking to leave other countries), for 'citizens of the United Kingdom and Colonies' substitute 'British citizens, British Dependent Territories citizens or British Overseas citizens'.

5. In s 8(5) of the 1971 Act, for the words from 'settled' onwards (by virtue of which persons are not to be regarded for the purposes of the 1971 Act as having been settled in the United Kingdom while entitled to certain exemptions) substitute 'settled in the United Kingdom at any time when he was entitled under the former immigration laws to any exemption corresponding to any of those afforded by subsection (3) or (4)(b) or (c) above or by any order under subsection (2) above.'.

6. In s 25(5) of the 1971 Act (extension of provisions about offences of assisting illegal entry and harbouring to things done outside the United Kingdom by persons of certain descriptions), for paras (a)–(e) substitute—

'(a) by a British citizen, a British Dependent Territories citizen, or a British Overseas citizen;

(b) by a person who under the British Nationality Act 1981 is a British subject; or

(c) by a British protected person (within the meaning of that Act).'.

7. In s 33 of the 1971 Act (interpretation)—

(a) in subsection (1)—

(i) in the definition of 'settled', for the words from 'with' onwards substitute 'with subsection (2A) below;'; and

(ii) after the definition of 'ship' insert—

'"United Kingdom passport" means a current passport issued by the government of the United Kingdom, or by the Lieutenant-Governor of any of the Islands, or by the government of any territory which is for the time being a dependent territory within the meaning of the British Nationality Act 1981;'; and

(b) after subsection (2) insert—

'(2A) Subject to s 8(5) above, references to a person being settled in the United Kingdom are references to his being ordinarily resident there without being subject under the immigration laws to any restriction on the period for which he may remain.'

SCHEDULE 5

FORM OF OATH OF ALLEGIANCE

The form of the oath of allegiance is as shown below, with the insertion, after the words 'on becoming', of whichever of the following expressions is appropriate, namely—

'a British citizen'
'a British Dependent Territories citizen'
'a British Overseas citizen'
'a British subject'.

Oath of allegiance

I, A.B., swear by Almighty God that, on becoming

I will be faithful and bear true allegiance to Her Majesty Queen Elizabeth the Second Her Heirs and Successors according to law.

SCHEDULE 6

BRITISH DEPENDENT TERRITORIES

Anguilla
Bermuda
British Antarctic Territory
British Indian Ocean Territory
Cayman Islands
Falkland Islands and Dependencies
Gibraltar
Hong Kong
Montserrat
Pitcairn, Henderson, Ducie and Oeno Islands
St Christopher and Nevis
St Helena and Dependencies
The Sovereign Base Areas of Akrotiri and Dhekelia (that is to say the areas mentioned in s 2(1) of the Cyprus Act 1960)
Turks and Caicos Islands
Virgin Islands

SCHEDULE 7

CONSEQUENTIAL AMENDMENTS

ACT OF SETTLEMENT (12 AND 13 WILL. 3. C. 2.)

In s 3, the words from 'That after the said limitation shall take effect' to 'in trust for him'; (which impose certain disqualifications) shall not apply to Commonwealth citizens or citizens of the Republic of Ireland.

LEGITIMACY DECLARATION ACT 1858 (C. 93)

In s 9 (declaration that person is a subject of Her Majesty in Scottish action of declarator), for 'subject of Her Majesty; substitute 'Commonwealth citizen'.

SUBMARINE TELEGRAPH ACT 1885 (C.49)

In s 3(5) (offence for a subject of Her Majesty to abet breaking or injuring of submarine cable outside dominions), for 'a subject of Her Majesty' substitute 'a Commonwealth citizen'.

BRITISH NATIONALITY ACT 1948 (C.56)

In s 3 (limitation of criminal liability of citizens of certain countries), after subsection (3) insert—

> '(4) In this section 'foreign country' and 'British protected person' have the same meaning as in the British Nationality Act 1981.'.

IRELAND ACT 1949 (C.41)

1. In s 3(1)(a) (certain provisions not affected by fact that Republic of Ireland is not part of Her Majesty's dominions), for sub-para (i) (which lists the British Nationality Act 1948) substitute—

> '(i) s 3 of the British Nationality Act 1948;'.

2. For s 7(2) (interpretation of references to protectorates, etc by reference to 1948 Act) substitute—

> '(2) In this Act 'the United Kingdom' includes the Channel Islands and the Isle of Man.'.

DEFAMATION ACT 1952 (C.66)

In Part III of the Schedule (interpretation), in para 14, for 'subsection (3) of section one of that Act' substitute 'Schedule 3 to the British Nationality Act 1981'.

DEFAMATION ACT (NORTHERN IRELAND) 1955 (c.11) (N.I.)

In Part III of the Schedule (interpretation), in para 14, for 'subsection (3) of s 1 of that Act' substitute 'Schedule 3 to the British Nationality Act 1981'.

CYPRUS ACT 1960 (c.52)

In s 6(1) (power to remove Republic of Cyprus from s 1(3) of 1948 Act), for the words from 'specified' onwards substitute 'mentioned in Schedule 3 to the British Nationality Act 1981, Her Majesty may by Order in Council remove the Republic of Cyprus from that Schedule.'.

EMERGENCY LAWS (RE-ENACTMENTS AND REPEALS) ACT 1964 (c.60)

In s 9 (territorial extent of Part I), in subsection (2)—

(a) in the definition of 'British protected person', for 'the British Nationality Acts 1948 to 1964' substitute 'the British Nationality Act 1981'; and

(b) in the definition of 'excepted ship or aircraft', for 'section 1(3) of the British Nationality Act 1948' substitute 'Schedule 3 to the British Nationality Act 1981'.

DIPLOMATIC PRIVILEGES ACT 1964 (c.81)

For s 3(2) (disregard, in connection with citizenship of children of certain persons possessing diplomatic immunity, of Orders in Council withdrawing diplomatic privileges and immunities) substitute—

> '(2) An Order in Council under this section shall be disregarded for the purposes of s 50(4) of the British Nationality Act 1981 (circumstances in which certain persons entitled to exemption under s 8(3) of the Immigration Act 1971 are to be regarded for the purposes of s 1(1) of the said Act of 1981 as settled in the United Kingdom).'.

COMMONWEALTH SECRETARIAT ACT 1966 (c.10)

In Part II of the Schedule (staff of the Secretariat), in paras 5(1) and 7, for 'section 1(3) of the British Nationality Act 1948' substitute 'Schedule 3 to the British Nationality Act 1981'.

WEST INDIES ACT 1967 (c.4)

1. In s 13(3) (power to make changes in nationality or citizenship law in certain events), for 'citizens of the United Kingdom and Colonies' substitute 'British Dependent Territories citizens or British Overseas citizens'.

2. In Schedule 3 (modifications of British Nationality Acts)—

(a) for para 4(3) substitute—

> '(3) This paragraph applies to those functions of the Secretary of State under the British Nationality Act 1981 in the case of which he has power under s 43 of that Act to make arrangements for them to be exercised in a dependent territory which is for the time being a colony by the Governor; and subsection (4) of that section (approval of Secretary of State) shall apply in relation to a direction under this paragraph as it applies in relation to arrangements under that section.'; and

(b) in para 6, for the words from 'Section 26' to '1965)' substitute 'Section 44 of the British Nationality Act 1981'.

MARINE, ETC BROADCASTING (OFFENCES) ACT 1967 (C. 41)

In s 3(3) (persons prohibited from broadcasting whilst on or over high seas), for paras (a)–(e) substitute—

> '(a) a British citizen, a British Dependent Territories citizen or a British Overseas citizen; or
>
> (b) a person who under the British Nationality Act 1981 is a British subject; or
>
> (c) a British protected person (within the meaning of that Act).'

ANTARCTIC TREATY ACT 1967 (C. 65)

In s 1(3) (persons prohibited from harming Antarctic flora and fauna)—

(a) for paras (a)–(e) substitute—

> '(a) a British citizen, a British Dependent Territories citizen or a British Overseas citizen; or
>
> (b) a person who under the British Nationality Act 1981 is a British subject; or
>
> (c) a British protected person (within the meaning of that Act),'; and

(b) for '(a)–(e)' substitute '(a)–(c)'.

FUGITIVE OFFENDERS ACT 1967 (C. 68)

In s 2(1) (designated Commonwealth countries whose fugitives may be returned by United Kingdom), for 'subsection (3) of s 1 of the British Nationality Act 1948' substitute 'Schedule 3 to the British Nationality Act 1981'.

CONSULAR RELATIONS ACT 1968 (C. 18)

In s 1(2) (meaning of certain terms in Schedule 1), in the definition of 'national of the receiving State', for the words from 'as' onwards substitute 'as meaning—

(a) a British citizen, a British Dependent Territories citizen or a British Overseas citizen; or

(b) a person who under the British Nationality Act 1981 is a British subject; or

(c) a British protected person (within the meaning of that Act).'.

TANZANIA ACT 1969 (C. 29)

In s 4(3) (enactments excluded from power to apply statutory provisions to Tanzania), for 'the British Nationality Acts' substitute 'the British Nationality Act 1981'.

INCOME AND CORPORATION TAXES ACT 1970 (C. 10)

1. For 's 1(3) of the British Nationality Act 1948', wherever it occurs (that is, in ss 181(1), 214(1)(b) and 372(2)(b)) substitute 'Schedule 3 to the British Nationality Act 1981'.

2. In s 214, after subsection (5) insert—

> '(6) In subsection (1)(b) above, the references to a country mentioned in Schedule 3 to the British Nationality Act 1981 do not include any country which, immediately before the commencement of the British Nationality Act 1981, was mentioned in s 1(3) of the British Nationality Act 1948 otherwise than by virtue of an enactment passed after 1956.'.

MERCHANT SHIPPING ACT 1970 (C. 36)

1. In s 70(3) (meaning of 'British seamen' in s 70), for 'the British Nationality Act 1948' substitute 'the British Nationality Act 1981'.

2. In s 93(3) (meaning of 'independent Commonwealth country' in s 93), for 'section 1(3) of the British Nationality Act 1948' substitute 'Schedule 3 to the British Nationality Act 1981'.

HIJACKING ACT 1971 (C. 70)

In s 1(3) (persons not within exceptions to offence of hijacking), for paras (a)–(e) substitute—

'(a) a British citizen, a British Dependent Territories citizen or a British Overseas citizen; or

(b) a person who under the British Nationality Act 1981 is a British subject; or

(c) a British protected person (within the meaning of that Act).'

CIVIL AVIATION ACT 1971 (C. 75)

In s 64(1) (interpretation), in the definition of 'United Kingdom national', for paras (a)–(e) substitute—

'(a) a British citizen, a British Dependent Territories citizen or a British Overseas citizen; or

(b) a person who under the British Nationality Act 1981 is a British subject; or

(c) a British protected person (within the meaning of that Act).'

PROTECTION OF AIRCRAFT ACT 1973 (C. 47)

In s 1(5) (persons not within exception to offence of destroying, etc aircraft), for paras (a)–(e) substitute—

'(a) a British citizen, a British Dependent Territories citizen or a British Overseas citizen; or

(b) a person who under the British Nationality Act 1981 is a British subject; or

(c) a British protected person (within the meaning of that Act).'.

CHILDREN ACT 1975 (C. 72)

1. In Part II of Schedule 1 (adoption orders)—

(a) in para 7(2)(a), for 'the British Nationality Acts 1948–65' substitute 'the British Nationality Act 1981'; and

(b) in para 7(2)(d), for 'citizenship of the United Kingdom and Colonies' substitute 'British citizenship, British Dependent Territories citizenship or British Overseas citizenship.'.

2. In Schedule 2 (status conferred in Scotland by adoption)—

(a) in para 1(4)(a), for 'the British Nationality Acts 1948–65' substitute 'the British Nationality Act 1981'; and

(b) in para 1(4)(d), for 'citizenship of the United Kingdom and Colonies' substitute 'British citizenship, British Dependent Territories citizenship or British Overseas citizenship'.

ADOPTION ACT 1976 (C. 36)

In s 47(2) (nationality enactments)—

(a) in para (a), for 'the British Nationality Acts 1948–65' substitute 'the British Nationality Act 1981'; and

(b) in para (d), for 'citizenship of the United Kingdom and Colonies' substitute 'British citizenship, British Dependent Territories citizenship or British Overseas citizenship'.

NATIONAL HEALTH SERVICE ACT 1977 (C. 49)

In para 3 of Schedule 11 (territorial extent)—

(a) in the definition of 'British protected person', for 'the British Nationality Acts 1948–65' substitute 'the British Nationality Act 1981'; and

(b) in the definition of 'excepted ship or aircraft', for 's 1(3) of the British Nationality Act 1948' substitute 'Schedule 3 to the British Nationality Act 1981'.

SOLOMON ISLANDS ACT 1978 (C. 15)

In s 6 (construction of nationality provisions)—

(a) in subsection (1), for 's 1(3) of the 1948 Act' substitute 'Schedule 3 to the British Nationality Act 1981';

(b) for subsection (2) substitute—

> '(2) The following provisions of the British Nationality Act 1981, namely ss 45 (evidence), 46 (offences and proceedings), 48 (posthumous children) and 50 (interpretation) shall have effect for the purposes of ss 2 to 6 of this Act as if those sections of this Act were included in that Act.'; and

(c) in subsection (3), for 's 23(2) of the 1948 Act' substitute 's 47(2) of the British Nationality Act 1981'.

ADOPTION (SCOTLAND) ACT 1978 (C. 28)

In s 41(2) (nationality enactments)—

(a) in para (a), for 'the British Nationality Acts 1948–65' substitute 'the British Nationality Act 1981'; and

(b) in para (d), for 'citizenship of the United Kingdom and Colonies' substitute 'British citizenship, British Dependent Territories citizenship or British Overseas citizenship'.

NATIONAL HEALTH SERVICE (SCOTLAND) ACT 1978 (C. 29)

In para 3 of Schedule 10 (territorial extent)—

(a) in the definition of 'British protected person', for 'the British Nationality Acts 1948–65' substitute 'the British Nationality Act 1981'; and

(b) in the definition of 'excepted ship or aircraft', for 's 1(3) of the British Nationality Act 1948' substitute 'Schedule 3 to the British Nationality Act 1981'.

STATE IMMUNITY ACT 1978 (C. 33)

In s 4(5) (definition of 'national of the United Kingdom'), for the words from 'means' onwards substitute 'means—

(a) a British citizen, a British Dependent Territories citizen or a British Overseas citizen; or

(b) a person who under the British Nationality Act 1981 is a British subject; or

(c) a British protected person (within the meaning of that Act)'.

DEEP SEA MINING (TEMPORARY PROVISIONS) ACT 1981 (C. 53)

1. In s 1 (prohibition of unlicensed deep sea mining)—

(a) in subsection (4), for 'citizen of the United Kingdom and Colonies' substitute 'United Kingdom national';

(b) in subsection (5)(a), for 'citizens of the United Kingdom and Colonies' and 'such citizens' substitute respectively 'United Kingdom nationals' and 'such nationals'; and

(c) in subsection (6), for the words from 'and references' onwards substitute—

'"United Kingdom national" means—

(a) a British citizen, a British Dependent Territories citizen or a British Overseas citizen;

(b) a person who under the British Nationality Act 1981 is a British subject; or

(c) a British protected person (within the meaning of that Act).'.

2. In s 14(3) (persons who may be guilty of offences under regulations), for 'a citizen of the United Kingdom and Colonies' substitute 'a British citizen, a British Dependent Territories citizen or a British Overseas citizen'.

SCHEDULE 8

TRANSITIONAL PROVISIONS

Applications for naturalisation or registration pending at commencement

1.—(1) This paragraph applies to any application—

(a) for registration under any provision of the British Nationality Acts 1948–65 as a citizen of the United Kingdom and Colonies or as a British subject; or

(b) for a certificate of naturalisation under s 10 of the 1948 Act,

which is received before commencement by a person authorised to receive it on behalf of the person to whom it is made but which at commencement has not been determined.

(2) In relation to any application to which this paragraph applies—

(a) the British Nationality Acts 1948–65 and all regulations and arrangements in force under them immediately before commencement shall (so far as applicable) continue to apply; and

(b) this Act shall not apply;

but on the granting of such an application and the taking under those Acts of such other steps as are necessary for the person in question to become—

(i) a citizen of the United Kingdom and Colonies by virtue of any provision of those Acts; or

(ii) a British subject by virtue of registration under any provision of those Acts,

that person, instead of becoming a citizen or subject of that description, shall become under this Act such a citizen or subject as he would have become at commencement if, immediately before commencement, he had been such a citizen or subject as is mentioned in para (i) or (ii), as the case may be.

(3) Sub-para (2) shall have effect as if the references in it to the British Nationality Acts 1948–65 did, and as if the reference in para (b) of it to this Act did not, include s 49 of this Act.

2. Where a person who has been registered or to whom a certificate of naturalisation has been granted before the passing of this Act has at commencement not yet taken the oath of allegiance, para 1(2) shall apply as if the application on which he was registered or the certificate was granted were an application to which para 1 applies.

Registration at the United Kingdom consulate, after commencement, of certain births occurring in foreign countries less than a year before commencement

3.—(1) This paragraph applies to a person born less than a year before commencement if—

(a) the birth occurred in a place in a foreign country (within the meaning of the 1948 Act); and

(b) at the time of the birth his father was a citizen of the United Kingdom and Colonies by descent only; and

(c) the birth was not registered at a United Kingdom consulate before commencement.

(2) If the birth of a person to whom this paragraph applies is registered at a United Kingdom consulate within one year of its occurrence, he shall be deemed for the purposes of this Act to have been, immediately before commencement, a citizen of the United Kingdom and Colonies by virtue of s 5 of the 1948 Act (citizenship by descent).

(3) References in this paragraph to the 1948 Act are references to that Act if in force at the time of the birth in question.

Declarations by certain persons who by virtue of an Order in Council under s 4 of the Cyprus Act 1960 have ceased to be citizens of the United Kingdom and Colonies

4.—(1) Where—

(a) a person has before commencement duly made a declaration under s 4(2) of the Cyprus Act 1960 of his intention to resume citizenship of the United Kingdom and Colonies; but

(b) at commencement the declaration has not been registered. the Secretary of State shall cause the declaration to be registered.

(2) If—

(a) a person who in consequence of anything done before he attained the age of 16 years ceased by virtue of an Order in Council under s 4 of the Cyprus Act 1960 to be a citizen of the United Kingdom and Colonies makes, in such a manner as the Secretary of State may direct, a declaration of his intention to accept the citizenship available to him under this paragraph; and

(b) the declaration is made by him after commencement and within one year after his attaining the age of 21 years,

the Secretary of State shall cause the declaration to be registered.

(3) On the registration under sub-para (1) or (2) of any such declaration as is there mentioned the person who made it shall become under this Act such a citizen as he would have become at commencement if, immediately before commencement, he had been a citizen of the United Kingdom and Colonies by virtue of s 4(2) of the Cyprus Act 1960.

Applications for certificates of patriality pending at commencement

5. Any application for a certificate of patriality under the Immigration Act 1971 duly made but not determined before commencement shall be treated as if it were an application for a certificate of entitlement under that Act as amended by this Act.

Appeals under Part II of Immigration Act 1971

6. Where a person who has been refused a certificate of patriality under the Immigration Act 1971 before commencement has immediately before commencement a right of appeal under Part II (appeals) of that Act against the refusal, the provisions of that Part shall have effect in relation to the refusal as if he had applied for, and been refused, a certificate of entitlement under that Act as amended by this Act.

7. Any appeal under Part II of the Immigration Act 1971 against a refusal of a certificate of patriality under that Act which is pending immediately before commencement shall be treated as if it were an appeal against a refusal of a certificate of entitlement under that Act as amended by this Act.

8. In relation to appeals against any decision taken or other thing done under the Immigration Act 1971 before commencement, other than a refusal of a certificate of patriality under that Act, the provisions of that Act shall continue to apply as in force immediately before commencement, and not as amended by this Act.

SCHEDULE 9

REPEALS

Chapter	Short title	Extent of repeal
11 & 12 Geo.6. c. 3.	Burma Independence Act 1947.	Section 2. Schedule 1.
11 &12 Geo.6. c. 56.	British Nationality Act 1948.	The whole Act except— (a) s 3; (b) s 32(3); (c) s 33(1) from the beginning to the words 'Isle of Man'; and (d) s 34(1).
12, 33 & 14 Geo. 6. c. 41	Ireland Act 1949.	Section 5.
14 Geo. 6. c. 5.	Newfoundland (Consequential Provisions) Act 1950.	The whole Act.
15 & 16 Geo.6 & I Eliz. 2. c. 67.	Visiting Forces Act 1952.	Section 15(3)(c) and (d).
5 & 6 Eliz. c. 6.	Ghana Independence Act 1957.	Section 2.
5 & 6 Eliz. 2. c. 60.	Federation of Malaya Independence Act 1957.	In Schedule 1, para l.
6 & 7 Eliz. 2. c. 10.	British Nationality Act 1958.	The whole Act.
7 & 8 Eliz. 2. c. 5.	Adoption Act 1958. In s 60(2), the words 'section nineteen, and'.	Section 19.
8 & 9 Eliz. 2. c. 52	Cyprus Act 1960. In the Schedule, para 1.	Section 4(2)–(4) and (7).
8 & 9 Eliz. 2. c. 55.	Nigeria Independence Act 1960.	Section 2.
9 & 10 Eliz. 2. c. 16.	Sierra Leone Independence Act 1961.	Section 2.
10 Eliz. 2. c. 1.	Tanganyika Independence Act 1961.	Section 2.
10 & 11 Eliz. 2. c. 8.	Civil Aviation (Eurocontrol) Act 1962.	Section 9(2).
10 & 11 Eliz. 2. c. 21.	Commonwealth Immigrants Act 1962.	Section 12(2) and (4).
10 & 11 Eliz. 2. c. 23.	South Africa Act 1962.	Schedule 1, Section 1(2).
10 & 11 Eliz.2. c. 40.	Jamaica Independence Act 1962.	Section 2.
10 & 11 Eliz.2. c. 54.	Trinidad and Tobago Independence Act 1962.	Section 2.
10 & 11 Eliz.2. c. 57.	Uganda Independence Act 1962.	Section 2.

Chapter	Short title	Extent of repeal
1963 c. 35.	Malaysia Act 1963.	Section 2. Schedule 1.
1963 c. 54.	Kenya Independence Act 1963.	Sections 2 and 3.
1963 c. 55.	Zanzibar Act 1963.	Section 2. Schedule 2.
1964 c. 5.	International Headquarters and Defence Organisations Act 1964.	Section 2(1)(e). In s 2(1)(d), the reference to para (e).
1964 c. 22.	British Nationality Act 1964.	The whole Act.
1964 c. 46.	Malawi Independence Act 1964.	Sections 2 and 3.
1964 c. 54.	British Nationality (No. 2) Act 1964.	The whole Act.
1964 c. 57.	Adoption Act 1964.	Section 1(3). In s 4(4), the words from 'except' to '1958'.
1964 c. 65.	Zambia Independence Act 1964.	Sections 3 and 4.
1964 c. 81.	Diplomatic Privileges Act 1964.	Section 5(2).
1964 c. 86.	Malta Independence Act 1964.	Sections 2 and 3.
1964 c. 93.	Gambia Independence Act 1964.	Sections 2 and 3.
1965 c. 34	British Nationality Act 1965.	The whole Act.
1966 c. 14.	Guyana Independence Act 1966.	Sections 2 and 3.
1966 c. 23.	Botswana Independence Act 1966.	Sections 3 and 4.
1966 c. 24.	Lesotho Independence Act 1966.	Sections 3 and 4.
1966 c. 29.	Singapore Act 1966.	In the Schedule. para 1.
1966 c. 37.	Barbados Independence Act 1966.	Sections 2 and 3.
1967 c. 4.	West Indies Act 1967.	Section 12. In Schedule 3, paras 1–3, 5 and 7 and, in para 4(1), the words from 'subject' to 'Schedule'.
1967 c. 71.	Aden, Perim and Kuria Muria Islands Act 1967.	Section 2. Schedule.
1968 c. 8.	Mauritius Independence Act 1968.	Sections 2 and 3.
1968 c. 18.	Consular Relations Act 1968.	Section 7.

Chapter	Short title	Extent of repeal
1968 c. 53.	Adoption Act 1968.	Section 9(5). In s 14(3), the words 'except ss 9(5) and this section'.
1968 c. 56.	Swaziland Independence Act 1968.	Sections 3 and 4.
1968 c. 59.	Hovercraft Act 1968.	In the Schedule, para 1(d).
1969 c. 29.	Tanzania Act 1969.	Section 1. Section 7(1)(a) and (2).
1969 c. 46.	Family Law Reform Act 1969.	Section 28(4)(a). In Schedule 1, the entry relating to the British Nationality Act 1948.
1970 c. 22.	Tonga Act 1970.	Section 2.
1970 c. 50.	Fiji Independence Act 1970.	Sections 2 and 3.
1971 c. 62.	Tribunals and Inquiries Act 1971.	In s 14(3), the words from 'affect' to '1948 or'.
1971 c. 77.	Immigration Act 1971.	In s 9(5), the words from 'other' to 'section 2'. Section 30(1). In s 31(a), the words from '(including' to 'Act)'. Schedule 1 (including Appendices A to C).
1972 c. 55.	Sri Lanka Republic Act 1972.	Section 1(3) and (5).
1973 c. 27.	Bahamas Independence Act 1973.	Section 2(1), (2) and (6).
1973 c. 48.	Pakistan Act 1973.	Section 1. Schedules 1 and 2.
1973 c. 49.	Bangladesh Act 1973.	Section 2.
1975 c. 31.	Malta Republic Act 1975.	Section 1(3).
1975 c. 72.	Children Act 1975.	In s 109(2)(b), the words 'and 63' and 'and'. Section 109(2)(c). In Schedule 3, para 63.
1976 c. 19.	Seychelles Act 1976.	Sections 3 and 4. Section 5(3)
1976 c. 36.	Adoption Act 1976.	Section 40. In s 47(2), the words 'Without prejudice to s 40'. In s 74(4), the words from 'except' to '1968'.
1976 c. 54.	Trinidad and Tobago Republic Act 1976.	Section 1(3).

Chapter	Short title	Extent of repeal
1978 c. 15.	Solomon Islands Act 1978.	Section 2(1). Section 4(5). Section 5(1) and (3).
1978 c. 20.	Tuvalu Act 1978.	Sections 2, 3 and 5(2).
1978 c. 23.	Judicature (Northern Ireland) Act 1978.	Section 22(2)(a).
1978 c. 28.	Adoption (Scotland) Act 1978.	Section 40. In s 41(2), the words 'Without prejudice to s40'
1978 c. 30.	Interpretation Act 1978.	In s 24(4), the words 'British subject and Commonwealth citizen;'. In Schedule 1, the entry defining 'British subject' and 'Commonwealth citizen'. In Schedule 2, in para 6, the words 'British subject and Commonwealth citizen;'.
1979 c. 27.	Kiribati Act 1979.	Section 3(3). Sections 4 and 5. Section 7(2).
1979 c. 60.	Zimbabwe Act 1979.	Section 2. In s 5(2) (a) para (a); and (b) in para (b), the words '1 or'. Schedule 1.
1980 c. 2.	Papua New Guinea, Western Samoa Nauru (Miscellaneous Provisions) Act 1980.	In s 1, subsection (1) and, and in subsection (3), the reference to s 3(2). Section 2. Section 3(2).
1980 c. 16.	New Hebrides Act 1980.	Section 1. In s 4(2), the reference to s 1(2).
1981 c. 52.	Belize Act 1981.	Section 4(1).
1981 c. 61.	British Nationality Act 1981.	Section 49.

Asylum and Immigration Appeals Act 1993

CHAPTER 23

ARRANGEMENT OF SECTIONS

Introductory

Section
1. Interpretation.
2. Primacy of Convention.

Treatment of persons who claim asylum

3. Fingerprinting.
4. Housing of asylum-seekers and their dependants.
5. Housing: interpretative provisions.
6. Protection of claimants from deportation, etc.
7. Curtailment of leave to enter or remain.

Rights of appeal

8. Appeals to special adjudicator.
9. Appeals from Immigration Appeal Tribunal.
10. Visitors, short-term and prospective students and their dependants.
11. Refusals which are mandatory under immigration rules.

Visas for transit passengers

12. Carriers' liability for transit passengers.

Supplementary

13. Financial provision.
14. Commencement.
15. Extent.
16. Short title.

SCHEDULES—

Schedule 1—Housing of asylum-seekers and their dependants: supplementary.

Schedule 2—Appeals to special adjudicator: supplementary.

Asylum and Immigration Appeals Act 1993

1993 CHAPTER 23

An Act to make provision about persons who claim asylum in the United Kingdom and their dependants; to amend the law with respect to certain rights of appeal under the Immigration Act 1971; and to extend the provisions of the Immigration (Carriers' Liability) Act 1987 to transit passengers.

[1 July 1993]

BE IT ENACTED by the Queen's most Excellent Majesty, by and with the advice and consent of the Lords Spiritual and Temporal, and Commons, in this present Parliament assembled, and by the authority of the same, as follows—

Introductory

Interpretation

1. In this Act—

'the 1971 Act' means the Immigration Act 1971;

'claim for asylum' means a claim made by a person (whether before or after the coming into force of this section) that it would be contrary to the United Kingdom's obligations under the Convention for him to be removed from, or required to leave, the United Kingdom; and

'the Convention' means the Convention relating to the Status of Refugees done at Geneva on 28 July 1951 and the Protocol to that Convention.

Primacy of Convention

2. Nothing in the immigration rules (within the meaning of the 1971 Act) shall lay down any practice which would be contrary to the Convention.

Treatment of persons who claim asylum

Fingerprinting

3.—(1) Where a person ('the claimant') has made a claim for asylum, an immigration officer, constable, prison officer or officer of the Secretary of State authorised for the purposes of this section may—

(a) take such steps as may be reasonably necessary for taking the claimant's fingerprints; or

(b) by notice in writing require the claimant to attend at a place specified in the notice in order that such steps may be taken.

(2) The powers conferred by subsection (1) above may be exercised not only in relation to the claimant but also in relation to any dependant of his;

but in the exercise of the power conferred by para (a) of that subsection, fingerprints shall not be taken from a person under the age of 16 ('the child') except in the presence of a person of full age who is—

(a) the child's parent or guardian; or

(b) a person who for the time being takes responsibility for the child and is not an immigration officer, constable, prison officer or officer of the Secretary of State.

(3) Where the claimant's claim for asylum has been finally determined or abandoned—

(a) the powers conferred by subsection (1) above shall not be exerciseable in relation to him or any dependant of his; and

(b) any requirement imposed on him or any dependant of his by a notice under subsection (1)(b) above shall no longer have effect.

(4) A notice given to any person under para (b) of subsection (1) above—

(a) shall give him a period of at least seven days within which he is to attend as mentioned in that paragraph; and

(b) may require him so to attend at a specified time of day or between specified times of day.

(5) Any immigration officer or constable may arrest without warrant a person who has failed to comply with a requirement imposed on him by a notice under subsection (1)(b) above (unless the requirement no longer has effect) and, where a person is arrested under this subsection,—

(a) he may be removed to a place where his fingerprints may conveniently be taken, and

(b) (whether or not he is so removed) there may be taken such steps as may be reasonably necessary for taking his fingerprints,

before he is released.

(6) Fingerprints of a person which are taken by virtue of this section must be destroyed not later than the earlier of—

(a) the end of the period of one month beginning with any day on which he is given indefinite leave under the 1971 Act to enter or remain in the United Kingdom; and

(b) the end of the period of 10 years beginning with the day on which the fingerprints are taken.

(7) Where fingerprints taken by virtue of this section are destroyed—

(a) any copies of the fingerprints shall also be destroyed; and

(b) if there are any computer data relating to the fingerprints, the Secretary of State shall, as soon as it is practicable to do so, make it impossible for access to be gained to the data.

(8) If—

(a) subsection (7)(b) above falls to be complied with, and

(b) the person to whose fingerprints the data relate asks for a certificate that it has been complied with,

such a certificate shall be issued to him by the Secretary of State not later than the end of the period of three months beginning with the day on which he asks for it.

(9) In this section—

(a) 'immigration officer' means an immigration officer appointed for the purposes of the 1971 Act; and

(b) 'dependant', in relation to the claimant, means a person—

(i) who is his spouse or a child of his under the age of 18; and

(ii) who has neither a right of abode in the United Kingdom nor indefinite leave under the 1971 Act to enter or remain in the United Kingdom.

(10) Nothing in this section shall be taken to limit the power conferred by para 18(2) of Schedule 2 to the 1971 Act.

Housing of asylum-seekers and their dependants

4.—(1) If a person ('the applicant') makes an application under the homelessness legislation for accommodation or assistance in obtaining accommodation and the housing authority who are dealing with his case are satisfied—

(a) that he is an asylum-seeker or the dependant of an asylum-seeker, and

(b) that he has or has available for his occupation any accommodation, however temporary, which it would be reasonable for him to occupy,

nothing in the homelessness legislation shall require the housing authority to secure that accommodation is made available for his occupation.

(2) In determining for the purposes of subsection (1)(b) above whether it would be reasonable for the applicant to occupy accommodation, regard may be had to the general circumstances prevailing in relation to housing in the district of the housing authority who are dealing with the applicant's case.

(3) Where, on an application made as mentioned in subsection (1) above, the housing authority are satisfied that the applicant is an asylum-seeker or the dependant of an asylum-seeker, but are not satisfied as mentioned in para (b) of that subsection, then, subject to subsection (4) below,—

(a) any duty under the homelessness legislation to secure that accommodation is made available for the applicant's occupation shall not continue after he ceases to be an asylum-seeker or a dependant of an asylum-seeker; and

(b) accordingly, so long as the applicant remains an asylum-seeker or the dependant of an asylum-seeker, any need of his for accommodation shall be regarded as temporary only.

(4) If, immediately before he ceases to be an asylum-seeker or the dependant of an asylum-seeker, the applicant is occupying accommodation (whether temporary or not) made available in pursuance of the homelessness legislation, that legislation shall apply as if, at that time—

(a) he were not occupying that accommodation; and

(b) he had made an application under that legislation for accommodation or assistance in obtaining accommodation to the housing authority who secured that accommodation was made available.

(5) Schedule 1 to this Act (which makes supplementary provision with respect to housing of asylum-seekers and their dependants) shall have effect.

Housing: interpretative provisions

5.—(1) The provisions of this section have effect for the purposes of s 4 above and Schedule 1 to this Act; and that section and Schedule are in the following provisions of this section referred to as 'the housing provisions'.

(2) For the purposes of the housing provisions a person who makes a claim for asylum—

(a) becomes an asylum-seeker at the time when his claim is recorded by the Secretary of State as having been made; and

(b) ceases to be an asylum-seeker at the time when his claim is recorded by the Secretary of State as having been finally determined or abandoned.

(3) For the purposes of the housing provisions, a person—

(a) becomes a dependant of an asylum-seeker at the time when he is recorded by the Secretary of State as being a dependant of the asylum-seeker; and

(b) ceases to be a dependant of an asylum-seeker at the time when the person whose dependant he is ceases to be an asylum-seeker or, if it is earlier, at the time when he is recorded by the Secretary of State as ceasing to be a dependant of the asylum-seeker.

(4) References in subsections (2) and (3) above to a time when an event occurs include references to a time before as well as after the passing of this Act.

(5) In relation to an asylum-seeker, 'dependant' means a person—

(a) who is his spouse or a child of his under the age of 18; and

(b) who has neither a right of abode in the United Kingdom nor indefinite leave under the 1971 Act to enter or remain in the United Kingdom.

(6) Except in their application to Northern Ireland, in the housing provisions—

(a) 'the homelessness legislation' means, in relation to England and Wales, Part III of the Housing Act 1985 and, in relation to Scotland, Part II of the Housing (Scotland) Act 1987;

(b) 'housing authority' means—

(i) in relation to England and Wales, any authority which is a local housing authority for the purposes of Part III of the Housing Act 1985; and

(ii) in relation to Scotland, any authority which is a local authority for the purposes of Part II of the Housing (Scotland) Act 1987;

and references to a housing authority who are dealing with an applicant's case shall be construed as references to the authority to whom the application is made or (as the case may be) the authority who under the homelessness legislation are the notified authority in relation to the applicant.

(7) In the application of the housing provisions to Northern Ireland—

(a) 'the homelessness legislation' means Part II of the Housing (Northern Ireland) Order 1988;

(b) 'housing authority' means the Northern Ireland Housing Executive and references to a housing authority who are dealing with an applicant's case shall be construed as references to that Executive; and

(c) references to the district of a housing authority shall be construed as references to Northern Ireland.

(8) For the purposes of the housing provisions accommodation shall be regarded as available for the applicant's occupation only if it is available for occupation both by him and by any other person who might reasonably be expected to reside with him and references to securing accommodation for his occupation shall be construed accordingly.

Protection of claimants from deportation, etc

6. During the period beginning when a person makes a claim for asylum and ending when the Secretary of State gives him notice of the decision on the claim, he may not be removed from, or required to leave, the United Kingdom.

Curtailment of leave to enter or remain

7.—(1) Where—

(a) a person who has limited leave under the 1971 Act to enter or remain in the United Kingdom claims that it would be contrary to the United Kingdom's obligations under the Convention for him to be required to leave the United Kingdom after the time limited by the leave; and

(b) the Secretary of State has considered the claim and given to the person notice in writing of his rejection of it,

the Secretary of State may by notice in writing, given to the person concurrently with the notice under para (b) above, curtail the duration of the leave.

(2) No appeal may be brought under s 14 of the 1971 Act or s 8(2) below against the curtailment of leave under subsection (1) above.

(3) The power conferred by subsection (1) above is without prejudice to ss 3(3) and 4 of the 1971 Act and the immigration rules (within the meaning of that Act).

(4) Where—

(a) the duration of a person's leave under the 1971 Act to enter or remain in the United Kingdom has been curtailed under subsection (1) above; and

(b) the Secretary of State has decided to make a deportation order against him by virtue of s 3(5) of that Act,

he may be detained under the authority of the Secretary of State pending the making of the deportation order; and the references to sub-para (2) of para 2 of Schedule 3 to that Act in sub-paras (3), (4) and (6) of that paragraph (provisions about detention under sub-para (2)) shall include references to this subsection.

Rights of appeal

Appeals to special adjudicator

8.—(1) A person who is refused leave to enter the United Kingdom under the 1971 Act may appeal against the refusal to a special adjudicator on the ground that his removal in consequence of the refusal would be contrary to the United Kingdom's obligations under the Convention.

(2) A person who has limited leave under the 1971 Act to enter or remain in the United Kingdom may appeal to a special adjudicator against any variation of, or refusal to vary, the leave on the ground that it would be contrary to the United Kingdom's obligations under the Convention for him to be required to leave the United Kingdom after the time limited by the leave.

(3) Where the Secretary of State—

(a) has decided to make a deportation order against a person by virtue of s 3(5) of the 1971 Act, or

(b) has refused to revoke a deportation order made against a person by virtue of s 3(5) or (6) of that Act,

the person may appeal to a special adjudicator against the decision or refusal on the ground that his removal in pursuance of the order would be contrary to the United Kingdom's obligations under the Convention; but a person may not bring an appeal under both para (a) and para (b) above.

(4) Where directions are given as mentioned in s 16(1)(a) or (b) of the 1971 Act for a person's removal from the United Kingdom, the person may appeal to a special adjudicator against the directions on the ground that his removal in pursuance of the directions would be contrary to the United Kingdom's obligations under the Convention.

(5) The Lord Chancellor shall designate such number of the adjudicators appointed for the purposes of Part II of the 1971 Act as he thinks necessary to act as special adjudicators for the purposes of this section and may from time to time vary that number and the persons who are so designated.

(6) Schedule 2 to this Act (which makes supplementary provision about appeals under this section) shall have effect; and the preceding provisions of this section shall have effect subject to that Schedule.

Appeals from Immigration Appeal Tribunal

9.—(1) Where the Immigration Appeal Tribunal has made a final determination of an appeal brought under Part II of the 1971 Act (including that Part as it applies by virtue of Schedule 2 to this Act) any party to the appeal may bring a further appeal to the appropriate appeal court on any question of law material to that determination.

(2) An appeal under this section may be brought only with the leave of the Immigration Appeal Tribunal or, if such leave is refused, with the leave of the appropriate appeal court.

(3) In this section 'the appropriate appeal court' means—

(a) if the appeal is from the determination of an adjudicator or special adjudicator and that determination was made in Scotland, the Court of Session; and

(b) in any other case, the Court of Appeal.

(4) Rules of procedure under s 22 of the 1971 Act may include provision regulating, and prescribing the procedure to be followed on, applications to the Immigration Appeal Tribunal for leave to appeal under this section.

(5) In s 33(4) of the 1971 Act—

(a) for the words 'in the case of an appeal to an adjudicator, the' there shall be substituted 'an'; and

(b) after the words 'section 20' there shall be inserted 'or s 9 of the Asylum and Immigration Appeals Act 1993'.

Visitors, short-term and prospective students and their dependants

10. In s 13 of the 1971 Act (appeals against exclusion from United Kingdom), after subsection (3) there shall be inserted—

'(3A) A person who seeks to enter the United Kingdom—

(a) as a visitor, or

(b) in order to follow a course of study of not more than six months duration for which he has been accepted, or

(c) with the intention of studying but without having been accepted for any course of study, or

(d) as a dependant of a person within para (a), (b) or (c) above,

shall not be entitled to appeal against a refusal of an entry clearance and shall not be entitled to appeal against a refusal of leave to enter unless he held a current entry clearance at the time of the refusal.

(3AA) The Secretary of State shall appoint a person, not being an officer of his, to monitor, in such manner as the Secretary of State may determine, refusals of entry clearance in cases where there is, by virtue of subsection (3A) above, no right of appeal; and the person so appointed shall make an annual report on the discharge of his functions to the Secretary of State who shall lay a copy of it before each House of Parliament.

(3AB) The Secretary of State may pay to a person appointed under subsection (3AA) above such fees and allowances as he may with the approval of the Treasury determine.'

Refusals which are mandatory under immigration rules

11.—(1) In s 13 of the 1971 Act, after subsection (3AB) (which is inserted by s 10 above) there shall be inserted—

'(3B) A person shall not be entitled to appeal against a refusal of an entry clearance if the refusal is on the ground that—

(a) he or any person whose dependant he is does not hold a relevant document which is required by the immigration rules; or

(b) he or any person whose dependant he is does not satisfy a requirement of the immigration rules as to age or nationality or citizenship; or

(c) he or any person whose dependant he is seeks entry for a period exceeding that permitted by the immigration rules;

and a person shall not be entitled to appeal against a refusal of leave to enter if the refusal is on any of those grounds.

(3C) For the purposes of subsection (3B)(a) above, the following are 'relevant documents'—

(a) entry clearances;

(b) passports or other identity documents; and

(c) work permits.'

(2) In s 14 of the 1971 Act (appeals against refusals to vary leave to enter or remain), after subsection (2) there shall be inserted—

'(2A) A person shall not be entitled to appeal under subsection (1) above against any refusal to vary his leave if the refusal is on the ground that—

(a) a relevant document which is required by the immigration rules has not been issued; or

(b) the person or a person whose dependant he is does not satisfy a requirement of the immigration rules as to age or nationality or citizenship; or

(c) the variation would result in the duration of the person's leave exceeding what is permitted by the immigration rules; or

(d) any fee required by or under any enactment has not been paid.

(2B) For the purposes of subsection (2A)(a) above, the following are relevant documents—

(a) entry clearances;

(b) passports or other identity documents; and

(c) work permits.'

Visas for transit passengers

Carriers' liability for transit passengers

12.—(1) The Immigration (Carriers' Liability) Act 1987 shall be amended as follows.

(2) In subsection (l)(b) of s 1 (liability of carrier of person who requires a visa for entry but fails to produce one) for the words ', a visa valid for that purpose,' there shall be substituted the words 'or by virtue of s 1A below requires a visa for passing through the United Kingdom, a visa valid for the purpose of entering or (as the case may be) passing through the United Kingdom,'.

(3) After that section there shall be inserted—

'Visas for transit passengers

1A.—(1) The Secretary of State may by order require persons of any description specified in the order who on arrival in the United Kingdom pass through to another country or territory without entering the United Kingdom to hold a visa for that purpose.

(2) An order under this section—

(a) may specify a description of persons by reference to nationality, citizenship, origin or other connection with any particular country or territory, but not by reference to race, colour or religion;

(b) shall not provide for the requirement imposed by the order to apply to any person who under the Immigration Act 1971 has the right of abode in the United Kingdom and may provide for any category of persons of a description specified in the order to be exempted from the requirement imposed by the order; and

(c) may make provision about the method of application for visas required by the order.

(3) An order under this section shall be made by statutory instrument which shall be subject to annulment in pursuance of a resolution of either House of Parliament.'

Supplementary

Financial provision

13.—(1) There shall be paid out of money provided by Parliament—

(a) any expenditure incurred by the Secretary of State under this Act; and

(b) any increase attributable to this Act in the sums payable out of such money under any other enactment.

(2) Any sums received by the Secretary of State by virtue of this Act shall be paid into the Consolidated Fund.

Commencement

14.—(1) Sections 4–11 above (and s 1 above so far as it relates to those sections) shall not come into force until such day as the Secretary of State may by order appoint, and different days may be appointed for different provisions or for different purposes.

(2) An order under subsection (1) above—

(a) shall be made by statutory instrument; and

(b) may contain such transitional and supplemental provisions as the Secretary of State thinks necessary or expedient.

(3) Without prejudice to the generality of subsections (1) and (2) above, with respect to any provision of s 4 above an order under subsection (1) above may appoint different days in relation to different descriptions of asylum-seekers and dependants of asylum-seekers; and any such descriptions may be framed by reference to nationality, citizenship, origin or other connection with any particular country or territory, but not by reference to race, colour or religion.

Extent

15.—(1) Her Majesty may by Order in Council direct that any of the provisions of this Act shall extend, with such modifications as appear to Her Majesty to be appropriate, to any of the Channel Islands or the Isle of Man.

(2) This Act extends to Northern Ireland.

Short title

16. This Act may be cited as the Asylum and Immigration Appeals Act 1993.

SCHEDULES

SCHEDULE I

HOUSING OF ASYLUM-SEEKERS AND THEIR DEPENDANTS: SUPPLEMENTARY

Qualifying persons

1. In this Schedule the expression 'qualifying person' means an asylum-seeker or a dependant of an asylum-seeker.

Inquiries about applicants

2. If a housing authority to whom an application is made have reason to believe that the applicant is a qualifying person, they shall include in the inquiries that they are required to make under s 62 of the Housing Act 1985, s 28 of the Housing (Scotland) Act 1987 or, as the case may be, Article 7 of the Housing (Northern Ireland) Order 1988 such inquiries as are necessary to satisfy them as to whether—

(a) he is a qualifying person; and

(b) if so, whether any duty is owed to him to secure that accommodation is made available for his occupation.

Notification of decision and reasons

3.—(1) Subject to sub-para (2) below, if a housing authority who are dealing with an applicant's case are satisfied that he is a qualifying person they shall notify him—

(a) that they are so satisfied;

(b) that they are or, as the case may be, are not satisfied that a duty is owed to him to secure that accommodation is made available for his occupation;

(c) if they are the authority to whom the application is made, whether they have notified or propose to notify another housing authority under s 67 of the Act of 1985 or, as the case may be, s 33 of the Act of 1987 (referral of application on grounds of local connection) as modified by para 4 below;

and they shall at the same time notify him of their reasons.

(2) In its application to Northern Ireland, sub-para (1) above shall have effect as if para (c) were omitted.

(3) The notice required to be given to the applicant under sub-para (1) above shall be given in writing and shall, if not received by him, be treated as having been given to him only if it is made available at the authority's office for a reasonable period for collection by him or on his behalf.

(4) Where notice is given under sub-para (1) above, no notice need be given under s 64 of the Act of 1985, s 30 of the Act of 1987 or, as the case may be, Article 9 of the Order of 1988 (notification of decision and reasons).

Referral of application to another housing authority

4.—(1) If a housing authority to whom an application is made are satisfied that the applicant is a qualifying person and that a duty to secure that accommodation is made available for his occupation is owed to him, the homelessness legislation shall have effect as if in s 67 of the Act of 1985 or, as the case may be, s 33 of the Act of 1987 for para (a) of subsection (1) there were substituted—

> '(a) are satisfied that an applicant is a qualifying person and that a duty to secure that accommodation is made available for his occupation is owed to him.'

(2) Sub-para (1) above does not apply in relation to Northern Ireland.

Offences

5. Section 74 of the Act of 1985, s 40 of the Act of 1987 or, as the case may be, Article 17 of the Order of 1988 applies to statements made or information withheld with intent to induce an authority to believe that a person is or is not an asylum-seeker or a dependant of an asylum-seeker as it applies to statements made or information withheld with the intent mentioned in subsection (1) of s 74, s 40 or, as the case may be, Article 17.

Security of tenure

6.—(1) A tenancy granted in pursuance of any duty under Part III of the Act of 1985 to a person who is a qualifying person cannot be—

(a) a tenancy which is a secure tenancy for the purposes of that Act, or

(b) a tenancy which is an assured tenancy for the purposes of the Housing Act 1988,

before the expiry of the period of 12 months beginning with the date on which the landlord is supplied with written information given by the Secretary of State under para 7 below that the person has ceased to be a qualifying person, unless before the expiry of that period the landlord notifies that person that the tenancy is to be regarded as a secure tenancy or, as the case may be, an assured tenancy.

(2) A tenancy granted in pursuance of any duty under Part II of the Order of 1988 to a person who is a qualifying person cannot be a tenancy which is a secure tenancy for the purposes of Part II of the Housing (Northern Ireland) Order 1983 before the expiry of the period of 12 months beginning with the date on which the landlord is supplied with written information given by the Secretary of State under para 7 below that the person has ceased to be a qualifying person, unless before the expiry of that period the landlord notifies that person that the tenancy is to be regarded as a secure tenancy.

Information

7.—(1) The Secretary of State shall, if requested to do so by a housing authority who are dealing with an applicant's case, inform the authority whether the applicant has become a qualifying person.

(2) Where information which the Secretary of State is required to give to a housing authority under sub-para (1) above is given otherwise than in writing, he shall confirm it in writing if a written request is made to him by the authority.

(3) If the Secretary of State informs an authority that an applicant has become a qualifying person, he shall, when the applicant ceases to be a qualifying person, inform the authority and the applicant in writing of that event and of the date on which it occurred.

Existing applicants

8.—(1) Nothing in s 4 or s 5 of this Act or this Schedule shall affect—

(a) the right of any person to occupy (or to have made available for his occupation) accommodation which, immediately before the day on which s 4 comes into force, is required to be made available for his occupation in pursuance of the homelessness legislation; or

(b) any application made to a housing authority which immediately before that day is a pending application.

(2) For the purposes of sub-para (1) above an application shall be regarded as pending if it is an application in respect of which the authority have not completed the inquiries that they are required to make under s 62 of the Housing Act 1985, s 28 of the Housing (Scotland) Act 1987 or, as the case may be, Article 7 of the Housing (Northern Ireland) Order 1988.

Isles of Scilly

9.—(1) The provisions of ss 4 and 5 of this Act and this Schedule shall apply to the Isles of Scilly subject to such exceptions, adaptations and modifications as the Secretary of State may by order direct.

(2) An order under sub-para (1) above shall be made by statutory instrument which shall be subject to annulment in pursuance of a resolution of either House of Parliament.

SCHEDULE 2

APPEALS TO SPECIAL ADJUDICATOR: SUPPLEMENTARY

New appeal rights to replace rights under the 1971 Act

1. No appeal may be brought under Part II of the 1971 Act on any of the grounds mentioned in subsections (1)–(4) of s 8 of this Act.

Scope of new rights of appeal

2. A person may not bring an appeal on any of the grounds mentioned in subsections (1)–(4) of s 8 of this Act unless, before the time of the refusal, variation, decision or directions (as the case may be), he has made a claim for asylum.

Other grounds of appeal

3. Where an appeal is brought by a person on any of the grounds mentioned in subsections (1) to (4) of s 8 of this Act, the special adjudicator shall in the same proceedings deal with—

(a) any appeal against the refusal, variation, decision or directions (as the case may be) which the person is entitled to bring under Part II of the 1971 Act on any other ground on which he seeks to rely; and

(b) any appeal brought by the person under that Part of that Act against any other decision or action.

Application of procedures in the 1971 Act

4.—(1) Subject to sub-paras (3) and (4) of this paragraph and to para 5 below, the provisions of the 1971 Act specified in sub-para (2) below shall have effect as if s 8 of this Act were contained in Part II of that Act.

(2) The provisions referred to in sub-para (1) above are—

(a) s 18 (notice of decisions appealable under that Part and statement of appeal rights, etc);

(b) s 19 (determination of appeals under that Part by adjudicators);

(c) s 20 (appeal from adjudicator to Immigration Appeal Tribunal);

(d) s 21 (references of cases by Secretary of Slate for further consideration);

(e) s 22(1)–(4), (6) and (7) (rules of procedure for appeals);

(f) s 23 (grants to voluntary organisations helping persons with rights of appeal); and

(g) Schedule 5 (provisions about adjudicators and Immigration Appeal Tribunal).

(3) Rules of procedure under s 22 may make special provision in relation to

(a) proceedings on appeals on any of the grounds mentioned in subsections (1)–(4) of s 8 of this Act; and

(b) proceedings in which. by virtue of para 3 above, a special adjudicator is required to deal both with an appeal on any of those grounds and another appeal.

(4) So much of para 5 of Schedule 5 as relates to the allocation of duties among the adjudicators shall have effect subject to subsection (5) of s 8 of this Act.

Special appeal procedures for claims without foundation

5.—(1) Subject to sub-para (2) below, this paragraph applies to an appeal by a person under subsection (1), (3)(b) or (4) of s 8 of this Act if the Secretary of State has certified that, in his opinion, the person's claim on the ground that it would be contrary to the United Kingdom's obligations under the Convention for him to be removed from the United Kingdom is without foundation.

(2) This paragraph does not apply to an appeal on the ground mentioned in subsection (1) of s 8 of this Act if, by virtue of s 13(3) of the 1971 Act (right of appeal for person with current entry clearance or work permit), the appellant seeks to rely on another ground.

(3) For the purposes of this paragraph a claim is without foundation if (and only if)—

(a) it does not raise any issue as to the United Kingdom's obligations under the Convention; or

(b) it is otherwise frivolous or vexatious.

(4) Rules of procedure under s 22 of the 1971 Act may make special provision in relation to appeals to which this paragraph applies.

(5) If on an appeal to which this paragraph applies the special adjudicator agrees that the claim is without foundation, s 20(1) of that Act shall not confer on the appellant any right to appeal to the Immigration Appeal Tribunal.

(6) If the special adjudicator does not agree that the claim is without foundation, he may (as an alternative to allowing or dismissing the appeal)

refer the case to the Secretary of State for reconsideration; and the making of such a reference shall, accordingly, be regarded as disposing of the appeal.

Exception for national security

6. Subsection (5) of s 13, subsection (3) of s 14 and subsections (3) and (4) of s 15 of the 1971 Act shall have effect in relation to the rights of appeal conferred by s 8(1), (2) and (3)(a) and (b) of this Act respectively as they have effect in relation to the rights of appeal conferred by subsection (1) of those sections of that Act but as if references to a person's exclusion, departure or deportation being conducive to the public good were references to its being in the interests of national security.

Suspension of variation of limited leave pending appeal

7. The limitation on the taking effect of a variation and on a requirement to leave the United Kingdom contained in subsection (1) of s 14 of the 1971 Act shall have effect as if appeals under s 8(2) of this Act were appeals under that subsection.

Deportation order not to be made while appeal pending

8. In s 15(2) of the 1971 Act references to an appeal against a decision to make a deportation order shall include references to an appeal against such a decision under s 8(3)(a) of this Act.

Stay of removal directions pending appeal and bail

9. Part II of Schedule 2, and para 3 of Schedule 3, to the 1971 Act shall have effect as if the references to appeals under s 13(1), 15(1)(a) and 16 of that Act included (respectively) appeals under s 8(1), (3) and (4) of this Act and as if sub-para (5) of para 28 of Schedule 2 were omitted.

Asylum and Immigration Act 1996

CHAPTER 49

ARRANGEMENT OF SECTIONS

Asylum claims

Section

1. Extension of special appeals procedures.
2. Removal, etc of asylum claimants to safe third countries.
3. Appeals against certificates under s 2.

Immigration offences

4. Obtaining leave by deception.
5. Assisting asylum claimants, and persons seeking to obtain leave by deception.
6. Increased penalties.
7. Power of arrest and search warrants.

Persons subject to immigration control

8. Restrictions on employment.
9. Entitlement to housing accommodation and assistance.
10. Entitlement to child benefit.
11. Saving for social security regulations.

Miscellaneous and supplemental

12. Other amendments and repeals.
13. Short title, interpretation, commencement and extent.

SCHEDULES—

Schedule I—Modifications of social security regulations.

Part I—Social Security (Persons From Abroad) Miscellaneous Amendments Regulations 1996.

Part II—Social Security (Persons From Abroad) (Miscellaneous Amendments) Regulations (Northern Ireland) 1996.

Schedule 2—Amendments of the 1971 Act and the Immigration Act 1988.

Schedule 3—Amendments of the 1993 Act.

Schedule 4—Repeals.

Asylum and Immigration Act 1996

1996 CHAPTER 49

An Act to amend and supplement the Immigration Act 1971 and the Asylum and Immigration Appeals Act 1993; to make further provision with respect to persons subject to immigration control and the employment of such persons; and for connected purposes.

[24 July 1996]

BE IT ENACTED by the Queen s most Excellent Majesty, by and with the advice and consent of the Lords Spiritual and Temporal, and Commons, in this present Parliament assembled, and by the authority of the same, as follows—

Asylum claims

Extension of special appeals procedures

1. For para 5 of Schedule 2 to the Asylum and Immigration Appeals Act 1993 ('the 1993 Act') there shall be substituted the following paragraph—

'5.—(1) This paragraph applies to an appeal by a person on any of the grounds mentioned in subsections (1)–(4) of s 8 of this Act if the Secretary of State has certified that, in his opinion, the person's claim on the ground that it would be contrary to the United Kingdom's obligations under the Convention for him to be removed from, or be required to leave, the United Kingdom is one to which—

(a) sub-para (2), (3) or (4) below applies; and

(b) sub-para (5) below does not apply.

(2) This sub-paragraph applies to a claim if the country or territory to which the appellant is to be sent is designated in an order made by the Secretary of State by statutory instrument as a country or territory in which it appears to him that there is in general no serious risk of persecution.

(3) This sub-paragraph applies to a claim if, on his arrival in the United Kingdom, the appellant was required by an immigration officer to produce a valid passport and either—

(a) he failed to produce a passport without giving a reasonable explanation for his failure to do so; or

(b) he produced a passport which was not in fact valid and failed to inform the officer of that fact.

(4) This sub-paragraph applies to a claim if—

(a) it does not show a fear of persecution by reason of the appellant's race, religion, nationality, membership of a particular social group, or political opinion;

(b) it shows a fear of such persecution, but the fear is manifestly unfounded or the circumstances which gave rise to the fear no longer subsist;

(c) it is made at any time after the appellant—

(i) has been refused leave to enter under the 1971 Act,

(ii) has been recommended for deportation by a court empowered by that Act to do so,

(iii) has been notified of the Secretary of State's decision to make a deportation order against him by virtue of s 3(5) of that Act, or

(iv) has been notified of his liability to removal under para 9 of Schedule 2 to that Act;

(d) it is manifestly fraudulent, or any of the evidence adduced in its support is manifestly false; or

(e) it is frivolous or vexatious.

(5) This sub-paragraph applies to a claim if the evidence adduced in its support establishes a reasonable likelihood that the appellant has been tortured in the country or territory to which he is to be sent.

(6) Rules of procedure under s 22 of the 1971 Act may make special provision in relation to appeals to which this paragraph applies.

(7) If on an appeal to which this paragraph applies the special adjudicator agrees that the claim is one to which—

(a) sub-para (2), (3) or (4) above applies; and

(b) sub-para (5) above does not apply,

s 20(1) of that Act shall not confer on the appellant any right to appeal to the Immigration Appeal Tribunal.

(8) The first order under this paragraph shall not be made unless a draft of the order has been laid before and approved by a resolution of each House of Parliament.

(9) A statutory instrument containing a subsequent order under this paragraph shall be subject to annulment in pursuance of a resolution of either House of Parliament.

(10) In this paragraph—

'immigration officer' means an immigration officer appointed for the purposes of the 1971 Act;

'passport', in relation to an appellant, means a passport with photograph or some other document satisfactorily establishing his identity and nationality or citizenship.'

Removal, etc of asylum claimants to safe third countries

2.—(1) Nothing in s 6 of the 1993 Act (protection of claimants from deportation, etc) shall prevent a person who has made a claim for asylum being removed from the United Kingdom if—

(a) the Secretary of State has certified that, in his opinion, the conditions mentioned in subsection (2) below are fulfilled;

(b) the certificate has not been set aside on an appeal under s 3 below; and

(c) except in the case of a person who is to be sent to a country or territory to which subsection (3) below applies, the time for giving notice of such an appeal has expired and no such appeal is pending.

(2) The conditions are—

(a) that the person is not a national or citizen of the country or territory to which he is to be sent;

(b) that his life and liberty would not be threatened in that country or territory by reason of his race, religion, nationality, membership of a particular social group, or political opinion; and

(c) that the government of that country or territory would not send him to another country or territory otherwise than in accordance with the Convention.

(3) This subsection applies to any country or territory which is or forms part of a member State, or is designated for the purposes of this subsection in an order made by the Secretary of State by statutory instrument.

(4) The first order under this section shall not be made unless a draft of the order has been laid before and approved by a resolution of each House of Parliament.

(5) A statutory instrument containing a subsequent order under this section shall be subject to annulment in pursuance of a resolution of either House of Parliament.

(6) For the purposes of this section, an appeal under s 3 below is pending during the period beginning when notice of appeal is duly given and ending when the appeal is finally determined or withdrawn.

(7) In this section 'claim for asylum' and 'the Convention' have the same meanings as in the 1993 Act.

Appeals against certificates under s 2

3.—(1) Where a certificate has been issued under s 2(1) above in respect of any person—

(a) that person may appeal against the certificate to a special adjudicator on the ground that any of the conditions mentioned in s 2(2) above was not fulfilled when the certificate was issued, or has since ceased to be fulfilled; but

(b) unless and until the certificate is set aside on such an appeal, he shall not be entitled to bring or pursue any appeal under—

(i) Part II of the 1971 Act (appeals: general); or

(ii) s 8 of the 1993 Act (appeals to special adjudicator on Convention grounds),

as respects matters arising before his removal from the United Kingdom.

(2) A person who has been, or is to be, sent to a country or territory to which s 2(3) above applies shall not be entitled to bring or pursue an appeal under this section so long as he is in the United Kingdom.

(3) The Lord Chancellor shall designate such number of the adjudicators appointed for the purposes of Part II of the 1971 Act as he thinks necessary to act as special adjudicators for the purposes of this section and may from time to time vary that number and the persons who are so designated.

(4) Subject to subsection (5) below, the following provisions of the 1971 Act, namely—

(a) s 18 (notice of decisions appealable under that Part and statement of appeal rights, etc);

(b) s 19 (determination of appeals under that Part by adjudicators);

(c) s 21 (references of cases by Secretary of State for further consideration);

(d) s 22(1)–(4), (6) and (7) (rules of procedure for appeals);

(e) s 23 (grants to voluntary organisations helping persons with rights of appeal); and

(f) Schedule 5 (provisions about adjudicators and Immigration Appeal Tribunal),

shall have effect as if this section were contained in Part II of that Act.

(5) Rules of procedure under s 22 of the 1971 Act—

(a) may make special provision in relation to appeals under this section; and

(b) may make different provision in relation to appeals by persons who have been, or are to be, sent to countries or territories of different descriptions;

and so much of para 5 of Schedule 5 to that Act as relates to the allocation of duties among the adjudicators shall have effect subject to subsection (3) above.

(6) Paragraph 29 of Schedule 2 to the 1971 Act (grant of bail pending appeal) shall have effect as if the references to appeals under ss 13(1), 15(1)(a) and 16 of that Act included references to appeals under this section.

Immigration offences

Obtaining leave by deception

4. In subsection (1) of s 24 of the 1971 Act (illegal entry and similar offences), after para (a) there shall be inserted the following paragraph—

'(aa) if, by means which include deception by him, he obtains or seeks to obtain leave to enter or remain in the United Kingdom;'.

Assisting asylum claimants, and persons seeking to obtain leave by deception

5.—(1) In subsection (1) of s 25 of the 1971 Act (assisting illegal entry, and harbouring), for the words from 'the entry' to 'illegal entrant' there shall be substituted the following paragraphs—

'(a) the entry into the United Kingdom of anyone whom he knows or has reasonable cause for believing to be an illegal entrant;

(b) the entry into the United Kingdom of anyone whom he knows or has reasonable cause for believing to be an asylum claimant; or

(c) the obtaining by anyone of leave to remain in the United Kingdom by means which he knows or has reasonable cause for believing to include deception,'.

(2) After that subsection there shall be inserted the following subsection—

'(1A) Nothing in subsection (1)(b) above shall apply to anything which is done—

(a) by a person otherwise than for gain, or in the course of his employment by a *bona fide* organisation whose purpose it is to assist refugees; or

(b) in relation to a person who has been detained under para 16 of Schedule 2 to this Act, or has been granted temporary admission under para 21 of that Schedule;

and in that provision 'asylum claimant' means a person who intends to make a claim for asylum (within the meaning of the Asylum and Immigration Appeals Act 1993).'

(3) In subsection (5) of that section, for the words 'Subsection (1)' there shall be substituted the words 'Subsection (1)(a)'.

(4) In subsection (6) of that section, for the words 'subsection (1)' there shall be substituted the words 'subsection (1)(a) or (b)'.

Increased penalties

6. In the following provisions, namely—

(a) subsection (1) of s 24 of the 1971 Act (illegal entry and similar offences);

(b) subsection (1) of s 26 (general offences in connection with administration of Act); and

(c) s 27 (offences by persons connected with ships or aircraft or with ports),

for the words 'level 4' there shall be substituted the words 'level 5'.

Power of arrest and search warrants

7.—(1) A constable or immigration officer may arrest without warrant anyone whom he has reasonable grounds for suspecting to have committed an offence to which this section applies.

(2) If—

(a) a justice of the peace is by written information on oath satisfied that there is reasonable ground for suspecting that a person who is liable to be arrested under subsection (1) above is to be found on any premises; or

(b) in Scotland, a sheriff, or a justice of the peace, having jurisdiction in the place where the premises are situated is by evidence on oath so satisfied,

he may grant a warrant authorising any constable to enter, if need be by force, the premises named in the warrant for the purposes of searching for and arresting that person.

(3) The following provisions, namely—

(a) s 8 of the Police and Criminal Evidence Act 1984 (power of justice to authorise entry and search of premises); and

(b) Article 10 of the Police and Criminal Evidence (Northern Ireland) Order 1989 (corresponding provision for Northern Ireland),

shall have effect as if the reference in subsection (1) of that section or, as the case may be, para (1) of that Article to a serious arrestable offence included a reference to an offence to which this section applies.

(4) This section applies to the following offences under s 24(1) of the 1971 Act, namely—

(a) an offence under para (a) (illegal entry);

(b) an offence under para (aa) (obtaining leave to enter or remain by deception); and

(c) an offence under para (b) (remaining beyond time limited by leave or failing to observe condition of leave).

(5) In this section 'immigration officer' has the same meaning as in the 1971 Act.

Persons subject to immigration control

Restrictions on employment

8.—(1) Subject to subsection (2) below, if any person ('the employer') employs a person subject to immigration control ('the employee') who has attained the age of 16, the employer shall be guilty of an offence if—

(a) the employee has not been granted leave to enter or remain in the United Kingdom; or

(b) the employee's leave is not valid and subsisting, or is subject to a condition precluding him from taking up the employment,

and (in either case) the employee does not satisfy such conditions as may be specified in an order made by the Secretary of State.

(2) Subject to subsection (3) below, in proceedings under this section, it shall be a defence to prove that—

(a) before the employment began, there was produced to the employer a document which appeared to him to relate to the employee and to be of a description specified in an order made by the Secretary of State; and

(b) either the document was retained by the employer, or a copy or other record of it was made by the employer in a manner specified in the order in relation to documents of that description.

(3) The defence afforded by subsection (2) above shall not be available in any case where the employer knew that his employment of the employee would constitute an offence under this section.

(4) A person guilty of an offence under this section shall be liable on summary conviction to a fine not exceeding level 5 on the standard scale.

(5) Where an offence under this section committed by a body corporate is proved to have been committed with the consent or connivance of, or to be attributable to any neglect on the part of—

(a) any director, manager, secretary or other similar officer of the body corporate; or

(b) any person who was purporting to act in any such capacity,

he as well as the body corporate shall be guilty of the offence and shall be liable to be proceeded against and punished accordingly.

(6) Where the affairs of a body corporate are managed by its members, subsection (5) above shall apply in relation to the acts and defaults of a member in connection with his functions of management as if he were a director of the body corporate.

(7) An order under this section shall be made by statutory instrument which shall be subject to annulment in pursuance of a resolution of either House of Parliament.

(8) In this section—

'contract of employment' means a contract of service or apprenticeship, whether express or implied, and (if it is express) whether it is oral or in writing;

'employ' means employ under a contract of employment and 'employment' shall be construed accordingly.

Entitlement to housing accommodation and assistance

9.—(1) Each housing authority shall secure that, so far as practicable, no tenancy of, or licence to occupy, housing accommodation provided under the accommodation Part is granted to a person subject to immigration control unless he is of a class specified in an order made by the Secretary of State.

(2) A person subject to immigration control—

(a) shall not be eligible for accommodation or assistance under the homelessness Part; and

(b) shall be disregarded in determining, for the purposes of that Part, whether another person—

(i) is homeless or is threatened with homelessness; or

(ii) has a priority need for accommodation,

unless he is of a class specified in an order made by the Secretary of State.

(3) An order under this section—

(a) may make different provision for different circumstances or for accommodation or assistance of different descriptions; and

(b) shall be made by statutory instrument which shall be subject to annulment in pursuance of a resolution of either House of Parliament.

(4) In this section—

'the accommodation Part' and 'the homelessness Part' mean respectively—

(a) in relation to England and Wales, Parts II and III of the Housing Act 1985;

(b) in relation to Scotland, Parts I and II of the Housing (Scotland) Act 1987;

(c) in relation to Northern Ireland, Part II of the Housing (Northern Ireland) Order 1981 and Part II of the Housing (Northern Ireland) Order 1988;

'housing authority' means-—

(a) in relation to England and Wales, a local housing authority within the meaning of the Housing Act 1985;

(b) in relation to Scotland, a local authority within the meaning of the Housing (Scotland) Act 1987;

(c) in relation to Northern Ireland, the Northern Ireland Housing Executive;

'licence to occupy', in relation to Scotland, means a permission or right to occupy;

'tenancy', in relation to England and Wales, has the same meaning as it has in the Housing Act 1985.

Entitlement to child benefit

10.—(1) The provision set out in subsection (2) below shall be inserted—

(a) after s 146 of the Social Security Contributions and Benefits Act 1992, as s 146A of that Act; and

(b) after s 142 of the Social Security Contributions and Benefits (Northern Ireland) Act 1992, as s 142A of that Act.

(2) The provision is as follows—

'**Persons subject to immigration control**.

No person subject to immigration control within the meaning of the Asylum and Immigration Act 1996 shall be entitled to child benefit for any week unless he satisfies prescribed conditions.'

Saving for social security regulations

11.—(1) Notwithstanding any enactment or rule of law, regulations may exclude any person who has made a claim for asylum from entitlement to any of the following benefits, namely—

(a) income support, housing benefit and council tax benefit under the Social Security Contributions and Benefits Act 1992;

(b) income support and housing benefit under the Social Security Contributions and Benefits (Northern Ireland) Act 1992; and

(c) jobseeker's allowance under the Jobseekers Act 1995 or the Jobseekers (Northern Ireland) Order 1995.

(2) Regulations may provide that, where such a person who is so excluded is subsequently recorded by the Secretary of State as a refugee within the meaning of the Convention—

(a) that person may, within a prescribed period, claim the whole or any prescribed proportion of any income support, housing benefit or council tax benefit to which he would have been entitled had he been recorded as a refugee immediately after he made the claim for asylum; and

(b) where he makes such a claim as is mentioned in para (a) above in respect of housing benefit or council tax benefit having resided in the areas of two or more local authorities in Great Britain, the claim shall be investigated and determined, and any benefit awarded shall be paid or allowed, by such one of those authorities as may be prescribed.

(3) Regulations making such provision as is mentioned in subsection (2)(b) above may require the other authorities there mentioned to supply the

prescribed authority with such information as it may reasonably require in connection with the exercise of its functions under the regulations.

(4) Schedule 1 to this Act—

(a) Part I of which modifies the Social Security (Persons from Abroad) Miscellaneous Amendments Regulations 1996; and

(b) Part II of which modifies the Social Security (Persons from Abroad) (Miscellaneous Amendments) Regulations (Northern Ireland) 1996,

shall have effect.

(5) The Jobseeker's Allowance (Amendment) Regulations 1996 shall have effect as if they had been made on the day on which this Act is passed.

(6) In this section—

'claim for asylum' and 'the Convention' have the same meanings as in the 1993 Act;

'prescribed' means prescribed by regulations;

'regulations'—

(a) in relation to income support, housing benefit or council tax benefit under the Social Security Contributions and Benefits Act 1992, means regulations under that Act or the Social Security Administration Act 1992;

(b) in relation to income support or housing benefit under the Social Security Contributions and Benefits (Northern Ireland) Act 1992, means regulations under that Act or the Social Security Administration (Northern Ireland) Act 1992;

(c) in relation to jobseeker's allowance under the Jobseekers Act 1995, means regulations under that Act or the Social Security Administration Act 1992;

(d) in relation to jobseeker's allowance under the Jobseekers (Northern Ireland) Order 1995, means regulations under that Order or the Social Security Administration (Northern Ireland) Act 1992.

Miscellaneous and supplemental

Other amendments and repeals

12.—(1) Schedule 2 to this Act (which contains amendments of the 1971 Act and a related amendment of the Immigration Act 1988) shall have effect.

(2) Schedule 3 to this Act (which contains amendments of the 1993 Act) shall have effect.

(3) The enactments specified in Schedule 4 to this Act are hereby repealed to the extent specified in the third column of that Schedule.

Short title, interpretation, commencement and extent

13.—(1) This Act may be cited as the Asylum and Immigration Act 1996.

(2) In this Act—

'the 1971 Act' means the Immigration Act 1971;

'the 1993 Act' means the Asylum and Immigration Appeals Act 1993;

'person subject to immigration control' means a person who under the 1971 Act requires leave to enter or remain in the United Kingdom (whether or not such leave has been given).

(3) This Act, except s 11 and Schedule 1, shall come into force on such day as the Secretary of State may by order made by statutory instrument appoint, and different days may be appointed for different purposes.

(4) An order under subsection (3) above may make such transitional and supplemental provision as the Secretary of State thinks necessary or expedient.

(5) Her Majesty may by Order in Council direct that any of the provisions of this Act shall extend, with such modifications as appear to Her Majesty to be appropriate, to any of the Channel Islands or the Isle of Man.

(6) This Act extends to Northern Ireland.

SCHEDULES

SCHEDULE I

MODIFICATION OF SOCIAL SECURITY REGULATIONS

PART I

SOCIAL SECURITY (PERSONS FROM ABROAD) MISCELLANEOUS AMENDMENTS REGULATIONS 1996

Preliminary

1. In this Part of this Schedule—

(a) 'the 1996 Regulations' means the Social Security (Persons from Abroad) Miscellaneous Amendments Regulations 1996; and

(b) expressions which are used in the 1996 Regulations have the same meanings as in those Regulations.

Income support

2. In regulation 8 of the 1996 Regulations Amendment of the Income Support Regulations—

(a) para (2) so far as relating to the sub-paragraph added to regulation 21(3) of the Income Support Regulations as sub-para (j); and

(b) para (3)(c) and (d),

shall have effect as if the 1996 Regulations had been made, and had come into force, on the day on which this Act is passed.

Housing benefit

3. In regulation 7 of the 1996 Regulations (amendment of regulation 7A of the Housing Benefit Regulations)—

(a) para (a) so far as relating to the sub-paragraph added to regulation 7A(4) of the Housing Benefit Regulations as sub-para (g);

(b) para (b) so far as relating to sub-paras (a) and (b) of the paragraph substituted for regulation 7A(5) of those Regulations; and

(c) para (c),

shall have effect as if the 1996 Regulations had been made, and had come into force, on the day on which this Act is passed.

Council tax benefit

4. In regulation 3 of the 1996 Regulations (amendment of regulation 4A of the Council Tax Benefit Regulations)—

(a) para (a) so far as relating to the sub-paragraph added to regulation 4A(4) of the Council Tax Benefit Regulations as sub-para (g);

(b) para (b) so far as relating to sub-paras (a) and (b) of the paragraph substituted for regulation 4A(5) of those Regulations; and

(c) para (c),

shall have effect as if the 1996 Regulations had been made, and had come into force, on the day on which this Act is passed.

General

5. Regulation 12(1) of the 1996 Regulations (saving) shall have effect as if after the words 'shall continue to have effect' there were inserted the words '(both as regards him and as regards persons who are members of his family at the coming into force of these Regulations)'.

6.—(1) Subject to sub-para (2) below, any person who is excluded from entitlement to income support, housing benefit or council tax benefit by any of the provisions which are modified by the preceding provisions of this Part of this Schedule—

(a) shall not be entitled to the benefit for any period beginning on or after the day on which this Act is passed; and

(b) shall not be entitled to the benefit for any period beginning on or after 5th February 1996 except on a claim made before the day on which this Act is passed, or an application made before that day for the review of a decision.

(2) Nothing in this paragraph shall apply in any case where a person is entitled to the benefit in question either—

(a) by virtue of regulation 12(1) of the 1996 Regulations (saving); or

(b) by virtue of regulations making such provision as is mentioned in s 11(2) of this Act.

PART II

SOCIAL SECURITY (PERSONS FROM ABROAD) (MISCELLANEOUS AMENDMENTS) REGULATIONS (NORTHERN IRELAND) 1996

Preliminary

7. In this Part of this Schedule 'the 1996 Regulations' means the Social Security (Persons from Abroad) (Miscellaneous Amendments) Regulations (Northern Ireland) 1996.

Income support

8. In regulation 4 of the 1996 Regulations (amendment of the Income Support (General) Regulations)—

(a) para (2) so far as relating to the paragraph added to regulation 21(3) of the Income Support (General) Regulations (Northern Ireland) 1987 as para (1); and

(b) para (3)(b),

shall have effect as if the 1996 Regulations had been made, and had come into operation, on the day on which this Act is passed.

Housing benefit

9. In regulation 5 of the 1996 Regulations (amendment of the Housing Benefit (General) Regulations)—

(a) para (a) so far as relating to the sub-paragraph added to regulation 7A(4) of the Housing Benefit (General) Regulations (Northern Ireland) 1987 as sub-para (g);

(b) para (b) so far as relating to sub-paras (a) and (b) of the paragraph substituted for regulation 7A(5) of those Regulations; and

(c) para (c),

shall have effect as if the 1996 Regulations had been made. and had come into operation, on the day on which this Act is passed.

General

10. Regulation 11(1) of the 1996 Regulations (saving) shall have effect as if after the words 'shall have effect' there were inserted the words '(both as regards him and as regards persons who are members of his family at the coming into operation of these Regulations)'.

11.—(1) Subject to sub-para (2) below, any person who is excluded from entitlement to income support or housing benefit by any of the provisions which are modified by the preceding provisions of this Part of this Schedule—

(a) shall not be entitled to the benefit for any period beginning on or after the day on which this Act is passed; and

(b) shall not be entitled to the benefit for any period beginning on or after 5 February 1996 except on a claim made before the day on which this Act is passed, or an application made before that day for the review of a decision.

(2) Nothing in this paragraph shall apply in any case where a person is entitled to the benefit in question either—

(a) by virtue of regulation 11(1) of the 1996 Regulations (saving); or

(b) by virtue of regulations making such provision as is mentioned in s 11(2) of this Act.

SCHEDULE 2

AMENDMENTS OF THE 1971 ACT AND THE IMMIGRATION ACT 1988

General provisions for regulation and control, &c.

1.—(1) In subsection (1) of s 3 of the 1971 Act (general provisions for regulation and control), for para (c) there shall be substituted the following paragraph—

'(c) if he is given limited leave to enter or remain in the United Kingdom, it may be given subject to all or any of the following conditions, namely—

(i) a condition restricting his employment or occupation in the United Kingdom;

(ii) a condition requiring him to maintain and accommodate himself, and any dependants of his, without recourse to public funds; and

(iii) a condition requiring him to register with the police.'

(2) In subsection (5) (persons liable to deportation) of that section, after para (a) there shall be inserted the following paragraph—

'(aa) if he has obtained leave to remain by deception; or'.

(3) In subsection (1) of s 5 of the Immigration Act 1988 (restricted right of appeal against deportation), after para (a) there shall be inserted the following paragraph—

'(aa) by virtue of s 3(5)(aa) of that Act (leave obtained by deception); or'.

Persons belonging to another's family

2. In subsection (4) of s 5 of the 1971 Act (persons belonging to another's family), for para (b) there shall be substituted the following paragraph—

'(b) where that other person is a woman, her husband and her or his children under the age of 18;'.

Appeals against conditions

3.—(1) After subsection (2) of s 14 of the 1971 Act (appeals against conditions), there shall be inserted the following subsection—

'(2ZA) A person shall not be entitled to appeal under subsection (1) above against—

(a) a variation of his leave which adds such a condition as is mentioned in s 3(1)(c)(ii) above; or

(b) a refusal to vary his leave by revoking such a condition.'

(2) In subsection (2B) of that section, for para (c) there shall be substituted the following paragraph—

'(c) work permits, or equivalent documents issued after entry.'

Interpretation

4.—(1) In subsection (1) of s 33 of the 1971 Act (interpretation), for the definitions of 'entrant' and 'illegal entrant' there shall be substituted the following definitions—

'entrant' means a person entering or seeking to enter the United Kingdom and 'illegal entrant' means a person—

(a) unlawfully entering or seeking to enter in breach of a deportation order or of the immigration laws, or

(b) entering or seeking to enter by means which include deception by another person,

and includes also a person who has entered as mentioned in para (a) or (b) above;'.

(2) In subsection (4) of that section, after the words 'determined or withdrawn', in the first place where they occur, there shall be inserted the words 'or is abandoned by reason of the appellant leaving the United Kingdom'.

Information and documents

5.—(1) In sub-para (2)(b) of para 4 of Schedule 2 to the 1971 Act (information and documents), after the words 'is carrying or conveying', in the first place where they occur, there shall be inserted the words ', or has carried or conveyed,'.

(2) In sub-para (3) of that paragraph—

(a) after the words 'is carrying or conveying' there shall be inserted the words ', or has carried or conveyed,';

(b) for the words from 'he and any' to 'control' there shall be substituted the following paragraphs—

'(a) he and any baggage or vehicle belonging to him or under his control; and

(b) any ship, aircraft or vehicle in which he arrived in the United Kingdom,'; and

(c) after the words 'is doing' there shall be inserted the words 'or, as the case may be, has done'.

Removal of illegal entrants

6. Paragraph 9 of Schedule 2 to the 1971 Act (removal of illegal entrants) shall be renumbered as sub-para (1) of that paragraph; and after that provision as so renumbered there shall be inserted the following sub-paragraph—

'(2) Any leave to enter the United Kingdom which is obtained by deception shall be disregarded for the purposes of this paragraph.'

Arrest of persons liable to detention

7. In sub-para (2)(b) of para 17 of Schedule 2 to the 1971 Act (arrest of persons liable to detention), the words 'magistrate or' shall cease to have effect.

Recovery of expenses incurred in detaining persons refused leave to enter

8. In sub-para (1) of para 19 of Schedule 2 to the 1971 Act (recovery of expenses incurred in detaining persons refused leave to enter), for the words 'at any time' there shall be substituted the words 'for any period (not exceeding 14 days)'.

Recovery of expenses incurred in detaining illegal entrants

9.—(1) In sub-para (1) of para 20 of Schedule 2 to the 1971 Act (recovery of expenses incurred in detaining illegal entrants), for the words 'at any time' there shall be substituted the words 'for any period (not exceeding 14 days)'.

(2) After that sub-paragraph there shall be inserted the following sub-paragraph—

'(1A) Sub-para (1) above shall not apply to expenses in respect of an illegal entrant if he obtained leave to enter by deception and the leave has not been cancelled under para 6(2) above.'

Temporary admission of persons liable to detention

10. After sub-para (2) of para 21 of Schedule 2 to the 1971 Act (temporary admission of persons liable to detention) there shall be inserted the following sub-paragraphs—

'(3) Sub-para (4) below applies where a person who is at large in the United Kingdom by virtue of this paragraph is subject to a restriction as to reporting to an immigration officer with a view to the conclusion of his examination under para 2 above.

(4) If the person fails at any time to comply with that restriction—

(a) an immigration officer may direct that the person's examination under para 2 above shall be treated as concluded at that time; but

(b) nothing in para 6 above shall require the notice giving or refusing him leave to enter the United Kingdom to be given within 24 hours after that time.'

Temporary release of persons liable to detention

11.—(1) For sub-para (1) of para 22 of Schedule 2 to the 1971 Act (temporary release of persons liable to detention) there shall be substituted the following sub-paragraphs—

'(1) The following, namely—

(a) a person detained under para 16(1) above pending examination; and

(b) a person detained under para 16(2) above pending the giving of directions,

may be released on bail in accordance with this paragraph.

(1A) An immigration officer not below the rank of chief immigration officer or an adjudicator may release a person so detained on his entering into a recognizance or, in Scotland, bail bond conditioned for his appearance before an immigration officer at a time and place named in the recognizance or bail bond or at such other time and place as may in the meantime be notified to him in writing by an immigration officer.

(1B) Sub-paragraph (l)(a) above shall not apply unless seven days have elapsed since the date of the person's arrival in the United Kingdom.'

(2) In sub-paragraph (2) of that paragraph—

(a) for the word 'adjudicator', in the first place where it occurs, there shall be substituted the words 'immigration officer or adjudicator'; and

(b) for the word 'adjudicator', in the second place where it occurs, there shall be substituted the words 'officer or adjudicator'.

(3) In sub-para (3) of that paragraph—

(a) for the word 'adjudicator', in the first place where it occurs, there shall be substituted the words 'immigration officer or adjudicator'; and

(b) for the word 'adjudicator', in the second and third places where it occurs, there shall be substituted the words 'officer or adjudicator'.

Grant of bail pending removal

12. After para 33 of Schedule 2 to the 1971 Act there shall be inserted the following paragraph—

'*Grant of bail pending removal*

34.—(1) Paragraph 22 above shall apply in relation to a person—

(a) directions for whose removal from the United Kingdom are for the time being in force; and

(b) who is for the time being detained under Part I of this Schedule,

as it applies in relation to a person detained under para 16(1) above pending examination or detained under para 16(2) above pending the giving of directions.

(2) Paragraphs 23–25 above shall apply as if any reference to para 22 above included a reference to that paragraph as it applies by virtue of this paragraph.'

Supplementary provisions as to deportation

13. In para 2(5) of Schedule 3 to the 1971 Act (supplementary provisions as to deportation), after the words 'the police' there shall be inserted the words 'or an immigration officer'.

SCHEDULE 3

AMENDMENTS OF THE 1993 ACT

Curtailment of leave to enter or remain

1.—(1) After subsection (1) of s 7 of the 1993 Act (curtailment of leave to enter or remain) there shall be inserted the following subsection—

'(1A) Where the Secretary of State by notice under subsection (1) above curtails the duration of any person's leave to enter or remain in the United Kingdom, he may also by notice in writing given to any dependant of that person curtail to the same extent the duration of that dependant's leave so to enter or remain.'

(2) In subsections (2), (3) and (4) of that section, for the words 'subsection (1) above' there shall be substituted the words 'subsection (1) or (lA) above'.

Appeals to special adjudicator

2.—(1) In subsection (3) of s 8 of the 1993 Act (appeals to special adjudicator), the words from 'but a person' to the end shall cease to have effect.

(2) Alter that subsection there shall be inserted the following subsection—

'(3A) A person may not appeal under para (b) of subsection (3) above if he has had the right to appeal under para (a) of that subsection, whether or not he has exercised it.'

Bail pending appeal from Immigration Appeal Tribunal

3. After s 9 of the 1993 Act there shall be inserted the following section—

'*Bail pending appeal from Immigration Appeal Tribunal*

9A.—(1) Where a person ('an appellant')—

(a) has an appeal under Part II of the 1971 Act which is pending by reason of an appeal, or an application for leave to appeal, under s 9 above; and

(b) is for the time being detained under Part I of Schedule 2 to that Act (general provisions as to control on entry, etc),

he may be released on bail in accordance with this section.

(2) An immigration officer not below the rank of chief immigration officer, a police officer not below the rank of inspector or an adjudicator may release an appellant on his entering into a recognizance or, in Scotland, bail bond conditioned for his appearance before the appropriate appeal court at a time and place named in the recognizance or bail bond.

(3) The Immigration Appeal Tribunal may release an appellant on his entering into a recognizance or, in Scotland, bail bond conditioned for his appearance before the appropriate appeal court at a time and place named in the recognizance or bail bond; and where—

(a) the appeal, or the application for leave to appeal, under s 9 above is by the Secretary of State; or

(b) the appellant has been granted leave to appeal under that section, and has duly given notice of appeal,

the Tribunal shall, if the appellant so requests, exercise its powers under this subsection.

(4) Sub-paragraphs (5) and (6) of para 29 (grant of bail pending appeal) of Schedule 2 to the 1971 Act shall apply for the purposes of this section as they apply for the purposes of that paragraph.

(5) Paragraphs 30 to 33 of that Schedule shall apply as if—

(a) any reference to para 29 included a reference to this section;

(b) the reference in para 30(2) to para 29(3) or (4) included a reference to subsection (3) above; and

(c) any reference in paras 31–33 to the Immigration Appeal Tribunal included a reference to the appropriate appeal court.

(6) In this section 'the appropriate appeal court' has the same meaning as in s 9 above.'

Security of tenure

4. In para 6(1) of Schedule I to the 1993 Act (security of tenure)—

(a) after the words 'Part III of the Act of 1985' there shall be inserted the words 'or Part II of the Act of 1987'; and

(b) after the words 'the Housing Act 1988' there shall be inserted the words 'or the Housing (Scotland) Act 1988'.

Appeals to special adjudicator: supplementary

5. In para 4(2) of Schedule 2 to the 1993 Act (appeals to special adjudicator: supplementary), for the word 'and' immediately following para (1) there shall be substituted the following paragraph—

'(ff) s 33(4) (duration of appeals); and'.

SCHEDULE 4

REPEALS

Chapter	Short title	Extent of repeal
1971 c. 77.	Immigration Act 1971.	In Schedule 2, in para 17(2)(b), the words magistrate or'.
1993 c. 23.	Asylum and Immigration Appeals Act 1993.	In s 8(3), the words from 'but a person' to the end.

Appendix II

Statement of Changes in Immigration Rules

Laid before Parliament on 23 May 1994

under s 3(2) of the Immigration Act 1971

CONTENTS

Paragraphs

Introduction 1–2

Implementation and transitional provisions 4

Application 5

Interpretation 6

Part 1: General provisions regarding leave to enter or remain in the United Kingdom

Leave to enter the United Kingdom 7–9

Exercise of the power to refuse leave to enter the United Kingdom ...10

Requirement for persons arriving in the United Kingdom or seeking entry through the Channel Tunnel to produce evidence of identity and nationality 11

Requirement for a person not requiring leave to enter the United Kingdom to prove that he has the right of abode 12–14

Common Travel Area 15

Admission for certain British passport holders 16–17

Returning residents 18–20

Holders of restricted travel documents and passports 21–23

Entry clearance 24–30

Variation of leave to enter or remain in the United Kingdom ...31–33

Withdrawn applications for variation of leave to enter or remain in the United Kingdom 34

Undertakings 35

Medical 36–39

Part 2: Persons seeking to enter or remain in the United Kingdom for visits

Visitors ... 40–46
Visitors in transit ... 47–50
Visitors seeking to enter or remain for private medical treatment 51–56

Part 3: Persons seeking to enter or remain in the United Kingdom for studies

Students ... 57–62
Student nurses ... 63–69
Postgraduate doctors and dentists ... 70–75
Spouses of students ... 76–78
Children of students ... 79–81
Prospective students ... 82–87

Part 4: Persons seeking to enter or remain in the United Kingdom in an 'au pair' placement, as a working holidaymaker or for training or work experience

'Au pair' placements ... 88–94
Working holidaymakers ... 95–100
Children of working holidaymakers ... 101–03
Seasonal workers at agricultural camps ... 104–09
Teachers and language assistants coming to the United Kingdom under approved exchange schemes ... 110–15
Department of Employment approved training or work experience ... 116–21
Spouses of persons with limited leave to enter or remain under paras 110–21 ... 122–24
Children of persons with limited leave to enter or remain under paras 110–21 ... 125–27

Part 5: Persons seeking to enter or remain in the United Kingdom for employment

Work permit employment ... 128–35
Representatives of overseas newspapers, news agencies and broadcasting organisations ... 136–43
Sole representatives ... 144–51
Private servants in diplomatic households ... 152–59
Overseas government employees ... 160–68

Ministers of religion, missionaries and members of religious orders 169–77
Airport-based operational ground staff of overseas-owned airlines 178–85
Persons with United Kingdom ancestry 186–93
Spouses of persons with limited leave to enter or remain under paras 128–93..... 194–96
Children of persons with limited leave to enter or remain under paras 128–93 197-99

Part 6: Persons seeking to enter or remain in the United Kingdom as a businessman, self-employed person, investor, writer, composer or artist

Persons intending to establish themselves in business 200–10
Persons intending to establish themselves in business under the provisions of EC Association Agreements 211–23
Investors 224–31
Writers, composers and artists 232–39
Spouses of persons with limited leave to enter or remain under paras 200–39 240–42
Children of persons with limited leave to enter or remain under paras 200–39 243–45

Part 7: Other Categories

Persons exercising rights of access to a child resident in the United Kingdom 246–48
Holders of special vouchers and their dependants 249–54
EEA nationals and their families 255–62
Retired persons of independent means 263–70
Spouses of persons with limited leave to enter or remain in the United Kingdom as retired persons of independent means 271–73
Children of persons with limited leave to enter or remain in the United Kingdom as retired persons of independent means 274–76

Part 8: Family Members

Spouses 277-89
Fiance(e)s 290–95
Children 296–316
Parents, grandparents and other dependent relatives 317–19

Part 9: General grounds for the refusal of entry clearance, leave to enter or variation of leave to enter or remain in the United Kingdom

Refusal of entry clearance or leave to enter the United Kingdom ... 320

Refusal of leave to enter in relation to a person in possession of an entry clearance ... 321

Refusal of variation of leave to enter or remain or curtailment of leave ... 322–23

Crew members ... 324

Part 10: Registration with the police ... 325–26

Part 11: Asylum ... 327–52

Part 12: Rights of appeal ... 353–61

Part 13: Deportation ... 362–95

Appendix

Visa requirements for the United Kingdom

INTRODUCTION

The Home Secretary has made changes in the Rules laid down by him as to the practice to be followed in the administration of the Immigration Acts for regulating entry into and the stay of persons in the United Kingdom and contained in the statement laid before Parliament on 23 March 1990 (HC 251) (as amended). This statement contains the Rules as changed and replaces the provisions of HC 251 (as amended).

2. Immigration Officers, Entry Clearance Officers and all staff of the Home Office Immigration and Nationality Department will carry out their duties without regard to the race, colour or religion of persons seeking to enter or remain in the United Kingdom.

3. In these Rules words importing the masculine gender include the feminine unless the contrary intention appears.

IMPLEMENTATION AND TRANSITIONAL PROVISIONS

4. These Rules come into effect on 1 October 1994 and will apply to all decisions taken on or after that date save that any application made before 1 October 1994 for entry clearance, leave to enter or remain or variation of leave to enter or remain shall be decided under the provisions of HC 251, as amended, as if these Rules had not been made.

APPLICATION

5. Save where expressly indicated, these Rules do not apply to a European Economic Area (EEA) national or the family member of such a national who is entitled to enter or remain in the United Kingdom by virtue of the

provisions of the Immigration (European Economic Area) Order 1994. But an EEA national or his family member who is not entitled to rely on the provisions of that Order is covered by these Rules.

INTERPRETATION

6. In these Rules the following interpretations apply—

'the Immigration Acts' mean the Immigration Act 1971 and the Immigration Act 1988.

'the 1993 Act' is the Asylum and Immigration Appeals Act 1993.

'the 1994 EEA Order' is the Immigration (European Economic Area) Order 1994.

'United Kingdom passport' bears the meaning it has in the Immigration Act 1971.

'Immigration Officer' includes a Customs Officer acting as an Immigration Officer.

'public funds' means—

(a) housing under Part III of the Housing Act 1985, Part II of the Housing (Scotland) Act 1987 or Part II of the Housing (Northern Ireland) Order 1983;

(b) income support, family credit, council tax benefit and housing benefit under Part VII of the Social Security Contributions and Benefits Act 1992; and

(c) income support, family credit and housing benefit under the Social Security Contributions and Benefits (Northern Ireland) Act 1992.

'Department of Employment' includes, where appropriate, the equivalent government Department for Northern Ireland.

'settled in the United Kingdom' means that the person concerned—

(a) is free from any restriction on the period for which he may remain save that a person entitled to an exemption under s 8 of the Immigration Act 1971 (otherwise than as a member of the home forces) is not to be regarded as settled in the United Kingdom except in so far as s 8(5A) so provides; and

(b) is either—

(i) ordinarily resident in the United Kingdom without having entered or remained in breach of the immigration laws; or

(ii) despite having entered or remained in breach of the immigration laws, has subsequently entered lawfully or has been granted leave to remain and is ordinarily resident.

'a parent' includes—

(a) the stepfather of a child whose father is dead;

(b) the stepmother of a child whose mother is dead;

(c) the father as well as the mother of an illegitimate child where he is proved to be the father;

(d) an adoptive parent but only where a child was adopted in accordance with a decision taken by the competent administrative authority or court in a country whose adoption orders are recognised by the United Kingdom (except where an application for leave to enter or remain is made under paras 310–16);

(e) in the case of a child born in the United Kingdom who is not a British citizen, a person to whom there has been a genuine transfer of parental responsibility on the ground of the original parent(s)' inability to care for the child.

'visa nationals' are the persons specified in the Appendix to these Rules who need a visa for the United Kingdom.

'employment', unless the contrary intention appears, includes paid and unpaid employment, self-employment and engaging in business or any professional activity.

'EEA national' means a national of a State which is a Contracting Party to the European Economic Area Agreement other than the United Kingdom, but until the EEA Agreement comes into force in relation to Liechtenstein does not include a national of the State of Liechtenstein.

'family member' in relation to an EEA national has the same meaning as in the 1994 EEA Order.

PART 1: GENERAL PROVISIONS REGARDING LEAVE TO ENTER OR REMAIN IN THE UNITED KINGDOM

Leave to enter the United Kingdom

7. A person who is neither a British citizen nor a Commonwealth citizen with the right of abode nor an EEA national or the family member of such a national who is entitled to enter or remain in the United Kingdom by virtue of the provisions of the Immigration (European Economic Area) Order 1994 requires leave to enter the United Kingdom.

8. Under ss 3 and 4 of the Immigration Act 1971 an Immigration Officer when admitting to the United Kingdom a person subject to control under that Act may give leave to enter for a limited period and, if he does, may impose conditions restricting or prohibiting employment or occupation in the United Kingdom or requiring the person to register with the police or both. He may also require him to report to the appropriate Medical Officer of Environmental Health. Under s 24 of the 1971 Act it is an offence knowingly to remain beyond the time limit or to fail to comply with such a condition or requirement.

9. The time limit and any conditions attached will be made known to the person concerned by a written notice which will normally be given to him or be endorsed by the Immigration Officer in his passport or travel document.

Exercise of the power to refuse leave to enter the United Kingdom

10. The power to refuse leave to enter the United Kingdom is not to be exercised by an Immigration Officer acting on his own. The authority of a Chief Immigration Officer or of an Immigration Inspector must always be obtained.

Requirement for persons arriving in the United Kingdom or seeking entry through the Channel Tunnel to produce evidence of identity and nationality

11. A person must, on arrival in the United Kingdom or when seeking entry through the Channel Tunnel, produce on request by the Immigration Officer—

(i) a valid national passport or other document satisfactorily establishing his identity and nationality; and

(ii) such information as may be required to establish whether he requires leave to enter the United Kingdom and, if so, whether and on what terms leave to enter should be given.

Requirement for a person not requiring leave to enter the United Kingdom to prove that he has the right of abode

12. A person claiming to be a British citizen must prove that he has the right of abode in the United Kingdom by producing either—

(i) a United Kingdom passport describing him as a British citizen or as a citizen of the United Kingdom and Colonies having the right of abode in the United Kingdom; or

(ii) a certificate of entitlement duly issued by or on behalf of the government of the United Kingdom certifying that he has the right of abode.

13. A person claiming to be a Commonwealth citizen with the right of abode in the United Kingdom must prove that he has the right of abode by producing a certificate of entitlement duly issued to him by or on behalf of the government of the United Kingdom certifying that he has the right of abode.

14. A Commonwealth citizen who has been given limited leave to enter the United Kingdom may later claim to have the right of abode. The time limit on his stay may be removed if he is able to establish a claim to the right of abode, for example, by showing that—

(i) immediately before the commencement of the British Nationality Act 1981 he was a Commonwealth citizen born to or legally adopted by a parent who at the time of the birth had citizenship of the United Kingdom and Colonies by his birth in the United Kingdom or any of the Islands; and

(ii) he has not ceased to be a Commonwealth citizen in the meanwhile.

Common Travel Area

15. The United Kingdom, the Channel Islands, the Isle of Man and the Republic of Ireland collectively form a common travel area. A person who has been examined for the purpose of immigration control at the point at which he entered the area does not normally require leave to enter any other part of it. However, certain persons subject to the Immigration (Control of Entry through the Republic of Ireland) Order 1972 (as amended) who enter the United Kingdom through the Republic of Ireland do require leave to enter. This includes—

(i) those who merely passed through the Republic of Ireland;

(ii) persons requiring visas;

(iii) persons who entered the Republic of Ireland unlawfully;

(iv) persons who are subject to directions given by the Secretary of State for their exclusion from the United Kingdom on the ground that their exclusion is conducive to the public good;

(v) persons who entered the Republic from the United Kingdom and Islands after entering there unlawfully or overstaying their leave.

Admission of certain British passport holders

16. A person in any of the following categories may be admitted freely to the United Kingdom on production of a United Kingdom passport issued in the United Kingdom and Islands or the Republic of Ireland prior to 1 January 1973, unless his passport has been endorsed to show that he was subject to immigration control—

(i) a British Dependent Territories citizen;

(ii) a British National (Overseas);

(iii) a British Overseas citizen;

(iv) a British protected person;

(v) a British subject by virtue of s 30(a) of the British Nationality Act 1981, (who, immediately before the commencement of the 1981 Act, would have been a British subject not possessing citizenship of the United Kingdom and Colonies or the citizenship of any other Commonwealth country or territory).

17. British Overseas citizens who hold United Kingdom passports wherever issued and who satisfy the Immigration Officer that they have, since 1 March 1968, been given indefinite leave to enter or remain in the United Kingdom may be given indefinite leave to enter.

Returning Residents

18. A person seeking leave to enter the United Kingdom as a returning resident may be admitted for settlement provided the Immigration Officer is satisfied that the person concerned—

- (i) had indefinite leave to enter or remain in the United Kingdom when he last left; and
- (ii) has not been away from the United Kingdom for more than two years; and
- (iii) did not receive assistance from public funds towards the cost of leaving the United Kingdom; and
- (iv) now seeks admission for the purpose of settlement.

19. A person who does not benefit from the preceding paragraph by reason only of having been away from the United Kingdom too long may nevertheless be admitted as a returning resident if, for example, he has lived here for most of his life.

20. The leave of a person whose stay in the United Kingdom is subject to a time limit lapses on his going to a country or territory outside the common travel area. Such a person who returns after a temporary absence abroad within the period of this earlier leave has no claim to admission as a returning resident. His application to re-enter the United Kingdom should be considered in the light of all the relevant circumstances. The same time limit and any conditions attached will normally be reimposed if he meets the requirements of these Rules, unless he is seeking admission in a different capacity from the one in which he was last given leave to enter or remain.

Holders of restricted travel documents and passports

21. The leave to enter or remain in the United Kingdom of the holder of a passport or travel document whose permission to enter another country has to be exercised before a given date may be restricted so as to terminate at least two months before that date.

22. If his passport or travel document is endorsed with a restriction on the period for which he may remain outside his country of normal residence, his leave to enter or remain in the United Kingdom may be limited so as not to extend beyond the period of authorised absence.

23. The holder of a travel document issued by the Home Office should not be given leave to enter or remain for a period extending beyond the validity of that document. This paragraph and paras 21–22 do not apply to a person who is eligible for admission for settlement or to a spouse who is eligible for admission under para 282 or to a person who qualifies for the removal of the time limit on his stay.

Entry Clearance

24. A visa national and any other person who is seeking entry for a purpose for which prior entry clearance is required under these Rules must produce to the Immigration Officer a valid passport or other identity document endorsed with a United Kingdom entry clearance issued to him for the purpose for which he seeks entry. Such a person will be refused leave to enter if he has no such current entry clearance. Any other person who wishes to ascertain in advance whether he is eligible for admission to the United Kingdom may apply for the issue of an entry clearance.

25. Entry clearance takes the form of a visa (for visa nationals) or an entry certificate (for non-visa nationals). These documents are to be taken as evidence of the holder's eligibility for entry into the United Kingdom, and accordingly accepted as 'entry clearances' within the meaning of the Immigration Act 1971.

26. An application for entry clearance will be considered in accordance with the provisions in these Rules governing the grant or refusal of leave to enter. Where appropriate, the term 'Entry Clearance Officer' should be substituted for ' Immigration Officer'.

27. An application for entry clearance is to be decided in the light of the circumstances existing at the time of the decision, except that an applicant will not be refused an entry clearance where entry is sought in one of the categories contained in paras 296–316 solely on account of his attaining the age of 18 years between receipt of his application and the date of the decision on it.

28. An applicant for an entry clearance must be outside the United Kingdom and Islands at the time of the application. An applicant for an entry clearance who is seeking entry as a visitor must apply to a post designated by the Secretary of State to accept applications for entry clearance for that purpose and from that category of applicant. Any other application must be made to the post in the country or territory where the applicant is living which has been designated by the Secretary of State to accept applications for entry clearance for that purpose and from that category of applicant. Where there is no such post the applicant must apply to the appropriate designated post outside the country or territory where he is living.

29. For the purposes of para 28 'post' means a British Diplomatic Mission, British Consular post or the office of any person outside the United Kingdom and Islands who has been authorised by the Secretary of State to accept applications for entry clearance. A list of designated posts is published by the Foreign and Commonwealth Office.

30. An application for an entry clearance is not made until any fee required to be paid under the Consular Fees Act 1980 (including any Regulations or Orders made under that Act) has been paid.

Variation of leave to enter or remain in the United Kingdom

31. Under s 3(3) of the 1971 Act a limited leave to enter or remain in the United Kingdom may be varied by extending or restricting its duration, by adding, varying or revoking conditions or by removing the time limit (whereupon any condition attached to the leave ceases to apply). When leave to enter or remain is varied an entry is to be made in the applicant's passport or travel document (and his registration certificate where appropriate) or the decision may be made known in writing in some other appropriate way.

32. After admission to the United Kingdom any application for an extension of the time limit on or variation of conditions attached to a person's stay in the United Kingdom must be made to the Home Office before the applicant's current leave to enter or remain expires.

33. Where the application is in respect of employment for which a work permit or a permit for training or work experience is required or is in respect of the spouse or child of a person who is making such an application, the application should be made direct to the Department of Employment Overseas Labour Service.

Withdrawn applications for variation of leave to enter or remain in the United Kingdom

34. Where a person whose application for variation of leave to enter or remain is being considered requests the return of his passport for the purpose of travel outside the common travel area, the application for variation of leave shall, provided it has not already been determined, be treated as withdrawn as soon as the passport is returned in response to that request and the provisions of the Immigration (Variation of Leave) Order 1976 (as amended) will apply.

Undertakings

35. A sponsor of a person seeking leave to enter or variation of leave to enter or remain in the United Kingdom may be asked to give an undertaking in writing to be responsible for that person's maintenance and accommodation for the period of any leave granted, including any further variation. Under the Social Security Administration Act 1992 and the Social Security Administration (Northern Ireland) Act 1992, the Department of Social Security or, as the case may be, the Department of Health and Social Services in Northern Ireland may seek to recover from the person giving such an undertaking any income support paid to meet the needs of the person in respect of whom the undertaking has been given.

Medical

36. A person who intends to remain in the United Kingdom for more than six months should normally be referred to the Medical Inspector for examination. If he produces a medical certificate he should be advised to

hand it to the Medical Inspector. Any person seeking entry who mentions health or medical treatment as a reason for his visit, or who appears not to be in good mental or physical health, should also be referred to the Medical Inspector; and the Immigration Officer has discretion, which should be exercised sparingly, to refer for examination in any other case.

37. Where the Medical Inspector advises that a person seeking entry is suffering from a specified disease or condition which may interfere with his ability to support himself or his dependants the Immigration Officer should take account of this, in conjunction with other factors, in deciding whether to admit that person. The Immigration Officer should also take account of the Medical Inspector's assessment of the likely course of treatment in deciding whether a person seeking entry for private medical treatment has sufficient means at his disposal.

38. A returning resident should not be refused leave to enter on medical grounds. But where a person would be refused leave to enter on medical grounds if he were not a returning resident, or in any case where it is decided on compassionate grounds not to exercise the power to refuse leave to enter, or in any other case where the Medical Inspector so recommends, the Immigration Officer should give the person concerned a notice requiring him to report to the Medical Officer of Environmental Health designated by the Medical Inspector with a view to further examination and any necessary treatment.

39. The Entry Clearance Officer has the same discretion as an Immigration Officer to refer applicants for entry clearance for medical examination and the same principles will apply to the decision whether or not to issue an entry clearance.

PART 2: PERSONS SEEKING TO ENTER OR REMAIN IN THE UNITED KINGDOM FOR VISITS

VISITORS

Requirements for leave to enter as a visitor

40. For the purpose of paras 41–46 a visitor includes a person living and working outside the United Kingdom who comes to the United Kingdom to transact business (such as attending meetings and briefings, fact finding, negotiating or making contracts with United Kingdom businesses to buy or sell goods or services). A visitor seeking leave to enter or remain for private medical treatment must meet the requirements of paras 51 or 54.

41. The requirements to be met by a person seeking leave to enter the United Kingdom as a visitor are that he—

(i) is genuinely seeking entry as a visitor for a limited period as stated by him, not exceeding six months; and

(ii) intends to leave the United Kingdom at the end of the period of the visit as stated by him; and

(iii) does not intend to take employment in the United Kingdom; and

(iv) does not intend to produce goods or provide services within the United Kingdom, including the selling of goods or services direct to members of the public; and

(v) does not intend to study at a maintained school; and

(vi) will maintain and accommodate himself and any dependants adequately out of resources available to him without recourse to public funds or taking employment; or will, with any dependants, be maintained and accommodated adequately by relatives or friends; and

(vii) can meet the cost of the return or onward journey.

Leave to enter as a visitor

42. A person seeking leave to enter the United Kingdom as a visitor may be admitted for a period not exceeding six months, subject to a condition prohibiting employment, provided the Immigration Officer is satisfied that each of the requirements of para 41 is met.

Refusal of leave to enter as a visitor

43. Leave to enter as a visitor is to be refused if the Immigration Officer is not satisfied that each of the requirements of para 41 is met.

Requirements for an extension of stay as a visitor

44. Six months is the maximum permitted leave which may be granted to a visitor. The requirements for an extension of stay as a visitor are that the applicant—

(i) meets the requirements of para 41 (ii)–(vii); and

(ii) has not already spent, or would not as a result of an extension of stay spend more than six months in total in the United Kingdom as a visitor.

Any period spent as a seasonal agricultural worker is to be counted as a period spent as a visitor.

Extension of stay as a visitor

45. An extension of stay as a visitor may be granted, subject to a condition prohibiting employment, provided the Secretary of State is satisfied that each of the requirements of para 44 is met.

Refusal of extension of stay as a visitor

46. An extension of stay as a visitor is to be refused if the Secretary of State is not satisfied that each of the requirements of para 44 is met.

VISITORS IN TRANSIT

Requirements for admission as a visitor in transit to another country

47. The requirements to be met by a person (not being a member of the crew of a ship, aircraft, hovercraft, hydrofoil or train) seeking leave to enter the United Kingdom as a visitor in transit to another country are that he—

(i) is in transit to a country outside the common travel area; and

(ii) has both the means and the intention of proceeding at once to another country; and

(iii) is assured of entry there; and

(iv) intends and is able to leave the United Kingdom within 48 hours.

Leave to enter as a visitor in transit

48. A person seeking leave to enter the United Kingdom as a visitor in transit may be admitted for a period not exceeding 48 hours with a prohibition on employment provided the Immigration Officer is satisfied that each of the requirements of para 47 is met.

Refusal of leave to enter as a visitor in transit

49. Leave to enter as a visitor in transit is to be refused if the Immigration Officer is not satisfied that each of the requirements of para 47 is met.

Extension of stay as a visitor in transit

50. The maximum permitted leave which may be granted to a visitor in transit is 48 hours. An application for an extension of stay beyond 48 hours from a person admitted in this category is to be refused.

VISITORS SEEKING TO ENTER OR REMAIN FOR PRIVATE MEDICAL TREATMENT

Requirements for leave to enter as a visitor for private medical treatment

51. The requirements to be met by a person seeking leave to enter the United Kingdom as a visitor for private medical treatment are that he—

(i) meets the requirements set out in para 41 (iii)–(vii) for entry as a visitor; and

(ii) in the case of a person suffering from a communicable disease, has satisfied the Medical Inspector that there is no danger to public health; and

(iii) can show, if required to do so, that any proposed course of treatment is of finite duration; and

(iv) intends to leave the United Kingdom at the end of his treatment; and

(v) can produce satisfactory evidence, if required to do so, of—
  (a) the medical condition requiring consultation or treatment; and
  (b) satisfactory arrangements for the necessary consultation or treatment at his own expense; and
  (c) the estimated costs of such consultation or treatment; and
  (d) the likely duration of his visit; and
  (e) sufficient funds available to him in the United Kingdom to meet the estimated costs and his undertaking to do so.

Leave to enter as a visitor for private medical treatment

52. A person seeking leave to enter the United Kingdom as a visitor for private medical treatment may be admitted for a period not exceeding six months, subject to a condition prohibiting employment, provided the Immigration Officer is satisfied that each of the requirements of para 51 is met.

Refusal of leave to enter as a visitor for private medical treatment

53. Leave to enter as a visitor for private medical treatment is to be refused if the Immigration Officer is not satisfied that each of the requirements of para 51 is met.

Requirements for an extension of stay as a visitor for private medical treatment

54. The requirements for an extension of stay as a visitor to undergo or continue private medical treatment are that the applicant—

(i) meets the requirements set out in para 41 (iii)–(vii) and para 51 (ii)–(v); and

(ii) has produced evidence from a registered medical practitioner who holds an NHS consultant post of satisfactory arrangements for private medical consultation or treatment and its likely duration; and, where treatment has already begun, evidence as to its progress; and

(iii) can show that he has met, out of the resources available to him, any costs and expenses incurred in relation to his treatment in the United Kingdom; and

(iv) has sufficient funds available to him in the United Kingdom to meet the likely costs of his treatment and intends to meet those costs.

Extension of stay as a visitor for private medical treatment

55. An extension of stay to undergo or continue private medical treatment may be granted, with a prohibition on employment, provided the Secretary of State is satisfied that each of the requirements of para 54 is met.

Refusal of extension of stay as a visitor for private medical treatment

56. An extension of stay as a visitor to undergo or continue private medical treatment is to be refused if the Secretary of State is not satisfied that each of the requirements of para 54 is met.

PART 3: PERSONS SEEKING TO ENTER OR REMAIN IN THE UNITED KINGDOM FOR STUDIES

STUDENTS

Requirements for leave to enter as a student

57. The requirements to be met by a person seeking leave to enter the United Kingdom as a student are that he—

(i) has been accepted for a course of study at—

(a) a publicly funded institution of further or higher education; or

(b) a *bona fide* private education institution which maintains satisfactory records of enrolment and attendance; or

(c) an independent fee paying school outside the maintained sector; and

(ii) is able and intends to follow either—

(a) a recognised full-time degree course at a publicly funded institution of further or higher education; or

(b) a weekday full-time course involving attendance at a single institution for a minimum of 15 hours organised daytime study per week of a single subject or directly related subjects; or

(c) a full-time course of study at an independent fee paying school; and

(iii) if under the age of 16 years is enrolled at an independent fee paying school on a full-time course of studies which meets the requirements of the Education Act 1914; and

(iv) intends to leave the United Kingdom at the end of his studies; and

(v) does not intend to engage in business or to take employment except part-time or vacation work undertaken with the consent of the Secretary of State for Employment; and

(vi) is able to meet the costs of his course and accommodation and the maintenance of himself and any dependants without taking employment or engaging in business or having recourse to public funds.

Leave to enter as a student

58. A person seeking leave to enter the United Kingdom as a student may be admitted for an appropriate period depending on the length of his course of study and his means, and with a condition restricting his freedom to take employment provided the Immigration Officer is satisfied that each of the requirements of para 57 is met.

Refusal of leave to enter as a student

59. Leave to enter as a student is to be refused if the Immigration Officer is not satisfied that each of the requirements of para 57 is met.

Requirements for an extension of stay as a student

60. The requirements for all extension of stay as a student are that the applicant—

- (i) was admitted to the United Kingdom with a valid student entry clearance if he is a person specified in the Appendix to these Rules; and
- (ii) meets the requirements for admission as a student set out in para 57 (i)–(vi); and
- (iii) has produced evidence of his enrolment on a course which meets the requirements of para 57; and
- (iv) can produce satisfactory evidence of regular attendance during any course which he has already begun; or any other course for which he has been enrolled in the past; and
- (v) can show evidence of satisfactory progress in his course of study including the taking and passing of any relevant examinations; and
- (vi) would not as a result of an extension of stay spend more than four years on short courses (ie courses of less than two years duration or longer courses broken off before completion); and
- (vii) has not come to the end of a period of government or international scholarship agency sponsorship, or has the written consent of his original sponsor for a further period of study in the United Kingdom and satisfactory evidence that sufficient sponsorship funding is available.

Extension of stay as a student

61. An extension of stay as a student may be granted, subject to a restriction on his freedom to take employment, provided the Secretary of State is satisfied that the applicant meets each of the requirements of para 60.

Refusal of extension of stay as a student

62. An extension of stay as a student is to be refused if the Secretary of State is not satisfied that each of the requirements of para 60 is met.

STUDENT NURSES

Definition of student nurse

63. For the purposes of these Rules the term student nurse means a person accepted for training as a student nurse or midwife leading to a registered nursing qualification; or an overseas nurse or midwife who has been accepted on an adaptation course leading to registration as a nurse with the United Kingdom Central Council for Nursing, Midwifery and Health Visiting.

Requirements for leave to enter as a student nurse

64. The requirements to be met by a person seeking leave to enter the United Kingdom as a student nurse are that the person—

- (i) comes within the definition set out in para 63 above; and
- (ii) has been accepted for a course of study in a recognised nursing educational establishment offering nursing training which meets the requirements of the United Kingdom Central Council for Nursing, Midwifery and Health Visiting; and
- (iii) did not obtain acceptance by misrepresentation; and
- (iv) is able and intends to follow the course; and
- (v) does not intend to engage in business or take employment except in connection with the training course; and
- (vi) intends to leave the United Kingdom at the end of the course; and
- (vii) has sufficient funds available for accommodation and maintenance for himself and any dependants without engaging in business or taking employment (except in connection with the training course) or having recourse to public funds. The possession of a Department of Health bursary may be taken into account in assessing whether the student meets the maintenance requirement.

Leave to enter the United Kingdom as a student nurse

65. A person seeking leave to enter the United Kingdom as a student nurse may be admitted for the duration of the training course, with a restriction on his freedom to take employment, provided the Immigration Officer is satisfied that each of the requirements of para 64 is met.

Refusal of leave to enter as a student nurse

66. Leave to enter as a student nurse is to be refused if the Immigration Officer is not satisfied that each of the requirements of para 64 is met.

Requirements for an extension of stay as a student nurse

67. The requirements for an extension of stay as a student nurse are that the applicant—

(i) was admitted to the United Kingdom with a valid student entry clearance if he is a person specified in the Appendix to these Rules; and

(ii) meets the requirements set out in para 64 (i)–(vii); and

(iii) has produced evidence of enrolment at a recognised nursing educational establishment; and

(iv) can provide satisfactory evidence of regular attendance during any course which he has already begun; or any other course for which he has been enrolled in the past; and

(v) would not, as a result of an extension of stay, spend more than four years in obtaining the relevant qualification; and

(vi) has not come to the end of a period of government or international scholarship agency sponsorship, or has the written consent of his original sponsor for a further period of study in the United Kingdom and evidence that sufficient sponsorship funding is available.

Extension of stay as a student nurse

68. An extension of stay as a student nurse may be granted, subject to a restriction on his freedom to take employment, provided the Secretary of State is satisfied that the applicant meets each of the requirements of para 67.

Refusal of extension of stay as a student nurse

69. An extension of stay as a student nurse is to be refused if the Secretary of State is not satisfied that each of the requirements of para 67 is met.

POSTGRADUATE DOCTORS AND DENTISTS

Requirements for leave to enter as a postgraduate doctor or dentist

70. The requirements for leave to enter the United Kingdom for the purpose of training as a postgraduate doctor or dentist are that the applicant—

(i) (a) is a graduate from a United Kingdom medical school intending to undertake Pre-Registration House Officer employment for up to 12 months, as required for full registration with the General Medical Council; and

(b) has not spent more than 12 months in aggregate in Pre-Registration House Officer employment; or

(ii) (a) is a doctor or dentist eligible for full or limited registration with the General Medical Council or with the General Dental Council who intends to undertake postgraduate training in a hospital; and

(b) has not spent more than four years in aggregate in the United Kingdom as a postgraduate doctor or dentist, excluding any period spent in Pre-Registration House Officer employment; and

(iii) intends to leave the United Kingdom on completion of his training period.

Leave to enter as a postgraduate doctor or dentist

71. A person seeking leave to enter the United Kingdom to study as a postgraduate doctor or dentist may be admitted for a period not exceeding 12 months provided the Immigration Officer is satisfied that each of the requirements of para 70 is met.

Refusal of leave to enter as a postgraduate doctor or dentist

72. Leave to enter as a postgraduate doctor or dentist is to be refused if the Immigration Officer is not satisfied that each of the requirements of para 70 is met.

Requirements for extension of stay as a postgraduate doctor or dentist

73. The requirements for an extension of stay as a postgraduate doctor or dentist are that the applicant—

(i) (a) meets the requirements of para 70 (i)(a); and

(b) would not, as a result of an extension of stay, spend more than 12 months in aggregate in Pre-Registration House Officer employment; or

(ii) (a) is a doctor or dentist who can provide satisfactory evidence of limited or full registration with the General Medical Council or registration with the General Dental Council and intends to undertake postgraduate training in a hospital; and

(b) would not, as a result of an extension of stay, spend more than four years in aggregate in the United Kingdom as a postgraduate doctor or dentist excluding any period spent in Pre-Registration House Officer employment; and

(iii) intends to leave the United Kingdom on completion of his training period.

Extension of stay as a postgraduate doctor or dentist

74. An extension of stay as a postgraduate doctor or dentist may be granted for a period not exceeding 12 months provided the Secretary of State is satisfied that each of the requirements of para 73 is met.

Refusal of extension of stay as a postgraduate doctor or dentist

75. An extension of stay as a postgraduate doctor or dentist is to be refused if the Secretary of State is not satisfied that each of the requirements of para 73 is met.

SPOUSES OF STUDENTS

Requirements for leave to enter or remain as the spouse of a student

76. The requirements to be met by a person seeking leave to enter or remain in the United Kingdom as the spouse of a student are that—

- (i) the applicant is married to a person admitted to or allowed to remain in the United Kingdom under paras 57–75; and
- (ii) each of the parties intends to live with the other as his or her spouse during the applicant's stay and the marriage is subsisting; and
- (iii) there will be adequate accommodation for the parties and any dependants without recourse to public funds; and
- (iv) the parties will be able to maintain themselves and any dependants adequately without recourse to public funds; and
- (v) the applicant does not intend to take employment except as permitted under para 77 below; and
- (vi) the applicant intends to leave the United Kingdom at the end of any period of leave granted to him.

Leave to enter or remain as the spouse of a student

77. A person seeking leave to enter or remain in the United Kingdom as the spouse of a student may be admitted or allowed to remain for a period not in excess of that granted to the student provided the Immigration Officer or, in the case of an application for limited leave to remain the Secretary of State, is satisfied that each of the requirements of para 76 is met. Employment is to be prohibited except where the period of leave being granted is 12 months or more.

Refusal of leave to enter or remain as the spouse of a student

78. Leave to enter or remain as the spouse of a student is to be refused if the Immigration Officer or, in the case of an application for limited leave to remain, the Secretary of State is not satisfied that each of the requirements of para 76 is met.

CHILDREN OF STUDENTS

Requirements for leave to enter or remain as the child of a student

79. The requirements to be met by a person seeking leave to enter or remain in the United Kingdom as the child of a student are that he—

- (i) is the child of a parent admitted to or allowed to remain in the United Kingdom as a student under paras 57–75; and
- (ii) is under the age of 18 or has current leave to enter or remain in this capacity; and

(iii) is unmarried, has not formed an independent family unit and is not leading an independent life; and

(iv) can, and will, be maintained and accommodated adequately without recourse to public funds; and

(v) will not stay in the United Kingdom beyond any period of leave granted to his parent.

Leave to enter or remain as the child of a student

80. A person seeking leave to enter or remain in the United Kingdom as the child of a student may be admitted or allowed to remain for a period of leave not in excess of that granted to the student provided the Immigration Officer or in the case of an application for limited leave to remain, the Secretary of State is satisfied that each of the requirements of para 79 is met. Employment is to be prohibited except where the period of leave being granted is 12 months or more.

Refusal of leave to enter or remain as the child of a student

81. Leave to enter or remain in the United Kingdom as the child of a student is to be refused if the Immigration Officer or, in the case of an application for limited leave to remain, the Secretary of State is not satisfied that each of the requirements of para 79 is met.

PROSPECTIVE STUDENTS

Requirements for leave to enter as a prospective student

82. The requirements to be met by a person seeking leave to enter the United Kingdom as a prospective student are that he—

(i) can demonstrate a genuine and realistic intention of undertaking within six months of his date of entry a course of study which would meet the requirements for an extension of stay as a student set out in paras 60 or 67; and

(ii) intends to leave the United Kingdom on completion of his studies or on the expiry of his leave to enter if he is not able to meet the requirements for an extension of stay as a student set out in paras 60 or 67; and

(iii) is able without working or recourse to public funds to meet the costs of his intended course and accommodation and the maintenance of himself and any dependants while making arrangements to study and during the course of his studies.

Leave to enter as a prospective student

83. A person seeking leave to enter the United Kingdom as a prospective student may be admitted for a period not exceeding six months with a

condition prohibiting employment provided the Immigration Officer is satisfied that each of the requirements of para 82 is met.

Refusal of leave to enter as a prospective student

84. Leave to enter as a prospective student is to be refused if the Immigration Officer is not satisfied that each of the requirements of para 82 is met.

Requirements for extension of stay as a prospective student

85. Six months is the maximum permitted leave which may be granted to a prospective student. The requirements for an extension of stay as a prospective student are that the applicant—

- (i) was admitted to the United Kingdom with a valid prospective student entry clearance if he is a person specified in the Appendix to these Rules; and
- (ii) meets the requirements of para 82; and
- (iii) would not, as a result of all extension of stay, spend more than six months in the United Kingdom.

Extension of stay as a prospective student

86. An extension of stay as a prospective student may be granted, with a prohibition on employment, provided the Secretary of State is satisfied that each of the requirements of para 85 is met.

Refusal of extension of stay as a prospective student

87. An extension of stay as a prospective student is to be refused if the Secretary of State is not satisfied that each of the requirements of para 85 is met.

PART 4: PERSONS SEEKING TO ENTER OR REMAIN IN THE UNITED KINGDOM IN AN 'AU PAIR' PLACEMENT, AS A WORKING HOLIDAYMAKER, OR FOR TRAINING OR WORK EXPERIENCE

'AU PAIR' PLACEMENTS

Definition of an 'au pair' placement

88. For the purposes of these Rules an 'au pair' placement is an arrangement whereby a young person—

- (a) comes to the United Kingdom for the purpose of learning the English language; and
- (b) lives for a time as a member of an English speaking family with appropriate opportunities for study; and
- (c) helps in the home for a maximum of five hours per day in return for a reasonable allowance and with two free days per week.

Requirements for leave to enter as an 'au pair'

89. The requirements to be met by a person seeking leave to enter the United Kingdom as an 'au pair' are that he—

(i) is seeking entry for the purpose of taking up an arranged placement which can be shown to fall within the definition set out in para 88; and
(ii) is aged between 17–27 inclusive or was so aged when first given leave to enter in this capacity; and
(iii) is unmarried; and
(iv) is without dependants; and
(v) is a national of one of the following countries: Andorra, Bosnia-Herzegovina, Croatia, Cyprus, Czech Republic, The Faeroes, Greenland, Hungary, Liechtenstein, Macedonia, Malta, Monaco, San Marino, Slovak Republic, Slovenia, Switzerland, or Turkey; and
(vi) does not intend to stay in the United Kingdom for more than two years as an 'au pair'; and
(vii) intends to leave the United Kingdom on completion of his stay as an 'au pair'; and
(viii) if he has previously spent time in the United Kingdom as an 'au pair', is not seeking leave to enter to a date beyond two years from the date on which he was first given leave to enter the United Kingdom in this capacity.

Leave to enter as an 'au pair'

90. A person seeking leave to enter the United Kingdom as an 'au pair' may be admitted for a period not exceeding two years with a prohibition on employment except as an 'au pair', provided the Immigration Officer is satisfied that each of the requirements of para 89 is met. (A non-visa national who wishes to ascertain in advance whether a proposed 'au pair' placement is likely to meet the requirements of para 89 is advised to obtain an entry clearance before travelling to the United Kingdom).

Refusal of leave to enter as an 'au pair'

91. An application for leave to enter as an 'au pair' is to be refused if the Immigration Officer is not satisfied that each of the requirements of para 89 is met.

Requirements for an extension of stay as an 'au pair'

92. The requirements for an extension of stay as an 'au pair' are that the applicant—

(i) was given leave to enter the United Kingdom as an 'au pair' under para 90; and

(ii) is undertaking an arranged 'au pair' placement which can be shown to fall within the definition set out in para 88; and

(iii) meets the requirements of para 89 (ii)–(vii); and

(iv) would not, as a result of an extension of stay, remain in the United Kingdom as an 'au pair' to a date beyond two years from the date on which he was first given leave to enter the United Kingdom in this capacity.

Extension of stay as an 'au pair'

93. An extension of stay as an 'au pair' may be granted with a prohibition on employment except as an 'au pair', provided the Secretary of State is satisfied that each of the requirements of para 92 is met.

Refusal of extension of stay as an 'au pair'

94. An extension of stay as an 'au pair' is to be refused if the Secretary of State is not satisfied that each of the requirements of para 92 is met.

WORKING HOLIDAYMAKERS

Requirements for leave to enter as a working holidaymaker

95. The requirements to be met by a person seeking leave to enter the United Kingdom as a working holidaymaker are that he—

(i) is a Commonwealth citizen; and

(ii) is aged 17-27 inclusive or was so aged when first given leave to enter in this capacity; and

(iii) is unmarried or is married to a person who meets the requirements of this paragraph and the parties to the marriage intend to take a working holiday together; and

(iv) has the means to pay for his return or onward journey; and

(v) is able and intends to maintain and accommodate himself without recourse to public funds; and

(vi) is intending to take employment incidental to a holiday but not to engage in business, provide services as a professional sportsman or entertainer or pursue a career in the United Kingdom; and

(vii) does not have dependent children any of whom are five years of age or over or who will reach five years of age before the applicant completes his working holiday; or commitments which would require him to earn a regular income; and

(viii) intends to leave the United Kingdom at the end of his working holiday; and

(ix) if he has previously spent time in the United Kingdom as a working holidaymaker, is not seeking leave to enter to a date beyond two years from the date he was first given leave to enter in this capacity; and,

(x) holds a valid United Kingdom entry clearance for entry in this capacity.

Leave to enter as a working holidaymaker

96. A person seeking leave to enter the United Kingdom as a working holidaymaker may be admitted for a period not exceeding two years with a condition restricting his freedom to take employment, provided he is able to produce to the Immigration Officer, on arrival, a valid United Kingdom entry clearance for entry in this capacity.

Refusal of leave to enter as a working holidaymaker

97. Leave to enter as a working holidaymaker is to be refused if a valid United Kingdom entry clearance for entry in this capacity is not produced to the Immigration Officer on arrival.

Requirements for an extension of stay as a working holidaymaker

98. The requirements for an extension of stay as a working holidaymaker are that the applicant—

(i) entered the United Kingdom with a valid United Kingdom entry clearance as a working holidaymaker; and

(ii) meets the requirements of para 95 (i)–(viii); and

(iii) would not, as a result of an extension of stay, remain in the United Kingdom as a working holidaymaker to a date beyond two years from the date on which he was first given leave to enter the United Kingdom in this capacity.

Extension of stay as a working holidaymaker

99. An extension of stay as a working holidaymaker may be granted, with a condition restricting his freedom to take employment, provided the Secretary of State is satisfied that the applicant meets each of the requirements of para 98.

Refusal of extension of stay as a working holidaymaker

100. An extension of stay as a working holidaymaker is to be refused if the Secretary of State is not satisfied that each of the requirements of para 98 is met.

CHILDREN OF WORKING HOLIDAYMAKERS

Requirements for leave to enter or remain as the child of a working holidaymaker

101. The requirements to be met by a person seeking leave to enter or remain in the United Kingdom as the child of a working holidaymaker are that—

- (i) he is the child of a parent admitted to or allowed to remain in the United Kingdom as a working holidaymaker; and
- (ii) he is under the age of five and will leave the United Kingdom before reaching that age; and
- (iii) he can and will be maintained and accommodated adequately without recourse to public funds or without his parent(s) engaging in business or taking employment except as provided by para 95 above; and
- (iv) both parents are being or have been admitted to or allowed to remain in the United Kingdom save where—
  - (a) the parent he is accompanying or joining is his sole surviving parent; or
  - (b) the parent he is accompanying or joining has had sole responsibility for his upbringing; or
  - (c) there are serious and compelling family or other considerations which make exclusion from the United Kingdom undesirable and suitable arrangements have been made for his care; and
- (v) if seeking leave to enter, he holds a valid United Kingdom entry clearance for entry in this capacity or, if seeking leave to remain, was admitted with a valid United Kingdom entry clearance for entry in this capacity.

Leave to enter or remain as the child of a working holidaymaker

102. A person seeking leave to enter or remain in the United Kingdom as the child of a working holidaymaker may be admitted or allowed to remain for the same period of leave as that granted to the working holidaymaker provided that, in relation to an application for leave to enter, a valid United Kingdom entry clearance for entry in this capacity is produced to the Immigration Officer on arrival or, in the case of an application for leave to remain, he was admitted with a valid United Kingdom entry clearance for entry in this capacity and is able to satisfy the Secretary of State that each of the requirements of para 101 (i)–(iv) is met.

Refusal of leave to enter or remain as the child of a working holiday-maker

103. Leave to enter or remain in the United Kingdom as the child of a working holidaymaker is to be refused if, in relation to an application for leave to enter, a valid United Kingdom entry clearance for entry in this capacity is not produced to the Immigration Officer on arrival or, in the case of an application for leave to remain, the applicant was not admitted with a valid United Kingdom entry clearance for entry in this capacity or is unable to satisfy the Secretary of State that each of the requirements of para 101(i)–(iv) is met.

SEASONAL WORKERS AT AGRICULTURAL CAMPS

Requirements for leave to enter as a seasonal worker at an agricultural camp

104. The requirements to be met by a person seeking leave to enter the United Kingdom as a seasonal worker at an agricultural camp are that he—

(i) is a student in full-time education aged between 18-25 years inclusive, except if returning for another season at the specific invitation of a farmer; and

(ii) holds a valid Home Office work card issued by the operator of a scheme approved by the Secretary of State; and

(iii) intends to leave the United Kingdom at the end of his period of leave as a seasonal worker; and

(iv) does not intend to take employment except in the terms of this paragraph.

Leave to enter as a seasonal worker at an agricultural camp

105. A person seeking leave to enter the United Kingdom as a seasonal worker at an agricultural camp may be admitted with a condition restricting his freedom to take employment for a period not exceeding 3 months or until 30 November of the year in question, whichever is the shorter period, provided the Immigration Officer is satisfied that each of the requirements of para 104 is met.

Refusal of leave to enter as a seasonal worker at an agricultural camp

106. Leave to enter the United Kingdom as a seasonal worker at an agricultural camp is to be refused if the Immigration Officer is not satisfied that each of the requirements of para 104 is met.

Requirements for extension of stay as a seasonal worker at an agricultural camp

107. The requirements for an extension of stay as a seasonal worker at an agricultural camp are that the applicant—

(i) entered the United Kingdom as a seasonal worker with a valid Home Office work card under para 105; and

(ii) meets the requirements of para 104 (iii)-(iv); and

(iii) can show that there is further farm work available under the approved scheme; and

(iv) would not, as a result of an extension of stay, remain in the United Kingdom as a seasonal worker for longer than six months in aggregate or beyond 30 November of the year in question, whichever is the shorter period.

Extension of stay as a seasonal worker at an agricultural camp

108. An extension of stay as a seasonal worker may be granted with a condition restricting his freedom to take employment for a further period not exceeding three months or until 30 November of the year in question, whichever is the shorter period, provided the Secretary of State is satisfied that the applicant meets each of the requirements of para 107.

Refusal of extension of stay as a seasonal worker at an agricultural camp

109. An extension of stay as a seasonal worker at an agricultural camp is to be refused if the Secretary of State is not satisfied that each of the requirements of para 107 is met.

TEACHERS AND LANGUAGE ASSISTANTS COMING TO THE UNITED KINGDOM UNDER APPROVED EXCHANGE SCHEMES

Requirements for leave to enter as a teacher or language assistant under an approved exchange scheme

110. The requirements to be met by a person seeking leave to enter the United Kingdom as a teacher or language assistant on an approved exchange scheme are that he—

(i) is coming to an educational establishment in the United Kingdom under an exchange scheme approved by the Education Departments or administered by the Central Bureau for Educational Visits and Exchanges or the League for the Exchange of Commonwealth Teachers; and

(ii) intends to leave the United Kingdom at the end of his exchange period; and

(iii) does not intend to take employment except in the terms of this paragraph; and

(iv) is able to maintain and accommodate himself and any dependants without recourse to public funds; and

(v) holds a valid United Kingdom entry clearance for entry in this capacity.

Leave to enter as a teacher or language assistant under an exchange scheme

111. A person seeking leave to enter the United Kingdom as a teacher or language assistant under an approved exchange scheme may be given leave to enter for a period not exceeding 12 months provided he is able to produce to the Immigration Officer, on arrival, a valid United Kingdom entry clearance for entry in this capacity.

Refusal of leave to enter as a teacher or language assistant under an approved exchange scheme

112. Leave to enter the United Kingdom as a teacher or language assistant under an approved exchange scheme is to be refused if a valid United Kingdom entry clearance for entry in this capacity is not produced to the Immigration Officer on arrival.

Requirements for extension of stay as a teacher or language assistant under an approved exchange scheme

113. The requirements for an extension of stay as a teacher or language assistant under an approved exchange scheme are that the applicant—

(i) entered the United Kingdom with a valid United Kingdom entry clearance as a teacher or language assistant; and

(ii) is still engaged in the employment for which his entry clearance was granted; and

(iii) is still required for the employment in question, as certified by the employer; and

(iv) meets the requirements of para 110 (ii)-(iv); and

(v) would not, as a result of an extension of stay, remain in the United Kingdom as an exchange teacher or language assistant for more than two years from the date on which he was first given leave to enter the United Kingdom in this capacity.

Extension of stay as a teacher or language assistant under an approved exchange scheme

114. An extension of stay as a teacher or language assistant under an approved exchange scheme may be granted for a further period not exceeding 12 months provided the Secretary of State is satisfied that each of the requirements of para 113 is met.

Refusal of extension of stay as a teacher or language assistant under an approved exchange scheme

115. An extension of stay as a teacher or language assistant under an approved exchange scheme is to be refused if the Secretary of State is not satisfied that each of the requirements of para 113 is met.

DEPARTMENT OF EMPLOYMENT APPROVED TRAINING OR WORK EXPERIENCE

Requirements for leave to enter for Department of Employment approved training or work experience

116. The requirements to be met by a person seeking leave to enter the United Kingdom for Department of Employment approved training or work experience are that he—

- (i) holds a valid work permit from the Department of Employment issued under the Training and Work Experience Scheme; and
- (ii) is not of an age which puts him outside the limits for employment; and
- (iii) is capable of undertaking the training or work experience as specified in his work permit; and
- (iv) intends to leave the United Kingdom on the completion of his training or work experience; and
- (v) does not intend to take employment except as specified in his work permit; and
- (vi) is able to maintain and accommodate himself and any dependants adequately without recourse to public funds.

Leave to enter for Department of Employment approved training or work experience

117. A person seeking leave to enter the United Kingdom for approved training may be admitted to the United Kingdom for a period not exceeding three years and a person seeking entry for approved work experience may be admitted for a period not exceeding 12 months, provided the Immigration Officer is satisfied that each of the requirements of para 116 is met. Leave to enter is to be subject to a condition permitting the person to take or change employment only with the permission of the Department of Employment.

Refusal of leave to enter for Department of Employment approved training or work experience

118. Leave to enter the United Kingdom for Department of Employment approved training or work experience is to be refused if the Immigration Officer is not satisfied that each of the requirements of para 116 is met.

Requirements for extension of stay for Department of Employment approved training or work experience

119. The requirements for an extension of stay for Department of Employment approved training or work experience are that the applicant—

- (i) entered the United Kingdom with a valid work permit under para 117 or was admitted or allowed to remain in the United Kingdom as a student; and

(ii) has written approval from the Department of Employment for an extension of stay in this category; and

(iii) meets the requirements of para 116 (ii)–(vi); and

(iv) would not as a result of an extension of stay spend more than two years in the United Kingdom for Department of Employment approved work experience.

Extension of stay for Department of Employment approved training or work experience

120. An extension of stay for approved training may be granted for a further period not exceeding three years; and an extension of stay for approved work experience may be granted for a further period not exceeding 12 months provided the Secretary of State is satisfied that each of the requirements of para 119 is met. An extension of stay is to be subject to a condition permitting the applicant to take or change employment only with the permission of the Department of Employment.

Refusal of extension of stay for Department of Employment approved training or work experience

121. An extension of stay for Department of Employment approved training or work experience is to be refused if the Secretary of State is not satisfied that each of the requirements of para 119 is met.

SPOUSES OF PERSONS WITH LIMITED LEAVE TO ENTER OR REMAIN UNDER PARAGRAPHS 111–21

Requirements for leave to enter or remain as the spouse of a person with limited leave to enter or remain in the United Kingdom under paras 110–21

122. The requirements to be met by a person seeking leave to enter or remain in the United Kingdom as the spouse of a person with limited leave to enter or remain in the United Kingdom under paras 110–21 are that—

(i) the applicant is married to a person with limited leave to enter or remain in the United Kingdom under paras 110–21; and

(ii) each of the parties intends to live with the other as his or her spouse during the applicant's stay and the marriage is subsisting; and

(iii) there will be adequate accommodation for the parties and any dependants without recourse to public funds in accommodation which they own or occupy exclusively; and

(iv) the parties will be able to maintain themselves and any dependants adequately without recourse to public funds; and

(v) the applicant does not intend to stay in the United Kingdom beyond any period of leave granted to his spouse; and

(vi) if seeking leave to enter, the applicant holds a valid United Kingdom entry clearance for entry in this capacity or, if seeking leave to remain, was admitted with a valid United Kingdom entry clearance for entry in this capacity.

Leave to enter or remain as the spouse of a person with limited leave to enter or remain in the United Kingdom under paras 110–21

123. A person seeking leave to enter or remain in the United Kingdom as the spouse of a person with limited leave to enter or remain in the United Kingdom under paras 110–121 may be given leave to enter or remain in the United Kingdom for a period of leave not in excess of that granted to the person with limited leave to enter or remain under paras 110–121 provided that, in relation to an application for leave to enter, he is able, on arrival to produce to the Immigration Officer a valid United Kingdom entry clearance for entry in this capacity or, in the case of an application for limited leave to remain, was admitted with a valid United Kingdom entry clearance for entry in this capacity and is able to satisfy the Secretary of State that each of the requirements of para 122 (i)–(v) is met.

Refusal of leave to enter or remain as the spouse of a person with limited leave to enter or remain in the United Kingdom under paras 110–21

124. Leave to enter or remain in the United Kingdom as the spouse of a person with limited leave to enter or remain in the United Kingdom under paras 110–21 is to be refused if, in relation to an application for leave to enter, a valid United Kingdom entry clearance for entry in this capacity is not produced to the Immigration Officer on arrival or, in the case of an application for limited leave to remain, if the applicant was not admitted with a valid United Kingdom entry clearance for entry in this capacity or is unable to satisfy the Secretary of State that each of the requirements of para 122 (i)–(v) is met.

CHILDREN OF PERSONS ADMITTED OR ALLOWED TO REMAIN UNDER PARAGRAPHS 110–21

Requirements for leave to enter or remain as the child of a person with limited leave to enter or remain in the United Kingdom under paras 110–21

125. The requirements to be met by a person seeking leave to enter or remain in the United Kingdom as the child of a person with limited leave to enter or remain in the United Kingdom under paras 110–21 are that—

(i) he is the child of a parent who has limited leave to enter or remain in the United Kingdom under paras 110–21; and

(ii) he is under the age of 18 or has current leave to enter or remain in this capacity; and

(iii) he is unmarried, has not formed an independent family unit and is not leading an independent life; and

(iv) he can, and will, be maintained and accommodated adequately without recourse to public funds in accommodation which his parent(s) own or occupy exclusively; and

(v) he will not stay in the United Kingdom beyond any period of leave granted to his parent(s); and

(vi) both parents are being or have been admitted to or allowed to remain in the United Kingdom save where—

(a) the parent he is accompanying or joining is his sole surviving parent; or

(b) the parent he is accompanying or joining has had sole responsibility for his upbringing; or

(c) there are serious and compelling family or other considerations which make exclusion from the United Kingdom undesirable and suitable arrangements have been made for his care; and

(vii) if seeking leave to enter, he holds a valid United Kingdom entry clearance for entry in this capacity or, if seeking leave to remain, was admitted with a valid United Kingdom entry clearance for entry in this capacity.

Leave to enter or remain as the child of a person with limited leave to enter or remain in the United Kingdom under paras 110–21

126. A person seeking leave to enter or remain in the United Kingdom as the child of a person with limited leave to enter or remain in the United Kingdom under paras 110–21 may be given leave to enter or remain in the United Kingdom for a period of leave not in excess of that granted to the person with limited leave to enter or remain under paras 110–21 provided that, in relation to an application for leave to enter, he is able, on arrival, to produce to the Immigration Officer a valid United Kingdom entry clearance for entry in this capacity or, in the case of an application for limited leave to remain, he was admitted with a valid United Kingdom entry clearance for entry in this capacity and is able to satisfy the Secretary of State that each of the requirements of para 125 (i)–(vi) is met.

Refusal of leave to enter or remain as the child of a person with limited leave to enter or remain in the United Kingdom under paras 110–21

127. Leave to enter or remain in the United Kingdom as the child of a person with limited leave to enter or remain in the United Kingdom under paras 110–21 is to be refused if, in relation to an application for leave to enter, a valid United Kingdom entry clearance for entry in this capacity is not produced to the Immigration Officer on arrival or in the case of an application for limited leave to remain, if the applicant was not admitted with a valid United Kingdom entry clearance for entry in this capacity or is unable to satisfy the Secretary of State that each of the requirements of para 125 (i)–(vi) is met.

PART 5: PERSONS SEEKING TO ENTER OR REMAIN IN THE UNITED KINGDOM FOR EMPLOYMENT

WORK PERMIT EMPLOYMENT

Requirements for leave to enter the United Kingdom for work permit employment

128. The requirements to be met by a person coming to the United Kingdom to seek or take employment (unless he is otherwise eligible for admission for employment under these Rules or is eligible for admission as a seaman under contract to join a ship due to leave British waters) are that he—

- (i) holds a valid Department of Employment work permit; and
- (ii) is not of an age which puts him outside the limits for employment; and
- (iii) is capable of undertaking the employment specified in the work permit; and
- (iv) does not intend to take employment except as specified in his work permit; and
- (v) is able to maintain and accommodate himself and any dependants adequately without recourse to public funds; and
- (vi) in the case of a person in possession of a work permit which is valid for a period of 12 months or less, intends to leave the United Kingdom at the end of his approved employment.

Leave to enter for work permit employment

129. A person seeking leave to enter the United Kingdom for the purpose of work permit employment may he admitted for a period not exceeding four years (normally as specified in his work permit), subject to a condition restricting him to employment approved by the Department of Employment, provided the Immigration Officer is satisfied that each of the requirements of para 128 is met.

Refusal of leave to enter for employment

130. Leave to enter for the purpose of employment is to be refused if the Immigration Officer is not satisfied that each of the requirements of para 128 is met (unless he is otherwise eligible for admission for employment under these Rules or is eligible for admission as a seaman under contract to join a ship due to leave British waters).

Requirements for an extension of stay for work permit employment

131. The requirements for an extension of stay to seek or take employment (unless the applicant is otherwise eligible for an extension of stay for employment under these Rules) are that the applicant—

(i) entered the United Kingdom with a valid work permit under para 124; and

(ii) has written approval from the Department of Employment for the continuation of his employment; and

(iii) meets the requirements of para 128 (ii)–(v).

Extension of stay for work permit employment

132. An extension of stay for work permit employment may be granted for a period not exceeding the period of approved employment recommended by the Department of Employment provided the Secretary of State is satisfied that each of the requirements of para 131 is met. An extension of stay is to be subject to a condition restricting the applicant to employment approved by the Department of Employment.

Refusal of extension of stay for employment

133. An extension of stay for employment is to be refused if the Secretary of State is not satisfied that each of the requirements of para 131 is met (unless the applicant is otherwise eligible for an extension of stay for employment under these Rules).

Indefinite leave to remain for a work permit holder

134. Indefinite leave to remain may be granted on application, to a person admitted as a work permit holder provided—

(i) he has spent a continuous period of four years in the United Kingdom in this capacity; and

(ii) he has met the requirements of para 131 throughout the four year period; and

(iii) he is still required for the employment in question, as certified by his employer.

Refusal of indefinite leave to remain for a work permit holder

135. Indefinite leave to remain in the United Kingdom for a work permit holder is to be refused if the Secretary of State is not satisfied that each of the requirements of para 134 is met.

REPRESENTATIVES OF OVERSEAS NEWSPAPERS, NEWS AGENCIES AND BROADCASTING ORGANISATIONS

Requirements for leave to enter as a representative of an overseas newspaper, news agency or broadcasting organisation

136. The requirements to be met by a person seeking leave to enter the United Kingdom as a representative of an overseas newspaper, news agency or broadcasting organisation are that he—

- (i) has been engaged by that organisation outside the United Kingdom and is being posted to the United Kingdom on a long-term assignment as a representative; and
- (ii) intends to work full-time as a representative of that overseas newspaper, news agency or broadcasting organisation; and
- (iii) does not intend to take employment except within the terms of this paragraph; and
- (iv) can maintain and accommodate himself and any dependants adequately without recourse to public funds; and
- (v) holds a valid United Kingdom entry clearance for entry in this capacity.

Leave to enter as a representative of an overseas newspaper, news agency or broadcasting organisation

137. A person seeking leave to enter the United Kingdom as a representative of an overseas newspaper, news agency or broadcasting organisation may be admitted for a period not exceeding 12 months provided he is able to produce to the Immigration Officer, on arrival, a valid United Kingdom entry clearance for entry in this capacity.

Refusal of leave to enter as a representative of an overseas newspaper, news agency or broadcasting organisation

138. Leave to enter as a representative of an overseas newspaper, news agency or broadcasting organisation is to be refused if a valid United Kingdom entry clearance for entry in this capacity is not produced to the Immigration Officer on arrival.

Requirements for an extension of stay as a representative of an overseas newspaper, news agency or broadcasting organisation

139. The requirements for an extension of stay as a representative of an overseas newspaper, news agency or broadcasting organisation are that the applicant—

(i) entered the United Kingdom with a valid United Kingdom entry clearance as a representative of an overseas newspaper, news agency or broadcasting organisation; and
(ii) is still engaged in the employment for which his entry clearance was granted, and
(iii) is still required for the employment in question, as certified by his employer; and
(iv) meets the requirements of para 136(ii)–(iv).

Extension of stay as a representative of an overseas newspaper, news agency or broadcasting organisation

140. An extension of stay as a representative of an overseas newspaper, news agency or broadcasting organisation may be granted for a period not exceeding three years provided the Secretary of State is satisfied that each of the requirements of para 139 is met.

Refusal of extension of stay as a representative of an overseas newspaper, news agency or broadcasting organisation

141. An extension of stay as a representative of an overseas newspaper, news agency or broadcasting organisation is to be refused if the Secretary of State is not satisfied that each of the requirements of para 139 is met.

Indefinite leave to remain for a representative of an overseas newspaper, news agency or broadcasting organisation

142. Indefinite leave to remain may be granted on application to a representative of an overseas newspaper news agency or broadcasting organisation provided—

(i) he has spent a continuous period of four years in the United Kingdom in this capacity; and
(ii) he has met the requirements of para 139 throughout the four year period; and
(iii) he is still required for the employment in question, as certified by his employer.

Refusal of indefinite leave to remain for a representative of an overseas newspaper, news agency or broadcasting organisation

143. Indefinite leave to remain in the United Kingdom for a representative of an overseas newspaper, news agency or broadcasting organisation is to be refused if the Secretary of State is not satisfied that each of the requirements of para 112 is met.

REPRESENTATIVES OF OVERSEAS FIRMS WHICH HAVE NO BRANCH, SUBSIDIARY OR OTHER REPRESENTATIVE IN THE UNITED KINGDOM (SOLE REPRESENTATIVES)

Requirements for leave to enter as a sole representative

144. The requirements to be met by a person seeking leave to enter the United Kingdom as a sole representative are that he—

- (i) has been recruited and taken on as an employee outside the United Kingdom as a representative of a firm which has its headquarters and principal place of business outside the United Kingdom and which has no branch, subsidiary or other representative in the United Kingdom;
- (ii) seeks entry to the United Kingdom as a senior employee with full authority to take operational decisions on behalf of the overseas firm for the purpose of representing it in the United Kingdom by establishing and operating a registered branch or wholly-owned subsidiary of that overseas firm; and
- (iii) intends to be employed full-time as a representative of that overseas firm; and
- (iv) is not a majority shareholder in that overseas firm; and
- (v) does not intend to take employment except within the terms of this paragraph; and
- (vi) can maintain and accommodate himself and any dependants adequately without recourse to public funds; and
- (vii) holds a valid United Kingdom entry clearance for entry in this capacity.

Leave to enter as a sole representative

145. A person seeking leave to enter the United Kingdom as a sole representative may be admitted for a period not exceeding 12 months provided he is able to produce to the Immigration Officer, on arrival, a valid United Kingdom entry clearance for entry in this capacity.

Refusal of leave to enter as a sole representative

146. Leave to enter as a sole representative is to be refused if a valid United Kingdom entry clearance for entry in this capacity is not produced to the Immigration Officer on arrival.

Requirements for an extension of stay as a sole representative

147. The requirements for an extension of stay as a sole representative are that the applicant—

- (i) entered the United Kingdom with a valid United Kingdom entry clearance as a sole representative of an overseas firm; and

(ii) can show that the overseas firm still has its headquarters and principal place of business outside the United Kingdom; and
(iii) is employed full-time as a representative of that overseas firm and has established and is in charge of its registered branch or wholly-owned subsidiary; and
(iv) is still required for the employment in question, as certified by his employer; and
(v) meets the requirements of para 144 (iii)–(vi).

Extension of stay as a sole representative

148. An extension of stay not exceeding three years as a sole representative may be granted provided the Secretary of State is satisfied that each of the requirements of para 147 is met.

Refusal of extension of stay as a sole representative

149. An extension of stay as a sole representative is to be refused if the Secretary of State is not satisfied that each of the requirements of para 117 is met.

Indefinite leave to remain for a sole representative

150. Indefinite leave to remain may be granted, on application, to a sole representative provided—

(i) he has spent a continuous period of four years in the United Kingdom in this capacity; and
(ii) he has met the requirements of para 147 throughout the four year period; and
(iii) he is still required for the employment in question, as certified by his employer.

Refusal of indefinite leave to remain for a sole representative

151. Indefinite leave to remain in the United Kingdom for a sole representative is to be refused if the Secretary of State is not satisfied that each of the requirements of para 150 is met.

PRIVATE SERVANTS IN DIPLOMATIC HOUSEHOLDS

Requirements for leave to enter as a private servant in a diplomatic household

152. The requirements to be met by a person seeking leave to enter the United Kingdom as a private servant in a diplomatic household are that he—

(i) is aged 18 or over; and
(ii) is employed as a private servant in the household of a member of staff of a diplomatic or consular mission who enjoys diplomatic privileges and immunity within the meaning of the Vienna

Convention on Diplomatic and Consular Relations or a member of the family forming part of the household of such a person; and

(iii) intends to work full-time as a private servant within the terms of this paragraph; and

(iv) does not intend to take employment except within the terms of this paragraph; and

(v) can maintain and accommodate himself and any dependants adequately without recourse to public funds; and

(vi) holds a valid United Kingdom entry clearance for entry in this capacity.

Leave to enter as a private servant in a diplomatic household

153. A person seeking leave to enter the United Kingdom as a private servant in a diplomatic household may be given leave to enter for a period not exceeding 12 months provided he is able to produce to the Immigration Officer on arrival a valid United Kingdom entry clearance for entry in this capacity.

Refusal of leave to enter as a private servant in a diplomatic household

154. Leave to enter as a private servant in a diplomatic household is to be refused if a valid United Kingdom entry clearance for entry in this capacity is not produced to the Immigration Officer on arrival.

Requirements for an extension of stay as a private servant in a diplomatic household

155. The requirements for an extension of stay as a private servant in a diplomatic household are that the applicant—

(i) entered the United Kingdom with a valid United Kingdom entry clearance as a private servant in a diplomatic household; and

(ii) is still engaged in the employment for which his entry clearance was granted; and

(iii) is still required for the employment in question as certified by the employer; and

(iv) meets the requirements of para 152 (iii)–(v).

Extension of stay as a private servant in a diplomatic household

156. An extension of stay as a private servant in a diplomatic household may be granted for a period not exceeding 12 months provided the Secretary of State is satisfied that each of the requirements of para 155 is met.

Refusal of extension of stay as a private servant in a diplomatic household

157. An extension of stay as a private servant in a diplomatic household is to be refused if the Secretary of State is not satisfied that each of the requirements of para 155 is met.

Indefinite leave to remain for a servant in a diplomatic household

158. Indefinite leave to remain may be granted, on application to a private servant in a diplomatic household provided—

- (i) he has spent a continuous period of four years in the United Kingdom in this capacity; and
- (ii) he has met the requirements of para 155 throughout the four year period; and
- (iii) he is still required for the employment in question, as certified by his employer.

Refusal of indefinite leave to remain for a servant in a diplomatic household

159. Indefinite leave to remain in the United Kingdom for a private servant in a diplomatic household is to be refused if the Secretary of State is not satisfied that each of the requirements of para 158 is met.

OVERSEAS GOVERNMENT EMPLOYEES

Requirements for leave to enter as an overseas government employee

160. For the purposes of these Rules an overseas government employee means a person coming for employment by an overseas government or employed by the United Nations organisation or other international organisation of which the United Kingdom is a member.

161. The requirements to be met by a person seeking leave to enter the United Kingdom as an overseas government employee are that he—

- (i) is able to produce either a valid United Kingdom entry clearance for entry in this capacity or satisfactory documentary evidence of his status as an overseas government employee; and
- (ii) intends to work full time for the government or organisation concerned; and
- (iii) does not intend to take employment except within the terms of this paragraph; and
- (iv) can maintain and accommodate himself and any dependants adequately without recourse to public funds.

Leave to enter as an overseas government employee

162. A person seeking leave to enter the United Kingdom as an overseas government employee may be given leave to enter for a period not exceeding

12 months, provided he is able on arrival to produce to the Immigration Officer a valid United Kingdom entry clearance for entry in this capacity or satisfy the Immigration Officer that each of the requirements of para 161 is met.

Refusal of leave to enter as an overseas government employee

163. Leave to enter as an overseas government employee is to be refused if a valid United Kingdom entry clearance for entry in this capacity is not produced to the Immigration Officer on arrival or if the Immigration Officer is not satisfied that each of the requirements of para 161 is met.

Requirements for an extension of stay as an overseas government employee

164. The requirements to be met by a person seeking an extension of stay as an overseas government employee are that the applicant—

(i) was given leave to enter the United Kingdom under para 162 as an overseas government employee; and

(ii) is still engaged in the employment in question; and

(iii) is still required for the employment in question, as certified by the employer; and

(iv) meets the requirements of para 161 (ii)–(iv).

Extension of stay as an overseas government employee

165. An extension of stay as an overseas government employee may be granted for a period not exceeding three years provided the Secretary of State is satisfied that each of the requirements of para 164 is met.

Refusal of extension of stay as an overseas government employee

166. An extension of stay as an overseas government employee is to be refused if the Secretary of State is not satisfied that each of the requirements of para 161 is met.

Indefinite leave to remain for an overseas government employee

167. Indefinite leave to remain may be granted, on application, to an overseas government employee provided—

(i) he has spent a continuous period of four years in the United Kingdom in this capacity; and

(ii) he has met the requirements of para 164 throughout the four year period; and

(iii) he is still required for the employment in question, as certified by his employer.

Refusal of indefinite leave to remain for an overseas government employee

168. Indefinite leave to remain in the United Kingdom for an overseas government employee is to be refused if the Secretary of State is not satisfied that each of the requirements of para 167 is met.

MINISTERS OF RELIGION, MISSIONARIES AND MEMBERS OF RELIGIOUS ORDERS

169. For the purposes of these Rules—

(i) a minister of religion means a religious functionary whose main regular duties comprise the leading of a congregation in performing the rites and rituals of the faith and in preaching the essentials of the creed;

(ii) a missionary means a person who is directly engaged in spreading a religious doctrine and whose work is not in essence administrative or clerical;

(iii) a member of a religious order means a person who is coming to live in a community run by that order.

Requirements for leave to enter as a minister of religion, missionary or member of a religious order

170. The requirements to be met by a person seeking leave to enter the United Kingdom as a minister of religion, missionary or member of a religious order are that he—

(i) (a) if seeking leave to enter as a minister of religion has either been working for at least one year as a minister of religion or, where ordination is prescribed by a religious faith as the sole means of entering the ministry, has been ordained as a minister of religion following at least one year's full-time or two years' part-time training for the ministry; or

(b) if seeking leave to enter as a missionary has been trained as a missionary or has worked as a missionary and is being sent to the United Kingdom by an overseas organisation; or

(c) if seeking leave to enter as a member of a religious order is coming to live in a community maintained by the religious order of which he is a member and, if intending to teach, does not intend to do so save at an establishment maintained by his order; and

(ii) intends to work full-time as a minister of religion, missionary or for the religious order of which he is a member; and

(iii) does not intend to take employment except within the terms of this paragraph; and

(iv) can maintain and accommodate himself and any dependants adequately without recourse to public funds; and

(v) holds a valid United Kingdom entry clearance for entry in this capacity.

Leave to enter as a minister of religion, missionary or member of a religious order

171. A person seeking leave to enter the United Kingdom as a minister of religion, missionary or member of a religious order may be admitted for a period not exceeding 12 months provided he is able to produce to the Immigration Officer, on arrival, a valid United Kingdom entry clearance for entry in this capacity.

Refusal of leave to enter as a minister of religion, missionary or member of a religious order

172. Leave to enter as a minister of religion, missionary or member of a religious order is to be refused if a valid United Kingdom entry clearance for entry in this capacity is not produced to the Immigration Officer on arrival.

Requirements for an extension of stay as a minister of religion, missionary or member of a religious order

173. The requirements for an extension of stay as a minister of religion, missionary or member of a religious order are that the applicant—

(i) entered the United Kingdom with a valid United Kingdom entry clearance as a minister of religion, missionary or member of a religious order; and

(ii) is still engaged in the employment for which his entry clearance was granted; and

(iii) is still required for the employment in question as certified by the leadership of his congregation, his employer or the head of his religious order; and

(iv) meets the requirements of para 170 (ii)–(iv).

Extension of stay as a minister of religion, missionary or member of a religious order

174. An extension of stay as a minister of religion, missionary or member of a religious order may be granted for a period not exceeding three years provided the Secretary of State is satisfied that each of the requirements of para 173 is met.

Refusal of extension of stay as a minister of religion, missionary or member of a religious order

175. An extension of stay as a minister of religion, missionary or member of a religious order is to be refused if the Secretary of State is not satisfied that each of the requirements of para 173 is met.

Indefinite leave to remain for a minister of religion, missionary or member of a religious order

176. Indefinite leave to remain may be granted, on application to a person admitted as a minister of religion, missionary or member of a religious order provided—

(i) he has spent a continuous period of four years in the United Kingdom in this capacity; and

(ii) he has met the requirements of para 173 throughout the four year period; and

(iii) he is still required for the employment in question as certified by the leadership of his congregation or the head of the religious order to which he belongs.

Refusal of indefinite leave to remain for a minister of' religion, missionary or member of a religious order

177. Indefinite leave to remain in the United Kingdom for a minister of religion, missionary or member of a religious order is to be refused if the Secretary of State is not satisfied that each of the requirements of para 176 is met.

AIRPORT-BASED OPERATIONAL GROUND STAFF OF OVERSEAS-OWNED AIRLINES

Requirements for leave to enter the United Kingdom as a member of the operational ground staff of an overseas-owned airline

178. The requirements to be met by a person seeking leave to enter the United Kingdom as a member of the operational ground staff of an overseas-owned airline are that he—

(i) has been transferred to the United Kingdom by an overseas-owned airline operating services to and from the United Kingdom to take up duty at an international airport as station manager, security manager or technical manager; and

(ii) intends to work full-time for the airline concerned; and

(iii) does not intend to take employment except within the terms of this paragraph; and

(iv) can maintain and accommodate himself and any dependants without recourse to public funds; and

(v) holds a valid United Kingdom entry clearance for entry in this capacity.

Leave to enter as a member of the operational ground staff of an overseas-owned airline

179. A person seeking leave to enter the United Kingdom as a member of the operational ground staff of an overseas-owned airline may be given leave

to enter for a period not exceeding 12 months, provided he is able to produce to the Immigration Officer, on arrival, a valid United Kingdom entry clearance for entry in this capacity.

Refusal of leave to enter as a member of the operational ground staff of an overseas-owned airline

180. Leave to enter as a member of the operational ground staff of an overseas-owned airline is to be refused if a valid United Kingdom entry clearance for entry in this capacity is not produced to the Immigration Officer on arrival.

Requirements for an extension of stay as a member of the operational ground staff of an overseas-owned airline

181. The requirements to be met by a person seeking an extension of stay as a member of the operational ground staff of an overseas-owned airline are that the applicant—

- (i) entered the United Kingdom with a valid United Kingdom entry clearance as a member of the operational ground staff of an overseas-owned airline; and
- (ii) is still engaged in the employment for which entry was granted; and
- (iii) is still required for the employment in question, as certified by the employer; and
- (iv) meets the requirements of para 178 (ii)–(iv).

Extension of stay as a member of the operational ground staff of an overseas-owned airline

182. An extension of stay as a member of the operational ground staff of an overseas-owned airline may be granted for a period not exceeding three years, provided the Secretary of State is satisfied that each of the requirements of para 181 is met.

Refusal of extension of stay as a member of the operational ground staff of an overseas-owned airline

183. An extension of stay as a member of the operational ground staff of an overseas-owned airline is to be refused if the Secretary of State is not satisfied that each of the requirements of para 181 is met.

Indefinite leave to remain for a member of the operational ground staff of an overseas-owned airline

184. Indefinite leave to remain may be granted, on application, to a member of the operational ground staff of an overseas-owned airline provided—

- (i) he has spent a continuous period of four years in the United Kingdom in this capacity; and

(ii) he has met the requirements of para 181 throughout the four year period; and

(iii) he is still required for the employment in question, as certified by the employer.

Refusal of indefinite leave to remain for a member of the operational ground staff of an overseas-owned airline

185. Indefinite leave to remain in the United Kingdom for a member of the operational ground staff of an overseas-owned airline is to be refused if the Secretary of State is not satisfied that each of the requirements of para 184 is met.

PERSONS WITH UNITED KINGDOM ANCESTRY

Requirements for leave to enter on the grounds of United Kingdom ancestry

186. The requirements to be met by a person seeking leave to enter the United Kingdom on the grounds of his United Kingdom ancestry are that he—

(i) is a Commonwealth citizen; and

(ii) is aged 17 or over; and

(iii) is able to provide proof that one of his grandparents was born in the United Kingdom and Islands; and

(iv) is able to work and intends to take or seek employment in the United Kingdom; and

(v) will be able to maintain and accommodate himself and any dependants adequately without recourse to public funds; and

(vi) holds a valid United Kingdom entry clearance for entry in this capacity.

Leave to enter the United Kingdom on the grounds of United Kingdom ancestry

187. A person seeking leave to enter the United Kingdom on the grounds of his United Kingdom ancestry may be given leave to enter for a period not exceeding four years provided he is able to produce to the Immigration Officer, on arrival, a valid United Kingdom entry clearance for entry in this capacity.

Refusal of leave to enter on the grounds of United Kingdom ancestry

188. Leave to enter the United Kingdom on the grounds of United Kingdom ancestry is to be refused if a valid United Kingdom entry clearance for entry in this capacity is not produced to the Immigration Officer on arrival.

Requirements for an extension of stay on the grounds of United Kingdom ancestry

189. The requirements to be met by a person seeking an extension of stay on the grounds of United Kingdom ancestry are that he is able to meet each of the requirements of para 186 (v).

Extension of stay on the grounds of United Kingdom ancestry

190. An extension of stay on the grounds of United Kingdom ancestry may be granted for a period not exceeding four years provided the Secretary of State is satisfied that each of the requirements of para 186 (i)–(v) is met.

Refusal of extension of stay on the grounds of United Kingdom ancestry

191. An extension of stay on the grounds of United Kingdom ancestry is to be refused if the Secretary of State is not satisfied that each of the requirements of para 186 (i)–(v) is met.

Indefinite leave to remain on the grounds of United Kingdom ancestry

192. Indefinite leave to remain may be granted, on application, to a Commonwealth citizen with a United Kingdom born grandparent provided—

- (i) he meets the requirements of para 186 (i)–(v); and
- (ii) he has spent a continuous period of four years in the United Kingdom in this capacity.

Refusal of indefinite leave to remain on the grounds of United Kingdom ancestry

193. Indefinite leave to remain in the United Kingdom on the grounds of a United Kingdom born grandparent is to be refused if the Secretary of State is not satisfied that each of the requirements of para 192 is met.

SPOUSES OF PERSONS WITH LIMITED LEAVE TO ENTER OR REMAIN UNDER PARAGRAPHS 128–93

Requirements for leave to enter or remain as the spouse of a person with limited leave to enter or remain in the United Kingdom under paras 128–93

194. The requirements to be met by a person seeking leave to enter or remain in the United Kingdom as the spouse of a person with limited leave to enter or remain in the United Kingdom under paras 128–93 are that—

- (i) the applicant is married to a person with limited leave to enter or remain in the United Kingdom under paras 128-193; and
- (ii) each of the parties intends to live with the other as his or her spouse during the applicant's stay and the marriage is subsisting; and

(iii) there will be adequate accommodation for the parties and any dependants without recourse to public funds in accommodation which they own or occupy exclusively; and

(iv) the parties will be able to maintain themselves and any dependants adequately without recourse to public funds; and

(v) the applicant does not intend to stay in the United Kingdom beyond any period of leave granted to his spouse; and

(vi) if seeking leave to enter, the applicant holds a valid United Kingdom entry clearance for entry in this capacity or, if seeking leave to remain, was admitted with a valid United Kingdom entry clearance for entry in this capacity.

Leave to enter or remain as the spouse of a person with limited leave to enter or remain in the United Kingdom under paras 128–93

195. A person seeking leave to enter or remain in the United Kingdom as the spouse of a person with limited leave to enter or remain in the United Kingdom under paras 128–93 may be given leave to enter or remain in the United Kingdom for a period of leave not in excess of that granted to the person with limited leave to enter or remain under paras 128–93 provided that, in relation to an application for leave to enter, he is able, on arrival, to produce to the Immigration Officer a valid United Kingdom entry clearance for entry in this capacity or, in the case of an application for limited leave to remain, he was admitted with a valid United Kingdom entry clearance for entry in this capacity and is able to satisfy the Secretary of State that each of the requirements of para 194 (i)–(v) is met. An application for indefinite leave to remain in this category may be granted provided the applicant was admitted with a valid United Kingdom entry clearance for entry in this capacity and is able to satisfy the Secretary of State that each of the requirements of para 194 (i)–(v) is met and provided indefinite leave to remain is, at the same time, being granted to the person with limited leave to enter or remain under paras 128–93.

Refusal of leave to enter or remain as the spouse of a person with limited leave to enter or remain in the United Kingdom under paras 128–93

196. Leave to enter or remain in the United Kingdom as the spouse of a person with limited leave to enter or remain in the United Kingdom under paras 128–93 is to be refused if, in relation to an application for leave to enter, a valid United Kingdom entry clearance for entry in this capacity is not produced to the Immigration Officer on arrival or, in the case of an application for limited leave to remain, if the applicant was not admitted with a valid United Kingdom entry clearance for entry in this capacity or is unable to satisfy the Secretary of State that each of the requirements of para 194 (i)–(v) is met. An application for indefinite leave to remain in this category

is to be refused if the applicant was not admitted with a valid United Kingdom entry clearance for entry in this capacity or is unable to satisfy the Secretary of State that each of the requirements of para 194 (i)–(v) is met or if indefinite leave to remain is not, at the same time, being granted to the person with limited leave to enter or remain under paras 128–93.

CHILDREN OF PERSONS WITH LIMITED LEAVE TO ENTER OR REMAIN IN THE UNITED KINGDOM UNDER PARAGRAPHS 128–93

Requirements for leave to enter or remain as the child of a person with limited leave to enter or remain in the United Kingdom under paras 128–93

197. The requirements to be met by a person seeking leave to enter or remain in the United Kingdom as a child of a person with limited leave to enter or remain in the United Kingdom under paras 128–93 are that—

- (i) he is the child of a parent with limited leave to enter or remain in the United Kingdom under paras 128–93; and
- (ii) he is under the age of 18 or has current leave to enter or remain in this capacity; and
- (iii) he is unmarried, has not formed an independent family unit and is not leading an independent life; and
- (iv) he can and will be maintained and accommodated adequately without recourse to public funds in accommodation which his parent(s) own or occupy exclusively; and
- (v) he will not stay in the United Kingdom beyond any period of leave granted to his parent(s); and
- (vi) both parents are being or have been admitted to or allowed to remain in the United Kingdom save where—
  - (a) the parent he is accompanying or joining is his sole surviving parent; or
  - (b) the parent he is accompanying or joining has had sole responsibility for his upbringing; or
  - (c) there are serious and compelling family or other considerations which make exclusion from the United Kingdom undesirable and suitable arrangements have been made for his care; and
- (vii) if seeking leave to enter, he holds a valid United Kingdom entry clearance for entry in this capacity or, if seeking leave to remain, was admitted with a valid United Kingdom entry clearance for entry in this capacity.

Leave to enter or remain as the child of a person with limited leave to enter or remain in the United Kingdom under paras 128–93

198. A person seeking leave to enter or remain in the United Kingdom as the child of a person with limited leave to enter or remain in the United Kingdom under paras 128–93 may be given leave to enter or remain in the United Kingdom for a period of leave not in excess of that granted to the person with limited leave to enter or remain under paras 128–93 provided that, in relation to an application for leave to enter, he is able to produce to the Immigration Officer, on arrival, a valid United Kingdom entry clearance for entry in this capacity or, in the case of an application for limited leave to remain, he was admitted with a valid United Kingdom entry clearance for entry in this capacity and is able to satisfy the Secretary of State that each of the requirements of para 197 (i)–(vi) is met. An application for indefinite leave to remain in this category may be granted provided the applicant was admitted with a valid United Kingdom entry clearance for entry in this capacity and is able to satisfy the Secretary of State that each of the requirements of para 197 (i)–(vi) is met and provided indefinite leave to remain is, at the same time, being granted to the person with limited leave to enter or remain under paras 128–93.

Refusal of leave to enter or remain as the child of a person with limited leave to enter or remain in the United Kingdom under paras 128–93

199. Leave to enter or remain in the United Kingdom as the child of a person with limited leave to enter or remain in the United Kingdom under paras 128–93 is to be refused if, in relation to an application for leave to enter, a valid United Kingdom entry clearance for entry in this capacity is not produced to the Immigration Officer on arrival or, in the case of an application for limited leave to remain, if the applicant was not admitted with a valid United Kingdom entry clearance for entry in this capacity or is unable to satisfy the Secretary of State that each of the requirements of para 197 (i)–(vi) is met. An application for indefinite leave to remain in this category is to be refused if the applicant was not admitted with a valid United Kingdom entry clearance for entry in this capacity or is unable to satisfy the Secretary of State that each of the requirements of para 197(i)–(vi) is met or if indefinite leave to remain is not, at the same time, being granted to the person with limited leave to enter or remain under paras 128–93.

PART 6: PERSONS SEEKING TO ENTER OR REMAIN IN THE UNITED KINGDOM AS A BUSINESSMAN, SELF-EMPLOYED PERSON, INVESTOR, WRITER, COMPOSER OR ARTIST

PERSONS INTENDING TO ESTABLISH THEMSELVES IN BUSINESS

Requirements for leave to enter the United Kingdom as a person intending to establish himself in business

200. For the purpose of paras 201–10 a business means an enterprise as—

- a sole trader; or
- a partnership; or
- a company registered in the United Kingdom.

201. The requirements to be met by a person seeking leave to enter the United Kingdom to establish himself in business are—

(i) that he satisfies the requirements of either para 202 or para 203; and

(ii) that he has not less than £200,000 of his own money under his control and disposable, in the United Kingdom which is held in his own name and not by a trust or other investment vehicle and which he will be investing in the business in the United Kingdom; and

(iii) that until his business provides him with an income he will have sufficient additional funds to maintain and accommodate himself and any dependants without recourse to employment (other than his work for the business) or to public funds; and

(iv) that he will be actively involved full-time in trading or providing services on his own account or in partnership, or in the promotion and management of the company as a director; and

(v) that his level of financial investment will be proportional to his interest in the business; and

(vi) that he will have either a controlling or equal interest in the business and that any partnership or directorship does not amount to disguised employment; and

(vii) that he will be able to bear his share of liabilities; and

(viii) that there is a genuine need for his investment and services in the United Kingdom; and

(ix) that his share of the profits of the business will be sufficient to maintain and accommodate himself and any dependants without recourse to employment (other than his work for the business) or to public funds; and

(x) that he does not intend to supplement his business activities by taking or seeking employment in the United Kingdom other than his work for the business; and

(xi) that he holds a valid United Kingdom entry clearance for entry in this capacity.

202. Where a person intends to take over or join as a partner or director an existing business in the United Kingdom he will need, in addition to meeting the requirements at para 201, to produce—

(i) a written statement of the terms on which he is to take over or join the business; and

(ii) audited accounts for the business for previous years; and

(iii) evidence that his services and investment will result in a net increase in the employment provided by the business to persons settled here to the extent of creating at least two new full-time jobs.

203. Where a person intends to establish a new business in the United Kingdom he will need, in addition to meeting the requirements at para 201 above, to produce evidence—

(i) that he will be bringing into the country sufficient funds of his own to establish a business; and

(ii) that the business will create full-time paid employment for at least two persons already settled in the United Kingdom.

Leave to enter the United Kingdom as a person seeking to establish himself in business

204. A person seeking leave to enter the United Kingdom to establish himself in business may be admitted for a period not exceeding 12 months with a condition restricting his freedom to take employment provided he is able to produce to the Immigration Officer, on arrival, a valid United Kingdom entry clearance for entry in this capacity.

Refusal of leave to enter the United Kingdom as a person seeking to establish himself in business

205. Leave to enter the United Kingdom as a person seeking to establish himself in business is to be refused if a valid United Kingdom entry clearance for entry in this capacity is not produced to the Immigration Officer on arrival.

Requirements for an extension of stay in order to remain in business

206. The requirements for an extension of stay in order to remain in business in the United Kingdom are that the applicant can show—

(i) that he entered the United Kingdom with a valid United Kingdom entry clearance as a businessman; and

(ii) audited accounts which show the precise financial position of the business and which confirm that he has invested not less than £200,000 of his own money directly into the business in the United Kingdom; and

(iii) that he is actively involved on a full-time basis in trading or providing services on his own account or in partnership or in the promotion and management of the company as a director; and

(iv) that his level of financial investment is proportional to his interest in the business; and

(v) that he has either a controlling or equal interest in the business and that any partnership or directorship does not amount to disguised employment; and

(vi) that he is able to bear his share of any liability the business may incur; and

(vii) that there is a genuine need for his investment and services in the United Kingdom; and

(viii) (a) that where he has established a new business, new full-time paid employment has been created in the business for at least two persons settled in the United Kingdom; or

(b) that where he has taken over or joined an existing business, his services and investment have resulted in a net increase in the employment provided by the business to persons settled here to the extent of creating at least two new full-time jobs; and

(ix) that his share of the profits of the business is sufficient to maintain and accommodate him and any dependants without recourse to employment (other than his work for the business) or to public funds; and

(x) that he does not and will not have to supplement his business activities by taking or seeking employment in the United Kingdom other than his work for the business.

Extension of stay in order to remain in business

207. An extension of stay in order to remain in business with a condition restricting his freedom to take employment may be granted for a period not exceeding three years provided the Secretary of State is satisfied that each of the requirements of para 206 is met.

Refusal of extension of stay in order to remain in business

208. An extension of stay in order to remain in business is to be refused if the Secretary of State is not satisfied that each of the requirements of para 206 is met.

Indefinite leave to remain for a person established in business

209. Indefinite leave to remain may be granted, on application, to a person established in business provided he—

(i) has spent a continuous period of four years in the United Kingdom in this capacity and is still engaged in the business in question; and

(ii) has met the requirements of para 206 throughout the four year period; and

(iii) submits audited accounts for the first three years of trading and management accounts for the fourth year.

Refusal of indefinite leave to remain for a person established in business

210. Indefinite leave to remain in the United Kingdom for a person established in business is to be refused if the Secretary of State is not satisfied that each of the requirements of para 209 is met.

PERSONS INTENDING TO ESTABLISH THEMSELVES IN BUSINESS UNDER PROVISIONS OF EC ASSOCIATION AGREEMENTS

Requirements for leave to enter the United Kingdom as a person intending to establish himself in business under the provisions of an EC Association Agreement

211. For the purpose of paras 212–23 a business means an enterprise as—

- a sole trader; or
- a partnership; or
- a company registered in the United Kingdom.

212. The requirements to be met by a person seeking leave to enter the United Kingdom to establish himself in business are that—

(i) he satisfies the requirements of either para 213 or para 214; and

(ii) the money he is putting into the business is under his control and sufficient to establish himself in business in the United Kingdom; and

(iii) until his business provides him with an income he will have sufficient additional funds to maintain and accommodate himself and any dependants without recourse to employment (other than his work for the business) or to public funds; and

(iv) his share of the profits of the business will be sufficient to maintain and accommodate himself and any dependants without recourse to employment (other than his work for the business) or to public funds; and

(v) he does not intend to supplement his business activities by taking or seeking employment in the United Kingdom other than his work for the business; and

(vi) he holds a valid United Kingdom entry clearance for entry in this capacity.

213. Where a person intends to establish himself in a company in the United Kingdom which he effectively controls he will need, in addition to meeting the requirements at para 212, to show—

(i) that he is a national of Hungary or Poland; and

(ii) that he will have a controlling interest in the company; and

(iii) that he will be actively involved in the promotion and management of the company; and

(iv) that the company will be registered in the United Kingdom and be trading or providing services in the United Kingdom; and

(v) that the company will be the owner of the assets of the business; and

(vi) where he is taking over an existing company, a written statement of the terms on which he is to take over the business and audited accounts for the business for previous years.

214. Where a person intends to establish himself in self-employment or in partnership in the United Kingdom he will need, in addition to meeting the requirements at 212 above, to show—

(i) that he is a national of Poland; and

(ii) that he will be actively involved in trading or providing services on his own account or in partnership in the United Kingdom; and

(iii) that he, or he together with his partners, will be the owner of the assets of the business; and

(iv) in the case of a partnership, that his part in the business will not amount to disguised employment; and

(v) where he is taking over or joining an existing business a written statement of the terms on which he is to take over or join the business and audited accounts for the business for previous years

Leave to enter the United Kingdom as a person seeking to establish himself in business under the provisions of an EC Association Agreement

215. A person seeking leave to enter the United Kingdom to establish himself in business may be admitted for a period not exceeding 12 months with a condition restricting his freedom to take employment provided he is able to produce to the Immigration Officer, on arrival, a valid United Kingdom entry clearance for entry in this capacity.

Refusal of leave to enter the United Kingdom as a person seeking to establish himself in business under the provisions of an EC Association Agreement

216. Leave to enter the United Kingdom as a person seeking to establish himself in business is to be refused if a valid United Kingdom entry clearance for entry in this capacity is not produced to the Immigration Officer on arrival.

Requirements for an extension of stay in order to remain in business under the provisions of an EC Association Agreement

217. The requirements for an extension of stay in order to remain in business in the United Kingdom are that the applicant can show that—

- (i) he has established himself in business in the United Kingdom; and
- (ii) his share of the profits of the business is sufficient to maintain and accommodate himself and any dependants without recourse to employment (other than his work for the business) or to public funds; and
- (iii) he does not and will not supplement his business activities by taking or seeking employment in the United Kingdom other than his work for the business; and
- (iv) in addition he satisfies the requirements of either para 218 or para 219.

218. Where a person has established himself in a company in the United Kingdom which he effectively controls he will need, in addition to meeting the requirements at para 217 above, to show—

- (i) that he is a national of Hungary or Poland; and
- (ii) that he is actively involved in the promotion and management of the company; and
- (iii) that he has a controlling interest in the company; and
- (iv) that the company is registered in the United Kingdom and trading or providing services in the United Kingdom; and
- (v) that the company is the owner of the assets of the business; and

(vi) the current financial position in the form of audited accounts for the company.

219. Where a person has established himself as a sole trader or in partnership in the United Kingdom he will need, in addition to meeting the requirements at 217 above, to show—

(i) that he is a national of Poland; and

(ii) that he is actively involved in trading or providing services on his own account or in partnership in the United Kingdom; and

(iii) that he, or he together with his partners, is the owner of the assets of the business; and

(iv) in the case of a partnership, that his part in the business does not amount to disguised employment; and

(v) the current financial position in the form of audited accounts for the business.

Extension of stay in order to remain in business under the provisions of an EC Association Agreement

220. An extension of stay in order to remain in business with a condition restricting his freedom to take employment may be granted for a period not exceeding three years provided the Secretary of State is satisfied that each of the requirements of paras 217 and 218 or 219 is met.

Refusal of extension of stay in order to remain in business under the provisions of an EC Association Agreement

221. An extension of stay in order to remain in business is to be refused if the Secretary of State is not satisfied that each of the requirements of paras 217 and 218 or 219 is met.

Indefinite leave to remain for a person established in business under the provisions of an EC Association Agreement

222. Indefinite leave to remain may be granted, on application, to a person established in business provided he—

(i) has spent a continuous period of four years in the United Kingdom in this capacity and is still so engaged; and

(ii) has met the requirements of paras 217 and 218 or 219 throughout the four years; and

(iii) submits audited accounts for the first three years of trading and management accounts for the fourth year.

Refusal of indefinite leave to remain for a person established in business under the provisions of an EC Association Agreement

223. Indefinite leave to remain in the United Kingdom for a person established in business is to be refused if the Secretary of State is not satisfied that each of the requirements of para 222 is met.

INVESTORS

Requirements for leave to enter the United Kingdom as an investor

224. The requirements to be met by a person seeking leave to enter the United Kingdom as an investor are that he—

(i) has money of his own under his control and disposable in the United Kingdom amounting to no less than £1 million; and

(ii) intends to invest not less than £750,000 of his capital in the United Kingdom by way of United Kingdom government bonds, share capital or loan capital in active and trading United Kingdom registered companies (other than those principally engaged in property investment and excluding investment by the applicant by way of deposits with a bank, building society or other enterprise whose normal course of business includes the acceptance of deposits); and

(iii) intends to make the United Kingdom his main home; and

(iv) is able to maintain and accommodate himself and any dependants without taking employment (other than self-employment or business) or recourse to public funds; and

(v) holds a valid United Kingdom entry clearance for entry in this capacity.

Leave to enter as an investor

225. A person seeking leave to enter the United Kingdom as an investor may be admitted for a period not exceeding 12 months with a restriction on his right to take employment, provided he is able to produce to the Immigration Officer, on arrival, a valid United Kingdom entry clearance for entry in this capacity.

Refusal of leave to enter as an investor

226. Leave to enter as an investor is to be refused if a valid United Kingdom entry clearance for entry in this capacity is not produced to the Immigration Officer on arrival.

Requirements for an extension of stay as an investor

227. The requirements for an extension of stay as an investor are that the applicant—

(i) entered the United Kingdom with a valid United Kingdom entry clearance as an investor; and

(ii) has no less than £1 million of his own money under his control in the United Kingdom; and

(iii) has invested not less than £750,000 of his capital in the United Kingdom on the terms set out in para 224 (ii) above and intends to maintain that investment on the terms set out in para 224 (ii); and

(iv) has made the United Kingdom his main home; and

(v) is able to maintain and accommodate himself and any dependants without taking employment (other than his self-employment or business) or recourse to public funds.

Extension of stay as an investor

228. An extension of stay as an investor, with a restriction on the taking of employment, may be granted for a maximum period of three years, provided the Secretary of State is satisfied that each of the requirements of para 227 is met.

Refusal of extension of stay as an investor

229. An extension of stay as an investor is to be refused if the Secretary of State is not satisfied that each of the requirements of para 227 is met.

Indefinite leave to remain for an investor

230. Indefinite leave to remain may be granted, on application, to a person admitted as an investor provided he—

(i) has spent a continuous period of four years in the United Kingdom in this capacity; and

(ii) has met the requirements of para 227 throughout the four year period including the requirement as to the investment of £750,000 and continues to do so.

Refusal of indefinite leave to remain for an investor

231. Indefinite leave to remain in the United Kingdom for an investor is to be refused if the Secretary of State is not satisfied that each of the requirements of para 230 is met.

WRITERS, COMPOSERS AND ARTISTS

Requirements for leave to enter the United Kingdom as a writer, composer or artist

232. The requirements to be met by a person seeking leave to enter the United Kingdom as a writer, composer or artist are that he—

(i) has established himself outside the United Kingdom as a writer, composer or artist primarily engaged in producing original work which has been published (other than exclusively in newspapers or magazines), performed or exhibited for its literary, musical or artistic merit; and

(ii) does not intend to work except as related to his self-employment as a writer, composer or artist; and

(iii) has for the preceding year been able to maintain and accommodate himself and any dependants from his own resources without working except as a writer, composer or artist; and

(iv) will be able to maintain and accommodate himself and any dependants from his own resources without working except as a writer, composer or artist and without recourse to public funds; and

(v) holds a valid United Kingdom entry clearance for entry in this capacity.

Leave to enter as a writer, composer or artist

233. A person seeking leave to enter the United Kingdom as a writer, composer or artist may be admitted for a period not exceeding 12 months, subject to a condition restricting his freedom to take employment, provided he is able to produce to the Immigration Officer, on arrival, a valid United Kingdom entry clearance for entry in this capacity.

Refusal of leave to enter as a writer, composer or artist

234. Leave to enter as a writer, composer or artist is to be refused if a valid United Kingdom entry clearance for entry in this capacity is not produced to the Immigration Officer on arrival.

Requirements for an extension of stay as a writer, composer or artist

235. The requirements for an extension of stay as a writer, composer or artist are that the applicant—

(i) entered the United Kingdom with a valid United Kingdom entry clearance as a writer, composer or artist; and

(ii) meets the requirements of para 232 (ii)–(iv).

Extension of stay as a writer, composer or artist

236. An extension of stay as a writer, composer or artist may be granted for a period not exceeding three years with a restriction on his freedom to take employment, provided the Secretary of State is satisfied that each of the requirements of para 235 is met.

Refusal of extension of stay as a writer, composer or artist

237. An extension of stay as a writer, composer or artist is to be refused if the Secretary of State is not satisfied that each of the requirements of para 235 is met.

Indefinite leave to remain for a writer, composer or artist

238. Indefinite leave to remain may be granted, on application, to a person admitted as a writer, composer or artist provided he—

(i) has spent a continuous period of four years in the United Kingdom in this capacity; and

(ii) has met the requirements of para 235 throughout the four year period.

Refusal of indefinite leave to remain for a writer, composer or artist

239. Indefinite leave to remain for a writer, composer or artist is to be refused if the Secretary of State is not satisfied that each of the requirements of para 238 is met.

SPOUSES OF PERSONS WITH LIMITED LEAVE TO ENTER OR REMAIN UNDER PARAGRAPHS 200–39

Requirements for leave to enter or remain as the spouse of a person with limited leave to enter or remain under paras 200–39

240. The requirements to be met by a person seeking leave to enter or remain in the United Kingdom as the spouse of a person with limited leave to enter or remain in the United Kingdom under paras 200–39 are that—

(i) the applicant is married to a person with limited leave to enter or remain in the United Kingdom under paras 200–39; and

(ii) each of the parties intends to live with the other as his or her spouse during the applicant's stay and the marriage is subsisting; and

(iii) there will be adequate accommodation for the parties and any dependants without recourse to public funds in accommodation which they own or occupy exclusively; and

(iv) the parties will be able to maintain themselves and any dependants adequately without recourse to public funds; and

(v) the applicant does not intend to stay in the United Kingdom beyond any period of leave granted to his spouse; and

(vi) if seeking leave to enter, the applicant holds a valid United Kingdom entry clearance for entry in this capacity or, if seeking leave to remain, was admitted with a valid United Kingdom entry clearance for entry in this capacity.

Leave to enter or remain as the spouse of a person with limited leave to enter or remain in the United Kingdom under paras 200–39

241. A person seeking leave to enter or remain in the United Kingdom as the spouse of a person with limited leave to enter or remain in the United Kingdom under paras 200–39 may be given leave to enter or remain in the United Kingdom for a period of leave not in excess of that granted to the person with limited leave to enter or remain under paras 200–39 provided that, in relation to an application for leave to enter, he is able, on arrival, to produce to the Immigration Officer a valid United Kingdom entry clearance for entry in this capacity or, in the case of an application for limited leave to

remain, he was admitted with a valid United Kingdom entry clearance for entry in this capacity and is able to satisfy the Secretary of State that each of the requirements of para 240 (i)–(v) is met. An application for indefinite leave to remain in this category may be granted provided the applicant was admitted with a valid United Kingdom entry clearance for entry in this capacity and is able to satisfy the Secretary of State that each of the requirements of para 240 (i)–(v) is met and provided indefinite leave to remain is, at the same time, being granted to the person with limited leave to remain under paras 200–39.

Refusal of leave to enter or remain as the spouse of a person with limited leave to enter or remain in the United Kingdom under paras 200–239

242. Leave to enter or remain in the United Kingdom as the spouse of a person with limited leave to enter or remain in the United Kingdom under paras 200-39 is to be refused if, in relation to an application for leave to enter, a valid United Kingdom entry clearance for entry in this capacity is not produced to the Immigration Officer on arrival or, in the case of an application for limited leave to remain, if the applicant was not admitted with a valid United Kingdom entry clearance for entry in this capacity or is unable to satisfy the Secretary of State that each of the requirements of para 240 (i)–(v) is met. An application for indefinite leave to remain in this category is to be refused if the applicant was not admitted with a valid United Kingdom entry clearance for entry in this capacity or is unable to satisfy the Secretary of State that each of the requirements of para 240 (i)–(v) is met or if indefinite leave to remain is not, at the same time, being granted to the person with limited leave to remain under paras 200–39.

CHILDREN OF PERSONS WITH LIMITED LEAVE TO ENTER OR REMAIN UNDER PARAGRAPHS 200–39

Requirements for leave to enter or remain as the child of a person with limited leave to enter or remain in the United Kingdom under paras 200–39

243. The requirements to be met by a person seeking leave to enter or remain in the United Kingdom as a child of a person with limited leave to enter or remain in the United Kingdom under paras 200–39 are that—

- (i) he is the child of a parent who has leave to enter or remain in the United Kingdom under paras 200–39; and
- (ii) he is under the age of 18 or has current leave to enter or remain in this capacity; and
- (iii) he is unmarried, has not formed an independent family unit and is not leading an independent life; and

(iv) he can and will be maintained and accommodated adequately without recourse to public funds in accommodation which his parent(s) own or occupy exclusively; and

(v) he will not stay in the United Kingdom beyond any period of leave granted to his parent(s); and

(vi) both parents are being or have been admitted to or allowed to remain in the United Kingdom save where—

(a) the parent he is accompanying or joining is his sole surviving parent; or

(b) the parent he is accompanying or joining has had sole responsibility for his upbringing; or

(c) there are serious and compelling family or other considerations which make exclusion from the United Kingdom undesirable and suitable arrangements have been made for his care; and

(vii) if seeking leave to enter, he holds a valid United Kingdom entry clearance for entry in this capacity or, if seeking leave to remain, was admitted with a valid United Kingdom entry clearance for entry in this capacity.

Leave to enter or remain as the child of a person with limited leave to enter or remain in the United Kingdom under paras 200–39

244. A person seeking leave to enter or remain in the United Kingdom as the child of a person with limited leave to enter or remain in the United Kingdom under paras 200–39 may be admitted to or allowed to remain in the United Kingdom for the same period of leave as that granted to the person given limited leave to enter or remain under paras 200–39 provided that, in relation to an application for leave to enter, he is able to produce to the Immigration Officer, on arrival, a valid United Kingdom entry clearance for entry in this capacity or, in the case of an application for limited leave to remain, he was admitted with a valid United Kingdom entry clearance for entry in this capacity and is able to satisfy the Secretary of State that each of the requirements of para 243 (i)–(vi) is met. An application for indefinite leave to remain in this category may be granted provided the applicant was admitted with a valid United Kingdom entry clearance for entry in this capacity and is able to satisfy the Secretary of State that each of the requirements of para 243 (i)–(vi) is met and provided indefinite leave to remain is, at the same time, being granted to the person with limited leave to remain under paras 200–39.

Refusal of leave to enter or remain as the child of a person with limited leave to enter or remain in the United Kingdom under paras 200–39

245. Leave to enter or remain in the United Kingdom as the child of a person with limited leave to enter or remain in the United Kingdom under paras 200–39 is to be refused if, in relation to an application for leave to enter, a valid United Kingdom entry clearance for entry in this capacity is not produced to the Immigration Officer on arrival or, in the case of an application for limited leave to remain, if the applicant was not admitted with a valid United Kingdom entry clearance for entry in this capacity or is unable to satisfy the Secretary of State that each of the requirements of para 243 (i)–(vi) is met. An application for indefinite leave to remain in this capacity is to be refused if the applicant was not admitted with a valid United Kingdom entry clearance for entry in this capacity or is unable to satisfy the Secretary of State that each of the requirements of para 243 (i)–(vi) is met or if indefinite leave to remain is not, at the same time, being granted to the person with limited leave to remain under paras 200–39.

PART 7: OTHER CATEGORIES

PERSONS EXERCISING RIGHTS OF ACCESS TO A CHILD RESIDENT IN THE UNITED KINGDOM

Requirements for leave to enter the United Kingdom as a person exercising rights of access to a child resident in the United Kingdom

246. The requirements to be met by a person seeking leave to enter the United Kingdom to exercise access rights to a child resident in the United Kingdom are that he—

- (i) produces evidence that a court in the United Kingdom has granted him access rights to his child; and
- (ii) is seeking leave to enter for the purpose of exercising access rights to his child; and
- (iii) is either divorced or legally separated from the other parent of the child; and
- (iv) intends to leave the United Kingdom at the expiry of his leave to enter; and
- (v) does not intend to take employment in the United Kingdom; and
- (vi) does not intend to produce goods or provide services within the United Kingdom, including the selling of goods or services direct to members of the public; and
- (vii) will maintain and accommodate himself and any dependants adequately out of resources available to him without recourse to public funds or taking employment; or will, with any depen-

dants, be maintained and accommodated adequately by relatives or friends; and

(viii) can meet the cost of the onward or return journey; and

(ix) holds a valid United Kingdom entry clearance for entry in this capacity.

Leave to enter as a person exercising rights of access to a child resident in the United Kingdom

247. A person seeking leave to enter the United Kingdom to exercise rights of access to a child resident in the United Kingdom may be granted leave to enter for a period which will enable him to exercise his access rights but in any case for no longer than 12 months provided he is able to produce to the Immigration Officer, on arrival, a valid United Kingdom entry clearance for entry in this capacity. Leave to enter is to be subject to a condition prohibiting employment.

Refusal of leave to enter as a person exercising rights of access to a child resident in the United Kingdom

248. Leave to enter as a person exercising rights of access to a child resident in the United Kingdom is to be refused if a valid United Kingdom entry clearance for entry in this capacity is not produced to the Immigration Officer on arrival.

HOLDERS OF SPECIAL VOUCHERS

Requirements for indefinite leave to enter as the holder of a special voucher

249. The requirements for indefinite leave to enter as the holder of a special voucher are that the person concerned—

(i) is a British Overseas citizen; and

(ii) is in possession of a special voucher issued to him by a British government representative overseas or a valid United Kingdom entry clearance for settlement in the United Kingdom in this capacity.

Indefinite leave to enter as the holder of a special voucher

250. A British Overseas citizen may be granted indefinite leave to enter the United Kingdom provided he is able to produce to the Immigration Officer, on arrival, either a special voucher issued to him by a British government representative or a valid United Kingdom entry clearance for settlement in this capacity.

Refusal of indefinite leave to enter as the holder of a special voucher

251. Indefinite leave to enter as the holder of a special voucher is to be refused if neither a special voucher issued by a British government

representative nor a valid United Kingdom entry clearance for settlement in this capacity is produced to the Immigration officer on arrival.

Requirements for indefinite leave to enter as the spouse or child of a special voucher holder

252. The requirements for indefinite leave to enter the United Kingdom as the spouse or child of a special voucher holder are that the person concerned—

(i) is in possession of a valid United Kingdom entry clearance for settlement in the United Kingdom in this capacity; and

(ii) can and will be maintained and accommodated adequately by the special voucher holder without recourse to public funds.

Indefinite leave to enter as the spouse or child of a special voucher holder

253. Indefinite leave to enter as the spouse or child of a special voucher holder may be granted provided a valid United Kingdom entry clearance for settlement is produced to the Immigration Officer on arrival.

Refusal of indefinite leave to enter as the spouse or child of a special voucher holder

254. Indefinite leave to enter as the spouse or child of a special voucher holder is to be refused if a valid United Kingdom entry clearance for settlement is not produced to the Immigration Officer on arrival.

EEA NATIONALS AND THEIR FAMILIES

Settlement

255. An EEA national (other than a student) and the family member of such a person, who has been issued with a residence permit or residence document valid for five years, and who has remained in the United Kingdom in accordance with the provisions of the 1994 EEA Order for four years and continues to do so may, on application, have his residence permit or residence document (as the case may be) endorsed to show permission to remain in the United Kingdom indefinitely.

256. A self-employed EEA national who has a right to reside in the United Kingdom by virtue of having ceased such activity in the United Kingdom within the meaning of the 1994 EEA Order, and the family member of such a person, will be permitted to remain in the United Kingdom indefinitely.

257. In addition, the following persons will be permitted to remain in the United Kingdom indefinitely—

(i) an EEA national who has been continuously resident in the United Kingdom for at least three years, has been in employment in the United Kingdom or any other Member State of the EEA for the preceding 12 months, and has reached the age of entitlement to a State retirement pension;

(ii) an EEA national who has ceased to be employed owing to a permanent incapacity for work arising out of an accident at work or an occupational disease entitling him to a State disability pension;

(iii) an EEA national who has been continuously resident in the United Kingdom for at least two years, and who has ceased to be employed owing to a permanent incapacity for work;

(iv) a member of the family of an EEA national as (defined in the 1994 EEA Order) to whom (i), (ii) or (iii) above applies;

(v) a member of the family of an EEA national (as defined in the 1994 EEA Order) who dies during his working life after having resided continuously in the United Kingdom for at least two years, or whose death results from an accident at work or an occupational disease.

The EEA family permit

258. An 'EEA family permit' means an entry clearance issued, free of charge, to a family member (as defined in the 1994 EEA Order) who is not an EEA national and who is a visa national or a person who wishes to install himself in the United Kingdom with an EEA national who is a qualified person in the terms of the 1994 EEA Order.

Requirements for the issue of an EEA family permit

259. The requirements for the issue of an EEA family permit are that—

(i) the applicant is the family member (as defined the 1994 EEA Order) of an EEA national who is a qualified person in the terms of the 1994 EEA Order; and

(ii) the applicant is coming to the United Kingdom for a purpose provided for in the 1994 EEA Order; and

(iii) the applicant is not a person who falls to be excluded on grounds of public policy, public security or public health.

Issue of an EEA family permit

260. An application for an EEA family permit shall be granted provided the Entry Clearance Officer is satisfied that each of the requirements of para 259 is met.

Refusal of an application for an EEA family permit

261. An application for an EEA family permit is to be refused if the Entry Clearance Officer is not satisfied that each of the requirements of para 259 is met.

Registration with the police for family members of EEA nationals

262. The requirements relating to registration with the police are set out in Part 10.

RETIRED PERSONS OF INDEPENDENT MEANS

Requirements for leave to enter the United Kingdom as a retired person of independent means

263. The requirements to be met by a person seeking leave to enter the United Kingdom as a retired person of independent means are that he—

(i) is at least 60 years old; and

(ii) has under his control and disposable in the United Kingdom an income of his own of not less than £25,000 per annum; and

(iii) is able and willing to maintain and accommodate himself and any dependants indefinitely in the United Kingdom from his own resources with no assistance from any other person and without taking employment or having recourse to public funds; and

(iv) can demonstrate a close connection with the United Kingdom; and

(v) intends to make the United Kingdom his main home; and

(vi) holds a valid United Kingdom entry clearance for entry in this capacity.

Leave to enter as a retired person of independent means

264. A person seeking leave to enter the United Kingdom as a retired person of independent means may be admitted subject to a condition prohibiting employment for a period not exceeding four years, provided he is able to produce to the Immigration Officer, on arrival, a valid United Kingdom entry clearance for entry in this capacity.

Refusal of leave to enter as a retired person of independent means

265. Leave to enter as a retired person of independent means is to be refused if a valid United Kingdom entry clearance for entry in this capacity is not produced to the Immigration Officer on arrival.

Requirements for an extension of stay as a retired person of independent means

266. The requirements for an extension of stay as a retired person of independent means are that the applicant—

(i) entered the United Kingdom with a valid United Kingdom entry clearance as a retired person of independent means; and

(ii) meets the requirements of para 263 (ii)–(iv); and

(iii) has made the United Kingdom his main home.

Extension of stay as a retired person of independent means

267. An extension of stay as a retired person of independent means, with a prohibition on the taking of employment, may be granted so as to bring

the person's stay in this category up to a maximum of four years in aggregate, provided the Secretary of State is satisfied that each of the requirements of para 266.

Refusal of extension of stay as a retired person of independent means

268. An extension of stay as a retired person of independent means is to be refused if the Secretary of State is not satisfied that each of the requirements of para 266 is met.

Indefinite leave to remain for a retired person of independent means

269. Indefinite leave to remain may be granted, on application, to a person admitted as a retired person of independent means provided he—

(i) has spent a continuous period of four years in the United Kingdom in this capacity; and

(ii) has met the requirements of para 266 throughout the four year period and continues to do so.

Refusal of indefinite leave to remain for a retired person of independent means

270. Indefinite leave to remain in the United Kingdom for a retired person of independent means is to be refused if the Secretary of State is not satisfied that each of the requirements of para 266 is met.

SPOUSES OF PERSONS WITH LIMITED LEAVE TO ENTER OR REMAIN IN THE UNITED KINGDOM AS RETIRED PERSONS OF INDEPENDENT MEANS

Requirements for leave to enter or remain as the spouse of a person with limited leave to enter or remain in the United Kingdom as a retired person of independent means

271. The requirements to be met by a person seeking leave to enter or remain in the United Kingdom as the spouse of a person with limited leave to enter or remain in the United Kingdom as a retired person of independent means are that—

(i) the applicant is married to a person with limited leave to enter or remain in the United Kingdom as a retired person of independent means; and

(ii) each of the parties intends to live with the other as his or her spouse during the applicant's stay and the marriage is subsisting; and

(iii) there will be adequate accommodation for the parties and any dependants without recourse to public funds in accommodation which they own or occupy exclusively; and

(iv) the parties will be able to maintain themselves and any dependants adequately without recourse to public funds; and

(v) the applicant does not intend to stay in the United Kingdom beyond any period of leave granted to his spouse; and

(vi) if seeking leave to enter, the applicant holds a valid United Kingdom entry clearance for entry in this capacity or, if seeking leave to remain, was admitted with a valid United Kingdom entry clearance for entry in this capacity.

Leave to enter or remain as the spouse of a person with limited leave to enter or remain in the United Kingdom as a retired person of independent means

272. A person seeking leave to enter or remain in the United Kingdom as the spouse of a person with limited leave to enter or remain in the United Kingdom as a retired person of independent means may be given leave to enter or remain in the United Kingdom for a period not in excess of that granted to the person given limited leave to enter or remain as a retired person of independent means provided that, in relation to an application for leave to enter, he is able to produce to the Immigration Officer, on arrival, a valid United Kingdom entry clearance for entry in this capacity, or, in the case of an application for limited leave to remain, he was admitted with a valid United Kingdom entry clearance for entry in this capacity and is able to satisfy the Secretary of State that each of the requirements of para 271(i)–(v) is met. An application for indefinite leave to remain in this category may be granted provided the applicant was admitted with a valid United Kingdom entry clearance for entry in this capacity and is able to satisfy the Secretary of State that each of the requirements of para 271(i)–(v) is met and provided indefinite leave to remain is, at the same time, being granted to the person with limited leave to enter or remain as a retired person of independent means. Leave to enter or remain is to be subject to a condition prohibiting employment except in relation to the grant of indefinite leave to remain.

Refusal of leave to enter or remain as the spouse of a person with limited leave to enter or remain in the United Kingdom as a retired person of independent means

273. Leave to enter or remain in the United Kingdom as the spouse of a person with limited leave to enter or remain in the United Kingdom as a retired person of independent means is to be refused if, in relation to an application for leave to enter, a valid United Kingdom entry clearance for entry in this capacity is not produced to the Immigration Officer on arrival or, in the case of an application for limited leave to remain, if the applicant was not admitted with a valid United Kingdom entry clearance for entry in this capacity or is unable to satisfy the Secretary of State that each of the requirements of para 271 (i)–(v) is met. An application for indefinite leave to remain in this category is to be refused if the applicant was not admitted with a valid United Kingdom entry clearance for entry in this capacity or is unable to

satisfy the Secretary of State that each of the requirements of para 271(i)–(v) is met or if indefinite leave to remain is not, at the same time, being granted to the person with limited leave to enter or remain as a retired person of independent means.

CHILDREN OF PERSONS WITH LIMITED LEAVE TO ENTER OR REMAIN IN THE UNITED KINGDOM AS RETIRED PERSONS OF INDEPENDENT MEANS

Requirements for leave to enter or remain as the child of a person with limited leave to enter or remain in the United Kingdom as a retired person of independent means

274. The requirements to be met by a person seeking leave to enter or remain in the United Kingdom as the child of a person with limited leave to enter or remain in the United Kingdom as a retired person of independent means are that—

(i) he is the child of a parent who has been admitted to or allowed to remain in the United Kingdom as a retired person of independent means; and

(ii) he is under the age of 18 or has current leave to enter or remain in this capacity; and

(iii) he is unmarried, has not formed an independent family unit and is not leading an independent life; and

(iv) he can, and will, be maintained and accommodated adequately without recourse to public funds in accommodation which his parent(s) own or occupy exclusively; and

(v) he will not stay in the United Kingdom beyond any period of leave granted to his parent(s); and

(vi) both parents are being or have been admitted to or allowed to remain in the United Kingdom save where—

- (a) the parent he is accompanying or joining is his sole surviving parent; or
- (b) the parent he is accompanying or joining has had sole responsibility for his upbringing; or
- (c) there are serious and compelling family or other considerations which make exclusion from the United Kingdom undesirable and suitable arrangements have been made for his care; and

(vii) if seeking leave to enter, he holds a valid United Kingdom entry clearance for entry in this capacity or, if seeking leave to remain, was admitted with a valid United Kingdom entry clearance for entry in this capacity.

Leave to enter or remain as the child of a person with limited leave to enter or remain in the United Kingdom as a retired person of independent means

275. A person seeking leave to enter or remain in the United Kingdom as the child of a person with limited leave to enter or remain in the United Kingdom as a retired person of independent means may be given leave to enter or remain in the United Kingdom for a period of leave not in excess of that granted to the person with limited leave to enter or remain as a retired person of independent means provided that, in relation to an application for leave to enter, he is able to produce to the Immigration Officer, on arrival, a valid United Kingdom entry clearance for entry in this capacity or, in the case of an application for limited leave to remain, he was admitted with a valid United Kingdom entry clearance for entry in this capacity and is able to satisfy the Secretary of State that each of the requirements of para 274 (i)–(vi) is met. An application for indefinite leave to remain in this category may be granted provided the applicant was admitted to the United Kingdom with a valid United Kingdom entry clearance for entry in this capacity and is able to satisfy the Secretary of State that each of the requirements of para 274 (i)–(vi) is met and provided indefinite leave to remain is, at the same time, being granted to the person with limited leave to enter or remain as a retired person of independent means. Leave to enter or remain is to be subject to a condition prohibiting employment except in relation to the grant of indefinite leave to remain.

Refusal of leave to enter or remain as the child of a person with limited leave to enter or remain in the United Kingdom as a retired person of independent means

276. Leave to enter or remain in the United Kingdom as the child of a person with limited leave to enter or remain in the United Kingdom as a retired person of independent means is to be refused if in relation to an application for leave to enter, a valid United Kingdom entry clearance for entry in this capacity is not produced to the Immigration Officer on arrival, or in the case of an application for limited leave to remain, if the applicant was not admitted with a valid United Kingdom entry clearance for entry in this capacity or is unable to satisfy the Secretary of State that each of the requirements of para 274 (i)–(vi) is met. An application for indefinite leave to remain in this category is to be refused if the applicant was not admitted with a valid United Kingdom entry clearance for entry in this capacity or is unable to satisfy the Secretary of State that each of the requirements of para 274 (i)–(vi) is met or if indefinite leave to remain is not, at the same time, being granted to the person with limited leave to enter or remain as a retired person of independent means.

PART 8: FAMILY MEMBERS

SPOUSES

277. Nothing in these Rules shall be construed as permitting a person to be granted entry clearance, leave to enter, leave to remain or variation of leave as a spouse of another if either party to the marriage will be aged under 16 on the date of arrival in the United Kingdom or (as the case may be) on the date on which the leave to remain or variation of leave would be granted.

278. Nothing in these Rules shall be construed as allowing a woman to be granted entry clearance, leave to enter, leave to remain or variation of leave as the wife of a man ('the husband') if—

- (i) her marriage to the husband is polygamous; and
- (ii) there is another woman living who is the wife of the husband and who—
  - (a) is, or at any time since her marriage to the husband has been, in the United Kingdom; or
  - (b) has been granted a certificate of entitlement in respect of the right of abode mentioned in s 2(1)(a) of the Immigration Act 1988 or an entry clearance to enter the United Kingdom as the wife of the husband.

For the purpose of this paragraph a marriage may be polygamous although at its inception neither party had any other spouse.

279. Paragraph 278 does not apply to any woman who seeks entry clearance, leave to enter, leave to remain or variation of leave where—

- (i) she has been in the United Kingdom before 1 August 1988 having been admitted for the purpose of settlement as the wife of the husband; or
- (ii) she has, since her marriage to the husband, been in the United Kingdom at any time when there was no such other woman living as is mentioned in para 278 (ii),

but where a woman claims that para 278 does not apply to her because she has been in the United Kingdom in circumstances which cause her to fall within sub-paras (i) or (ii) of that paragraph it shall be for her to prove that fact.

280. For the purposes of paras 278 and 279 the presence of any wife in the United Kingdom in any of the following circumstances shall be disregarded—

- (i) as a visitor; or
- (ii) an illegal entrant; or
- (iii) in circumstances whereby a person is deemed by s 11 (1) of the Immigration Act 1971 not to have entered the United Kingdom.

SPOUSES OF PERSONS PRESENT AND SETTLED IN THE UNITED KINGDOM OR BEING ADMITTED ON THE SAME OCCASION FOR SETTLEMENT

Requirements for leave to enter the United Kingdom with a view to settlement as the spouse of a person present and settled in the United Kingdom or being admitted on the same occasion for settlement

281. The requirements to be met by a person seeking leave to enter the United Kingdom with a view to settlement as the spouse of a person present and settled in the United Kingdom or who is on the same occasion being admitted for settlement are that—

- (i) the applicant is married to a person present and settled in the United Kingdom or who is on the same occasion being admitted for settlement; and
- (ii) the marriage was not entered into primarily to obtain admission to the United Kingdom; and
- (iii) the parties to the marriage have met; and
- (iv) each of the parties intends to live permanently with the other as his or her spouse and the marriage is subsisting; and
- (v) there will be adequate accommodation for the parties and any dependants without recourse to public funds in accommodation which they own or occupy exclusively; and
- (vi) the parties will be able to maintain themselves and any dependants adequately without recourse to public funds; and
- (vii) the applicant holds a valid United Kingdom entry clearance for entry in this capacity.

For the purposes of this paragraph, a member of HM Forces based in the United Kingdom but serving overseas is to be regarded as present and settled in the United Kingdom.

Leave to enter as the spouse of a person present and settled in the United Kingdom or being admitted for settlement on the same occasion

282. A person seeking leave to enter the United Kingdom as the spouse of a person present and settled in the United Kingdom or who is on the same occasion being admitted for settlement may be admitted for an initial period not exceeding 12 months provided a valid United Kingdom entry clearance for entry in this capacity is produced to the Immigration Officer on arrival.

Refusal of leave to enter as the spouse of a person present and settled in the United Kingdom or being admitted on the same occasion for settlement

283. Leave to enter the United Kingdom as the spouse of a person present and settled in the United Kingdom or who is on the same occasion being

admitted for settlement is to be refused if a valid United Kingdom entry clearance for entry in this capacity is not produced to the Immigration Officer on arrival.

Requirements for an extension of stay as the spouse of a person present and settled in the United Kingdom

284. The requirements for an extension of stay as the spouse of a person present and settled in the United Kingdom are that—

- (i) the applicant has limited leave to remain in the United Kingdom; and
- (ii) is married to a person present and settled in the United Kingdom; and
- (iii) the marriage was not entered into primarily to obtain settlement here; and
- (iv) the parties to the marriage have met; and
- (v) the applicant has not remained in breach of the immigration laws; and
- (vi) the marriage has not taken place after a decision has been made to deport the applicant or he has been recommended for deportation or been given notice under s 6(2) of the Immigration Act 1971; and
- (vii) each of the parties intends to live permanently with the other as his or her spouse and the marriage is subsisting; and
- (viii) there will be adequate accommodation for the parties and any dependants without recourse to public funds in accommodation which they own or occupy exclusively; and
- (ix) the parties will be able to maintain themselves and any dependants adequately without recourse to public funds.

Extension of stay as the spouse of a person present and settled in the United Kingdom

285. An extension of stay as the spouse of a person present and settled in the United Kingdom may be granted for a period of 12 months in the first instance, provided the Secretary of State is satisfied that each of the requirements of para 284 is met.

Refusal of extension of stay as the spouse of a person present and settled in the United Kingdom

286. An extension of stay as the spouse of a person present and settled in the United Kingdom is to be refused if the Secretary of State is not satisfied that each of the requirements of para 284 is met.

Requirements for indefinite leave to remain for the spouse of a person present and settled in the United Kingdom

287. The requirements for indefinite leave to remain for the spouse of a person present and settled in the United Kingdom are that—

(i) the applicant was admitted to the United Kingdom or given an extension of stay for a period of 12 months and has completed a period of 12 months as the spouse of a person present and settled here; and

(ii) the applicant is still the spouse of the person he or she was admitted or granted an extension of stay to join and the marriage is subsisting; and

(iii) each of the parties intends to live permanently with the other as his or her spouse.

Indefinite leave to remain for the spouse of a person present and settled in the United Kingdom

288. Indefinite leave to remain for the spouse of a person present and settled in the United Kingdom may be granted provided the Secretary of State is satisfied that each of the requirements of para 287 is met.

Refusal of indefinite leave to remain for the spouse of a person present and settled in the United Kingdom

289. Indefinite leave to remain for the spouse of a person present and settled in the United Kingdom is to be refused if the Secretary of State is not satisfied that each of the requirements of para 287 is met.

FIANCE(E)S

Requirements for leave to enter the United Kingdom as a fiance(e) (ie with a view to marriage and permanent settlement in the United Kingdom)

290. The requirements to be met by a person seeking leave to enter the United Kingdom as a fiance(e) are that—

(i) the applicant is seeking leave to enter the United Kingdom for marriage to a person present and settled in the United Kingdom or who is on the same occasion being admitted for settlement; and

(ii) it is not the primary purpose of the intended marriage to obtain admission to the United Kingdom; and

(iii) the parties to the proposed marriage have met; and

(iv) each of the parties intends to live permanently with the other as his or her spouse after the marriage; and

(v) adequate maintenance and accommodation without recourse to public funds will be available for the applicant until the date of the marriage; and

(vi) there will, after the marriage, be adequate accommodation for the parties and any dependants without recourse to public funds in accommodation which they own or occupy exclusively; and

(vii) the parties will be able after the marriage to maintain themselves and any dependants adequately without recourse to public funds; and

(viii) the applicant holds a valid United Kingdom entry clearance for entry in this capacity.

Leave to enter as a fiance(e)

291. A person seeking leave to enter the United Kingdom as a fiance(e) may be admitted, with a prohibition on employment, for a period not exceeding six months to enable the marriage to take place provided a valid United Kingdom entry clearance for entry in this capacity is produced to the Immigration Officer on arrival.

Refusal of leave to enter as a fiance(e)

292. Leave to enter the United Kingdom as a fiance(e) is to be refused if a valid United Kingdom entry clearance for entry in this capacity is not produced to the Immigration officer on arrival.

Requirements for an extension of stay as a fiance(e)

293. The requirements for an extension of stay as a fiance(e) are that—

(i) the applicant was admitted to the United Kingdom with a valid United Kingdom entry clearance as a fiance(e); and

(ii) good cause is shown why the marriage did not take place within the initial period of leave granted under para 291; and

(iii) there is satisfactory evidence that the marriage will take place at an early date; and

(iv) the requirements of para 290 (ii)–(vii) are met.

Extension of stay as a fiance(e)

294. An extension of stay as a fiance(e) may be granted for an appropriate period with a prohibition on employment to enable the marriage to take place provided the Secretary of State is satisfied that each of the requirements of para 293 is met.

Refusal of extension of stay as a fiance(e)

295. An extension of stay is to be refused if the Secretary of State is not satisfied that each of the requirements of para 293 is met.

CHILDREN

296. Nothing in these Rules shall be construed as permitting a child to be granted entry clearance, leave to enter or remain, or variation of leave where his mother is party to a polygamous marriage and any application by her for admission or leave to remain for settlement or with a view to settlement would be refused pursuant to para 278.

LEAVE TO ENTER OR REMAIN IN THE UNITED KINGDOM AS THE CHILD OF A PARENT, PARENTS OR A RELATIVE PRESENT AND SETTLED OR BEING ADMITTED FOR SETTLEMENT IN THE UNITED KINGDOM

Requirements for indefinite leave to enter the United Kingdom as the child of a parent, parents or a relative present and settled or being admitted for settlement in the United Kingdom

297. The requirements to be met by a person seeking indefinite leave to enter the United Kingdom as the child of a parent, parents or a relative present and settled or being admitted for settlement in the United Kingdom are that he—

(i) is seeking leave to enter to accompany or join a parent, parents or a relative in one of the following circumstances—

(a) both parents are present and settled in the United Kingdom; or

(b) both parents are being admitted on the same occasion for settlement; or

(c) one parent is present and settled in the United Kingdom and the other is being admitted on the same occasion for settlement; or

(d) one parent is present and settled in the United Kingdom or being admitted on the same occasion for settlement and the other parent is dead; or

(e) one parent is present and settled in the United Kingdom or being admitted on the same occasion for settlement and has had sole responsibility for the child's upbringing; or

(f) one parent or a relative is present and settled in the United Kingdom or being admitted on the same occasion for settlement and there are serious and compelling family or other considerations which make exclusion of the child undesirable and suitable arrangements have been made for the child's care; and

(ii) is under the age of 18; and

(iii) is not leading an independent life, is unmarried, and has not formed an independent family unit; and

(iv) can, and will, be maintained and accommodated adequately without recourse to public funds in accommodation which the parent, parents or relative own or occupy exclusively; and

(v) holds a valid United Kingdom entry clearance for entry in this capacity.

Requirements for indefinite leave to remain in the United Kingdom as the child of a parent, parents or a relative present and settled or being admitted for settlement in the United Kingdom

298. The requirements to be met by a person seeking indefinite leave to remain in the United Kingdom as the child of a parent, parents or a relative present and settled in the United Kingdom are that he—

(i) is seeking to remain with a parent, parents or a relative in one of the following circumstances—

(a) both parents are present and settled in the United Kingdom; or

(b) one parent is present and settled in the United Kingdom and the other parent is dead; or

(c) one parent is present and settled in the United Kingdom and has had sole responsibility for the child's upbringing; or

(d) one parent or a relative is present and settled in the United Kingdom and there are serious and compelling family or other considerations which make exclusion of the child undesirable and suitable arrangements have been made for the child's care; and

(ii) has limited leave to enter or remain in the United Kingdom, and

(a) is under the age of 18; or

(b) was given leave to enter or remain with a view to settlement under para 302; and

(iii) is not leading an independent life, is unmarried, and has not formed an independent family unit; and

(iv) can, and will, be maintained and accommodated adequately without recourse to public funds in accommodation which the parent, parents or relative own or occupy exclusively.

Indefinite leave to enter or remain in the United Kingdom as the child of a parent, parents or a relative present and settled or being admitted for settlement in the United Kingdom

299. Indefinite leave to enter the United Kingdom as the child of a parent, parents or a relative present and settled or being admitted for settlement in

the United Kingdom may be granted provided a valid United Kingdom entry clearance for entry in this capacity is produced to the Immigration Officer on arrival. Indefinite leave to remain in the United Kingdom as the child of a parent, parents or a relative present and settled in the United Kingdom may be granted provided the Secretary of Stale is satisfied that each of the requirements of para 298 is met.

Refusal of indefinite leave to enter or remain in the United Kingdom as the child of a parent, parents or a relative present and settled or being admitted for settlement in the United Kingdom

300. Indefinite leave to enter the United Kingdom as the child of a parent, parents or a relative present and settled or being admitted for settlement in the United Kingdom is to be refused if a valid United Kingdom entry clearance for entry in this capacity is not produced to the Immigration Officer on arrival. Indefinite leave to remain in the United Kingdom as the child of a parent, parents or a relative present and settled in the United Kingdom is to be refused if the Secretary of State is not satisfied that each of the requirements of para 298 is met.

Requirements for limited leave to enter or remain in the United Kingdom with a view to settlement as the child of a parent or parents given limited leave to enter or remain in the United Kingdom with a view to settlement

301. The requirements to be met by a person seeking limited leave to enter or remain in the United Kingdom with a view to settlement as the child of a parent or parents given limited leave to enter or remain in the United Kingdom with a view to settlement are that he—

(i) is seeking leave to enter to accompany or join or remain with a parent or parents in one of the following circumstances—

(a) one parent is present and settled in the United Kingdom or being admitted on the same occasion for settlement and the other parent is being or has been given limited leave to enter or remain in the United Kingdom with a view to settlement; or

(b) one parent is being or has been given limited leave to enter or remain in the United Kingdom with a view to settlement and has had sole responsibility for the child's upbringing; or

(c) one parent is being or has been given limited leave to enter or remain in the United Kingdom with a view to settlement and there are serious and compelling family or other considerations which make exclusion of the child undesirable and suitable arrangements have been made for the child's care; and

(ii) is under the age of 18; and
(iii) is not leading an independent life, is unmarried, and has not formed an independent family unit; and
(iv) can, and will, be maintained and accommodated adequately without recourse to public funds in accommodation which the parent or parents own or occupy exclusively; and
(v) (where an application is made for limited leave to remain with a view to settlement) has limited leave to enter or remain in the United Kingdom; and
(vi) if seeking leave to enter, holds a valid United Kingdom entry clearance for entry in this capacity or, if seeking leave to remain, was admitted with a valid United Kingdom entry clearance for entry in this capacity.

Limited leave to enter or remain in the United Kingdom with a view to settlement as the child of a parent or parents given limited leave to enter or remain in the United Kingdom with a view to settlement

302. A person seeking limited leave to enter the United Kingdom with a view to settlement as the child of a parent or parents given limited leave to enter or remain in the United Kingdom with a view to settlement may be admitted for a period not exceeding 12 months provided he is able, on arrival, to produce to the Immigration Officer a valid United Kingdom entry clearance for entry in this capacity. A person seeking limited leave to remain in the United Kingdom with a view to settlement as the child of a parent or parents given limited leave to enter or remain in the United Kingdom with a view to settlement may be given limited leave to remain for a period not exceeding 12 months provided the Secretary of State is satisfied that each of the requirements of para 301(i)–(v) is met.

Refusal of limited leave to enter or remain in the United Kingdom with a view to settlement as the child of a parent or parents given limited leave to enter or remain in the United Kingdom with a view to settlement

303. Limited leave to enter the United Kingdom with a view to settlement as the child of a parent or parents given limited leave to enter or remain in the United Kingdom with a view to settlement is to be refused if a valid United Kingdom entry clearance for entry in this capacity is not produced to the Immigration Officer on arrival. Limited leave to remain in the United Kingdom with a view to settlement as the child of a parent or parents given limited leave to enter or remain in the United Kingdom with a view to settlement is to be refused if the Secretary of State is not satisfied that each of the requirements of para 301(i)–(v) is met.

CHILDREN BORN IN THE UNITED KINGDOM WHO ARE NOT BRITISH CITIZENS

304. This paragraph and paras 305–09 apply only to unmarried dependent children under 18 years of age who were horn in the United Kingdom on or after 1 January 1983 (when the British Nationality Act 1981 came into force) but who, because neither of their parents was a British citizen or settled in the United Kingdom at the time of their birth, are not British citizens and are therefore subject to immigration control. Such a child requires leave to enter where admission to the United Kingdom is sought, and leave to remain where permission is sought for the child to be allowed to stay in the United Kingdom. If he qualifies for entry clearance, leave to enter or leave to remain under any other part of these Rules, a child who was born in the United Kingdom but is not a British citizen may be granted entry clearance, leave to enter or leave to remain in accordance with the provisions of that other part.

Requirements for leave to enter or remain in the United Kingdom as the child of a parent or parents given leave to enter or remain in the United Kingdom

305. The requirements to be met by a child born in the United Kingdom who is not a British citizen who seeks leave to enter or remain in the United Kingdom as the child of a parent or parents given leave to enter or remain in the United Kingdom are that he—

- (i) (a) is accompanying or seeking to join or remain with a parent or parents who have, or are given, leave to enter or remain in the United Kingdom; or
  - (b) is accompanying or seeking to join or remain with a parent or parents one of whom is a British citizen or has the right of abode in the United Kingdom; or
  - (c) is a child in respect of whom the parental rights and duties are vested solely in a local authority; and
- (ii) is under the age of 18; and
- (iii) was born in the United Kingdom; and
- (iv) is not leading an independent life, is unmarried, and has not formed an independent family unit; and
- (v) (where an application is made for leave to enter) has not been away from the United Kingdom for more than two years.

Leave to enter or remain in the United Kingdom

306. A child born in the United Kingdom who is not a British citizen and who requires leave to enter or remain in the circumstances set out in para 304 may be given leave to enter for the same period as his parent or parents

where para 305 (i)(a) applies, provided the Immigration Officer is satisfied that each of the requirements of para 305 (ii)–(v) is met. Where leave to remain is sought, the child may be granted leave to remain for the same period as his parent or parents where para 305 (i)(a) applies, provided the Secretary of State is satisfied that each of the requirements of para 305 (ii)–(iv) is met. Where the parent or parents have or are given periods of leave of different duration, the child may be given leave to whichever period is longer except that if the parents are living apart the child should be given leave for the same period as the parent who has day to day responsibility for him.

307. If a child does not qualify for leave to enter or remain because neither of his parents has a current leave (and neither of them is a British citizen or has the right of abode), he will normally be refused leave to enter or remain, even if each of the requirements of para 305 (ii)–(v) has been satisfied. However, he may be granted leave to enter or remain for a period not exceeding three months if both of his parents are in the United Kingdom and it appears unlikely that they will be removed in the immediate future, and there is no other person outside the United Kingdom who could reasonably be expected to care for him.

308. A child born in the United Kingdom who is not a British citizen and who requires leave to enter or remain in the United Kingdom in the circumstances set out in para 304 may be given indefinite leave to enter where para 305 (i)(b) or (i)(c) applies provided the Immigration Officer is satisfied that each of the requirements of para 305 (ii)–(v) is met. Where an application is for leave to remain, such a child may be granted indefinite leave to remain where para 305 (i)(b) or (i)(c) applies, provided the Secretary of State is satisfied that each of the requirements of para 305 (ii)–(iv) is met.

Refusal of leave to enter or remain in the United Kingdom

309. Leave to enter the United Kingdom where the circumstances set out in para 304 apply is to be refused if the Immigration Officer is not satisfied that each of the requirements of para 305 is met. Leave to remain for such a child is to be refused if the Secretary of State is not satisfied that each of the requirements of para 305 (i)–(iv) is met.

ADOPTED CHILDREN

Requirements for indefinite leave to enter the United Kingdom as the adopted child of a parent or parents present and settled or being admitted for settlement in the United Kingdom

310. The requirements to be met in the case of a child seeking indefinite leave to enter the United Kingdom as the adopted child of a parent or parents present and settled or being admitted for settlement in the United Kingdom are that he—

(i) is seeking leave to enter to accompany or join an adoptive parent or parents in one of the following circumstances;
   (a) both parents are present and settled in the United Kingdom; or
   (b) both parents are being admitted on the same occasion for settlement; or
   (c) one parent is present and settled in the United Kingdom and the other is being admitted on the same occasion for settlement; or
   (d) one parent is present and settled in the United Kingdom or being admitted on the same occasion for settlement and the other parent is dead; or
   (e) one parent is present and settled in the United Kingdom or being admitted on the same occasion for settlement and has had sole responsibility for the child's upbringing; or
   (f) one parent is present and settled in the United Kingdom or being admitted on the same occasion for settlement and there are serious and compelling family or other considerations which make exclusion of the child undesirable and suitable arrangements have been made for the child's care; and

(ii) is under the age of 18; and

(iii) is not leading an independent life, is unmarried, and has not formed an independent family unit; and

(iv) can, and will, be maintained and accommodated adequately without recourse to public funds in accommodation which the adoptive parent or parents own or occupy exclusively; and

(v) was adopted in accordance with a decision taken by the competent administrative authority or court in his country of origin or the country in which he is resident; and

(vi) was adopted at a time when—
   (a) both adoptive parents were resident together abroad; or
   (b) either or both adoptive parents were settled in the United Kingdom; and

(vii) has the same rights and obligations as any other child of the marriage; and

(viii) was adopted due to the inability of the original parent(s) or current carer(s) to care for him and there has been a genuine transfer of parental responsibility to the adoptive parents; and

(ix) has lost or broken his ties with his family of origin; and

(x) was adopted, but the adoption is not one of convenience arranged to facilitate his admission to or remaining in the United Kingdom; and

(xi) holds a valid United Kingdom entry clearance for entry in this capacity.

Requirements for indefinite leave to remain in the United Kingdom as the adopted child of a parent or parents present and settled in the United Kingdom

311. The requirements to be met in the case of a child seeking indefinite leave to remain in the United Kingdom as the adopted child of a parent or parents present and settled in the United Kingdom are that he—

(i) is seeking to remain with an adoptive parent or parents in one of the following circumstances—

- (a) both parents are present and settled in the United Kingdom; or
- (b) one parent is present and settled in the United Kingdom and the other parent is dead; or
- (c) one parent is present and settled in the United Kingdom and has had sole responsibility for the child's upbringing; or
- (d) one parent is present and settled in the United Kingdom and there are serious and compelling family or other considerations which make exclusion of the child undesirable and suitable arrangements have been made for the child's care; and

(ii) has limited leave to enter or remain in the United Kingdom; and

- (a) is under the age of 18; or
- (b) was given leave to enter or remain with a view to settlement under para 315; and

(iii) is not leading an independent life, is unmarried, and has not formed an independent family unit; and

(iv) can, and will, be maintained and accommodated adequately without recourse to public funds in accommodation which the adoptive parent or parents own or occupy exclusively; and

(v) was adopted in accordance with a decision taken by the competent administrative authority or court in his country of origin or the country in which he is resident; and

(vi) was adopted at a time when—

- (a) both adoptive parents were resident together abroad; or
- (b) either or both adoptive parents were settled in the United Kingdom; and

(vii) has the same rights and obligations as any other child of the marriage; and

(viii) was adopted due to the inability of the original parent(s) or current carer(s) to care for him and there has been a genuine transfer of parental responsibility to the adoptive parents; and

(ix) has lost or broken his ties with his family of origin; and

(x) was adopted, but the adoption is not one of convenience arranged to facilitate his admission to or remaining in the United Kingdom.

Indefinite leave to enter or remain in the United Kingdom as the adopted child of a parent or parents present and settled or being admitted for settlement in the United Kingdom

312. Indefinite leave to enter the United Kingdom as the adopted child of a parent or parents present and settled or being admitted for settlement in the United Kingdom may be granted provided a valid United Kingdom entry clearance for entry in this capacity is produced to the Immigration Officer on arrival. Indefinite leave to remain in the United Kingdom as the adopted child of a parent or parents present and settled in the United Kingdom may be granted provided the Secretary of State is satisfied that each of the requirements of para 311 is met.

Refusal of indefinite leave to enter or remain in the United Kingdom as the adopted child of a parent or parents present and settled or being admitted for settlement in the United Kingdom

313. Indefinite leave to enter the United Kingdom as the adopted child of a parent or parents present and settled or being admitted for settlement in the United Kingdom is to be refused if a valid United Kingdom entry clearance for entry in this capacity is not produced to the Immigration Officer on arrival. Indefinite leave to remain in the United Kingdom as the adopted child of a parent or parents present and settled in the United Kingdom is to be refused if the Secretary of State is not satisfied that each of the requirements of para 311 is met.

Requirements for limited leave to enter or remain in the United Kingdom with a view to settlement as the adopted child of a parent or parents given limited leave to enter or remain in the United Kingdom with a view to settlement

314. The requirements to be met in the case of a child seeking limited leave to enter or remain in the United Kingdom with a view to settlement as the adopted child of a parent or parents given limited leave to enter or remain in the United Kingdom with a view to settlement are that he—

(i) is seeking leave to enter to accompany or join or remain with a parent or parents in one of the following circumstances—

(a) one parent is present and settled in the United Kingdom or being admitted on the same occasion for settlement and the other parent is being or has been given limited leave to enter or remain in the United Kingdom with a view to settlement; or

(b) one parent is being or has been given limited leave to enter or remain in the United Kingdom with a view to settlement and has had sole responsibility for the child's upbringing; or

(c) one parent is being or has been given limited leave to enter or remain in the United Kingdom with a view to settlement and there are serious and compelling family or other considerations which make exclusion of the child undesirable and suitable arrangements have been made for the child's care; and

(ii) is under the age of 18; and

(iii) is not leading an independent life, is unmarried, and has not formed an independent family unit; and

(iv) can, and will, be maintained and accommodated adequately without recourse to public funds in accommodation which the adoptive parent or parents own or occupy exclusively; and

(v) was adopted in accordance with a decision taken by the competent administrative authority or court in his country of origin or the country in which he is resident; and

(vi) was adopted at a time when—

(a) both adoptive parents were resident together abroad; or

(b) either or both adoptive parents were settled in the United Kingdom; and

(vii) has the same rights and obligations as any other child of the marriage; and

(viii) was adopted due to the inability of the original parent(s) or current carer(s) to care for him and there has been a genuine transfer of parental responsibility to the adoptive parents; and

(ix) has lost or broken his ties with his family of origin; and

(x) was adopted, but the adoption is not one of convenience arranged to facilitate his admission to the United Kingdom; and

(xi) (where an application is made for limited leave to remain with a view to settlement) has limited leave to enter or remain in the United Kingdom; and

(xii) if seeking leave to enter, holds a valid United Kingdom entry clearance for entry in this capacity.

Limited leave to enter or remain in the United Kingdom with a view to settlement as the adopted child of a parent or parents given limited leave to enter or remain in the United Kingdom with a view to settlement

315. A person seeking limited leave to enter the United Kingdom with a view to settlement as the adopted child of a parent or parents given limited leave to enter or remain in the United Kingdom with a view to settlement may be admitted for a period not exceeding 12 months provided he is able, on arrival, to produce to the Immigration Officer a valid United Kingdom entry clearance for entry in this capacity. A person seeking limited leave to remain in the United Kingdom with a view to settlement as the adopted child of a parent or parents given limited leave to enter or remain in the United Kingdom with a view to settlement may be granted limited leave for a period not exceeding 12 months provided the Secretary of State is satisfied that each of the requirements of para 314 (i)–(xi) is met.

Refusal of limited leave to enter or remain in the United Kingdom with a view to settlement as the adopted child of a parent or parents given limited leave to enter or remain in the United Kingdom with a view to settlement

316. Limited leave to enter the United Kingdom with a view to settlement as the adopted child of a parent or parents given limited leave to enter or remain in the United Kingdom with a view to settlement is to be refused if a valid United Kingdom entry clearance for entry in this capacity is not produced to the Immigration Officer on arrival. Limited leave to remain in the United Kingdom with a view to settlement as the adopted child of a parent or parents given limited leave to enter or remain in the United Kingdom with a view to settlement is to be refused if the Secretary of State is not satisfied that each of the requirements of para 314 (i)–(xi) is met.

PARENTS, GRANDPARENTS AND OTHER DEPENDENT RELATIVES OF PERSONS PRESENT AND SETTLED IN THE UNITED KINGDOM

Requirements for indefinite leave to enter or remain in the United Kingdom as the parent, grandparent or other dependent relative of a person present and settled in the United Kingdom

317. The requirements to be met by a person seeking indefinite leave to enter or remain in the United Kingdom as the parent, grandparent or other dependent relative of a person present and settled in the United Kingdom are that the person—

(i) is related to a person present and settled in the United Kingdom in one of the following ways—

(a) mother or grandmother who is a widow aged 65 years or over; or

(b) father or grandfather who is a widower aged 65 years or over; or

(c) parent or grandparents travelling together of whom at least one is aged 65 or over; or

(d) a parent or grandparent aged 65 or over who has remarried but cannot look to the spouse or children of the second marriage for financial support; and where the person settled in the United Kingdom is able and willing to maintain the parent or grandparent and any spouse or child of the second marriage who would be admissible as a dependant; or

(e) a parent or grandparent under the age of 65 if living alone outside the United Kingdom in the most exceptional compassionate circumstances and mainly dependent financially on relatives settled in the United Kingdom; or

(f) the son, daughter, sister, brother, uncle or aunt over the age of 18 if living alone outside the United Kingdom in the most exceptional compassionate circumstances and mainly dependent financially on relatives settled in the United Kingdom; and

(ii) is joining or accompanying a person who is present and settled in the United Kingdom or who is on the same occasion being admitted for settlement; and

(iii) is financially wholly or mainly dependent on the relative present and settled in the United Kingdom; and

(iv) can, and will, be maintained and accommodated adequately, together with any dependants, without recourse to public funds in accommodation which the sponsor owns or occupies exclusively; and

(v) has no other close relatives in his own country to whom he could turn for financial support; and

(vi) if seeking leave to enter, holds a valid United Kingdom entry clearance for entry in this capacity.

Indefinite leave to enter or remain as the parent, grandparent or other dependent relative of a person present and settled in the United Kingdom

318. Indefinite leave to enter the United Kingdom as the parent, grandparent or other dependent relative of a person present and settled in the United Kingdom may be granted provided a valid United Kingdom entry clearance for entry in this capacity is produced to the Immigration Officer on arrival. Indefinite leave to remain in the United Kingdom as the parent,

grandparent or other dependent relative of a person present and settled in the United Kingdom may be granted provided the Secretary of State is satisfied that each of the requirements of para 317 (i)–(v) is met.

Refusal of indefinite leave to enter or remain in the United Kingdom as the parent, grandparent or other dependent relative of a person present and settled in the United Kingdom

319. Indefinite leave to enter the United Kingdom as the parent, grandparent or other dependent relative of a person settled in the United Kingdom is to be refused if a valid United Kingdom entry clearance for entry in this capacity is not produced to the Immigration Officer on arrival. Indefinite leave to remain in the United Kingdom as the parent, grandparent or other dependent relative of a person present and settled in the United Kingdom is to be refused if the Secretary of State is not satisfied that each of the requirements of para 317 (i)–(v) is met.

PART 9: GENERAL GROUNDS FOR THE REFUSAL OF ENTRY CLEARANCE, LEAVE TO ENTER OR VARIATION OF LEAVE TO ENTER OR REMAIN IN THE UNITED KINGDOM

REFUSAL OF ENTRY CLEARANCE OR LEAVE TO ENTER THE UNITED KINGDOM

320. In addition to the grounds for refusal of entry clearance or leave to enter set out in Parts 2–8 of these Rules, and subject to para 321 below, the following grounds for the refusal of entry clearance or leave to enter apply—

Grounds on which entry clearance or leave to enter the United Kingdom is to be refused

(1) the fact that entry is being sought for a purpose not covered by these Rules;

(2) the fact that the person seeking entry to the United Kingdom is currently the subject of a deportation order;

(3) failure by the person seeking entry to the United Kingdom to produce to the Immigration Officer a valid national passport or other document satisfactorily establishing his identity and nationality;

(4) failure to satisfy the Immigration Officer, in the case of a person arriving in the United Kingdom or seeking entry through the Channel Tunnel with the intention of entering any other part of the common travel area, that he is acceptable to the immigration authorities there;

(5) failure, in the case of a visa national, to produce to the Immigration Officer a passport or other identity document endorsed with a valid and current United Kingdom entry clearance issued for the purpose for which entry is sought;

(6) where the Secretary of State has personally directed that the exclusion of a person from the United Kingdom is conducive to the public good;

(7) save in relation to a person settled in the United Kingdom or where the Immigration Officer is satisfied that there are strong compassionate reasons justifying admission, confirmation from the Medical Inspector that, for medical reasons, it is undesirable to admit a person seeking leave to enter the United Kingdom.

Grounds on which entry clearance or leave to enter the United Kingdom should normally be refused

(8) failure by a person arriving in the United Kingdom to furnish the Immigration Officer with such information as may be required for the purpose of deciding whether he requires leave to enter and, if so, whether and on what terms leave should be given;

(9) failure by a person seeking leave to enter as a returning resident to satisfy the Immigration Officer that he meets the requirements of para 18 of these Rules;

(10) production by the person seeking leave to enter the United Kingdom of a national passport or travel document issued by a territorial entity or authority which is not recognised by Her Majesty's government as a State or is not dealt with as a government by them, or which does not accept valid United Kingdom passports for the purpose of its own immigration control; or a passport or travel document which does not comply with international passport practice;

(11) failure to observe the time limit or conditions attached to any grant of leave to enter or remain in the United Kingdom;

(12) the obtaining of a previous leave to enter or remain by deception;

(13) failure, except by a person eligible for admission to the United Kingdom for settlement or a spouse eligible for admission under para 282, to satisfy the Immigration Officer that he will be admitted to another country after a stay in the United Kingdom;

(14) refusal by a sponsor of a person seeking leave to enter the United Kingdom to give, if requested to do so, an undertaking in writing to be responsible for that person's maintenance and accommodation for the period of any leave granted;

(15) whether or not to the holder's knowledge, the making of false representations or the failure to disclose any material fact for the purpose of obtaining a work permit;

(16) failure, in the case of a child under the age of 18 years seeking leave to enter the United Kingdom otherwise than in conjunction with an application made by his parent(s) or legal guardian, to provide the

Immigration Officer, if required to do so, with written consent to the application from his parent(s) or legal guardian; save that the requirement as to written consent does not apply in the case of a child seeking admission to the United Kingdom as an asylum seeker;

(17) save in relation to a person settled in the United Kingdom, refusal to undergo a medical examination when required to do so by the Immigration Officer;

(18) save where the Immigration Officer is satisfied that admission would be justified for strong compassionate reasons, conviction in any country including the United Kingdom of an offence which, if committed in the United Kingdom, is punishable with imprisonment for a term of 12 months or any greater punishment or, if committed outside the United Kingdom, would be so punishable if the conduct constituting the offence had occurred in the United Kingdom;

(19) where, from information available to the Immigration Officer, it seems right to refuse leave to enter on the ground that exclusion from the United Kingdom is conducive to the public good, if, for example, in the light of the character, conduct or associations of the person seeking leave to enter it is undesirable to give him leave to enter.

Refusal of leave to enter in relation to a person in possession of an entry clearance

321. A person seeking leave to enter the United Kingdom who holds an entry clearance which was duly issued to him and is still current may be refused leave to enter only where the Immigration Officer is satisfied that—

(i) whether or not to the holder's knowledge, false representations were employed or material facts were not disclosed, either in writing or orally, for the purpose of obtaining the entry clearance; or

(ii) a change of circumstances since it was issued has removed the basis of the holder's claim to admission, except where the change of circumstances amounts solely to the person becoming over age for entry in one of the categories contained in paras 296–316 of these Rules since the issue of the entry clearance; or

(iii) refusal is justified on grounds of restricted returnability; on medical grounds; on grounds of criminal record; because the person seeking leave to enter is the subject of a deportation order or because exclusion would be conducive to the public good.

REFUSAL OF VARIATION OF LEAVE TO ENTER OR REMAIN OR CURTAILMENT OF LEAVE

322. In addition to the grounds for refusal of extension of stay set out in Parts 2–8 of these Rules, the following provisions apply in relation to the refusal of an application for variation of leave to enter or remain or, where appropriate, the curtailment of leave—

Grounds on which an application to vary leave to enter or remain in the United Kingdom is to be refused

(1) the fact that variation of leave to enter or remain is being sought for a purpose not covered by these Rules.

Grounds on which an application to vary leave to enter or remain in the United Kingdom should normally be refused

(2) the making of false representations or the failure to disclose any material fact for the purpose of obtaining leave to enter or a previous variation of leave;

(3) failure to comply with any conditions attached to the grant of leave to enter or remain;

(4) failure by the person concerned to maintain or accommodate himself and any dependants without recourse to public funds;

(5) the undesirability of permitting the person concerned to remain in the United Kingdom in the light of his character, conduct or associations or the fact that he represents a threat to national security;

(6) refusal by a sponsor of the person concerned to give, if requested to do so, an undertaking in writing to be responsible for his maintenance and accommodation in the United Kingdom or failure to honour such an undertaking once given;

(7) failure by the person concerned to honour any declaration or undertaking given orally or in writing as to the intended duration and/or purpose of his stay;

(8) failure, except by a person who qualifies for settlement in the United Kingdom or by the spouse of a person settled in the United Kingdom, to satisfy the Secretary of State that he will be returnable to another country if allowed to remain in the United Kingdom for a further period;

(9) failure by an applicant to produce within a reasonable time documents or other evidence required by the Secretary of State to establish his claim to remain under these Rules;

(10) failure, without providing a reasonable explanation, to comply with a request made on behalf of the Secretary of State to attend for interview;

(11) failure, in the case of a child under the age of 18 years seeking a variation of his leave to enter or remain in the United Kingdom otherwise than in conjunction with an application by his parent(s) or legal guardian, to provide the Secretary of State, if required to do so, with written consent to the application from his parent(s) or legal guardian; save that the requirement as to written consent does not apply in the case of a child who has been admitted to the United Kingdom as an asylum seeker.

Grounds on which leave to enter or remain may be curtailed

323. A person's leave to enter or remain may be curtailed on any of the grounds set out in para 322 (2)–(5) above or if he ceases to meet the requirements of the Rules under which his leave to enter or remain was granted.

Crew members

324. A person who has been given leave to enter to join a ship, aircraft, hovercraft, hydrofoil or international train service as a member of its crew, or a crew member who has been given leave to enter for hospital treatment, repatriation or transfer to another ship, aircraft, hovercraft, hydrofoil or international train service in the United Kingdom, is to be refused leave to remain unless an extension of stay is necessary to fulfil the purpose for which he was given leave to enter or unless he meets the requirements for an extension of stay as a spouse in para 284.

PART 10: REGISTRATION WITH THE POLICE

325. A condition requiring registration with the police should normally be imposed on any foreign national aged 16 years or over who is given limited leave to enter the United Kingdom—

(i) for employment for longer than three months unless he has been admitted for permit free employment as a private servant in a diplomatic household or as a minister of religion; or

(ii) for longer than six months under the following categories of these Rules—

(a) students;

(b) 'au pair';

(c) businessmen and self-employed persons;

(d) investors or persons of independent means;

(e) creative artists;

(f) family members of European Economic Area nationals who are not themselves European Economic Area nationals; or

(iii) as the spouse or child of a person required to register with the police; or

(iv) exceptionally, in any other case where the Immigration Officer considers it necessary to ensure that a foreign national complies with the terms of a limited leave to enter.

326. A condition requiring registration with the police should also be imposed when a foreign national on whom a registration requirement was not imposed on arrival is granted an extension of stay which has the effect of allowing him to remain in the United Kingdom for employment for longer than three months, or otherwise for longer than six months, reckoned from the date of his arrival, save where—

(i) the person concerned is under the age of 16; or

(ii) the extension of stay was granted as a minister of religion or private servant in a diplomatic household; or

(iii) the extension of stay was granted on the basis of marriage to a person.

PART 11: ASYLUM

Definition of asylum applicant

327. Under these Rules an asylum applicant is a person who claims that it would be contrary to the United Kingdom's obligations under the United Nations Convention and Protocol relating to the Status of Refugees for him to be removed from or required to leave the United Kingdom. All such cases are referred to in these Rules as asylum applications.

Applications for asylum

328. All asylum applications will be determined by the Secretary of State in accordance with the United Kingdom's obligations under the United Nations Convention and Protocol relating to the Status of Refugees. Every asylum application made by a person at a port or airport in the United Kingdom will be referred by the Immigration Officer for determination by the Secretary of State in accordance with these Rules.

329. Until an asylum application has been determined by the Secretary of State, no action will be taken to require the departure of the asylum applicant or his dependants from the United Kingdom.

330. If the Secretary of State decides to grant asylum and the person has not yet been given leave to enter, the Immigration Officer will grant limited leave to enter.

331. If a person seeking leave to enter is refused asylum, the Immigration Officer will then resume his examination to determine whether or not to grant him leave to enter under any other provision of these Rules.

332. If a person who has been refused leave to enter applies for asylum and that application is refused, leave to enter will again be refused unless the applicant qualifies for admission under any other provision of these Rules.

333. A person who is refused leave to enter following the refusal of an asylum application will be provided with a notice informing him of the decision and of the reasons for refusal. The notice of refusal will also explain any rights of appeal available to the applicant and will inform him of the means by which he may exercise those rights. The applicant will not be removed from the United Kingdom so long as any appeal which he may bring is pending.

Grant of asylum

334. An asylum applicant will be granted asylum in the United Kingdom if the Secretary of State is satisfied that—

(i) he is in the United Kingdom or has arrived at a port of entry in the United Kingdom; and

(ii) he is a refugee, as defined by the Convention and Protocol; and

(iii) refusing his application would result in his being required to go (whether immediately or after the time limited by an existing leave to enter or remain) in breach of the Convention and Protocol, to a country in which his life or freedom would be threatened on account of his race, religion, nationality, political opinion or membership of a particular social group.

335. If the Secretary of State decides to grant asylum to a person who has been given leave to enter (whether or not the leave has expired) or to a person who has entered without leave, the Secretary of State will vary the existing leave or grant limited leave to remain.

Refusal of asylum

336. An application which does not meet the criteria set out in para 334 will be refused.

337. The Secretary of State may decide not to consider the substance of a person's claim to refugee status if he is satisfied that the person's removal to a third country does not raise any issue as to the United Kingdom's obligations under the Convention and Protocol. More details are given in paras 345 and 347.

338. When a person in the United Kingdom is notified that asylum has been refused he may, if he is liable to removal as an illegal entrant or to deportation, at the same time be notified of removal directions, served with a notice of intention to make a deportation order, or served with a deportation order, as appropriate.

339. When a person with limited leave is refused asylum the leave may be curtailed if he does not meet the requirements of the Rules under which leave was granted. When a person's leave is curtailed under s 7 of the Asylum and Immigration Appeals Act 1993, he may at the same time be served with a notice of intention to make a deportation order. Full account will be taken

of all the relevant circumstances known to the Secretary of State, including those listed in para 364.

Consideration of cases

340. A failure, without reasonable explanation, to make a prompt and full disclosure of material factors, either orally or in writing, or otherwise to assist the Secretary of State to the full in establishing the facts of the case may lead to refusal of an asylum application. This includes failure to comply with a notice issued by the Secretary of State requiring the applicant to report to a designated place to be fingerprinted, or failure to complete an asylum questionnaire, or failure to comply with a request to attend an interview concerning the application.

341. In determining an asylum application the Secretary of State will have regard to matters which may damage an asylum applicant's credibility if no reasonable explanation is given. Among such matters are—

(i) that the applicant has failed to apply forthwith upon arrival in the United Kingdom, unless the application is founded on events which have taken place since his arrival in the United Kingdom;

(ii) that the applicant has made false representations, either orally or in writing;

(iii) that the applicant has destroyed, damaged or disposed of any passport, other document or ticket relevant to his claim;

(iv) that the applicant has undertaken any activities in the United Kingdom before or after lodging his application which are inconsistent with his previous beliefs and behaviour and calculated to create or substantially enhance his claim to refugee status;

(v) that the applicant has lodged concurrent applications for asylum in the United Kingdom or in another country.

If the Secretary of State concludes for these or any other reasons that an asylum applicant's account is not credible, the application will be refused.

342. The actions of anyone acting as an agent of the asylum applicant may also be taken into account in regard to the matters set out in paras 340 and 341.

343. If there is a part of the country from which the applicant claims to be a refugee in which he would not have a well-founded fear of persecution, and to which it would be reasonable to expect him to go, the application may be refused.

344. Cases will normally be considered on an individual basis but if an applicant is part of a group whose claims are clearly not related to the criteria for refugee status in the Convention and Protocol he may be refused without examination of his individual claim. However, the Secretary of State will

have regard to any evidence produced by an individual to show that his claim should be distinguished from those of the rest of the group.

Third country cases

345. If the Secretary of State is satisfied that there is a safe country to which an asylum applicant can be sent, his application will normally be refused without substantive consideration of his claim to refugee status. A safe country is one in which the life or freedom of the asylum applicant would not be threatened (within the meaning of Article 33 of the Convention) and the government of which would not send the applicant elsewhere in a manner contrary to the principles of the Convention and Protocol. The Secretary of State shall not remove an asylum applicant without substantive consideration of his claim unless—

(i) the asylum applicant has not arrived in the United Kingdom directly from the country in which he claims to fear persecution and has had an opportunity at the border or within the territory of a third country to make contact with that country's authorities in order to seek their protection; or

(ii) there is other clear evidence of his admissibility to a third country.

Provided that he is satisfied that a case meets these criteria, the Secretary of State is under no obligation to consult the authorities of the third country before the removal of an asylum applicant.

Previously rejected applications

346. When an asylum applicant has previously been refused asylum in the United Kingdom and can demonstrate no relevant and substantial change in his circumstances since that date, his application will be refused.

347. When an asylum applicant has come to the United Kingdom from another country which is a party to the United Nations Convention relating to the Status of Refugees or its Protocol and which has considered and rejected an application for asylum from him, his application for asylum in the United Kingdom may be refused without substantive consideration of his claim to refugee status. He may be removed to that country, or another country meeting the criteria of para 345, and invited to raise any new circumstances with the authorities of the country which originally considered his application.

Rights of appeal

348. Special provisions governing appeals in asylum cases are set out in the Asylum and Immigration Appeals Act 1993 and the Asylum Appeals (Procedure) Rules 1993. Where asylum is refused the applicant will be provided with a notice informing him of the decision and of the reasons for refusal. At the same time that asylum is refused the applicant may be notified of removal directions or served with a notice of intention to deport, as appropriate. The

notice of refusal of asylum will also explain any rights of appeal available to the applicant and will inform him of the means by which he may exercise those rights.

Dependants

349. A husband or wife or minor children accompanying a principal applicant may be included in an application for asylum. If the principal applicant is granted asylum any such dependants will be granted leave to enter or remain of the same duration. The case of any dependant who claims asylum in his own right and who would otherwise be refused leave to enter or remain will be considered individually in accordance with para 334 above. It will not normally be necessary separately to interview or otherwise investigate the status of children accompanying a parent who is an asylum applicant except insofar as this is necessary to establish the child's identity. (In this paragraph and paras 350–52 a child means a person who is under 18 years of age or who, in the absence of documentary evidence, appears to be under that age).

Unaccompanied children

350. Unaccompanied children may also apply for asylum and, in view of their potential vulnerability, particular priority and care is to be given to the handling of their cases.

351. A person of any age may qualify for refugee status under the Convention and the criteria in para 334 apply to all cases. However, account should be taken of the applicant's maturity and in assessing the claim of a child more weight should be given to objective indications of risk than to the child's state of mind and understanding of his situation. An asylum application made on behalf of a child should not be refused solely because the child is too young to understand his situation or to have formed a well-founded fear of persecution. Close attention should be given to the welfare of the child at all times.

352. A child will not be interviewed about the substance of his claim to refugee status if it is possible to obtain by written enquiries or from other sources sufficient information properly to determine the claim. When an interview is necessary it should be conducted in the presence of a parent, guardian, representative or another adult who for the time being takes responsibility for the child and is not an Immigration Officer, an officer of the Secretary of State or a police officer. The interviewer should have particular regard to the possibility that a child will feel inhibited or alarmed. The child should be allowed to express himself in his own way and at his own speed. If he appears tired or distressed, the interview should be stopped.

PART 12: RIGHTS OF APPEAL

Notice of refusal of leave to enter

353. Where refusal of leave to enter is confirmed, the person concerned should be handed a notice informing him of the decision and of the reasons for refusal. This notice will also inform him whether he has a right of appeal under s 13 of the 1971 Act and, if so, how the right of appeal might be exercised. If he has difficulty in understanding the notice its meaning should be explained to him.

Rights of appeal in relation to a person claiming to have the right of abode

354. A person who claims to have the right of abode is not entitled to appeal against a decision that he requires leave to enter unless he holds either a United Kingdom passport describing him as a British citizen or as a citizen of the United Kingdom and Colonies having the right of abode in the United Kingdom, or a certificate of entitlement duly issued to him by or on behalf of the government of the United Kingdom certifying that he has such a right of abode.

Rights of appeal in relation to a person who holds an entry clearance or work permit

355. Subject to s 13(5) of the Immigration Act 1971, a person in possession of a valid United Kingdom entry clearance or named in a current work permit who is entitled to appeal against refusal of leave to enter the United Kingdom may exercise his right of appeal before removal from the United Kingdom. If such a person sought entry through the Channel Tunnel he may, upon giving notice of appeal, be brought through the tunnel to enable him to pursue his appeal.

Rights of appeal exerciseable from abroad

356. Except in cases involving an asylum application to which para 348 applies and cases described in paras 354 and 355 above, a person entitled to appeal against refusal of leave to enter, irrespective of his national status, may exercise that right only after he has left the United Kingdom.

Rights of appeal against a time limit or condition

357. A person aggrieved by the imposition on entry of a time limit or condition may apply to the Home Office for variation of his leave. Subject to para 358 below, he will have a right of appeal if variation is refused.

Rights of appeal against variation of leave to enter or refusal to vary it

358. A person may appeal against any variation of his leave to enter or any refusal to vary it except—

(i) when a refusal is on one of the grounds specified in s 14(2A) of the 1971 Act; or

(ii) if the case comes within s 14(3) of the 1971 Act following a decision taken personally by the Secretary of State and not by a person acting under his authority; or

(iii) when a variation of leave is made by statutory instrument; or

(iv) if leave is curtailed under s 7(1) of the Asylum and Immigration Appeals Act 1993.

Notice of appeal rights

359. Where an application for variation of leave to enter is refused; or a variation is made otherwise than on the application of the person concerned, or is less favourable than that for which he applied, notice of the decision and, if an appeal lies, of his right of appeal will normally be handed to the person concerned or sent to his last known address. Alternatively, it may be so given or sent to a person who has either made the application on behalf of another, or has subsequently been appointed to act on another's behalf in connection with an application.

Explanatory statement

360. If notice of appeal is given within the period allowed, an explanatory statement summarising the facts of the case on the basis of which the decision was taken will normally be prepared and be sent to the independent appellate authorities, who will notify the appellant of the arrangements for any appeal to be heard.

Rights of appeal in asylum cases

361. Rights of appeal in asylum cases are covered in para 348 above.

PART 13: DEPORTATION

A deportation order

362. A deportation order requires the subject to leave the United Kingdom and authorises his detention until he is removed. It also prohibits him from re-entering the country for as long as it is in force and invalidates any leave to enter or remain in the United Kingdom given him before the order was made or while it is in force.

363. The circumstances in which a person is liable to deportation are set out in the Immigration Act 1971 and include—

(i) failure to comply with a condition attached to his leave to enter or remain or remaining beyond the time limited by the leave;

(ii) where the Secretary of State deems the person's deportation to be conducive to the public good;

(iii) where the person is the wife or child under 18 of a person ordered to be deported; and

(iv) where a court recommends deportation in the case of a person over the age of 17 who has been convicted of an offence punishable with imprisonment.

364. In considering whether deportation is the right course on the merits, the public interest will be balanced against any compassionate circumstances of the case. While each case will be considered in the light of the particular circumstances, the aim is an exercise of the power of deportation which is consistent and fair as between one person and another, although one case will rarely be identical with another in all material respects. Deportation will normally be the proper course where a person has failed to comply with or has contravened a condition or has remained without authority. Before a decision to deport is reached the Secretary of State will take into account all relevant factors known to him including—

(i) age;

(ii) length of residence in the United Kingdom;

(iii) strength of connections with the United Kingdom;

(iv) personal history, including character, conduct and employment record;

(v) domestic circumstances;

(vi) previous criminal record and the nature of any offence of which the person has been convicted;

(vii) compassionate circumstances;

(viii) any representations received on the person's behalf.

Deportation of family members

365. Section 5 of the Immigration Act 1971 gives the Secretary of State power in certain circumstances to make a deportation order against the wife or child of a person against whom a deportation order has been made. The Secretary of State will not normally decide to deport the wife of a deportee where—

(i) she has qualified for settlement in her own right; or

(ii) she has been living apart from the deportee.

366. The Secretary of State will not normally decide to deport the child of a deportee where—

(i) he and his mother are living apart from the deportee; or

(ii) he has spent some years in the United Kingdom and is nearing the age of 18; or

(iii) he has left home and established himself on an independent basis; or

(iv) he married before deportation came into prospect.

367. In considering whether to require a wife or child to leave with the deportee the Secretary of State will take account of the factors listed in para 364 as well as the following—

- (i) the ability of the wife to maintain herself and any children in the United Kingdom, or to be maintained by relatives or friends without charge to public funds, not merely for a short period but for the foreseeable future; and
- (ii) in the case of a child of school age, the effect of removal on his education; and
- (iii) the practicability of any plans for a child's care and maintenance in this country if one or both of his parents were deported; and
- (iv) any representations made by or on behalf of the wife or child.

368. Where the Secretary of State decides that it would be appropriate to deport a member of a family as such, the decision, and the right of appeal, will be notified and it will at the same time be explained that it is open to the member of the family to leave the country voluntarily if he does not wish to appeal or if he appeals and his appeal is dismissed.

Right of appeal against destination

369. In all cases of deportation the person in respect of whom the order has been or is to be made has a right of appeal against the removal directions on the ground that he ought to be removed (if at all) to a country or territory specified by him, other than the one named in the direction (s 17 of the 1971 Act).

Restricted right of appeal against deportation in cases of breach of limited leave

370. By virtue of s 5(1) of the Immigration Act 1988, a person who was last given leave to enter the United Kingdom less than 7 years before the date of the decision to make a deportation order against him—

- (i) by virtue of s 3(5)(a) of the Immigration Act 1971 (breach of limited leave); or
- (ii) by virtue of s 3(5)(c) of that Act (as belonging to the family of a person who is or has been ordered to be deported by virtue of s 3(5)(a))

shall not be entitled to appeal under s 15 of the 1971 Act against that decision except on the ground that on the facts of his case there is in law no power to make the deportation order for the reasons stated in the notice of the decision.

Exemption to the restricted right of appeal

371. This restriction on the right of appeal does not apply to a person who is exempt by virtue of an order made under s 5(2) of the 1988 Act. The

Immigration (Restricted Right of Appeal against Deportation) (Exemption) Order 1993 provides that a person is exempt if he would last have been given leave to enter seven years or more before the date of the decision to deport but for his having obtained a subsequent leave after an absence from the United Kingdom within the period limited for the duration of the earlier leave.

372. The Order also provides that a person is exempt if his limited leave has been curtailed by the Secretary of State under s 7 of the 1993 Act.

A deportation order made on the recommendation of a Court

373. There is no appeal within the immigration appeal system against the making of a deportation order on the recommendation of a court, but there is a right of appeal to a higher court against the recommendation itself. An order may not be made while it is still open to the person to appeal against the relevant conviction, sentence or recommendation, or while an appeal is pending.

Where deportation is deemed to be conducive to the public good

374. There is no right of appeal except as to the country of destination (see para 369) where a deportation order is made on the ground that the Secretary of State deems the person's deportation to be conducive to the public good as being in the interests of national security or of the relations between the United Kingdom and any other country or for other reasons of a political nature. Such cases are subject to a non-statutory advisory procedure and the person proposed to be deported on that ground will be informed, so far as possible, of the nature of the allegations against him and will be given the opportunity to appear before the advisers, and to make representations to them, before they tender advice to the Secretary of State.

375. Where it is proposed to deport a person because it is deemed that his expulsion will be conducive to the public good on other than security or political grounds there is a right of appeal, under s 15 of the 1971 Act, direct to the Immigration Appeal Tribunal.

Hearing of appeals

376. An appeal against a decision to make a deportation order against a person lies to the Tribunal.

377. Where the appeal is against a decision to make a deportation order for breach of conditions or for remaining beyond the authorised time it will be heard by an adjudicator in the first instance, unless there is pending an appeal against a decision to make an order against a person as belonging to the family of the person alleged to have broken a condition or remained beyond the authorised time, in which case both appeals will be heard by the Tribunal.

378. An order may not be made while it is still open to the person to appeal against the Secretary of State's decision, or while an appeal is pending.

Persons who have claimed asylum

379. In addition to the rights of appeal mentioned above, except where the ground of the decision to make a deportation order is that it is conducive to the public good and is certified by the Secretary of State as being in the interests of national security, a person who has claimed asylum may also appeal under s 8 of the Asylum and Immigration Appeals Act 1993 against—

(i) a decision to make a deportation order against him by virtue of s 3(5) of the 1971 Act; or

(ii) a refusal to revoke a deportation order made against him by virtue of s 3(5) or (6) of the 1971 Act; or

(iii) directions for his removal from the United Kingdom given under s 16(1)(a) or (b) of the 1971 Act. In such circumstances the appeal will be before a special adjudicator who will also consider any appeal under Part II of the 1971 Act.

380. A deportation order will not be made against any person if his removal in pursuance of the order would be contrary to the United Kingdom's obligations under the Convention and Protocol relating to the Status of Refugees.

Procedure

381. When a decision to make a deportation order has been taken (otherwise than on the recommendation of a court) a notice will be given to the person concerned informing him of the decision and of his right of appeal, or facility to make representations in the case of the security and political cases subject to the advisory procedure.

382. Following the issue of such a notice the Secretary of State may make a detention order, or any order restricting a person as to residence, employment or occupation and requiring him to report to the police, pending the making of a deportation order.

383. Where a person is detained pending an appeal, he may apply to an adjudicator for release on bail.

384. If a notice of appeal is given within the period allowed, a summary of the facts of the case on the basis of which the decision was taken will be sent to the appellate authorities, who will notify the appellant of the arrangements for the appeal to be heard.

Arrangements for removal

385. A person against whom a deportation order has been made will normally be removed from the United Kingdom. The power is to be exercised so as to secure the person's return to the country of which he is a national, or which has most recently provided him with a travel document, unless he can show that another country will receive him. In considering any departure from the normal arrangements, regard will be had to the public interest generally, and to any additional expense that may fall on public funds.

386. The person will not be removed as the subject of a deportation order while an appeal may be brought against the removal directions or such an appeal is pending.

Supervised departure

387. A person liable to deportation may, in certain circumstances, leave the United Kingdom by means of supervised departure without having a deportation order made against him.

Returned deportees

388. Where a person returns to this country when a deportation order is in force against him, he may be deported under the original order. The Secretary of State will consider every such case in the light of all the relevant circumstances before deciding whether to enforce the order.

Returned family members

389. Persons deported in the circumstances set out in para 365–68 above (deportation of family members) may be able to seek re-admission to the United Kingdom under the Immigration Rules where—

(i) a child reaches 18 (when he ceases to be subject- to the deportation order); or

(ii) in the case of a wife, the marriage comes to an end.

Revocation of deportation order

390. An application for revocation of a deportation order will be considered in the light of all the circumstances including the following—

(i) the grounds on which the order was made;

(ii) any representations made in support of revocation;

(iii) the interests of the community, including the maintenance of an effective immigration control;

(iv) the interests of the applicant, including any compassionate circumstances.

391. In the case of an applicant with a serious criminal record continued exclusion for a long term of years will normally be the proper course. In other cases revocation of the order will not normally be authorised unless the situation has been materially altered, either by a change of circumstances since the order was made, or by fresh information coming to light which was not before the court which made the recommendation or the appellate authorities or the Secretary of State. The passage of time since the person was deported may also in itself amount to such a change of circumstances as to warrant revocation of the order. However, save in the most exceptional circumstances, the Secretary of State will not revoke the order unless the person has been absent from the United Kingdom for a period of at least three years since it was made.

392. Revocation of a deportation order does not entitle the person concerned to re-enter the United Kingdom; it renders him eligible to apply for admission under the Immigration Rules. Application for revocation of the order may be made to the Entry Clearance Officer or direct to the Home Office.

Rights of appeal in relation to a decision not to revoke a deportation order

393. Where an application for revocation is refused there is a right of appeal, in the first instance to an adjudicator, unless the order was made against a person as belonging to the family of another person in which case it lies to the Tribunal.

394. No appeal lies while the person is in the United Kingdom or where the Secretary of State personally decides that continued exclusion from the United Kingdom is conducive to the public good.

395. Where an appeal does lie the right of appeal will be notified at the same time as the decision to refuse to revoke the order.

APPENDIX

VISA REQUIREMENTS FOR THE UNITED KINGDOM

1. Subject to para 2 below the following persons need a visa for the United Kingdom—

(a) Nationals or citizens of the following countries or territorial entities—

Afghanistan
Albania
Algeria
Angola
Armenia
Azerbaijan
Bangladesh
Belarus
Benin
Bhutan
Bosnia-Herzegovina
Bulgaria
Burkina
Burma
Burundi
Cambodia
Cameroon
Cape Verde
Central African Republic
Gabon
Georgia
Ghana
Guinea
Guinea-Bissau
Haiti
India
Indonesia
Iran
Iraq
Jordan
Kazakhstan
Kirgizstan
Korea (North)
Laos
Lebanon
Liberia
Libya
Macedonia
Madagascar
Philippines
Romania
Russia
Rwanda
Sao Tome e Principe
Saudi Arabia
Senegal
Somalia
Sri Lanka
Sudan
Syria
Taiwan
Tajikistan
Thailand
Togo
Tunisia
Turkey
Turkmenistan
Uganda
Ukraine

Chad	Mali	Uzbekistan
China	Mauritania	Vietnam
Comoros	Moldova	Yemen
Congo	Mongolia	Zaire
Cuba	Morocco	The territories formerly comprising the Socialist Federal Republic of Yugoslavia excluding Croatia and Slovenia
Djibouti	Mozambique	
Egypt	Nepal	
Equatorial Guinea	Nigeria	
Eritrea	Oman	
Ethiopia	Pakistan	

(b) Persons who hold passports or travel documents issued by the former Soviet Union or by the former Socialist Federal Republic of Yugoslavia.

(c) Stateless persons.

(d) Persons who hold non-national documents.

2. The following persons do not need a visa for the United Kingdom—

(a) those who qualify for admission to the United Kingdom as returning residents in accordance with para 18;

(b) those who seek leave to enter the United Kingdom within the period of their earlier leave unless that leave;

(i) was for a period of six months or less; or

(ii) was extended by statutory instrument;

(c) those holding refugee travel documents issued under the 1951 Convention relating to the Status of Refugees by countries which are signatories of the Council of Europe Agreement of 1959 on the Abolition of Visas for Refugees if coming on visits of three months or less.

Statement of Changes in Immigration Rules

Presented to Parliament

by the Secretary of State for the Home Department

by Command of Her Majesty

January 1996

STATEMENT OF CHANGES IN IMMIGRATION RULES

The Home Secretary has, with effect from 5 January 1996, made the changes hereinafter stated in the Rules laid down by him as to the practice to be followed in the administration of the Immigration Act 1971 for regulating entry into and the stay of persons in the United Kingdom and contained in the statement laid before Parliament on 23 May 1994 (HC 395), as amended. The amending statements were laid before Parliament on 20 September 1994 (Cm 2663) and on 26 October 1995 (HC 797).

1. In the Appendix to HC 395 after 'Tajikistan' there shall be inserted 'Tanzania'.

2. Paragraph 60(i) of HC 395 of 1994 shall not apply to any application for an extension of stay for the purpose of studying made by a national of Tanzania whose current leave to enter or remain was granted before 5 January 1996.

Statement of Changes in Immigration Rules

Presented to Parliament by the Secretary of State for the Home Department by Command of Her Majesty

August 1996

STATEMENT OF CHANGES IN IMMIGRATION RULES

The Home Secretary has made the changes hereinafter stated in the Rules laid down by him as to the practice to be followed in the administration of the Immigration Act 1971 for regulating entry into and the stay of persons in the United Kingdom and contained in the Statement laid before Parliament on 23 May 1994 (HC 395), as amended. The amending Statements were laid before, or presented to, Parliament on 20 September 1994 (Cmnd 2663), 26 October I995 (HC 797), 4 January 1996 (Cmnd 3073), 7 March 1996 (HC 274) and 2 April l 996 (HC 329).

These changes take effect on 1 September 1996 except for the changes contained in—

(a) para 3, which take effect on l November 1996;

(b) para 14, which take effect on 21 October 1996; and

(c) paras 25–29, which take effect on 1 October 1996.

1. Paragraph 4 shall be amended by the insertion after the words 'variation of leave to enter or remain' of the words ', other than an application for leave by a person seeking asylum,'.

2. In para 6 after the words 'Asylum and Immigration Appeals Act 1993' there shall be inserted—

'"the 1996 Act" is the Asylum and Immigration Act 1996.'

3. For para 8 there shall be substituted—

'8. Under ss 3 and 4 of the Immigration Act 1971 an Immigration Officer when admitting to the United Kingdom a person subject to immigration control under that Act may give leave to enter for a limited period and, if he does, may impose all or any of the following conditions—

(i) a condition restricting employment or occupation in the United Kingdom;

(ii) a condition requiring the person to maintain and accommodate himself, and any dependants of his, without recourse to public funds; and

(iii) a condition requiring the person to register with the police.

He may also require him to report to the appropriate Medical Officer of Environmental Health. Under s 24 of the 1971 Act it is an offence knowingly to remain beyond the time limit or fail to comply with such a condition or requirement.'

4. In paras 214 and 219 (persons intending to enter or remain for self-employment in the United Kingdom pursuant to an EC Association Agreement) for 'Slovenia' there shall be substituted 'Slovakia'.

5. In para 270 (refusal of indefinite leave to remain for a retired person of independent means) for '266' there shall be substituted '269'.

6. At the end of para 287 (requirements for indefinite leave to remain for the spouse of a person present and settled in the United Kingdom) there shall be added—

'and

(iv) there will be adequate accommodation for the parties and any dependants without recourse to public funds in accommodation which they own or occupy exclusively; and

(v) the parties will be able to maintain themselves and any dependants adequately without recourse to public funds.'

7. For para 323 there shall be substituted—

'323. A person's leave to enter or remain may be curtailed—

(i) on any of the grounds set out in para 322 (2)–(5) above; or

(ii) if he ceases to meet the requirements of the Rules under which his leave to enter or remain was granted; or

(iii) if he is the dependant, or is seeking leave to remain as the dependant, of an asylum applicant whose claim has been refused and whose leave has been curtailed under s 7 of the 1993 Act, and he does not qualify for leave to remain in his own right.'

For para 329 there shall be substituted—

'329. Until an asylum application has been determined by the Secretary of State or the Secretary of State has issued a certificate under s 2(1)(a) of the 1996 Act, no action will be taken to require the departure of the asylum applicant or his dependants from the United Kingdom.'

9. For para 331 there shall be substituted—

'331. If a person seeking leave to enter is refused asylum, the Immigration Officer will then resume his examination to determine whether or not to grant him leave to enter under any other provision of these Rules. If the person fails at any time to comply with a requirement to report to an Immigration Officer for examination, the Immigration Officer may direct that the person's examination shall be treated as concluded at that time. The Immigration Officer will then consider any outstanding applications for entry on the basis of any evidence before him.'

10. For para 333 there shall be substituted—

'333. A person who is refused leave to enter following the refusal of an asylum application will be provided with a notice informing him of the decision and of the reasons for refusal. The notice of refusal will also explain any rights of appeal available to the applicant and will inform him of the means by which he may exercise those rights. Subject to para 356(ii) below, the applicant will not be removed from the United Kingdom so long as any appeal which he may bring or pursue in the United Kingdom is pending.'

11. Paragraph 337 shall be deleted.

12. For para 339 there shall be substituted—

'339. When a person's leave is curtailed under s 7(1) or 7(1A) of the Asylum and Immigration Appeals Act 1993, he may at the same time be served with a notice of the Secretary of State's intention to make a deportation order against him. Full account will be taken of all relevant circumstances known to the Secretary of State, including those listed in para 364.'

13. For para 340 there shall be substituted—

'340. A failure, without reasonable explanation, to make a prompt and full disclosure of material facts, either orally or in writing, or otherwise to assist the Secretary of State in establishing the facts of the case may lead to refusal of an asylum application. This includes failure to comply with a notice issued by the Secretary of State or an Immigration Officer requiring the applicant to report to a designated place to be fingerprinted, or failure to complete an asylum questionnaire, or failure to comply with a request to attend an interview concerning the application, or failure to comply with a requirement to report to an Immigration Officer for examination.'

14. For para 341 there shall be substituted—

'341. In determining an asylum application the Secretary of State will have regard to matters which may damage an asylum applicant's credibility. Among such matters are—

(i) that the applicant has failed without reasonable explanation to apply forthwith upon arrival in the United Kingdom unless the application is founded on events which have taken place since his arrival in the United Kingdom;

(ii) that the application is made after the applicant has been refused leave to enter under the 1971 Act, or has been recommended for deportation by a court empowered by the 1971 Act to do so, or has been notified of the Secretary of State's decision to make a deportation order against him or has been notified of his liability for removal;

(iii) that the applicant has adduced manifestly false evidence in support of his application, or has otherwise made false representations, either orally or in writing;

(iv) that on his arrival in the United Kingdom the applicant was required to produce a passport in accordance with para 11(i) and either—

(a) failed to do so without providing a reasonable explanation; or

(b) produced a passport which was not in fact valid, and failed to inform the immigration officer of that fact;

(v) that the applicant has otherwise, without reasonable explanation destroyed, damaged or disposed of any passport, other document, or ticket relevant to his claim;

(vi) that the applicant has undertaken any activities in the United Kingdom before or after lodging his application which are inconsistent with his previous beliefs and behaviour and calculated to create or substantially enhance his claim to refugee status;

(vii) that the applicant has lodged concurrent applications for asylum in the United Kingdom or in another country.

If the Secretary of State concludes for these or any other reasons that an asylum applicant's account is not credible, the application will be refused.

15. For para 345 there shall be substituted—

'345. (1) In a case where the Secretary of State is satisfied that the conditions set out in s 2(2) of the 1996 Act are fulfilled, he will normally refuse the asylum application and issue a certificate under s 2(1) of the 1996 Act without substantive consideration of the applicant's claim to refugee status. The conditions are—

(i) that the applicant is not a national or citizen of the country or territory to which he is to be sent;

(ii) that the applicant's life and liberty would not be threatened in that country by reason of his race, religion, nationality, membership of a particular social group, or political opinion; and

(iii) that the government of that country or territory would not send him to another country or territory otherwise than in accordance with the Convention.

(2) The Secretary of State shall not remove an asylum applicant without substantive consideration of his claim unless—

(i) the asylum applicant has not arrived in the United Kingdom directly from the country in which he claims to fear persecution and has had an opportunity at the border or within the third country or territory to make contact with the authorities of that third country or territory in order to seek their protection; or

(ii) there is other clear evidence of his admissibility to a third country or territory.

Provided that he is satisfied that a case meets these criteria, the Secretary of State is under no obligation to consult the authorities of the third country or territory before the removal of an asylum applicant to that country or territory.'

16. For para 346 there shall be substituted—

'346. Where an asylum applicant has previously been refused asylum during his stay in the United Kingdom, the Secretary of State will determine whether any further representations should be treated as a fresh application for asylum. The Secretary of State will treat representations as a fresh application for asylum if the claim advanced in the representations is sufficiently different from the earlier claim that there is a realistic prospect that the conditions set out in para 334 will be satisfied. In considering whether to treat the representations as a fresh claim, the Secretary of State will disregard any material which—

(i) is not significant; or

(ii) is not credible; or

(iii) was available to the applicant at the time when the previous application was refused or when any appeal was determined.

17. Paragraph 347 shall be deleted.

18. For para 348 there shall be substituted—

'348. Special provisions governing appeals in asylum cases are set out in the Asylum and Immigration Appeals Act 1993, the Asylum and Immigration Act 1996 and the Asylum Appeals (Procedure) Rules 1996. Where asylum is refused the applicant will be provided with a notice informing him of the decision and of the reasons for refusal. At the same time that asylum is refused the applicant may be notified of removal directions, or served with a notice of the Secretary of State's intention to deport him, as appropriate. The notice of refusal of asylum will also explain any rights of appeal available to the applicant and will inform him of the means by which he may exercise those rights.'

19. For para 349 there shall be substituted—

'349. A husband or wife or minor children accompanying a principal applicant may be included in an application for asylum. If the principal applicant is granted asylum any such dependants will be granted leave to enter or remain for the same duration. The case of any dependant who claims asylum in his own right and who would otherwise be refused leave to enter or remain will be considered individually in accordance with para 334 above. If the dependant has a claim in his own right, it should be made at the earliest opportunity. Any failure to do so will be taken into account and may damage credibility if no reasonable explanation for it is given. Where the principal applicant is refused asylum and the dependant has previously been refused asylum in his own right, the dependant may be removed forthwith, notwithstanding any outstanding right of appeal that may be available to the principal applicant. At the same time that asylum is refused the applicant may be notified of removal directions or served with a notice of the Secretary of State's intention to deport him, as appropriate. The notice of refusal of asylum will also explain any rights of appeal available to the applicant and will inform him of the means by which he may exercise those rights.'

20. For para 353 there shall be substituted—

'353. Where refusal of leave to enter is confirmed, the person concerned should be served with a notice informing him of the decision and of the reasons for refusal. This notice will also inform him whether he has a right of appeal under s 13 of the 1971 Act and, if so, how the right of appeal might be exercised.'

21. For para 355 there shall be substituted—

'355. Subject to s 13(5) of the Immigration Act 1971 and s 2(1) of the 1996 Act, a person in possession of a valid United Kingdom entry clearance or work permit who is entitled to appeal against refusal of leave to enter the United Kingdom may exercise his right of appeal before removal from the United Kingdom. If such a person sought entry through the Channel Tunnel he may, upon giving notice of appeal, be brought through the tunnel to enable him to pursue his appeal.'

22. For para 356 there shall be substituted—

'356. A person who is entitled to appeal against refusal of leave to enter may exercise that right only after he has left the United Kingdom, irrespective of his national status, unless—

(i) the person has applied for asylum; or

(ii) the circumstances described in para 354 or 355 above apply,

and the Secretary of State has not issued a certificate under s 2(1) of the 1996 Act.'

23. For para 358 there shall be substituted—

'358. A person may appeal against any variation of his leave to enter or any refusal to vary it except—

(i) when a refusal is on one of the grounds specified in s 14(2ZA) or s 14(2A) of the 1971 Act; or

(ii) if the case comes under s 14(3) of the 1971 Act following a decision taken personally by the Secretary of State and not by a person acting under his authority; or

(iii) when a variation of leave is made by statutory instrument; or

(iv) if leave is curtailed under s 7(1) or s 7(1A) of the 1993 Act.'

24. For para 359 there shall be substituted—

'359. Where an application for variation of leave to enter is refused, or a variation is made otherwise than on the application of the person concerned, or is less favourable than that for which he applied, notice of the decision and, if an appeal lies, of his right of appeal, will normally be handed to the person concerned or sent to his last known address. Applicants should therefore keep the Secretary of State informed of any change of address. The notice may alternatively be given or sent to a person who has either made the application on behalf of another, or has subsequently been appointed to act on another's behalf in connection with an application.'

25. In para 363(iii), for the word 'wife' there shall be substituted the word 'spouse'.

26. For para 365 there shall be substituted—

'365. Section 5 of the Immigration Act 1971 gives the Secretary of State power in certain circumstances to make a deportation order against the spouse or child of a person against whom a deportation order has been made. The Secretary of State will not normally decide to deport the spouse of a deportee where—

(i) he has qualified for settlement in his own right; or

(ii) he has been living apart from the deportee.'

27. For para 366 there shall be substituted—

'366. The Secretary of State will not normally decide to deport the child of a deportee where—

(i) he and his mother or father are living apart from the deportee; or

(ii) he has left home and has established himself on an independent basis; or

(iii) he married before deportation came into prospect.'

28. For para 367 there shall be substituted—

'367. In considering whether to require a spouse or child to leave with the deportee the Secretary of State will take account of the factors listed in para 364 as well as the following—

(i) the ability of the spouse to maintain himself and any children in the United Kingdom, or to be maintained by relatives or friends without charge to public funds, not merely for a short period but for the foreseeable future; and

(ii) in the case of a child of school age, the effect of removal on his education; and

(iii) the practicality of any plans for a child's care and maintenance in this country if one or both of his parents were deported; and

(iv) any representations made on behalf of the spouse or child.'

29. For para 370 there shall be substituted—

'370. By virtue of s 5(1) of the Immigration Act 1988, a person who was last given leave to enter the United Kingdom less than seven years before the date of the decision to make a deportation order against him—

(i) by virtue of s 3(5)(a) of the Immigration Act 1971 (breach of limited leave); or

(ii) by virtue of s 3(5)(aa) of that Act (leave to remain obtained by deception); or

(iii) by virtue of s 3(5)(c) of that Act (as belonging to the family of a person who is or has been ordered to be deported by virtue of s 3(5)(a)),

shall not be entitled to appeal under s 15 of the 1971 Act against that decision except on the ground that on the facts of his case there is in law no power to make a deportation order for the reasons stated in the notice of decision.

30. For para 372 there shall be substituted—

'372. The Order also provides that a person is exempted if his limited leave has been curtailed by the Secretary of State under s 7(1) or s 7(1A) of the 1993 Act.'

31. Paragraphs 375 and 376 shall be deleted.

32. For para 377 there shall be substituted—

'377. An appeal against a decision to make a deportation order will be heard by the Tribunal when—

(i) the ground of the decision was that the deportation of the applicant is conducive to the public good, on other than security or political grounds;

(ii) it is an appeal against a decision to make a deportation order against a person as belonging to the family of another person, or an appeal against a refusal to revoke such an order;

(iii) there is a pending appeal under (ii) and the appellant is that other person and the appeal is not under s 8 of the 1 993 Act.'

33. For para 379 there shall be substituted—

'379. In addition to the rights of appeal mentioned above, a person who has claimed asylum may, unless para 379A below applies, also appeal under s 8 of the 1993 Act against—

(i) a decision to make a deportation order against him by virtue of s 3(5) of the 1971 Act; or

(ii) a refusal to revoke a deportation order made against him by virtue of s 3(5) or (6) of the 1971 Act; or

(iii) directions for his removal from the United Kingdom given under s 16(1)(a) or (b) of the 1971 Act. In such circumstances the appeal will be before a special adjudicator who will also consider any appeal under Part II of the 1971 Act.'

34. After para 379 there shall be substituted para 379A—

'379A. A person who has claimed asylum may not appeal under s 8 of the 1993 Act if—

(i) a deportation order has been made against him on the ground that it is conducive to the public good; or

(ii) the Secretary of State has issued a third country certificate under s 2(1) of the 1996 Act in respect of his application for asylum, and that certificate has not been set aside upon appeal.'

Statement of Changes in Immigration Rules

Laid before Parliament on 31 October 1996 under s 3(2) of the Immigration Act 1971.

Ordered by The House of Commons to be printed

31 October 1996

STATEMENT OF CHANGES IN IMMIGRATION RULES

The Home Secretary has made changes in the Rules laid down by him as to the practice to be followed in the administration of the Immigration Act 1971 for regulating entry into and the stay of persons in the United Kingdom and contained in the statement laid before Parliament on 23 May 1994 (HC 395), as amended. The amending statements were laid before, or presented to, Parliament on 20 September 1994 (Cmnd 2663), 26 October 1995 (HC 797), 4 January 1996 (Cmnd 3073), 7 March 1996 (HC 274), 2 April 1996 (HC 329) and 30 August 1996 (Cmnd 3365).

These changes take effect on 1 November 1996.

1. In para 6, for the definition of 'public funds' there shall be substituted—

'public funds' means

(a) housing under Part II or III of the Housing Act 1985, Part I or II of the Housing (Scotland) Act 1987, Part II of the Housing (Northern Ireland) Order 1981 or Part II of the Housing (Northern Ireland) Order 1988;

(b) attendance allowance, severe disablement allowance, invalid care allowance and disability living allowance under Part III, income support, family credit, council tax benefit, disability working allowance and housing benefit under Part VII and child benefit under Part IX of the Social Security Contribution and Benefits Act 1992;

(c) attendance allowance, severe disablement allowance, invalid care allowance and disability living allowance under Part III, income support, family credit, disability working allowance, housing benefit under Part VII and child benefit under Part IX of the Social Security Contributions and Benefits (Northern Ireland) Act 1992; and

(d) income-based jobseeker's allowance under the Jobseekers Act 1995.'

2. After para 30 there shall be inserted—

'30A. An entry clearance may be revoked if the Entry Clearance Officer is satisfied that—

(i) whether or not to the holder's knowledge, false representations were employed or material facts were not disclosed, either in writing or orally, for the purpose of obtaining the entry clearance; or

(ii) a change of circumstances since the entry clearance was issued has removed the basis of the holder's claim to be admitted to the United Kingdom, except where the change of circumstances amounts solely to his exceeding the age for entry in one of the categories contained in paras 296–316 of these Rules since the issue of the entry clearance; or

(iii) the holder's exclusion from the United Kingdom would be conducive to the public good.'

3. In paras 70 and 73 (postgraduate doctors and dentists), there shall be inserted after sub-para (iii)—

'; and (iv) is able to maintain and accommodate himself and any dependants without recourse to public funds.'

4. In each of the headings to paras 76–81 (spouses and children of students), after 'student' there shall be added 'or prospective student'.

5. In paras 76 and 79 (requirements for spouses and children of students), there shall be inserted after 'paras 57–75' in sub-para (i) 'or 82–87'.

6. In para 89 (requirements for 'au pairs'), there shall be inserted after sub-para (viii)—

'; and (ix) is able to maintain and accommodate himself without recourse to public funds.'

7. In para 92 (extension of stay as an 'au pair'), for '89(ii)–(viii)' in sub-para (iii) there shall be substituted '89(ii)–(ix)'.

8. In para 104 (requirements for seasonal workers at agricultural camps), there shall be inserted after sub-para (iv)—

'; and (v) is able to maintain and accommodate himself and any dependants without recourse to public funds.'

9. In para 107 (extension of stay as a seasonal worker), for '104(iii)–(iv)' in sub-para (ii) there shall be substituted '104(iii)–(v)'.

10. In para 320(9) (refusal of entry clearance or leave to enter) after 'para 18 of these Rules' there shall be inserted 'or that he seeks leave to enter for the same purpose as that for which his earlier leave was granted'.

11. In para 349 there shall be inserted at the end—

'In this paragraph and paras 350–52 a child means a person who is under 18 years of age or who, in the absence of documentary evidence, appears to be under that age.'

12. In the Appendix, for para 2(b) there shall be substituted—

'(b) those who seek leave to enter the United Kingdom within the period of their earlier leave and for the same purpose as that for which that leave was granted, unless it—

(i) was for a period of six months or less; or

(ii) was extended by statutory instrument;'.

Appendix III

Home Office Circulars on Deportation

DP/2/93
and instruction to IES (1) and (2)

MARRIAGE AND CHILDREN

Introduction

1. The instruction provides guidance on cases involving marriage and children, and takes into account the effect of the European Convention on Human Rights. Article 8 of the Convention guarantees the right to respect for family life and recent European Court cases have demonstrated that, *however unmeritorious the applicant's immigration history*, the Court is strongly disposed to find a breach of Article 8 where the effect of an immigration decision is to separate an applicant from his or her spouse or child.

2. The instruction is divided into two sections—

SECTION A: MARRIAGE POLICY

Paragraph 1	General considerations
Paragraphs 2–3	Presumption to concede
Paragraph 4	Presumption to proceed with enforcement action
Paragraphs 5–6	Divorced or separated parents
Paragraph 7	Common-law relationships
Paragraph 8	Criminal convictions
Paragraphs 9–10	Marriages of convenience to EC nationals

SECTION: CHILDREN

Part 1:	Adoption, wardship, custodianship and residence orders
Paragraph 11	Introduction
Paragraph 12	Definitions
Paragraphs 13–14	Intervention
Part 2:	Abandoned children
Paragraphs 15–16	Procedure and considerations

SECTION A: MARRIAGE POLICY

1. All deportation and illegal entry cases must be considered on their individual merits. Where enforcement action is under consideration or has been initiated and the offender is married a judgment will need to be reached on the weight to be attached to the marriage as a compassionate factor.

2. As a general rule deportation action under s 3(5)(a) or s 3(5)(b) (in non-criminal cases), or illegal entry action should not be initiated or pursued where the subject has a genuine and subsisting marriage to a person settled in the United Kingdom if—

(a) the marriage pre-dates enforcement action; and

(b) the marriage has lasted two years or more or, in the case of a common-law relationship (see para 7 below), the couple have cohabited for 2 years or more. It does not automatically follow, however, that deportation/removal is the right course where this test is not met. Full account should be taken of any evidence that a strong relationship has existed for more than two years (this will include any reasons why the couple did not marry earlier, eg waiting for a divorce to be finalised, saving to buy their own home); or

(c) the settled spouse has lived here from an early age or it is otherwise unreasonable to expect him/her to accompany on removal; or

(d) one or more children of the marriage has the right of abode in the United Kingdom, most commonly as a result of having been born in the United Kingdom to a parent settled here. It should be noted that an illegitimate child born in the United Kingdom only obtains British citizenship under the British Nationality Act 1981 if the mother is a British citizen or is settled in the United Kingdom. Under the 1981 Act the status of the father of an illegitimate child has no bearing on the nationality of the child unless he subsequently marries the mother and legitimises the child.

Note: (i) The subject's immigration history is of little relevance once it has been concluded that the marriage is genuine and subsisting.

(ii) Enforcement action may be inappropriate where the spouse or the foreign national is pregnant with a child who would have the right of abode here even if born outside the United Kingdom.

(iii) The presence of the settled spouse's children by a former relationship will also be an availing factor provided that the children have the right of abode in the United Kingdom, are still dependent and that we can be satisfied that they either live with or have frequent contact with the settled spouse.

3. In considering whether it is reasonable for a spouse to accompany on removal under para 2(c) above, whilst the onus is on the United Kingdom settled spouse to make out a case for why it is unreasonable for him or her

to join the family outside the United Kingdom, in general terms cases should be conceded if the United Kingdom settled spouse—

(a) has strong family ties in the United Kingdom; or

(b) has lengthy residence in the United Kingdom; or

(c) suffers from ill health such that his or her quality of life would be significantly impaired if he or she were to accompany his or her spouse on removal.

4. There will be a presumption to proceed with s 3(5)(a), 3(5)(b) (in non-criminal cases) or illegal entry action (subject to consideration of other relevant factors) in marriage cases where there are no children with the right of abode in the United Kingdom if—

(a) neither partner is settled in the United Kingdom; or

(b) the marriage is one of convenience: that is, the couple do not intend to live together permanently as husband and wife; or

(c) the couple are separated.

Divorced or separated parents

5. The fact that the European Court is strongly disposed to find a breach of Article 8 of the European Convention where the effect of an immigration decision is to separate a parent from his or her child is also relevant in cases involving divorced or separated parents. Where one parent is settled in the United Kingdom and the removal of the other would result in deprivation of frequent and regular access currently enjoyed by either parent, s 3(5)(a), 3(5)(b) (in non-criminal cases) or illegal entry action should be abandoned. Reliance cannot be placed on the argument that the United Kingdom settled parent can travel abroad to continue access.

6. Cases will arise where a person to be deported/removed has custody of a child with the right of abode in the United Kingdom by a previous partner who is no longer in contact with the child. Here, the crucial question is whether it is reasonable for the child to accompany the parent to live abroad. The factors to be considered are—

(a) the age of the child (in most cases a pre-school age child could reasonably be expected to adapt to life abroad);

(b) the strength of the child's ties with the United Kingdom, including other United Kingdom resident family members;

(c) any medical conditions which would be better treated here;

(d) the standard of living (including educational facilities) in the country to which the parent is being removed.

Common-law relationships

7. Where there is conclusive evidence that a genuine and subsisting common-law relationship akin to marriage exists, it should be considered under this

instruction as if it were a marriage. The onus rests firmly on the individual who seeks to benefit to provide conclusive evidence of the nature of the relationship.

Criminal convictions

8. The test in cases where someone liable to immigration control has family ties here which would normally benefit him or her under paras 1–6 above yet has criminal convictions is whether removal can be justified as 'necessary in the interests of a democratic society'. This is usually interpreted by the European Court as serious crime punished with imprisonment (for example, crimes of violence, drug offences (other than possession), murder, terrorism) but minor offences (even where the individual has a long criminal record) or a poor immigration history do not carry much weight. What is reasonable in any particular case will depend not only on the nature of the offence but also on the settled spouse's strength or ties with the United Kingdom. Where action is deemed to be in the interests of a democratic society it would normally be capable of being taken under s 3(5)(b) or 3(6) deportation powers.

Marriages of convenience to EC nationals

9. Foreign nationals who contract a valid marriage to an EC national exercising Treaty rights in the United Kingdom (for example, by working) have hitherto been accepted as benefiting from the provisions of Community law in line with his or her spouse, effectively preventing enforcement action (barring serious criminal convictions) at least while the spouse continues to exercise Treaty rights. It has become clear, however, that immigration offenders can exploit this approach by entering into marriages of convenience with EC nationals.

10. Current legal advice is that the removal of a person who has married an EC national exercising Treaty rights may be justified where there are *exceptionally strong grounds for suspicion* that the marriage was one of convenience, ie that the couple do not intend to live together permanently as man and wife and the marriage was contracted for immigration purposes.

SECTION B: CHILDREN

Part 1: Adoption, wardship, custodianship and residence orders

11. This part of the instruction provides guidance on handling cases where there is reason to believe that the purpose of the adoption, custodianship, wardship or residence order proceedings was to frustrate enforcement action.

Definitions

12. Adoption: A child adopted by order of a court in the United Kingdom is a British citizen (and thus not liable to immigration control) from the date of the order if an adoptive parent is a British citizen at that date. An adoption by order of

	a foreign court may not be recognised in United Kingdom law; in such cases advice should be sought from B2 Division.
Custodianship:	This represents a less final relationship than adoption and vests legal custody of the child in the adult(s) caring for him or her. Where a custodianship order is made the child's immigration status is unchanged but he or she should not be removed from the jurisdiction of the court while the order remains in force.
Wardship:	Children who are wards of court should not be removed from the United Kingdom without the court's leave.
Residence Orders:	Residence orders are very similar in effect to wardship and children subject to residence orders should not be removed from the United Kingdom without the leave of the court.

Intervention

13. The Family Court will generally attach much more weight to the child's welfare than to irregularities surrounding the immigration status of the child or a parent. Where however it is clear that the court proceedings are designed purely to enable the child or the parent to evade immigration control consideration may be given to instructing the Treasury Solicitor with a view to intervention in the proceedings. *There must be evidence, not just a suspicion, that there has been a serious attempt to circumvent the immigration control* and decisions to intervene must be taken at not less than SEO level.

14. Where intervention has been agreed, the papers should be copied to the Treasury Solicitor's office as soon as possible. Their normal practice is then to apply for the Secretary of State to be joined as a respondent, and to file an affidavit setting out the child's and/or parents' immigration history and the Secretary of State's objections.

Part 2: Abandoned children

15. Enforcement action against children and young persons under the age of 16 who are on their own in the United Kingdom should only be contemplated when the child's voluntary departure cannot be arranged. In all cases removal must not be enforced unless we are satisfied that the child will be met on arrival in his or her home country and that care arrangements are in place thereafter. To this end, caseworkers should contact the Welfare Section of the appropriate Embassy or High Commission as well as the local Social Services Department. If there is evidence, not just a suspicion, that the care arrangements are seriously below the standard normally provided in the country concerned or that they are so inadequate that the child would face a serious risk of harm if returned, consideration should be given to abandoning enforcement action.

16. Where deportation or removal remains the right course, consideration will need to be given to whether an escort is necessary on the journey.

Enforcement Policy Group
January 1993
IMG 89 47/558/5

DP 3/96
and instruction to IES(l) and IES(2)

MARRIAGE POLICY

Introduction

This notice provides guidance, in general terms, on the consideration of cases of those persons liable to be removed as illegal entrants or deported who have married a person settled in the United Kingdom. *This notice supersedes DP2/93 which is hereby cancelled*, subject to the transitional provisions set out in para 10 of this instruction. Deportation cases fall to be considered within the framework of the Immigration Rules and the attached guidance should be read in conjunction with those Rules. Although illegal entry cases are considered outside the Rules, any relevant compassionate circumstances, including those referred to below, should be considered before a decision to remove is taken.

Policy

2. Paragraph 364 of the Immigration Rules explains that deportation will normally be the proper course where a person has failed to comply with or has contravened a condition or has remained here without authority but that all the known relevant factors must be taken into account before a decision is reached. These include—

- (i) age;
- (ii) length of residence in the United Kingdom;
- (iii) strength of connections with the United Kingdom;
- (iv) personal history, including character, conduct and employment record;
- (v) domestic circumstances;
- (vi) previous criminal record and the nature of any offence;
- (vii) compassionate circumstances;
- (viii) any representations.

3. Where persons do not qualify for leave to remain under the Immigration Rules and are to be considered for deportation, or where they are illegal entrants liable to removal, but seek nevertheless to remain on the basis of

marriage in the United Kingdom, the following paragraphs of this guidance apply.

4. Where enforcement action is under consideration and the offender is married to someone settled here a judgement will need to be reached on the weight to be attached to the marriage as a compassionate factor. Caseworkers should bear in mind that para 284 of the Immigration Rules, which sets out the requirements to be met for an extension of stay as the spouse of a person present and settled in the United Kingdom, specifically requires, amongst other things, a person to have a limited leave to remain here and to have not remained here in breach of the immigration laws, in order to obtain leave to remain on that basis. Therefore, the fact that an offender is married to a person settled here does not give him or her any right to remain under the Rules.

Marriages that pre-date enforcement action

5. As a *general rule*, deportation action under 3(5)(a) or (3)(5)(b) (in non-criminal cases) or illegal entry action should not normally be initiated in the following circumstances (but see notes below)—

(a) where the subject has a genuine and subsisting marriage with someone settled here and the couple have lived together in this country continuously since their marriage for at least two years before the commencement of enforcement action; and

(b) it is unreasonable to expect the settled spouse to accompany his or her spouse on removal.

Notes

(i) In this instruction, 'settled' refers to British citizens who live in the United Kingdom or to other nationals who have ILE or ILR here.

(ii) In considering whether or not, under para 5(b) above, it would be unreasonable for a settled spouse to accompany the subject of enforcement action on removal the onus rests with the settled spouse to make out a case with supporting evidence as to why it is unreasonable for him or her to live outside the United Kingdom. Factors which caseworkers should take into account, if they are made known to them, will include whether the United Kingdom settled spouse—

(a) has very strong and close family ties in the United Kingdom such as older children from a previous relationship that form part of the family unit; or

(b) has been settled and living in the United Kingdom for at least the preceding 10 years; or

(c) suffers from ill-health and medical evidence conclusively shows that his or her life would be significantly impaired or endangered if he or she were to accompany his or her spouse on removal.

(iii) In this instruction commencement of enforcement action is to be taken as either—

(a) a specific instruction to leave with a warning of liability to deportation if the subject fails to do so; or

(b) service of a notice of intention to deport or service of illegal entry papers (including the service of papers during a previous stay in the United Kingdom where the subject has returned illegally); or

(c) a recommendation by a court that a person should be deported following a conviction.

(iv) The commencement of enforcement action 'stops the clock' in terms of the two year qualifying period referred to in para 5(a) above in which a marriage must have subsisted. No further time can then be accrued to meet this criterion, eg whilst making representations, appealing against the decision or applying for judicial review.

(v) This notice contains guidance as to the approach to be adopted in the generality of cases but it must be remembered that each case is to be decided on its individual merits and, for instance, a particularly poor immigration history may warrant the offender's enforced departure from the United Kingdom notwithstanding the factors referred to above.

Criminal convictions

6. In cases where someone liable to immigration control has family ties here which would normally benefit him or her under para 4 above but has criminal convictions, the severity of the offence should be balanced against the strength of the family ties. Serious crimes which are punishable with imprisonment or a series of lesser crimes which show a propensity to re-offend, would normally outweigh the family ties. A very poor immigration history may also be taken into account. Caseworkers must use their judgement to decide what is reasonable in any individual case.

Children

7. The presence of children with the right of abode in the United Kingdom (see note below) is a factor to be taken into account. In cases involving children who have the right of abode, the crucial question is whether it is reasonable for the child to accompany his or her parents abroad. Factors to be considered include—

(a) the age of the child (in most cases a child of 10 or younger could reasonably be expected to adapt to life abroad);

(b) serious ill-health for which treatment is not available in the country to which the family is going.

Note

(i) Children will have the right of abode most commonly as a result of having been born in the United Kingdom to a parent settled here. It should be noted that under the British Nationality Act 1981 an illegitimate child born in the United Kingdom obtains British citizenship only if the mother is a British citizen or is settled in the United Kingdom. Under the 1981 Act the status of the father of a child born illegitimate has no bearing on the nationality of the child unless he subsequently marries the mother and thus legitimises the child.

Marriages that post-date enforcement action

8. Where a person marries after the commencement of enforcement action removal should normally be enforced. The criteria set out in para 5 do not apply in such cases. Paragraph 284 of the Immigration Rules makes it clear that one of the requirements for an extension of stay as the spouse of a person present and settled in the United Kingdom is that 'the marriage has not taken place after a decision has been made to deport the applicant or he has been recommended for deportation or has been given notice under s 6(2) of the Immigration Act 1971'. Marriage cannot therefore in itself be considered a sufficiently compassionate factor to militate against removal. Detailed enquiries in order to ascertain whether the marriage is genuine and subsisting should *not* normally be undertaken. The onus is on the subject to put forward any compelling compassionate factors that he or she wishes to be considered which must be supported by documentary evidence. Only in the most *exceptional circumstances* should removal action be stopped and the person allowed to stay.

Marriage to European Economic Area (EEA) nationals

9. Any foreign national who contracts a marriage to an EEA national should have his or her case considered in the first instance by EC group, B6 Division to whom the case must be referred, irrespective of whether the marriage took place before or after the initiation of enforcement action.

Transitional arrangements

10. This instruction will not apply retrospectively. It has immediate effect in cases where the marriage came to the notice of the Immigration and Nationality Department after 13 March 1996 irrespective of the date on which the marriage took place. Cases where the marriage came to notice on or prior to 13 March 1996 should be considered under the terms of DP 2/93.

Enquiries

11. Any enquiries about this instruction should be addressed to the Enforcement Policy Group in Room 301 Apollo House. (Ext 8408/8409).

Enforcement Policy Group
13 March 1996
IMG 89 47/558/5

DP 4/96
and instruction to IES

CHILDREN

Introduction

This notice provides guidance, in general terms, on the consideration of cases of those persons liable to be removed as illegal entrants or deported who are either children on their own here or who are parents who have children present in the United Kingdom. It supplements the advice given in DP 3/96 about the consideration of marriage cases involving children with the right of abode, DP 5/96 which gives guidance on the consideration of cases involving children who have been resident for 10 or more years and DP 4/95 which gives guidance on the use of s 3(5)(c) of the Immigration Act 1971.

Policy

2. There is no bar to taking deportation/illegal entry action against children of any age who are liable to such action. However, enforcement action against children and young persons under the age of 16 *who are on their own* in the United Kingdom should only be contemplated when the child's voluntary departure cannot be arranged. In all cases removal must not be enforced unless we are satisfied that the child will be met on arrival in his or her home country and that care arrangements are in place thereafter. To this end, caseworkers should contact the Welfare Section of the appropriate Embassy or High Commission as well as the local Social Services Department.

3. If there is any evidence, not just a suspicion, that the care arrangements are seriously below the standard normally provided in the country concerned or that they are so inadequate that the child would face a serious risk of harm if returned, consideration should be given to abandoning enforcement action. Where deportation or removal remains the right course, consideration will need to be given to whether an escort is necessary on the journey.

4. Where deportation/removal action is being considered against a parent or parents the existence of children in the United Kingdom is a factor which must be taken into account when assessing the merits of such action. The weight to be attached to children as a compassionate factor will vary from case to case and has to be balanced against or along with the other factors.

5. In all cases the longer the child has been here the greater will be the weight to be attached to this as a factor; but the general presumption will be that a child who has spent less than 10 years in the United Kingdom would be able to adapt to life abroad. (See DP 5/96 for cases involving children who have been here for 10 years or more.)

Divorced and separated parents

6. Deportation or illegal entry action should not necessarily be conceded where a person liable to deportation or removal as an illegal entrant, whose marriage has broken down, has access rights to his or her child (who is entitled to remain here) and seeks to remain in order to exercise those rights. He or she should be advised that such an application should be made from abroad. Paragraphs 246–48 of the Immigration Rules provide a specific category for those who wish to enter the United Kingdom to exercise access rights to children. Entry clearance is required for this purpose which must be applied for from abroad, and there is a right of appeal against refusal. Recent legal advice indicates that in this type of case there is unlikely to be a breach of Article 8 of the ECHR as 'family life' has already broken down and that as there is no bar to someone applying to return to the United Kingdom for access visits and as a right of appeal is provided for, there can be no breach of Article 13 (the right to legal redress).

7. Enforcement action should normally proceed in these cases if, notwithstanding the advice provided, the offender fails to leave. A person who then becomes the subject of a deportation order should be informed that before he or she can apply to return in accordance with paras 246/248 of the Rules, he or she will need to apply for the revocation of the deportation order. Again, this must be done from abroad. Only in the most exceptional circumstances will it be right to concede a case to enable a parent to continue access visits, with agreement at no less than A/D level.

8. It should be noted that paras 246–48 of the rules apply only in cases where the parents of the child were married. It should also be noted that in cases where the parent is already the subject of a deportation order it may be unreasonable to expect him or her to return abroad to apply for entry clearance as he or she would normally be barred from re-entry for three years. In these cases it will be important to assess the quality and the regularity of access to the child in deciding how much weight should be attached to it as a compassionate factor.

Adoption, wardship, custodianship and residence orders

9. The following paragraphs provide advice on the handling of cases where there is reason to believe that the purpose of one or more of the above proceedings is to frustrate enforcement action. The definition of these proceedings are—

Adoption:	A child adopted by order of a court in the United Kingdom is a British citizen (and thus not liable to immigration

	control) from the date of the order if an adoptive-parent is a British citizen at that date. An adoption by order of a foreign court may not be recognised in United Kingdom law: in such cases advice should be sought from B2 Division.
Custodianship:	This represents a less final relationship than adoption and vests legal custody of the child in the adult(s) caring for him or her. Where a custodianship order is made the child's immigration status is unchanged but he or she should not be removed from the jurisdiction of the court while the order remains in force.
Wardship:	Children who are wards of court should not be removed from the United Kingdom without the court's leave.
Residence Orders:	Residence orders are very similar in effect to wardship and children subject to residence order should not be removed from the United Kingdom without the leave of the court.
Contact Order:	A court order allowing a person contact with a child and specifying the terms under which the contact is to take place.

Intervention in the above proceedings

10. The Family Court will generally attach much more weight to the child's welfare than to irregularities surrounding the immigration status of the child or a parent. Where, however, it is clear that the court proceedings are designed purely to enable the child or the parent to evade immigration control consideration may be given to instructing the Treasury Solicitor with a view to intervention in the proceedings. *There must be evidence. not just a suspicion, that there has been a serious attempt to circumvent the immigration control* and decisions to intervene must be taken at not less than SEO level.

11. Where intervention has been agreed the papers should be copied to the Treasury Solicitor's office as soon as possible. The normal practice is then to apply for the Secretary of State to be joined as a respondent, and to file an affidavit setting out the child's and/or parents' immigration history and the Secretary of State's objections.

12. It should be noted that where an order has been made under the Children Act this cannot in itself deprive the Secretary of State of the power conferred by the Immigration Act 1971 to remove or deport any party to the proceedings although it may be something to which he should have regard when deciding whether to exercise his powers under the Act.

Enquiries

13. Any enquiries about this instruction should be addressed to Enforcement Policy Group in Room 301, Apollo House, (extension 8408/8409).

Enforcement Policy Group
March 1996

DP 5/96
and instruction to IES

DEPORTATION IN CASES WHERE THERE ARE CHILDREN WITH LONG RESIDENCE

Introduction

1. The purpose of this instruction is to define more clearly the criteria to be applied when considering whether enforcement action should proceed or be initiated against parents who have children who were either born here and are aged 10 or over or where, having come to the United Kingdom at an early age, they have accumulated 10 years or more continuous residence.

Policy

2. Whilst it is important that each individual case must be considered on its merits, the following are factors which may be of particular relevance—

(a) the length of the parents' residence without leave;

(b) whether removal has been delayed through protracted (and often repetitive) representations or by the parents going to ground;

(c) the age of the children;

(d) whether the children were conceived at a time when either of the parents had a leave to remain;

(e) whether return to the parents' country of origin would cause extreme hardship for the children or put their health seriously at risk;

(f) whether either of the parents has a history of criminal behaviour or deception;

3. When notifying a decision to either concede or proceed with enforcement action it is important that full reasons be given making clear that each case is considered on its individual merits.

Enquiries

4. Any enquiries about this instruction should be addressed to Enforcement Policy Group in Room 301, Apollo House, (extension 8408/8409).

IS/94 51/290/1
Enforcement Policy Group
March 1996

Index

Abandoned children, 32–33, 44, 123, 359–60

Accommodation
  See Housing

Administration, 1–2, 54–55, 86–99

Adoption, 21–23
  age, 321
  applications, 21–22
  care, 318
  citizenship, 46, 50, 123–24, 135–36
  definition, 358–59
  deportation, 55, 358–60, 365–66
  entry clearance, 22–23, 319, 321–22
  housing, 318–19, 321
  Immigration Act 1971, 50, 55
  immigration officers, 320, 322
  immigration rules, 21–22
  leave to enter or remain, 21
  legislation, 22–23
  local authorities, 23
  mutual recognition, 23
  overseas, 22
  parents, 21–23, 319–21
  public funds, 318–19, 321
  settlement, 317–22
  welfare, 23

Age
  adopted children, 321
  au pairs, 256
  bail, 101
  deportation, 44, 53, 364
  diplomatic servants, 272
  fingerprinting, 196
  free movement of persons, 6
  immigration rules, 56
  leave to enter or remain, 6, 313, 314, 316
  marriage, 6, 18
  registration, 328, 329
  retired persons, 302, 305
  students, 14, 148, 253, 260
  training, 15
  work permits, 267
  working holidays, 14, 257, 259, 260

Aircraft, 2
  appeals, 66, 99
  births, on, 51
  citizenship, 51
  criminal offences, 75
  deportation, 58–59, 66, 104
  detention, 93, 94–95, 99
  disembarkation, 61
  forfeiture, 73
  harbouring, 73–74
  illegal entry, 71
  immigration officers, 54, 58–59, 87, 90–95, 98–99

Airport ground staff, 278–80

Ancestry, 280–81

Appeals
  See also Immigration Appeal Tribunals
  age, 101
  aircraft, 99
  asylum, 4, 25, 28, 200–02, 208–10, 212–15, 332–33, 335
  Asylum and Immigration Appeals Act 1993, 2
  bail, 100–03, 210
  Channel Islands, 106
  citizenship, 188–89
  conditions, 63–64, 334
  Convention relating to the Status of Refugees 1951, 200, 209
  decision-making, 1, 4–5
  dependants, 201–03
  deportation, 43, 57, 64–67, 105, 200, 210, 337–38, 341

detention, 95, 99, 101
directions for removal, 65–67
discretion, 68
entry clearance, 8, 63, 202, 334
evidence, 70–71
Immigration Act 1971, 57, 62–71, 80, 95, 99–103, 105–06, 208–09
Immigration Act 1988, 2, 113
immigration adjudicators, 4, 62–63, 68–70, 100–01, 200–01, 208–10, 214, 229–31
immigration officers, 95, 100
immigration rules, 68, 334–35, 349, 351
Isle of Man, 106
leave to appeal, 70, 100, 210
leave to enter or remain, 63, 70, 226, 334–35
legislation, 4
mental disorders, 101
national security, 210
notice, 67–68, 100–01, 335
patriality, 63–64
polygamy, 113
procedure, 69–71, 208–09, 215
recognizances, 100–03
reference of cases for further consideration, 69
right of abode, 334
Secretary of State, 69, 71, 202
ships, 99
special voucher schemes, 10
students, 201–02
time limits, 4, 334
visitors, 201–02
voluntary organisations, 71
women, 63
work permits, 334

Armed forces, 59–60

Arrest
asylum, 196, 217
Asylum and Immigration Act 1996, 227
bail, 102–03
detention, 94
fingerprinting, 196
harbouring, 72
illegal entry, 72
Immigration Act 1971, 72, 94, 97, 102–03
immigration officers, 72, 94, 97, 102–03
naturalisation, 173

Artists, 16, 293–95

Asylum, 25–29, 194–210
age, 333
appeals, 4, 25, 28, 200–02, 208–210, 212–14, 332–33, 335
arrest, 196, 217
Asylum and Immigration Act 1996, 2, 25, 212–31
Asylum and Immigration Appeals Act 1993, 2, 25, 194–210, 229–31
bail, 210
children, 25, 28–29, 333
Convention relating to the Status of Refugees 1951, 25–29, 195, 199, 209, 329–32
criminal offences, 206, 216–17
deception, 216
dependants, 195–99, 201–03, 205–08, 333
deportation, 199–200, 210, 213, 330, 339
detention, 200
documents, 202–03, 212
employers, 2
European Convention on Human Rights, 29
examinations, 329
families, 29
fear of persecution, 26–28, 212–13, 330, 331
fingerprinting, 195–97, 346
fraud, 2, 213
housing, 197–99, 205–08
Immigration Act 1971, 204, 210, 215

immigration
adjudicators, 200–01, 208–10, 214–15
Immigration Appeal
Tribunals, 201, 209, 213
immigration officers, 197, 213, 329
immigration rules, 25, 28, 202–03, 329–30, 345–52
leave to enter or
remain, 199–200, 216, 326, 328, 329–33
national security, 210
notice, 330, 331
port of entry, 27–28
refugees,
definition, 25–26
refusals, 202–03, 330–33, 346–49
removal to safe third
countries, 214, 332
search warrants, 217
Secretary of State, 200, 202
social groups, 26–27, 28
social security, 2, 25, 220
stay of removal, 210
students, 201–02
transit passengers, 203–04
unaccompanied children, 333
United Nations High
Commissioner for
Refugees *Handbook on Procedures and Criteria for Determining Refugee Status*, 25–26
visas, 203–04
visitors, 201–02

Asylum and Immigration
Act 1996, 2, 25, 211–31

Asylum and Immigration
Appeals Act 1993, 2, 25, 194–210, 229–31

Au pairs, 255–57, 354

Bail
age, 101
appeals, 100–01, 210
arrest, 102–03
asylum, 210
conditions, 101, 102
deportation, 339
detention, 101
forfeiture, 102
Immigration Act 1971, 96–98, 100–03
immigration
adjudicators, 100–02
Immigration Appeal
Tribunals, 100–02
immigration officers, 96–98, 100
mental disorders, 101
removal, 229
restrictions, 101–02
Scotland, 100
sureties, 101, 102–03

British Dependent Territories
citizenship, 126–27, 135–45, 179
leave to enter or remain, 240
naturalisation, 170–71
registration, 126–27
statelessness, 175

British Nationality
Act 1981, 3, 32, 120–193
See also Citizenship

British Overseas
Citizenship, 145–47, 156, 174, 240, 299

British protected persons, 149, 240

British subjects, 147–48, 156, 165, 174

Broadcasting organisations, 269–70

Business people, 16
definition, 285
employment, 285–86
entry clearance, 286–87, 289–90
EC association
agreements, 288–91
extensions, 286–88
immigration officers, 290
immigration rules, 285–91
investment, 285–87
leave to enter or
remain, 285–91

public funds, 285, 287, 289
self-employment, 289
time limits, 286

Care, 31–32, 312, 314
abandoned children, 33
adopted children, 318
deportation, 44, 364
local authorities, 31–32
parents, 31
rehabilitation, 31–32
Secretary of State, 32
supervision orders, 31, 33

Carriers' liability, 203

Channel Islands
appeals, 106
common travel area, 60–61, 240
deportation, 106
illegal entry, 106
Immigration Act 1971, 49, 60–61, 105–06
leave to enter or remain, 105–06, 239, 240
regulation of entry and stay, 49

Channel Tunnel, 239, 324, 349

Children
See also Adoption, Age, Care, Independent children, Parents
abandoned, 32–33, 44, 123, 359–60
access, 298–99
citizenship, 9, 32, 45–46, 123–25, 137–38, 145–46, 159, 167
definition, 5–6, 18
deportation, 44, 55, 336, 355–60, 359–60, 362–67
entry clearance, 9, 283, 298, 299, 312, 314–16
fingerprinting, 196
housing, 198, 283, 313, 318–20
immigration officers, 317, 320, 322
immigration rules, 9, 265–67, 283–84, 296–99, 312–22, 351, 354
leave to enter or remain, 265–67, 283–84, 296–99, 312–22, 325–26, 328
local authorities, 32
marriage, 18–20, 266–67
polygamy, 312
posthumous, 159
public funds, 283, 297, 298, 313
registration, 125–26, 137–38, 145–48
retired persons, 305–06
special voucher schemes, 300
students, 14, 17–18, 253–54
time limits, 316
unaccompanied, 333
United Kingdom, born in, 9–10
working holidays, 257, 259–60

Citizenship, 3, 32, 45–46, 120–93
abandoned children, 32, 123
adoption, 46, 50, 123–24, 135–36
appeals, 83, 188–89
birth, 45–46, 50, 51, 123–24, 135–36, 142
aircraft, on, 51
ships, on, 51
British Dependent Territories, 126–27, 135–45, 153–56, 179
British Overseas Citizenship, 145–47, 156
British protected persons, 149
British Subjects, 147–48, 156, 165
children, 9, 32, 45–46, 123–25, 137–38, 145–46, 159, 162

Commonwealth, 50, 51, 149, 150, 176–77
companies, 129
criminal offences, 157–59
Cyprus, 188
deportation, 83
deprivation, 152–53
descent, 46, 124–25, 134–37, 144, 148
diplomats, 154, 162, 187
discretion, 157
employment, 128–29
entry clearance, 45
European Union, 124, 127, 135–45
evidence, 157
foundlings, 45
fraud, 152
Governors, 156–57
harbouring, 72–73
illegitimacy, 159
Immigration Act 1971, 50–02, 72–73, 82–86, 149–51, 177–79, 188–89
international organisations, 128
Ireland, 147–48
leave to enter or remain, 239
marriage, 45, 51, 129–31, 139–40, 146–47
mental disability, 151
naturalisation, 46, 50, 127, 138–39, 143, 152–56, 160–63, 167–73, 186–87
oaths of allegiance, 155–56, 179
parents, 45, 50, 123–26, 130–32, 142
patriality, 52, 54, 188–89
posthumous children, 159
presumption, 45
registration, 46, 50–52, 82–86, 123–48, 154–56, 160, 187–88
regulation of entry and stay, 50–52
renunciation, 131–32, 135, 143, 145, 147, 148, 156
residence, 128–29, 132, 148
resumption, 133, 143, 156
right of abode, 132, 134, 149
Secretary of State, 129, 156–57
statelessness, 149, 173–76
time limits, 46, 128–30
war, 133
women, 54, 63, 81, 129–30, 134, 144, 148, 150

Common travel area
Channel Islands, 60–61, 240
definition, 62
disembarkation, 61–62
employment, 60
Immigration Act 1971, 50, 60–62
Ireland, 60–61, 240
Isle of Man, 60–61, 240
leave to enter or remain, 60, 240
national security, 60
overstaying, 240
patriality, 60
registration, 60
returning residents, 241
visas, 240
visitors, 246

Commonwealth
ancestry, 280
citizenship, 50, 51, 149, 150, 176–77
deportation, 57
families, 50
Immigration Act 1971, 50, 57, 81
leave to enter or remain, 239
working holidaymakers, 257

Companies, 129

Composers, 16, 293–95

Contact, 35–42

Convention relating to the Status of Refugees 1951, 2, 25–29, 195, 199, 209, 329–33

Courts
- deportation, 56–57, 359, 366
- Family Court, 359
- Immigration Act 1971, 56–57

Criminal offences
- aircraft, 75
- arrest, 72
- asylum, 206, 216–17
- citizenship, 157–59
- deception, 216
- deportation, 56–58, 104, 340, 358, 362
- embarkation cards, 74
- employment, 218
- examinations, 74
- harbouring, 72–74
- housing, 206
- illegal entry, 71–74
- Immigration Act 1971, 56–58, 71–76, 104
- immigration officers, 74
- information, 74
- landing cards, 74
- Northern Ireland, 76
- patriality, 74
- ships, 75
- time limits, 74, 75–76

Custodianship orders, 358–60, 365–66

Customs and excise officers, 86

Cyprus, 188

Decision-making, 3–5
- appeals, 1, 4–5
- challenges, 4–5
- delegated officers, 3
- deportation, 3, 4
- discretion, 4
- entry clearance, 5
  - officers, 3
- European Convention on Human Rights, 3, 5
- immigration officers, 3
- immigration rules, 4
- judicial review, 4, 5
- leave to enter or remain, 3, 5
- port of entry clearance, 3
- Secretary of State, 3
- visas, 3

Dentists, 251–52

Dependants
- appeals, 201–03
- asylum, 195–99, 201–03, 205–08, 333
- au pairs, 256
- fingerprinting, 195–97
- housing, 198
- immigration rules, 322–24, 346, 350–52
- leave to enter or remain, 13–16
- marriage, 264
- students, 248
- working holidays, 15, 257

Deportation, 43–44
- abandoned children, 359–60
- adoption, 55, 358–60, 365–66
- age, 44, 53, 364
- aircraft, 58–59, 66, 104
- appeals, 2, 43, 57, 64–67, 105, 200, 210, 337–38, 341
- armed forces, 59–60
- asylum, 199–200, 210, 330, 339
- Asylum and Immigration Act 1996, 229
- bail, 339
- care, 44, 364
- Channel Islands, 106
- children, 44, 55, 336, 355–60, 362–67
  - abandoned, 44
- common-law relationships, 357–58
- Commonwealth, 57
- contact, 39
- courts, 56–57, 338, 359, 366
- crews, 58–59, 66
- criminal offences, 56–58, 104, 338, 340, 358, 362

custodianship orders, 358–60, 365–66
decision-making, 3, 4
destination, objections to, 65–66, 337
detention, 104–05, 339
diplomatic immunity, 59
discretion, 44
entry clearance, 67, 324
European Convention on Human Rights, 44, 355, 357, 358
European Economic Area, 363
exemptions, 57
expenses, 56, 104
families, 43, 44, 55, 64–65, 336–37, 340
guidance, 43, 44
hearings, 338
Home Office circulars, 355–67
illegal entry, 65, 71, 356–57, 360–61
Immigration Act 1971, 53, 55–60, 64–67, 71, 80–81, 103–06, 335, 337–39
Immigration Act 1988, 2, 43
immigration adjudicators, 65–66
Immigration Appeal Tribunal, 65, 338
immigration officers, 58, 104
immigration rules, 44, 335–41, 360, 363
Ireland, 57
Isle of Man, 106
leave to enter or remain, 324, 335–41
legislation, 43
marriage, 19, 309, 336, 355–64
national security, 64, 338, 339
notice, 56, 66–67, 104, 339
overstaying, 43, 335
patriality, 53, 55, 56
procedure, 43–44, 55–56
public funds, 339
recommendations, 56–57, 80–81
removal, 103–05, 339–40
residence, 33, 57, 357, 358–60, 365–67
returns, 340
revocation of orders, 340–41
right of abode, 356–57, 362
Scotland, 56, 57
Secretary of State, 43, 44, 104
ships, 58–59, 66, 104
supervised departure, 340
time limits, 56, 57
wardship, 358–60
work permits, 67

Detention
aircraft, 93–94
arrest, 94, 87
asylum, 200
bail, 96–98, 101
deportation, 104–05, 339
examination, 93–99
Immigration Act 1971, 93–99, 101, 104–05
immigration officers, 93–99
leave to enter or remain, 94
naturalisation, 173
Scotland, 94
ships, 93–94
temporary admission or release, 96–97, 227–29

Diplomats
age, 272
citizenship, 154, 162, 167
deportation, 59
entry clearance, 242, 273
Immigration Act 1971, 59
Immigration Act 1988, 113–14
leave to enter or remain, 242, 272–74
naturalisation, 172
private servants, 272–74
public funds, 273
registration, 328, 329

Directives, 2

Discretion
appeals, 68
care, 37, 39
citizenship, 46, 157
contact, 39
decision-making, 4
leave to enter or remain, 33
deportation, 44

Secretary of State for the
Home Department, 1, 37, 39, 44

Disembarkation, 61–62

Doctors, 251–52

Embarkation, 74, 88

Employment
See also Work permits, Working holidays
age, 263
ancestry, 280
asylum, 2
Asylum and Immigration Act 1996, 218–19
business people, 285, 286
care, 37
citizenship, 128–29
common travel area, 60
criminal offences, 218
extension, 263–64
Immigration Act 1971, 50, 52, 60, 85
immigration rules, 244–46, 263–64, 267–80, 344
language assistants, 61
leave to enter or remain, 241, 324, 325, 327
marriage, 19
medical treatment, 245, 247
registration, 328
regulation of entry and stay, 50, 52
retired persons, 302, 304
seasonal workers, 245
self-employed, 289
students, 14, 17, 248–50, 253–55
teachers, 261
time limits, 264
training, 263–64
visitors, 245–46
work experience, 263–64

Entry clearance
access to children, 299
adoption, 22–23, 319, 321–22
airport ground staff, 279
ancestry, 280
appeals, 8, 63, 334
artists, 294
asylum, 326
business people, 286–87, 289–90
Channel Tunnel, 324
children, 9, 283, 298, 299, 312, 314–16
citizenship, 45
composers, 294
contact, 35
decision-making, 5
deportation, 324
diplomats, 242
European Economic Area, 301
families, 7–8
housing, 325
immigration officers, 324–26
immigration rules, 324–26, 353–54
information, 325, 326
investors, 292
language students, 261–62
leave to enter or remain, 242, 244, 324–26
marriage, 19, 282, 295–96, 307, 309, 311
medical examinations, 326
ministers of religion, 277
officers, 3, 244
overseas government employees, 274–75
parents, 16
polygamy, 112–13
refusal, 5, 326–27
retired persons, 304, 306
returning residents, 325
sole representatives, 271
special voucher schemes, 299–300
students, 249–50, 255
teachers, 261–62
time limits, 325
visas, 3, 242
work permits, 325
working holidays, 15, 258, 259–60
writers, 294

European Convention on
Human Rights, 2–3
asylum, 29
contact, 39, 40–41

decision-making, 3, 5
deportation, 44, 355, 357, 358
Secretary of State, 3

European Economic Area, 2
deportation, 363
entry clearances, 301
families, 10, 300–01
freedom of movement, 10
immigration rules, 300–01
incapacity for work, 301
leave to enter or remain, 300–01
registration, 301
residence permits, 10, 300
settlement, 300–01
time limits, 300

European Union, 1
citizenship, 124, 127, 135–45
directives, 2
EC Association Agreements, 288–93
families, 10
free movement of persons, 2
Immigration Act 1988, 115
immigration rules, 10
registration, 127

Evidence
appeals, 70–71
citizenship, 157
Immigration Act 1971, 70–71
leave to enter or remain, 249–50, 252
students, 249–50, 252

Examination
See also Medical examinations
asylum, 329
criminal offences, 74
detention, 93–99
Immigration Act 1971, 74, 87–89, 93–99
Immigration Act 1988, 115–16
immigration officers, 87–89, 93–99, 115–16
passengers, 115–16

Exchange schemes, 261–62

Expenses
deportation, 76, 104
detention, 94–95
illegal entry, 227
Immigration Act 1971, 56, 76, 77, 94–95, 104
Immigration Appeal Tribunals, 109
immigration officers, 94–95

Families
asylum, 29
Asylum and Immigration Act 1996, 226
Commonwealth, 50
contact, 39, 40
definition, 2
deportation, 43, 44, 55, 64–65, 336, 340
entry clearance, 7–8
European Economic Area, 10, 300–01
European Union, 10
free movement of persons, 2, 10
housing, 7
Immigration Act 1971, 50, 55, 64–65
immigration rules, 10, 300–01, 307–24
leave to enter or remain, 7–9, 300–01, 307–24
parents, 7–8
polygamous marriages, 11
port of entry, 7
primary purpose marriages, 11–12
public funds, 7
regulation of entry and stay, 50
relevant adults, 7–8
residence permits, 10
retired persons, 305
settlement, 7–12
social security, 7
special voucher schemes, 10–11

Fingerprinting, 195–97, 346

Floating structures, 62

Fraud, 2, 152, 213

Free movement of persons, 2, 6, 10

Governors, 156–57

Hague Convention on the Civil Aspects of International Child Abduction 1985, 37
Harbouring, 72–74
Holidays
 See Working holidays
Hotel records, 55
Housing
 adopted children, 318–20
 asylum, 197–99, 205–08
 Asylum and Immigration Act 1996, 219–20
 children, 198, 283, 313
 criminal offences, 206
 dependants, 198, 205–08
 entry clearance, 325
 families, 7
 homelessness, 199, 206–07, 219
 information, 206–07
 investors, 292
 Isles of Scilly, 208
 leave to enter or remain, 253, 264, 267
 legislation, 219
 marriage, 19, 198, 264, 282, 295, 309
 Northern Ireland, 199
 reasons, 205–06
 records, 55
 retired persons, 302, 303, 305
 right of abode, 198
 security of tenure, 206–07, 231
 social security, 220, 223, 224
 students, 253
 suitable accommodation, 7
 work permits, 267
Human rights
 See European Convention on Human Rights

Illegal entry
 aircraft, 71
 appeals, 65
 arrest, 72
 Channel Islands, 106
 criminal offences, 71–74
 deportation, 65, 71, 356–57, 360–61
 detention, 96
 expenses, 227
 harbouring, 72–74
 Immigration Act 1971, 65, 71–74, 90, 95–96, 106
 immigration officers, 71–72, 90, 95
 Isle of Man, 106
 marriage, 307
 medical examinations, 71
 overstaying, 1
 police, 71–72
 removal, 227
 ships, 71
 time limits, 72
 work permits, 267–68
Immigration Act 1971, 1, 47–111, 225–29, 344
Immigration Act 1988, 2, 43, 111–19
Immigration adjudicators
 appeals, 4, 68–70, 100, 200–01, 208–10, 214, 229–31
 asylum, 200–01, 208–10, 214
 bail, 100–03
 chief, 106
 deportation, 65–66
 entry clearance, 63
 Immigration Act 1971, 62, 65–66, 100–03, 106–07
 Immigration Appeal Tribunal, 68–71
 patriality, 62
 remuneration, 107
 resignation, 107
Immigration Appeal Tribunals, 4
 asylum, 201, 209, 213
 bail, 100–01
 immigration adjudicators, 68–71
 deportation, 65
 expenses, 109
 Immigration Act 1971, 62, 65, 68, 100–01, 107–09
 members, 62, 107–08

president, 107, 108
remuneration, 108, 109
resignation, 107
staff, 109

Immigration (Carriers' Liability) Act 1987, 2

Immigration officers
administration, 54, 86–99
adopted children, 320, 322
aircraft, 54, 58–59, 87, 90–95, 98–99
appeals, 95, 213
appointment, 86
arrest, 72, 94, 97, 102–03
asylum, 197, 213, 329
au pairs, 256
bail, 96–98, 100–03
business people, 290
children, 317
customs and excise officers, 86
decision-making, 4
deportation, 58, 104
detention, 93–99
diplomatic servants, 273
documents, 88
entry clearances, 324–25
examinations, 87–89, 93–99, 113–14
embarkation, 88
expenses, 94–95
harbouring, 72
illegal entry, 71–72, 90, 95
Immigration Act 1971, 54, 58, 71–72, 86–104
Immigration Act 1988, 115–16
immigration rules, 344
information, 88
landing cards, 88
leave to enter or remain, 87, 89–90, 94, 238–44, 324–26
marriage, 311
medical examinations, 89
medical treatment, 247
obstruction, 74
overseas government employees, 275
patriality, 87
retired persons, 302, 304
Secretary of State, 89–91
ships, 54, 58–59, 87, 90–95, 98–99
sole representatives, 271
students, 249–55
visitors, 245–46
women, 88
working holidays, 260

Immigration Rules, 1, 233–354
adoption, 21–22
age, 5–6
ancestry, 280–81
appeals, 68, 334–35, 349, 351
artists, 293–95
asylum, 25, 28, 202–03, 329–30, 345–52
au pairs, 255–57, 354
business people,
Channel Tunnel, 349
children, 9, 265–67, 283–84, 296–99, 312–22, 351, 354
composers, 293–95
dependants, 322–24
deportation, 44, 335–41, 346, 350–52, 360, 363
employment, 244–46, 263–64, 267–80, 344
entry clearance, 324–26, 353–54
European Economic Area, 300–01
European Union, 10
families, 10, 300–01, 307–24
housing, 345
Immigration Act 1971, 344
immigration officers, 344
investors, 292–93
leave to enter or remain, 238–367
marriage, 18, 264–65, 281–83, 295–96, 307–11, 350
medical treatment, 246–48
patriality, 53
polygamy, 11
public funds, 345, 354
regulation of entry and stay, 53

registration, 328–29, 344
retired persons, 302–06, 345
social security, 353
special voucher schemes, 10, 299–300
students, 14, 17–18, 248–55, 261–62, 354
Tanzania, 343
time limits, 345
training, 15, 244–46, 263–64
visas, 341–42
visitors, 14, 244–46
working holidays, 255–61
writers, 293–95

Independent children, 17–23

Information, 88, 207, 325–26

International organisations, 128

Investors, 16, 285, 286–87, 292–93

Ireland
citizenship, 147–48
common travel area, 60–61, 240
deportation, 57
Immigration Act 1971, 59, 60–61
leave to enter or remain, 240
regulation of entry and stay, 49

Islands
See Channel Islands, Isle of Man

Isle of Man, 106
appeals, 106
Channel Islands, 106
common travel area, 60–61, 240
deportation, 106
illegal entry, 106
Immigration Act 1971, 49, 60–61, 105–06
leave to enter or remain, 105–06, 240
regulation of entry and stay, 49

Isles of Scilly, 208

Journalists, 269–70

Judicial review, 1, 4, 5, 11

Landing cards, 74

Language, 168, 170, 261

Leave to enter or remain
adoption, 21
age, 6, 313, 314, 316
ancestry, 280–81
appeals, 63, 70, 226, 334–35
artists, 293–95
asylum, 199–200, 216, 326, 328, 329–33
British Dependent Territories, 240
British Overseas citizens, 240
British protected persons, 240
businessmen, 285–91
Channel Islands, 105–06, 240
Channel Tunnel, 239, 324
charges, 116
children, 265–67, 283–84, 296–99, 312–22, 325–26, 328
citizenship, 239
common travel area, 60, 240
Commonwealth, 239
composers, 293–95
conditions, 52, 327
contact, 35
crew, 328
curtailment, 229, 327–28, 345
deception, 216
decision-making, 3, 5
dependants, 13–16
deportation, 324, 335–41
detention, 94
diplomats, 242, 272–74
discretion, 33
documents, 241, 324, 325, 327
employment, 255–57, 267–80
entry clearance, 242, 244, 324–26
European Economic Area, 300–01
families, 7–9, 300–01, 307–24
Immigration Act 1971, 52–53, 60, 63, 70, 87, 89–90, 94, 105–06
Immigration Act 1988, 116

immigration officers, 87, 89–90, 94, 238–44, 324–26
immigration rules, 228–329
indefinite, 7–8, 33
information, 325–26
interviews, 327
investors, 292–93
Ireland, 240
Isle of Man, 105–06, 240
limited, 13–16, 52, 53, 238
marriage, 18, 264–68, 281–83, 295–96
medical examinations, 243–44, 326
medical treatment, 246–48
national security, 327
notice, 89, 238
overstaying, 240
parents, 13, 322–24
polygamy, 11
public funds, 325, 327
refusal, 5, 239, 324–28
registration, 328–29
regulation of entry and stay, 52–53
retired persons, 302–06
returning residents, 241, 325
right of abode, 239–40
Secretary of State, 327
social security, 243
special voucher schemes, 10, 299–300
students, 248–55, 261–62
time limits, 3, 238, 241, 325
training, 16, 255–57, 263–64
undertakings, 243
variation, 3, 243, 324–28, 334, 350
visas, 240, 242
visitors, 244–46
work experience, 255–57, 263–64
working holidays, 255–61
work permits, 325
writers, 293–95

Legal aid

Legislation, 1–3
See also Particular statutes
administration, 2
adoption, 22–23
appeals, 4
deportation, 43
housing, 219
mental patients, 77
social security, 220–25

Local authorities, 9, 23, 31–32

Marriage, 281–83
See also Polygamy
age, 6, 18, 266
children, 266–67
citizenship, 45, 51, 129–31, 139–40, 146–47
common-law relationships, 357–58
dependants, 264
deportation, 19, 309, 336, 355–64
divorce, 357, 365
employment, 19
entry clearance, 19, 266, 282, 295–96, 307, 309, 311
extension, 309, 311
fiance(e)s, 18–20, 310–11
housing, 19, 198, 264, 282, 295, 309
illegal entry, 307
Immigration Act 1971, 51
immigration officers, 311
immigration rules, 18, 264–65, 281–83, 293–96, 307–11, 350
independent children, 18–20
leave to enter or remain, 18, 264–68, 281–83, 295–96
primary purpose, 11–12, 19, 308–10
public funds, 19, 264, 266, 282, 295, 308–09, 311
refusals, 282–83, 311
registration, 129–30, 139–40, 146–47, 329
retired persons, 303–04
separation, 357, 365
settlement, 308–10
special voucher schemes, 300

students, 253
switching categories, 19
time limits, 18, 308, 310
visitors, 307
working holidays, 15, 257

Medical examinations
illegal entry, 71
Immigration Act 1971, 71, 87–89
immigration officers, 89
leave to enter or remain, 243–44
medical inspectors, 243–44, 326

Medical treatment
employment, 247
immigration officers, 247
immigration rules, 246–48
leave to enter or remain, 244, 246–48
mental patients, 76–77
time limits, 247
visitors, 14, 244, 246–48

Mental disorders
bail, 101
citizenship, 151
Immigration Act 1971, 76–77, 101
legislation, 77
naturalisation, 173
patients, 76–77
return, 76–77

Ministers of religion, 276–78, 329

Missionaries, 276–78

National security, 60, 64, 210, 327

Naturalisation, 46, 50
absence, 168, 172
arrest, 173
British Dependent Territories, 170–71
cancellation, 154
citizenship, 127, 138–39, 143, 152–56, 160–63, 167–73, 186–87
detention, 173
diplomats, 172
fraud, 152
language, 168, 170
mental disorders, 173
Secretary of State, 168
time limits, 168–69

News agencies, 269–70

Northern Ireland, 199, 224

Nurses, 250–51

Oaths, 155–56, 179

Overseas government employees, 274–76

Overstaying, 43, 71, 240

Parents
adoption, 21–23
care, 31
citizenship, 45, 50, 123–26, 130–32, 142
contact, 36–37, 42
definition, 7–8
divorce, 357
families, 7–8
Immigration Act 1971, 50
leave to enter or remain, 13, 283
local authorities, 9
separation, 357
statelessness, 174
training, 15–16
unmarried, 42
working holidays, 15

Patriality
appeals, 63–64
citizenship, 52, 54, 188–89
common travel area, 60
deportation, 53, 55, 56
Immigration Act 1971, 52, 53, 54, 55, 56, 60, 63–64, 87
immigration officers, 87
immigration rules, 53
women, 54

Polygamy
appeals, 113
children, 312
entry clearance, 112–13
families, 11

Immigration Act 1988, 2, 111–13
immigration rules, 11
leave to enter or remain, 11
right of abode, 111–13
women, 111–13

Port of entry clearance, 3, 7, 27–28

Primary purpose
marriages, 11–12, 19, 310

Public funds
See also Housing, Social security
access to children, 298
adopted children, 318–20
artists, 294
business people, 285, 287, 289
children, 283, 297, 298, 313
composers, 294
contact, 35
deportation, 339
diplomatic servants, 273
entry clearance, 325
families, 7
immigration rules, 345, 354
investors, 292
language students, 261
leave to enter or remain, 325, 327
marriage, 19, 264, 282, 295–96, 303, 308–09, 311
ministers of religion, 277
overseas government employees, 274
retired persons, 302, 305
sole representatives, 271
special voucher schemes, 10, 300
students, 14, 17, 248, 250, 253–54
teachers, 261
training, 15
visitors, 14, 245
work permits, 267
working holidays, 15, 257, 259
writers, 294

Recognizances
See Bail

Refugees
See Asylum

Registration
age, 328, 329
British Dependent Territories, 126–27
children, 125–26, 137–38, 145–48
citizenship, 46, 50–52, 82–86, 123–48, 154–56, 160, 187–88
common travel area, 60
conditions, 329
diplomats, 328, 329
employment, 328
European Economic Area, 301
European Union, 127
fees, 54
immigration rules, 328–29, 344
leave to enter or remain, 328–29
marriage, 129–30, 139–40, 146–47, 329
ministers of religion, 329
police, with, 52, 54
residence, 128
statelessness, 174–75
war, 133
women, 134, 148

Regulation of entry and stay
administration of control, 54–55
Channel Islands, 49
citizenship, 50–52
common travel area, 50, 60–61
Commonwealth, 50
deportation, 53, 55–60
employment, 50, 52
families, 50
Immigration Act 1971, 49–62
immigration rules, 53
Ireland, 49, 61
Isle of Man, 49
leave to enter or remain, 52–53
registration, 52
statement of right of abode, 50–52
students, 50
visitors, 50

Religious orders, 276–78

Residence
See also Residence permits

citizenship, 128–29, 154–56
contact, 42
deportation, 33, 57, 357, 358–60, 365–67
European Economic Area, 10, 300
Immigration Act 1971, 57
long-term, 33, 367
permits, 10, 300
registration, 128
returning residents, 241, 325
time limits, 33

Retired persons
age, 302, 305
children, 305–06
employment, 302, 304
entry clearance, 302, 304, 306
extension, 303
families, 205
housing, 302, 303, 305
immigration officers, 302, 304
immigration rules, 302–06
independent means, 302–06
leave to enter or remain, 302–06
marriage, 303–04
public funds, 302, 303, 305
time limits, 303

Scotland, 56, 57, 94, 100

Search warrants, 217

Seasonal workers, 245, 260–61

Secretary of State for the Home Department
administration, 1
appeals, 69, 71
asylum, 200, 202
care, 32, 37, 39
citizenship, 129, 156–57
contact, 39
decision-making, 3
delegation, 3
deportation, 43, 44, 104
discretion, 1, 37, 39, 44
European Convention on Human Rights, 3
Governors, 156
Immigration Act 1971, 89–91, 104
immigration officers, 89–91
leave to enter or remain, 327
naturalisation, 168

Self-employed, 289

Ships, 2
appeals, 66, 99
births, on, 51
citizenship, 51
deportation, 58–59, 66, 104
detention, 93, 94–95, 99
disembarkation, 61
forfeiture, 73
harbouring, 73–74
illegal entry, 71
immigration officers, 54, 58–59, 87, 90–95, 98–99
leave to enter or remain, 267
work permits, 267, 268

Social security
asylum, 2, 25, 220
Asylum and Immigration Act 1996, 220–21
child benefit, 220
council tax benefit, 220, 223
families, 7
housing benefit, 220, 223–24
immigration rules, 353
income support, 220, 222–24
jobseekers' allowance, 220–21
leave to enter or remain, 243
legislation, 220–25
Northern Ireland, 224
undertakings, 243

Sole representatives, 271–72

Special voucher schemes, 10–11, 299–300

Spouses
See Marriage

Statelessness, 149, 173–76

Statement of Changes in Immigration Rules
See Immigration Rules

Students
- age, 14, 248, 253, 260
- appeals, 201–02
- asylum, 201–02
- children, 14, 253–54
- dentists, 251–52
- dependants, 248
- doctors, 251–52
- employment, 14, 17, 248–50, 253, 255
- entry clearance, 249, 251, 255
- evidence, 49, 251, 252
- extension, 249, 250–51, 252
- housing, 253
- Immigration Act 1971, 50
- immigration officers, 249, 250, 252–55
- immigration rules, 17–18, 248–55, 261–62, 354
- independent children, 17–18
- leave to enter or remain, 245, 248–55, 260
- marriage, 253
- nurses, 50–51
- prospective, 254–55
- public funds, 14, 17, 248, 250, 253–54
- regulation of entry and stay, 50
- time limits, 252, 254
- visitors, 245
- working holidays, 260

Supervision orders, 31, 33

Tanzania, 343

Teachers, 261–62

Time limits
- ancestry, 280
- appeals, 4, 334
- artists, 294–95
- au pairs, 256
- broadcasting organisations, 269
- business people, 286
- children, 316
- citizenship, 128–30
- composers, 294–95
- contact, 36
- deportation, 56, 57, 335
- employment, 264
- entry clearance, 325
- European Economic Area, 300
- harbouring, 72
- illegal entry, 72
- Immigration Act 1971, 56, 57, 72
- immigration rules, 345
- investors, 292, 293
- journalists, 269
- language assistants, 262
- leave to enter or remain, 3, 238, 241, 325
- marriage, 18, 308, 310
- medical treatment, 247
- naturalisation, 168, 169
- news agencies, 269
- overseas government employees, 275
- residence, 33
- retired persons, 303
- sole representatives, 271
- students, 252, 254
- teachers, 262
- visitors, 13–14, 244–46
- work permits, 267
- working holidays, 258, 260
- writers, 294–95

Training, 15–16, 244–46, 263–64

Transit passengers, 203–04

United Nations High Commissioner for Refugees *Handbook on Procedures and Criteria for Determining Refugee Status*, 25–26

Visas
- asylum, 203–04
- common travel area, 240
- countries list, 341–42
- decision-making, 3
- entry clearance, 3, 242

immigration rules, 341–42
leave to enter or remain, 240, 242
transit passengers, 203–04

Visitors, 13–14
appeals, 201–02
asylum, 201–02
common travel area, 246
dependants, 245
employment, 245–46
extension, 245–46
Immigration Act 1971, 50
immigration officers, 245–46
immigration rules, 13–14, 244–46
leave to enter or remain, 244–46
marriage, 307
medical treatment, 14, 244, 246–48
public funds, 14, 245
regulation of entry and stay, 50
seasonal workers, 245
students, 245
time limits, 13–14, 244–46
transit, in, 246

Voluntary organisations, 71

War, 133

Wardship, 358–60

Welfare benefits
See Social security

Women
appeals, 63
citizenship, 54, 63, 81, 129–30, 134, 144, 148, 150
immigration officers, 88
patriality, 54
polygamy, 111–13
registration, 134, 148
searches, 88

Work experience, 263–64

Work permits
age, 267, 272
airport ground staff, 278–80
appeals, 334
broadcasting, 269–70
conditions, 268
deportation, 263
diplomats, 272–74
entry clearance, 271, 273–75, 277, 279, 325
extension, 268, 270, 271–74, 279
housing, 267
immigration officers, 267–68, 271, 273, 275
journalists, 269–70
leave to enter or remain, 325
ministers of religion, 276–78
missionaries, 276–78
news agencies, 269–70
overseas governments, 274–76
public funds, 267, 271, 273, 274, 277
refusal, 268, 269, 274, 278
ships, 267, 268
sole representatives, 271–72
time limits, 267, 269, 271, 275
United Nations, 274

Working holidays, 14–15
age, 14, 257, 259, 262
children, 257, 259–60
Commonwealth, 257
dependants, 15, 257
entry clearance, 15, 258, 259–60
extension, 258, 261
immigration officers, 260
immigration rules, 14–15, 255–61
leave to enter or remain, 257–61
marriage, 15, 257
parents, 15
public funds, 15, 257, 258
seasonal workers, 260–61
students, 260
time limits, 14, 258, 261

Writers, 16, 293–95